Oliver Franks

FOUNDING FATHER

Oliver Franks
Portrait by Karsh of Ottawa. *Photo: Camera Press (UK Ltd)*

Oliver Franks

FOUNDING FATHER

Alex Danchev

CLARENDON PRESS · OXFORD

1993

Oxford University Press, Walton Street, Oxford OX2 6DP
Oxford New York Toronto
Delhi Bombay Calcutta Madras Karachi
Kuala Lumpur Singapore Hong Kong Tokyo
Nairobi Dar es Salaam Cape Town
Melbourne Auckland Madrid
and associated companies in
Berlin Ibadan

Oxford is a trade mark of Oxford University Press

Published in the United States
by Oxford University Press Inc., New York

British Library Cataloguing in Publication Data
Data available

Library of Congress Cataloging in Publication Data
Data available
ISBN 0–19–821577–0

Set by Hope Services (Abingdon) Ltd.
Printed in Great Britain
on acid-free paper by
Biddles Ltd,
Guildford and King's Lynn

For zak

Whatever the world may say, he who hath not much meditated upon God, the human mind, and the *summum bonum*, may possibly make a thriving earthworm, but will most indubitably make a sorry patriot and a sorry statesman.

Bishop Berkeley

Preface

OLIVER FRANKS, an exceedingly deliberate man, was accident-prone. Things happened to him. He did not seek his various careers of don, mandarin, diplomat, banker, provost, pillar of state. They sought him. He did not collect committees, as some men do. Committees collected him. He did not pine for public recognition. Recognition came to him. 'Life', said Montaigne, 'is an unequal, irregular, and multiform movement.'[1] So it was for Oliver Franks.

A philosopher has remarked that each of us has an emotional interest in discerning coherent patterns of development in our own lives.[2] In Franks's case the interest was remarkably low. Discerning coherent patterns was a constant preoccupation; but not in his own life. Franks was averse to introspection. It was a waste of time. He grew impatient with the standard questions. Which part of his life did he find most enjoyable? Interesting? Rewarding? How was he influenced by his Nonconformist upbringing? Bristol schooling? Philosophical training? What lessons did he learn from his experience in London? Paris? Washington? These questions were practically meaningless to him. For one so attuned to history, he had surprisingly little sense of accumulated experience. He was highly task-orientated (an expression of which he would certainly have disapproved). He absorbed himself in the problem, or problems, of the moment. Recollected in tranquillity, this activity appeared as a succession of tasks of radically different duration, intensity, form, and substance. Neither at the time nor in retrospect did he expend much energy in comparing them. There was no point, he thought: they were, strictly, incomparable. Life, as Franks himself remarked, is not like a greatest-goal competition.[3] On the other hand, many of the tasks he undertook did have something in common, in form if not in substance. The proliferation of Franks Reports is only the most obvious example of this phenomenon. Were there, perhaps, other reasons to abstain from speculation about the past?

'He was a man of the greatest reticence, but with nothing to conceal; a man of intensely "private life", but wholly transparent.'[4] Franks attained what T. S. Eliot self-referentially admired in Spinoza. He was not the sort to attract many funny stories, but the best-known Franks story gives evidence of these very qualities.

When Sir Oliver Franks arrived in Washington at the height of the Cold War, he was rather taken aback by a telephone conversation he had with a local radio station before he had properly settled into his desk, a few days before Christmas. The man in the studio was welcoming him to the American capital, wishing him well during his time there, and seemed very anxious to know what Sir Oliver wanted for Christmas. Franks, not a man for small talk, spluttered a little as he groped for a seemly idea, and finally came up with something he thought might do. On Christmas morning the broadcasters came on the air, burbling goodwill across the District of Columbia. 'On this hallowed day,' crooned the announcer, 'we have a number of distinguished foreign residents in the capital city of the United States and we thought it would be appropriate to ask them what they would like most of all for Christmas 1948. First of all we asked His Excellency the French Ambassador what his choice would be . . .' The broadcast cut into a tape recording of a Parisian voice, pregnant with sincerity: 'Pour Noël, I want peace throughout all thee world.' 'Then we asked the Ambassador of the Soviet Union what he would like most of all today.' A dogmatic voice on the tape this time: 'For Chreesmas I want freedom for all the peoples enslaved by imperialism, wherever they may be.' 'Finally, folks, we asked Her Majesty the Queen's Ambassador from London, Sir Oliver Franks, what he would prefer on this day.' The diffident tones of Bristol Grammar School and Oxford came on the air. 'Well, as a matter of fact, it's very kind of you, I think I'd quite like a small box of candied fruit.'[5]

The essence of this story is contained in that small word 'seemly'. To grope for a seemly idea was the natural thing to do. Seemliness mattered to Oliver Franks. He lived by what was seemly and what was not. It was not seemly to spout pious platitudes on the radio. More importantly, it was not seemly to talk about oneself. Seemliness counselled silence. The living Lord Franks bore an uncanny resemblance to Aristotle's magnanimous man. 'He does not care for personal conversation; he will talk neither about himself nor about anyone else, because he does not care to be complimented himself or to hear others criticized; nor again is he inclined to pay compliments. For this reason he is not abusive either, not even of his enemies, unless he intends to be insulting.'[6]

Acknowledgements

To research and write a book over a lengthy period is to incur all manner of debts. Financially, I was assisted by a NATO Research Fellowship, a Fulbright Travel Grant, and a Keele University Research Award. Most of the American research for this book was done during a Fellowship at the Woodrow Wilson Centre in Washington, DC, in 1989. Most of the writing was done as Alistair Horne Fellow at St Antony's College, Oxford, in 1991. These two institutions are surely among the most stimulating and civilized scholarly confluences in the Western world. I feel privileged to have sampled them.

I have depended very heavily on the support of a certain few individuals to ease my passage in this world during the last few years, in particular Professor Lawrence Freedman, Professor Sir Michael Howard, and Professor Donald Cameron Watt. I am exceedingly grateful to all three. My colleagues in the Department of International Relations at Keele were remarkably tolerant of my frequent absences. Professor Peter Hennessy was a source of inspiration and encouragement from beginning to end. The draft manuscript was meticulously scrutinized by my friend Paul Edson, who knew nothing of Oliver Franks but left his mark on the whole work; and by the late Charles Wenden, who had observed Franks in his Oxford habitat over many years. To these original and enthusiastic readers I can only apologize for presuming to ignore so much of their advice. I am most grateful to Caroline Davidson in London and Robert Ducas in New York for negotiating on my behalf, and to Tony Morris at Oxford University Press for his sympathetic professionalism throughout.

A large number of people furnished me with written or oral evidence, sometimes both: Alice Acheson, David Acheson, Lord Armstrong, R. Gordon Arneson, John Bamborough, Dr Robert Barnes, Ambassador Lucius D. Battle, Sir Isaiah Berlin, Richard M. Bissell, Henry Brandon, Lord and Lady Briggs, Dr Michael Brock, J. D. Brown, Lord Bullock, Sir Alec Cairncross, Lord Callaghan, Brian Campbell, Lord Carr, Lord Dacre (Hugh Trevor-Roper), Jon Davey, Alan Davidson, Caroline, Emma, and Rachel Dinwiddy, Barbara Evans, Rosalind Fells, Jean Floud, Martin Franks, John Freeman, Lord Gladwyn, Ambassador Lincoln Gordon, Sir Anthony Gray, Sir John Habbakkuk, Professor A. H. Halsey, Sir William Hayter, Sir Nicholas Henderson, Professor T. F. Hewer, Dr Charles J. Hitch, the late Reverend John Huxtable, Lord Jay, Simon Jenkins, Ambassador Philip M. Kaiser, Professor George F. Kennan, Sir Patrick Kingsley, Matt Lethbridge, Lord Lever, James Littlewood, Canon Ronald Lunt, Ambassador George C. McGhee, Professor Donald Mackinnon,

Major R. Maclaran, James Meade, Leonard Miall, Sir Patrick Nairne, Sir Patrick Neill, the Bishop of Newcastle (Alec Graham), Ambassador Paul H. Nitze, Margery Ord, Professor C. B. Perry, Sir Henry Phelps Brown, Betty Pickup, Harry Pitt, Lord Plowden, John Prestwich, John Punshon, Anthony Rawsthorne, Merlyn Rees, James Reston, Dr Vernon Reynolds, Lord Richardson, Lord Roll, Dean Rusk, Sir Maurice Shock, Joanna Spencer, D. L. Stockton, W. de W. Symons, Sir Donald Tebbit, Humfrey and Helena Wakefield, Charles Wenden, Dr Anne Whiteman, Sir Geoffrey Wilson, and Professor A. D. Woozley.

Many others were most helpful in providing access to various documentary sources: Kathleen Burk; Christina Hardyment; Peter Hennessy; Alistair Horne; Edward Mortimer; Peter Snow; Stephen Tanner; Helen Langley at the Bodleian Library; Michael Booker and Maggie Lane at Bristol Grammar School; Malcolm Thomas at Friends House Library; Dr Alison M. Pearn of St John's College, Cambridge; Wilbert Mahoney at the National Archives in Washington, DC; Dr Brian Harrison and his colleagues in the History of the University offices in Oxford; Elaine Kaye, the historian of Mansfield College, Oxford; the Provost and Fellows of Queen's College, Oxford; the Provost and Fellows of Worcester College, Oxford; Anne Woolley at Redland High School; Benedict K. Zobrist and his staff at the Harry S. Truman Library; and Christina Lawson at Woodbrooke Settlement Library. Extracts from Crown Copyright documents appear by permission of the Controller of Her Majesty's Stationery Office.

I have left until last the most important and the most tantalizing debt of all. The subject of this book died in October 1992 at the age of 87. He was helpful to me in a number of ways. First, he never refused an interview. We met on a dozen occasions at his home in North Oxford, mostly in 1990-1 (when he was 85 or 86), for two or even three hours at a stretch, sometimes on broad prearranged topics, sometimes not. These encounters followed a simple format. I would ask questions. He would answer. He answered honestly (I believe), thoughtfully, and for the most part reliably, with a slightly unnerving relevancy. Old men forget, it is said; or else they ramble. The octogenarian Oliver Franks did not make a very convincing old man. He was punctilious alike in manner and conversation. Digression was foreign to him. He rarely repeated himself and seldom volunteered information. If I did not ask, he did not offer. He grew expansive only off the subject of himself. 'Now, waste five minutes', he might say, when it became apparent that I had exhausted my list of questions. 'What do you think about the situation in Russia? It seems to me . . .'— and he would kick out his legs, a sure sign that his interest was engaged, hook one over the arm of his favourite chair, and discourse freely, suddenly unconstrained.

I did not record these sessions, believing that the tape recorder somehow inhibits even the most experienced of interviewees. I scribbled notes on the pad in my lap, and filled them out around the next corner. They are cited here in undifferentiated fashion as 'Franks interviews'.

Secondly, Franks opened doors. Or rather, he permitted doors to open. 'I understand that you have been to see Isaiah Berlin', he remarked once, in a rare acknowledgement of the biographical enterprise. 'Yes,' I said, a little taken aback, 'you are very well informed.' 'Oh, they all ring up, you know', he said enigmatically, and the conversation was closed. Franks had spoken no more than the truth. In the tight-knit circles of the English middle class the social code is to check both ways before you speak—first with the subject, for approval, and then with the author, for verification. In this case the subject adopted a commendably *laisser-faire* approach, advising everyone to do just as they wished. One might almost have believed that it was no concern of his.

Thirdly, Franks allowed me to consult his private papers. These are by no means extensive. They amount to a cardboard box full of speeches and articles, largely from his period as British Ambassador in Washington (1948–52), kept at his home; and some early correspondence with his parents, deposited in the archives of Worcester College, Oxford. Franks's is an appropriately reticent documentary legacy. Unlike so many of his contemporaries, he kept no diary, amassed no personal correspondence, and appropriated no official papers. He would rather have a bonfire than an archive.

Finally, and perhaps most generously, he made no demands and no conditions. There was never any question, for example, of his reading the manuscript before its submission to the publisher. He did not know how I would set about his life, or what I would conclude. Now he will never know. I wonder if he would have approved?

ALEX DANCHEV
Keele, 1992

Contents

List of Plates

Abbreviations

BGS	Bristol Grammar School
BJSM	British Joint Services Mission in Washington
CAB	Cabinet Papers in the Public Record Office
CCS	Combined Chiefs of Staff
CEEC	Committee of European Economic Co-operation
CM	Cabinet Minutes
COHRC	Columbia University Oral History Record Collection
COS	Chiefs of Staff
CP	Cabinet Papers
CYB	*Congregational Yearbook*
DBPO	*Documents on British Policy Overseas*
DEA	Department of External Affairs, Ottawa
DEFE	Ministry of Defence Papers
DNB	*Dictionary of National Biography*
DO	Defence Committee Papers
ERP	European Recovery Programme
FO	Foreign Office Papers in the Public Record Office
FRUS	*Foreign Relations of the United States*
GATT	General Agreement on Tariffs and Trade
GCHQ	Government Communications Headquarters
HMSO	Her Majesty's Stationery Office
HSTL	Harry S. Truman Library
JCS	Joint Chiefs of Staff
LAB	Ministry of Labour Papers
LC	Library of Congress
LMH	Lady Margaret Hall, Oxford
LNU	League of Nations Union
LSE	London School of Economics
LSF	London Society of Friends
MAP	Ministry of Aircraft Production
MBZ	Ministerie voor Buitenlandse Zaken, The Hague
MRF	Marshall Research Foundation
NA	National Archives, Washington, DC
NAC	National Archives of Canada
NATO	North Atlantic Treaty Organization
OD	Defence and Overseas Policy Committee
OECD	Organization for Economic Co-operation and Development

OEEC	Organization for European Economic Co-operation
OHI	Oral History Interview
PHSC	Political Honours Scrutiny Committee
PPE	Philosophy, Politics, and Economics
PREM	Prime Minister's Papers in the Public Record Office
PRO	Public Record Office
REP	Reconstruction Programme Papers
RG	Record Group
T	Treasury Papers in the Public Record Office
UNC	United Nations Command in Korea
UNRRA	United Nations Relief and Rehabilitation Administration
WAC	Written Archives Centre

PART I

The Philosopher and the Garden

1 *Entry*

OLIVER FRANKS might have become a Congregational minister. His father was one, and his father before him; his three uncles; and his cousin, a near contemporary. Franks himself was steeped in the Dissenting tradition. William James Franks, 'Grandfather Franks' as they say in the family, was born in Leppington, near Malton, Yorkshire, in 1838.[1] *His* father, Richard Frank, was a small farmer and saddler at Leppington. (Both variants, Frank and Franks, seem to occur in this generation.) His mother, Charlotte Johnson, came from a farm in a nearby village. They were both Wesleyan Methodists. They had ten children, three of whom (all girls) died in infancy. William, the fourth son, left home at the age of 14 for Whitby, where he was apprenticed to a cabinet-maker and became a foreman. In those days cabinet-makers were also undertakers, and William Franks was a man of great strength. He could get coffins up and down stairs when others could not move them. In Whitby he lodged with Congregationalists and began to attend the local chapel. Encouraged by the pastor to offer himself for the ministry, he applied to train at the Cotton End Congregational Academy in Bedfordshire, under the direction of the Reverend John Frost, a dedicated and popular teacher. William Booth, later famous as 'God's soldier' in the Salvation Army, was a candidate for admission at about the same time. Regrettably Booth disapproved of the manner in which his examination on 'the disputed doctrines of Arminianism' was conducted by his sponsors, the Congregational Home Missionary Society, and withdrew.[2] Evidently William Franks had no such difficulty. He studied at Cotton End from 1861 to 1865. According to a contemporary report, the syllabus included, 'besides the common grammatical and literacy exercises, which in some cases are indispensable, Theology, . . . the Evidences of Christianity, Homiletics [the art of preaching], Logic, Ecclesiastical History, the Roman Catholic and Puseyite dogmas and forms, the Greek New Testament', and the preparation and delivery of sermons, not to mention Greek and Hebrew—in which one fellow student was proficient enough to be nicknamed 'The Rabbi'.[3]

Grandfather Franks's one and only ministry was in Redcar, Yorkshire, on the North Sea coast near Middlesbrough, where he had charge of the Congregational church for thirty-seven years, from 1865 to 1902. There, it is said, he exercised a remarkable influence, based not so much upon special pulpit gifts as upon force of character. 'Shrewdness, invincible uprightness, and the gift of sympathy were notably marked in him.'[4] His stipend was £150, but this was reduced to £140 when the church was in difficulties and the £10 cut was never restored. In later years there was also £80 a year from his widowed mother-in-law, who shared the same house. After a long and happy retirement, first in Bournemouth and then in Bakewell, he died peacefully in 1927 at the great age of 89, when his grandson Oliver was already 22. He was a wise man and a prescient one. Contemplating the blood-spattered early history of the Soviet Union, he was fond of saying that the Russians were excellent artillerymen and chess-players, but their entire experience was dictatorship or anarchy: there was nothing in between.

In 1868 he married Ann Eliza, daughter of Robert Sleightholm and Mary Pennock of Whitby. Ann's father was a ship's captain and shipowner. She came from an unusually small family. Her only brother was a doctor who trained at Manchester Royal Infirmary, a likeable man who died of drink. She and William Franks had six children: Robert, John, Ernest, Richard, Johnson, and Mary. Johnson died in infancy of meningitis. The other brothers all decided for the ministry; and so in a sense did Mary, who shared the home of the bachelor Richard, 'took her full part in the work of all his churches and cared for him lovingly through the long years of his illness', when increasingly serious asthmatic complaints forced his early retirement.[5] Ann died in 1888, aged 50. Six years later, William was married again: to Jane Ann Cowl. In the interval the household was run by William himself and 'Lizzie' (Elizabeth Williams), who came daily from eight in the morning until nine at night. Lizzie had an illegitimate child and was slightly simple, or so it appeared to the Franks children.

Robert Sleightholme Franks, Oliver's father, was born in 1871 and died in 1964, a venerable 92. Dr Franks, as he became, was a scholar and a theologian—one of the most distinguished of his day.[6] He was a shy, devout, and forbearing character, but his preaching and teaching had an unusual forcefulness and clarity.[7] He was interested in people, but truly at home with books. His appetite for ideas was insatiable. Bilingual in mathematics and theology, fluent in metaphysics and history, late in life he taught himself modern physics. Of his theological works, the most notable was an imposing historical tome on ecclesiastical doctrine, first published in two volumes in 1918 and republished in a single volume in 1962. It was for this work that he was awarded the Doctor of Letters by Oxford University, in 1919. More widely read, possibly, was his *Metaphysical Justification of Religion* (1929). In his eighties he published a substantial survey of the doctrine of the Trinity. Just before his death he completed a study of the relationship between Christianity and science.[8]

Robert Franks was a man of genuine humility. He used to say that Oliver was much abler than he.[9] Oliver for his part had no doubt that, intellectually, Robert was in a different class: he revered his father. Like his brothers, Robert was educated at Sir William Turner's Grammar School in Redcar. In 1888 he went up to St John's College, Cambridge to read mathematics. As a student mathematician he was something of a phenomenon. In rapid succession he won an Open Exhibition, a Foundation Scholarship, and a Wright's Prize. Simultaneously he took a degree in the same subject from London University, graduating with first-class honours in 1891, his third year at Cambridge. He played a lot of chess, and a little J. S. Bach on the piano. Perhaps the pace was too fast. Quietly, he had a nervous breakdown. The outcome was an *aegrotat* from Cambridge, but a full recovery.

In 1893 he went to Mansfield College, Oxford, recently established as 'a Free Church Faculty in theology' and a training college for ministers, to study under the doughty A. M. Fairbairn, the founding Principal. Fairbairn was a deeply religious man of wide learning, liberal spirit, and stimulating temperament; in Franks he discovered one of his most brilliant students. The college in this early period has been likened to a monastery, 'a community of devout and scholarly men engaged in hard reading and bent on winning University prizes and distinctions'.[10] In 1898 Robert Franks became Assistant Lecturer in Philosophy, Greek Testament, and Systematic Theology. So began a strong family connection with Mansfield. Robert's younger brothers duly followed him there after equally impressive first degrees, John at Cambridge, Ernest at Edinburgh, Richard at Glasgow; Ernest's son trod the same path a generation later.[11] In 1934 Dr Franks gave the prestigious Dale Lectures there, on 'The Atonement', with his son in the audience.[12] In the late 1930s Oliver himself sat on the Mansfield College Council and instigated a thought-provoking 'mini-inquiry' into its *modus operandi*.[13] In 1961 Robert Franks's children and grandchildren endowed a scholarship to honour his ninetieth birthday and commemorate his association with the college, to help Congregational ministerial ordinands to pursue postgraduate study in theology.[14]

Franks himself did not stay long as a lecturer. In 1900 he was ordained at Prenton Road Congregational Church, Birkenhead, near Liverpool, where 'the church [was] bravely doing its work amid many difficulties'.[15] Yoking the world and his work in a manner inherited by his son, he later wrote:

The four years that I spent at Prenton saw the beginning of the twentieth century, the death of Queen Victoria and the accession of King Edward VII, together with the end of the Boer War. It was a time of prosperity when the clouds that now [in 1937] darken the spiritual horizon were no bigger than a man's hand. Prenton was a very agreeable place to live in, and the Congregational church of those days, though small, was a happy and united community, of which Baptists, Methodists, Presbyterians and some Anglicans formed about three-quarters, so that those who were Congregationalists by tradition were quite in a minority.[16]

With the arrival of the new minister 'a great improvement set in'—so great that within two years 'the church and congregation [were] so encouraged by the state of things existing amongst them that they [began] to turn their attention towards the erection of a new chapel'.[17] Franks remembered 'a strong

Sunday School and a vigorous Band of Hope'.

> In addition to these I formed a small literary circle for young men. During the four years of my ministry, the church succeeded in freeing itself from the necessity of receiving a grant from the Cheshire County Union [of Congregational Churches]. In general, these years—if 'a day of small things' compared with the present state of the church—were a time of quiet growth and happy usefulness.[18]

In 1904 he moved on, to become Theology Lecturer at Woodbrooke, Selly Oak, Birmingham, which had opened its doors to students the previous year. Woodbrooke was initially a private venture founded on the enlightened munificence of the Cadbury and Rowntree families, with a Primitive Methodist as Director of Studies and a Congregationalist as Principal Lecturer. Nevertheless, it was (and is) essentially a Quaker foundation: 'a *permanent* Summer School', as John Wilhelm Rowntree envisaged it, 'open to either sex and to persons of any age . . . a Way-side Inn, a place where the dusty traveller, stepping aside for a moment from the thronged highway, shall find refreshment and repose'. The curriculum might be of special value to 'those who feel called to serve as teachers or as ministers of the gospel', but it should appeal to a wider circle. 'There must be means placed in the reach of any Friend, who feels the call to the ministry, for still further equipment, and for close study.'[19] As it turned out, Woodbrooke was neither a theological college nor a Bible school, though there was an emphasis on biblical study and Christian doctrine. For six years Robert Franks provided most of the main courses in these core subjects. He lectured unceasingly. He took countless small classes and individual tutorials. He led devotional meetings. He gave extra-curricular talks on poetry and literature. He played tennis; he went walking and cycling. As he himself observed, he was able to be useful—that cardinal virtue—and he was very happy.[20]

In this fashion the Woodbrooke experience fed into the two streams of English Nonconformism in which the Franks family has bathed throughout the twentieth century: the Congregational Church and the Religious Society of Friends. Thus it was entirely fitting that Oliver Shewell Franks was born there on 16 February 1905, and at a tender age narrowly escaped baptism by immersion in the Woodbrooke pond.[21] His father had fallen for a young woman from Redcar some years earlier—according to legend, on the tennis court. He pursued her with Franksian constancy, 'without haste, without rest', as he might have said. At Prenton, at last, he had enough money to marry; at Woodbrooke, where he was the highest-paid lecturer, they had enough to have children.[22] So, in 1902, at Redcar Friends Meeting House, he had married the love of his life, Katherine Shewell, the daughter of an engineer and iron-bridge builder.

Katherine, known as Kitty, was born in 1875 and died in 1971, living even longer than her husband. She was one of eleven children—a large brood of strong Quakers. As a matter of principle her father would carry out no work for the War Department. The Shewells were altogether a no-nonsense family. Oliver retained vivid memories of visiting them as a tubercular 7-year-old and being put out each day, rain or shine, to walk on the beach in the east wind. There was no school for Kitty until she was 15; she was too busy coping with her rumbustious younger brothers.[23] She was then sent to a Quaker school (Ackworth in Yorkshire) and later taught briefly at another (Saffron Walden in Essex). She held to her Quakerly beliefs resolutely all her life. Oliver's father used to say that she was *anima naturaliter Christiana*, a naturally Christian person, but one with absolutely no use for dogma. Pomposity of any kind was anathema to Kitty. In truth, she had no time for it. She moved fast; she had a propulsive energy. She was compassionate and kind, and at the same time brisk, efficient, definite, delightful. Kitty Shewell was an animating spirit in the Franks family. She was devoted to Dr Franks. Dr Franks thought she was wonderful. They complemented each other beautifully.

They had four children. After Oliver in 1905 came Rosalind in 1907, Martin in 1909, and Joanna in 1910. But there can be no doubt about who was the centre of attention in the Woodbrooke community:

The completion of his first year by Oliver S. Franks was marked by the presentation of a silver spoon; and this gift carried with it hearty good wishes, not only for the recipient, 'who could find no words to express his gratitude', but also for one to whom we owe so much, as he has lectured to us and moved among us at Woodbrooke.[24]

Soon the infant Oliver was scrabbling for cuckoo flowers down by the pool in the summer, or hunting for chestnut burrs among the fallen leaves in the autumn. At 5, when the family decided it was time to move on again, he was said to be the life of the kindergarten. 'Oliver', his father observed philosophically, 'certainly was a lively person.'[25]

They moved immediately after Joanna was born. Life at Woodbrooke, in many ways idyllic, was also a shade circumscribed. Robert Franks sought something more. In 1910 he found it. He became Principal of the Western College, Bristol, where he remained for almost thirty years until his retirement in 1939. So began what has been called his life's work, the rigorous intellectual training of young men for the Congregational ministry.[26] John Huxtable was a student there in the early 1930s. In a moving tribute on Franks's death in 1964, he wrote:

It is, perhaps, with his simplicity that I should begin, for part of my most precious recollection of him is the sound of his rather high-pitched voice leading us in prayer or expounding, as he sat in the Library . . ., some passage from Jeremiah or from one of the Gospels. It was all so direct, so profound, so simple. You knew that it came from a piety so deeply-rooted that the whole of the man's life was centred upon it; and there is the secret of his lack of worldly ambition, his somewhat austere kindness, his delight in all that was humane, his keenness for all that is righteous.[27]

Simplicity of character is a principal part of the Franks appeal.

Henceforth, Oliver became a West Countryman, and specifically a Bristolian. In Bristol he went first to a 'dame school', a small private establishment run by a species now almost extinct, where the punishment for misbehaviour was to do whatever you wanted. Rather like the historian A. J. P. Taylor—a contemporary of somewhat similar background who had the same experience—Oliver withdrew, and read by himself, voraciously.[28] There followed another private school, a little better, and then, from 1915 to 1923, the formative experience of Bristol Grammar School.

Chartered by Henry VIII, founded and financed by intrepid seafarers, Bristol Grammar School rightly considered itself one of the greatest of its kind in England. The best of the old-established city grammar schools cultivated an invincible ethos of local pride and national patriotism, enfolded in a continual awareness of the peculiar customs and traditions of their own institution. Bristol was no exception.[29] Many years later Oliver Franks himself deliberately invoked this ethos in an exhortatory message to his Alma Mater written from the British Embassy in Washington:

The westward tradition of the City of Bristol, I trust, will be maintained by the Grammar School whenever it has the opportunity to welcome American visitors, especially their own contemporaries. Thereby the School will add to the intermingling of our affairs and increase the web of [Anglo-American] friendship, the original strands of which were created by men like Cabot and the Merchant Venturers.[30]

Educationally, young Oliver was fortunate in the timing of his entry to the school. In 1915 the prodigious Cyril Norwood had been Headmaster for nearly a decade. He had stamped his exacting authority on every aspect of work and play. Standards and expectations had soared. For the school's historian, 'the Norwood era was a true renaissance'.[31] In 1917 Norwood was succeeded by the equally remarkable but very different J. E. Barton, whose study of Thomas Hardy was the one of which Hardy himself most approved, and who made an indelible impression on generations of pupils with his evangelistic teaching of art appreciation—'the art of just looking'—a great novelty in a classical book-bound culture.[32] Under Barton, Oliver experienced the school's most liberal and stimulating phase. Physically, however, the conditions in his junior years were rather less inspiring. Barton remembered his own arrival in the bitter January of 1917,

when street lighting was dimmed by war regulations, and the School clock forbidden to strike, lest it might excite the interest of hovering zeppelins. The School had something like 520 boys . . . There was no electric light in the School House, and many parts of the School were still lingering in the incandescent gas period. This I recall particularly, from the damage caused to all mantels in the classrooms below the Great Hall by the stamping exuberance of our Armistice Day assembly, summoned immediately the big news had been declared, and rapturous in the belief that the war to end war had achieved its aim.[33]

Oliver Franks's performance at Bristol offers no crumb of comfort for those who like their great men to be school dunces—what one might call the Churchill myth.[34] His school career was as brilliant as any of the others he pursued.[35] Every year with monotonous regularity he carried off the Form Prize and usually one or more besides. He departed the Classical Sixth with prizes in English Literature, Latin, and Greek Testament. He was also Best Debater and vice-chairman of the Literary and Debating Society, to which he contributed papers on 'Coleridge and Wordsworth in the Quantocks' and 'The Caliph Vathek', William Beckford's bizarre tale of a caliph who sold himself to the powers of evil.[36] He reached his modest ceiling as a Lance-Corporal in the Officers' Training Corps and never led his patrol in the 18th Bristol Scout Group, but this signal lack of leadership experience did not prevent him becoming House Prefect, School Prefect, House Captain, School Captain.

Franks—the boys barely knew each other's first names and never used them—was disgustingly good at every subject, much appreciated by the Masters, and not especially companionable. He even read books at break. He was, in short, a swot; but not an insufferable one. He was not averse to camping expeditions in the New Forest with an energetic Housemaster, the much-loved F. 'Billy' Beames; he was sometimes amusing in his serious-minded way; and if you got to know him, he could even be—there is a strong hint of surprise—fun.[37]

What is more, he was passably good at games—a redeeming feature of no small significance. Even under the enlightened Barton there were still vestiges of the Victorian nostrum that 'if a boy is not already a gentleman, football and cricket will soon serve to make him one'. On such criteria Franks's gentlemanly prospects at first appeared to be rather poor. He played no football and was but a humble scorer for the School First XI cricket team, his occasional batting record a ruinous 0, 9, 0, 1, 0. Yet the call to play up, play up, and play the game did not leave him entirely unmoved. Franks played First XI hockey: 'Rather slow in recovering from an attack on a forward. Clears well and hard, and is fairly safe when within reach of the ball. Inartistic stick play.' He also played First XV rugby, where his height (6 foot 2 inches) and weight (12 stone) told in the line-out: 'Must be careful not to bounce the ball on the ground in getting it away to the half. Dribbles well and packs low in the scrum. Should tackle harder and not hang out of a loose scrum. Kicks well with both feet.' Finally, there was fives. The dialogue in Erasmus would have appealed to him. Nicholas: 'We shall sweat less if we play with a racket.' Jerome: 'Let us leave nets to the fishermen; the game is prettier if played with the hands.'[38] Oliver played enthusiastically: 'Has improved a lot since last year. His left arm can be used to advantage, but he should practice [*sic*] with his right. He is still rather slow on his feet, and is hampered by bad eyesight.'

The sum of his academic achievement was an Open Scholarship in Classics to Queen's College, Oxford. This was a great day for the whole family. An absolute commitment to the best possible education—very probably an Oxbridge education—was one of the basic assumptions of their lives. In keeping with the Quaker value system, this held good for boys and girls alike. There was equality of esteem; and intellectually, if not socially, there was equality of treatment. In this sphere the Frankses, like the Webbs, were partners. A mettlesome air of intellectual enquiry pervaded the entire household. Oliver and his sisters and brother were expected to think, and think hard, for themselves.[39] They formed opinions of their own, and had every opportunity to define and defend them. Mealtimes were feasts of conversation. Dr Franks did not read the newspaper at breakfast; the family talked. More accurately, they *discussed*: tremendous, eager, open discussions about everything from the flowers in the fields to the Channel Fleet, the latter a boyhood vision of overwhelming power which haunted Franks throughout his adult life—a life coterminous with the long post-war recession, as he himself often remarked.[40] Correlli Barnett has written that 'the Great War has a fascination beyond the historical insights it gives'.

It is the fascination of events, of sentiments, as near as one's father's youth and yet as remote as the crusades: lances of the *Garde Ulanen* scratching the summer sky of 1914; the guns of Jellicoe's thirty-four capital ships firing the valedictory salute to British sea-power into the mists of Jutland; horizon blue and field grey; the Motherland, the Fatherland, *La Patrie.*[41]

The Franks family played seriously with words. They weighed their value, knew their meaning. If necessary they had recourse to *Chambers*. (Many things could be tolerated, but not a reckless imprecision. The children were taught to look things up. The elderly *Encyclopaedia Britannica* was as well used as the dictionary.) They analysed articles in *The Times*. On Sunday, over the midday meal, they dissected the sermon they had just heard. The opinions were sensible but the talk was unrestrained. This was a liberal household, in more than one sense. Within a clearly delineated moral framework there was great freedom, not only to talk, but also to climb on the Western College roof. It was a strong parental precept to be available, to be approachable, but never to interfere.

Socially, they had some advanced ideas. Sexual information was given early to the children. Politically, they were staunch believers in the unimpeachable virtue of Mr Gladstone—in moments of hilarity, the GOM (Grand Old Man). They voted Liberal, always. Young Oliver, 5 years old, sported a loyal rosette in the General Election of 1910. Around the meal table, however, there was little talk of party politics or politicians; they were more interested in the pattern of events, in the making of history, and its meaning. More than this, it was the natural world that engaged them, and they were avid for the poetry it inspired. In Wordsworth's preface to the *Lyrical Ballads* there is a resonant passage for any philosopher:

Aristotle, I have been told, hath said, that Poetry is the most philosophic of all writing: it is so: its object is truth, not individual and local, but general, and operative . . . Poetry is the image of man and nature. The obstacles that stand in the way of fidelity of the Biographer and Historian, and of their consequent utility, are incalculably greater than those which are to be encountered by the Poet who has an adequate notion of the dignity of his art. The Poet writes under one restriction only, namely, that of the necessity of giving immediate pleasure to a human Being possessed of that information which may be expected from him, not as a lawyer, a physician, a mariner, an astronomer or a natural philosopher, but as a Man.[42]

It is no accident that Oliver grew up a great quoter of Wordsworth. *Lyrical Ballads* was a favourite work of his father's. Oliver's paper on Wordsworth and Coleridge in the Quantocks was the fruit of numerous family walking holidays in those well-remembered hills, retracing the steps of the two poets, pausing now and then for Robert Franks to summon their ghostly presence by reading aloud from the book—on the ridge of Quantock Hill, for example, where Wordsworth had seen it (or its like) in 1798:

> There is a thorn; it looks so old,
> In truth you'll find it hard to say,
> How it could ever have been young,
> It looks so old and grey.
> Not higher than a two-years' child,
> It stands erect this aged thorn;
> No leaves it has, no thorny points;
> It is a mass of knotted joints,
> A wretched thing forlorn.
> It stands erect, and like a stone
> With lichens it is overgrown.[43]

Seventy years later Franks could still recall that rendition of 'The Thorn'. His holidays were always like this. Their frugality was at once essential and appealing. They stayed in farmhouses, occupying a sitting-room and three bedrooms, one for the parents, one for the girls, one for the boys. Kitty bought the food for the farmer's wife to cook. They walked and swam and walked again. They explored Alfoxden Manor (now Alfoxton) where Wordsworth lived with his sister, Dorothy; and Nether Stowey, where Coleridge pondered the Ancient Mariner in a dark little cottage nearby. They roamed the coombs and hills with a passion matching those 'three persons with one soul', as Coleridge once described them. They pursued their quarry with characteristic exactitude. As they went they pored over fallen leaves; they inspected new buds; with the help of Johns' *Flowers of the Field* (which accompanied them everywhere) they identified wild flowers; they watched the weather change. Skullcap, musk-mallow, meadow-cranesbill, arrowhead, and all manner of monocotyledons: in time, Oliver knew every one. He developed a keen botanical sense, an intellectual curiosity about natural phenomena, which found expression in an abiding love of gardening and an all-weather affection for walking the countryside. In the words of another poet:

> Between the hills are wooded coombes,
> The homes of solitude and peace.
> The whisp'ring trees and cool, dim air
> Bid all creation's turmoil cease.
>
> I love the quiet, shady glades,
> The scented gorse, the trickling rills.
> I wish I never had to leave
> The dear, old, peaceful Quantock Hills.

It seems Wordsworth and Coleridge were not the only poets around the house. These verses were written by Oliver's sister Joanna, aged 11. She spoke for all of them.[44]

The pronounced literary flavour of these holidays were entirely consistent with the normal daily round. Oliver had indeed 'lived among books and bookish people', as it says in the Queen's College entrance records.[45] As a child he was soaked in reading matter. Nothing in the house was deemed unsuitable. Foraging greedily among the shelves, he did a vast amount of reading. Oliver would do his homework in the study where his father worked from six until nine each evening. His reward was half an hour's reading—Dumas, perhaps, or Scott; or one of the many magazines to which his father subscribed: *Punch*, the *Strand*, *Blackwood's*, the *Spectator*, *Cornhill Magazine*. He devoured enormous quantities of poetry: as well as Coleridge and Wordsworth, Thomas Hardy (the influence of J. E. Barton), A. E. Housman (*A Shropshire Lad*, first published in 1896), Walter de la Mare—there is a cherished copy of *Peacock Pie* (1913) in the family still—John Donne, Henry Vaughan (those he called the 'quasi-mystical' poets), for whom childhood was a time of 'white Celestial light' and paradisal memories, Shakespeare, Milton, Spenser (*The Faerie Queene*, 'twice, but not recently'), the classics; *not* Tennyson or Longfellow or Kipling, the last rather scorned in youth but taken up afresh in old age. He could swallow a novel whole. Hardy again was a favourite—this time the influence of his mother, who read aloud selected passages from *Far From the Madding Crowd* (1874). Of course the children knew the poem, Gray's 'Elegy Written in a Country Churchyard', from which Hardy drew his inspiration:

> Far from the madding crowd's ignoble strife
>   Their sober wishes never learn'd to stray;
> Along the cool, sequester'd vale of life
>   They kept the noiseless tenor of their way.

And they never forgot the quiet roar of the burning hayrick, thrilling and exact as life itself.

A rick burns differently from a house. As the wind blows the fire inwards, the portion in flames completely disappears like melting sugar, and the outline is lost to the eye. However, a hay or a wheat rick, well put together, will resist combustion for a length of time if it begins on the outside.

This before Gabriel's eyes was a rick of straw, loosely put together, and the flames darted into it with lightning swiftness. It glowed on the windward side, rising and falling in intensity like the coal of a cigar. Then a superincumbent bundle rolled down with a whisking noise; flames elongated, and bent themselves about with a quiet roar, but no crackle. Banks of smoke went off horizontally at the back like passing clouds, and behind these burned hidden pyres, illuminating the semi-transparent sheet of smoke to a lustrous yellow uniformity. Individual straws in the foreground were consumed in a creeping movement of ruddy heat, as if they were knots of red worms, and above shone imaginary fiery faces, tongues hanging from lips, glaring eyes, and other impish forms, from which at intervals sparks flew in clusters like birds from a nest.

Above all, there was the Bible. When Oliver decided to teach himself German, in the long vacation at the end of his third year at Oxford, he did so in three somewhat unorthodox stages. He started with the familiar repetitions of the Gospel according to St John: 'In the beginning was the Word, and the Word was with God, and the Word was God . . .' When he had mastered the Gospel he turned to another key text from his childhood, Hans Andersen's fairy tales. After that he went straight on to his ultimate goal: Immanuel Kant's *Kritik der Reinen Vernunft (The Critique of Pure Reason)*. The foundation was appropriate. As far back as he could remember there had been Bible-reading at home. When he was very young his mother would read aloud from Amy Steadman's *Bible for Children*. When he was a little older there were family prayers after breakfast and before he went off to school. His mother would weave a narrative in daily instalments from the prophets of the Old Testament or the apostles of the New; or she would read them entrancing tales of heroism in strange lands—tales of 'The White Queen of Okodama', perhaps, otherwise known as Mary Slessor, a Scottish missionary who dared to venture among the cannibalistic tribes of the west coast of Africa.[46] On Sundays, naturally, they went to church. In the evening his father would play the piano and they would sing hymns. This was not at all a solemn occasion. Dr Franks relished playing every bit as much as his family enjoyed singing. Afterwards, a stillness would descend on the household. Oliver, Rosalind, and Joanna would be in different rooms, reading; Martin, of more practical bent, would be excavating in the garden or busy with his tools. Each absorbed new knowledge like a sponge. The openness of their parents, and their Goethe-like interest in the interrelatedness of things, did its work well.

In his final term at Bristol Grammar School, the School Captain penned an elegiac editorial, very much à la mode, for the school magazine: 'We have not much to record this term. All frivolous and pleasurable occupations have been neglected, and a staid and sober atmosphere of work has settled, at least, upon the upper forms of the School. Perforce, we shall have to fall back upon the perennial topic of polite English conversation', that is, the weather. The editorial continued: 'As this is the last time we shall occupy the editorial chair we must make our adieux. The parting is more bitter than wormwood, but the fate is inevitable. We shall endeavour to prove the truth of the saying, *Nec post obliviscemur.*'[47] This 'saying' was in fact a line from the last verse of the school song, written by Cyril Norwood. The verse was never sung, and they were few indeed who could quote from it. The final couplet runs:

> *Dum adsumus, augebimus,*
> *Nec post obliviscemur.*
>
> (While we are here, we shall grow in stature,
> And afterwards we shall not forget.)[48]

Oliver Franks had grown in stature. In the high summer of 1923, aged 18, he boarded the train for Oxford.

2 *Oxford Attained*

To his fellow students, he was 'Father Franks', preternaturally wise, solemn, seclusive, masterful. His tutors, 'eager for his good opinions, load him with gifts in the shape of Collections prizes'.[1] Summoned before the Provost, the ancient and other-worldly Reverend Dr J. R. Magrath, a wraith immured in the Provost's Lodgings since 1878, he was asked three questions. What was his religion? Did he take regular exercise? Did he own a horse? Father Franks was unperturbed by this strange catechism. To the first he answered Congregationalist. That was correct. To the second he answered yes. That too was correct. To the third he answered no. That was wrong—most definitely wrong. He should obtain a horse forthwith, and ride it daily. The Provost would advise him on the purchase. With that, the audience was over. Franks remembered it all his life. But he never bought a horse.

Initially, the appearance of complete self-possession was a little deceptive. Franks arrived at Oxford by no means as sure of himself as a perusal of the Bristol Grammar School magazine might suggest. The entrance examination had not been plain sailing. In fact, he fetched up at Queen's College only after a second attempt. He had tried first for a Classics scholarship at Corpus Christi College, without success. The next year he crept in, as he said, the second scholar at Queen's.[2] Undergraduate society in the college conformed to a rigid stratification, at once social and intellectual, complete with a president and various other elective offices. Obviously there were the different years. When Franks was in his freshman year the President of the Taberdars' Room (the Junior Common Room at Queen's) was Malcolm MacDonald, son of Ramsay MacDonald, soon to take office as the first Labour Prime Minister. Fundamentally, however, there were scholars (who had an award) and there were commoners (who did not). There were also exhibitioners (who held a minor award). The difference between scholars and commoners, already apparent in the terminology, was perfectly displayed in the gowns they wore. A scholar's gown was a splendid thing, immediately recognizable as such. It was fine and long and full. It made an ample cloak, like a musketeer's. When a scholar crossed the quad with a purposeful stride, it billowed satisfyingly behind. A commoner's gown allowed none of this. It was a skimpy article scarcely worthy of the name, sleeveless and short, vestigially hung with 'streamers' of limp cloth. It would not billow. Instead, it straggled. It was a garment that betokened an altogether humbler calling. At Oxford, as in life, style indicated station. 'In Hall,' Franks reported,

we have definite tables but not definite places. Our table consists of all the freshers who are scholars or exhibitioners—about 15 or 20 in all. The senior scholar . . . has to sit at the end of the table and if he is not there I as second scholar have to take his place. Apparently any Classical scholar takes precedence over any other scholar or exhibitioner. I got hold of a secondhand scholar's gown . . . and paid 8/-, not excessive I think, as they are 17/6 or 20/- in the shops.[3]

Dining, like dressing, had its own special meaning. The scholars were the élite. Classical scholars were the élite of the élite. Franks wore their gown, but only by the skin of his teeth. Fresh and rather ignorant, in his own estimation, he drew comfort from the family bookshelves. 'The great trouble with most of the scholars', he wrote home after a few weeks, 'is that they know a lot more classics than I do, at least they have read about five times as much, at school, but they know nothing about anything else. I lent a Thomas Hardy to one of them who had never heard of him before and most of them have hardly heard of classical authors outside the usual curriculum.'[4]

Financially he was not embarrassed; nor was he completely secure. In his first term he took up rowing. 'It will mean much ἀδγῶ τὸν ὄρρον [pain in the arse] but still it will not be too energetic, it is constant every afternoon and finishes before tea.' Hastening to reassure his mother, he wrote:

You ask what I am wearing for rowing: my attire is composed of 1 pr ordinary walking shoes, 1 pr ordinary army socks, 1 pr Rugger shorts, 1 zephyr [a light jersey] which I bought up here (3/6) and a sweater. So far at any rate it is much the cheapest of the games as in all the others a college shirt is used for which they rush at least 15/-.[5]

The family budget was still tight. Oliver's silver spoon was the exception rather than the rule. His pocket money was a penny a week until he was 16, when it was suddenly tripled. To give four children the chance to go to university, as his parents were determined to do, involved careful budgeting. 'At Oxford in the 1920s we were either rich or poor', wrote Douglas Jay, a near contemporary. To be poor was to be self-aware. Cyril Connolly once found Evelyn Waugh, no less, roaring drunk outside Balliol and asked him why he was making such a noise. 'I have to make a noise because I am poor', he said, with feeling.[6] Franks was poor, but made no noise—his whole life, one might say, was a noiseless one. In his first two years at Queen's his college bills (called battels) were around £50 per term. His annual income was £195. Of this, the scholarship contributed a much-needed £100. Money from his parents was topped up by a Bristol solicitor, Edgar Tanner, a widower and friend of the family, and a deacon of the chapel to which they all belonged. Each year Tanner put in £80—a generous sum. He assisted the others in similar fashion: Rosalind and Joanna read Mathematics and English, respectively, at Girton College, Cambridge; Martin read Engineering at Bristol. The arrangement had an exact parallel in the previous generation, when another deacon, Joseph Lister of Redcar, had helped to send Robert Franks to Cambridge. Like other Nonconformists, the Congregationalists were a tight-knit community who looked after their own.[7] To be accepted—fully accepted—'by the academic crowd at Oxford' must have meant a great deal to young Father Franks.[8]

With suitable economy, he enjoyed his early days at Oxford. 'Mr Franks, too, was admired by them that dally on the towpath.' He continued to row in spite of 'large raw patches' which prevented him from sitting down even in a soft armchair 'without instant repentance'.[9] He did not join the Oxford Union (the debating society) because he could not afford to. He went to the occasional free concert, and once a term to the sixpenny seats in the cinema. He slept well, relieved to find a bed long enough for his feet to project at the bottom without obstruction. He kept regular, and unfashionable, hours. 'There are truly many distractions from work: and one assumption on which most arguments are based when they draw me away in the evenings is that no-one should dream of going to bed before one. In fact all the visits I have had in the evening have been when I was well in bed.' He breakfasted on porridge, bacon and eggs, and toast, butter, and marmalade; lunched on bread and cheese (the habit of a lifetime); went out to tea; and dined in Hall. His letters home—written each Sunday afternoon, according to the unfailing family custom—identified new acquaintances with familiar exactitude. 'On Friday afternoon I went to tea with two freshers, Cousin a Scotch Presbyterian and Hall a Yorkshire Unitarian. We went to Cousin's rooms: we go to Hall's on Monday and mine next Friday. They seem interesting and intelligent chaps.'[10] He was naturally a frequent visitor to Mansfield College, and to the tea table of the long-serving Principal, W. B. Selbie, a friend of his father's. He also received regular invitations from that celebrated sage Gilbert Murray, Chairman of the League of Nations Union and Regius Professor of Greek, whose lectures he made a special point of attending. On Sunday mornings he went, 'all good', to the Mansfield College chapel, where he heard Selbie preach—on one occasion, 'an excellent sermon on the maniac and the Gadarene swine. He raised a considerable laugh when he said how he had left off saying that people had devils in them and called them complexes.'[11]

Two years into his degree came the event which, so to say, confirmed Father Franks to himself: the First Public Examination in *Literae Humaniores*: Honour Moderations—familiarly known as Mods—a first hurdle of fifteen papers in everything from Aristophanes to Virgil. Franks prepared himself for this test with exemplary thoroughness. 'With the approach of Mods, Mr Franks has withdrawn into an anchorite's seclusion, whence he only occasionally emerges, wearing the most remarkable stockings.'[12] The results were spectacular—fourteen alphas and a solitary beta in Latin Prose, some of the highest marks in the whole university, and the best First at Queen's since the Great War. With the éclat came a £5 book prize, invested in Ward's

Psychology, William James's *Psychology*, Bradley's *Appearance and Reality*, Broad's *Appearance, Perception and Reality*, and a bound volume of Wordsworth. He then permitted himself a little relaxation. 'Did not Mr Franks collect innumerable alphas in his recent encounter? Does he not now read paper-backs upon the river? Is not that the manifestation of real genius?'[13]

Thereafter, Franks never looked back. In 1925 he became President of the Taberdars' Room. When the General Strike was ordered in May 1926 he held a meeting of all junior members of the college to discuss what, if anything, they should do. The President exercised what he later called a judgement of Solomon: he determined that each individual should act according to the dictates of his conscience. Like most of his fellows—Hugh Gaitskell at New College and A. J. P. Taylor at Oriel were notable exceptions—Franks's own conscience told him that in the face of a potent constitutional threat it was necessary to strike-break. He therefore went to work as a docker at Hay's Wharf in London, shifting endless cheeses and sides of bacon. He returned to Oxford with an aching corset of muscles from his neck to his knees, the rich, rancid smell of the ship's hold wafting everywhere he went, clinging to his clothes, and lingering in his memory.[14]

He also became President of the Oxford Old Bristolians Society. The OBs dined together irregularly but formally, and in some style, at their various colleges. The 1929 Annual Dinner was held in the Senior Common Room of Merton College, courtesy of E. W. B. Gill. The menu makes impressive reading:

Hors d'Oeuvre Variés
Consommé Jardinière
Sole Meunière
Canard Sausage—Salade d'Orange
Omelette Soufflé en Surprise
Beignet au Parmesan
Café

For most of the company, though not for Father Franks—a teetotaller by upbringing and inclination—these dinners were bibulous affairs. The expected toasts were proposed and the expected replies made: the King, the Freshmen, the Visitors, the Senior Members, the School. Orotund minutes were kept. 'When we had done with orating . . . we adjourned to the smoke room where supplies of whisky and reinforcements of cigars were called for: both were obtained with some difficulty, the former with a not unwelcome scarcity of soda-water. When the turmoil for signatures had subsided and the owner had recovered the pencil, Mr Franks was discovered discussing metaphysics with Bro. Manson [of Blackfriars], while the rest of the company gathered in little knots exchanging stories of the usual sort.' At 11.45 or thereabouts they would disperse, like so many dinner-jacketed Cinderellas, 'each making for home with what speed he could command' before the college gates slammed shut at midnight. Inevitably there were those who had some late-night climbing to do.[15]

All this was diversion. Franks's chief responsibility was puritanically plain. Work came first. 'Mr Franks has become almost a legendary figure. There appear to be some doubts of his tangible existence at Queen's. One fact only has penetrated to us. Mr Franks, with characteristic wisdom, is reading St Thomas Aquinas for that most soul-destroying of all ordeals, Greats. We commend his example, for here is balm for the tortured spirit.'[16]

After Mods came Greats: two years of philosophy and ancient history culminating in the Second Public Examination—the dread finals, or in Oxford parlance, Schools. The voluptuous image of an Oxford populated entirely by the acolytes of Evelyn Waugh, trailing teddy bears palely in their wake and indulging in an endless round of eating, drinking, and expectorating, tends to conceal the almost obsessive seriousness with which many undergraduates addressed themselves to their books. For Oliver Franks, as for most others, *Vile Bodies* was a solipsistic dream, and *Brideshead* a foreign country.[17] Much more real, and more immediate, was C. S. Lewis on 'Moral Good', or H. J. Paton on 'Metaphysics', or Gilbert Ryle on 'The Theory of Knowledge, from Descartes to Hume', or the Wykeham Professor of Logic on 'The Judgement'. The Wykeham Professor, Harold Joachim, was a civilized neo-Hegelian, passionately fond of music. His lectures were said to be annotated with a musical score which varied from year to year, while the words remained the same. In spite of these idiosyncrasies, or perhaps because of them, it was Joachim's lectures that Franks particularly relished, as he recalled some sixty years later: 'Joachim held views, they were pure Hegelian views, with which I didn't agree at all, but it was a most *marvellous* performance—polished, learned, acute, sometimes witty, and I went for the sheer pleasure of hearing it, all the way through.'[18]

Franks imbibed philosophy with a will. He was reading prodigiously, as usual, encouraged by his father's example and conversation. Already acquainted with Plato and Socrates, Aristotle and Cicero, he embarked on an exploration of the whole canon, with Oxfordian emphasis on the native English empiricist tradition of Locke, Berkeley, Hume, and John Stuart Mill. In 1925 he read for the first time Aquinas's masterworks, *Summa contra gentiles* (*Summary against the Gentiles*, known in English translation as *On the Truth of the Catholic Faith*), a reasoned account of Christianity to non-believers; and *Summa theologiae* (*Summary of Theology*), a synthesis of Catholic theology beautifully articulated in three gigantic parts, *Prima pars*, on God and the going-out of all things from Him, *Secunda pars*, on the return of human beings to Him as their home, *Tertia pars*, on Christ and His sacraments. On reading this, Franks was deeply moved. He felt as if he had walked into a great medieval cathedral, brilliantly conceived, magnificently proportioned, exquisitely wrought, where everything fitted together with formal perfection. For Franks this was a new experience—an aesthetic experience—and an uplifting one.[19]

Now it was time for his self-instruction in German and the extreme demands of his most exciting discovery yet: the gloriously pure reason of Immanuel Kant.[20] For Kant, reason must never be *passive*. Literally, we should think for ourselves; that is, use our reason independently. To think for oneself is 'the supreme touchstone of truth'. It leads away from superstition (the complete subjugation of reason) towards enlightenment (the consistent application of reason). Kant thought that enlightenment tends to be confused with knowledge. As he remarked, 'those who are exceedingly rich in knowledge are often least enlightened in their use of it'. Rather, in striving for enlightenment it is necessary to cultivate 'the mental habit . . . of detaching ourselves from the subjective and personal conditions of our judgement, which cramp the mind of so many others, and reflect upon our judgement from a *universal point of view* which we can only do by adopting the point of view of others'. Thus the fundamental Kantian maxims of '*unprejudiced*' and '*enlarged*' thought.[21] Franks embraced them both, full-heartedly and for ever. With Immanuel Kant, he had found his first true intellectual home.

Oxford philosophy as Franks first sampled it—in the late 1920s—was witheringly characterized as 'surly and unadventurous' by A. J. Ayer, the precocious author of *Language, Truth and Logic* (1936). Ayer was naturally *parti pris*, but for Gilbert Ryle too, 'the philosophic kettle' in Oxford at this time was 'barely lukewarm'.[22] There was clearly something lacking. Tutorials were taken 'both seriously and lightly', as Franks remarked. His own tutor at Queen's was H. J. Paton, soon to become Professor of Logic at Glasgow. Paton was a man for deep ponderation, a Kantian scholar and a heavy smoker. In tutorial he was quite unfathomable. At some point he might enquire, 'Now, Franks, what *exactly* do you mean by . . .?', but otherwise he seldom spoke. Each week Franks was quietly kippered in a corner of his study. In his absence the best of his students were sent to H. A. Prichard, then a don at Trinity, later White's Professor of Moral Philosophy. A marvellous picture of Prichard has been drawn by Maurice Bowra:

He wore rough, shabby clothes, and had a dirty moustache and closely cropped hair. In lecturing he tied himself up in knots or began to climb the mantelpiece. There was no doubt to his passionate commitment to his subject. He went through fearful self-lacerations to find the right ideas and the right words for them. One term he lectured on 'What do we see?' He began hopefully with the idea that we see colours, but he abandoned it in the third week, and argued that we saw things. But that would not do either, and by the end of the term he admitted ruefully, 'I'm damned if I know what we do see.' This was magnificently humble, and I attended every lecture by Prichard that I could. . . . He had very eccentric views on duty, which had to be obeyed without hesitation but was never in the least explicable. Since his examples of it were getting up early in the morning and having one's hair cut short, it fell short of my ideal of a good life. Not that Prichard himself did not suffer in trying to decipher its messages, and we all read with avidity an article which he had written called 'Is moral philosophy based on a mistake?' But, as Jack Haldane pointed out, it was not the kind of mistake we hoped.[23]

Prichard was probably the most rigorous and minute thinker to be found in Oxford at that time. As a tutor, he was conscientious to the point of fanaticism. Franks had eight tutorials with him, 'the shortest of which lasted three hours, and I was never allowed to get beyond the second sentence of my essay in any one'. He complained to Queen's and to Prichard—who reacted with a characteristic 'I quite understand'—and was promptly switched to the advanced young Gilbert Ryle at Christ Church.[24]

Ryle was a clubbable Queensman, only five years Franks's senior, who had first taught him to row. The two men became friends. They went on holiday together, and Ryle later officiated at Franks's wedding. From the start, Ryle was 'philosophically eager', as he said of himself. As a student, unbidden, he had acquired a reading knowledge of Italian and a modest grasp of Italian philosophy, much to the surprise of his tutors. As a don he taught himself German and browsed contentedly for a while in the rarified fields of phenomenology and anti-psychologistic theories of meaning. One outcome of this browsing was an unwanted course of lectures on 'Logical Objectivism: Bolzano, Brentano, Husserl and Meinong'—known in Oxford as 'Ryle's three Austrian railway stations and one Chinese game of chance'.[25] Philosophically, Ryle moved on. In intellectual style and approach he had an important influence on Franks in these early years. As to tutorials: 'We agreed that essays were a bore, so eight times during term we went and played golf at Frilford, and talked a bit of philosophy going round the course.' This was a refreshing change from Paton and Prichard. 'It was fairly agreeable, I learnt a certain amount, it was entirely satisfactory.'[26]

In the summer of 1927 he took Schools. 'Is prudence a duty?' 'Can evil be done for its own sake?' 'Is a moral act more rational than an immoral?' 'Signs do not mean anything. It is we who mean. Discuss this.' 'Are thought and action in the same sense free?' 'Do scientific conclusions claim to be true or convenient?' 'Did Plato succeed in showing that the just life is more pleasant and profitable in itself than the unjust?' 'Is Aristotle's account of pleasure and pain an advance upon Plato's?' Such were the questions with which he had to grapple.[27] Manifestly he grappled well. In those days all candidates faced a viva (an oral examination) after their written papers had been marked. As A. L. Rowse painfully recalled, 'Schools over, I was by no means through with Schools: the viva voce loomed ahead at the end of July and intending Firsts were well advised to prepare themselves for the further ordeal, caulking leaks, filling in gaps, strengthening the weak spots divined by our enemies, the examiners.'[28] It was well understood that there were two possible variations. A short viva meant that the class of degree was already decided (though *which* class remained for the moment in doubt). A long viva meant that the outcome was entirely imponderable, and was invariably the cause of great anguish to all concerned. Franks's viva lasted a cursory six minutes—the merest formality. He had secured an unimpeachable First. The examiners tendered ceremonious congratulations. He had also secured the offer of a Fellowship in Philosophy at Queen's, an offer made and accepted before the viva was held. The college needed a successor for the departing Paton. Franks was chosen as 'the best philosopher of his year'. Could he now become *der schöne Magister*, like Kant himself?[29]

Franks considered the fellowship as a teacher first and a philosopher second. The offer had come as a complete surprise. Characteristically, he took time to reflect upon it. He was certainly interested in philosophy. He liked Oxford. His ancestry was littered with teachers. It would be appropriate. He thought he could do it. He had no distractions and no other plans. Unlike his younger brother Martin, who seemed to know from at least the age of 4 that he wanted to be an engineer, and happily became one, Oliver had no particular bent. Indeed, he did not have the slightest idea what he wanted to do or be. He had, however, already made certain choices: primarily, not to become a Congregational minister (thereby foregoing a closed scholarship to Oxford), or a chartered accountant (rejecting an attractive offer from the deacon of his uncle's church)—'two painful negatives arrived at'.[30] In the wake of Schools, he had also determined not to try for the Civil Service, unable to face the thought of yet another examination. After his summons to Queen's he consulted his father, who advised (as expected) that he should do what he thought best. As for himself, Dr Franks added, if he had been offered a fellowship, he had always thought he would have liked it. 'How children dance to the unlived lives of their parents', said Rilke, wisely.

In the event, the question of teaching was deferred. Having appointed him, the college immediately gave him a year's leave of absence and instructions to 'go to Europe and grow older', with the princely sum of £400 to help him on his way.[31] Franks needed no further encouragement. With Gilbert Ryle, he set off for Heidelberg, the hotbed of German philosophical activity. There he stayed for three months, attending lectures and seminars by such luminaries as Husserl, the father of phenomenology, and Jaspers, the existentialist. For an *émigré* from Oxford this was novel fare indeed.[32]

From Heidelberg, inspired possibly by the phenomenology, Franks composed some limericks for his sisters:

> There once was a lady of Girton
> Who got quite a liking for Burton
> She drank off so much
> That she talked Double Dutch
> And dined with the Mistress's skirt on.

There was an old lady of Ghent
Whose legs were exceedingly bent;
   She rode in a pram
   And kept a pet lamb
Whose wool paid the quarterly rent.[33]

When inspiration flagged, there was a need for the customary cold bath. This caused an unexpected problem.

Did I ever tell you of the surprise and amazement which greeted my petition for cold baths? I went without and performed with the normal jug and basin arrangement in the bedroom for a day or two, but it was so difficult to keep awake and so impossible to feel lively that I asked about a cold bath. At this I was introduced to the bathroom in which the bath stands in a solitary place looking unutterably grotesque. . . . Well, people took quite kindly to the idea when they saw I meant what I said. The first morning I had to discourage the servant whose idea of a cold bath was to run a hot one a half hour too soon so that it was tepid when I got to it. All is well now . . . [34]

There were other lacunae. 'At present I sigh plaintively for a Pontefract cake: you can't get low-down liquorice sweets anywhere in Germany. Now we know what made England great.'[35] For want of a Pontefract cake, and in truth a little bored, he quit Heidelberg for Berlin in January 1928. His departure was noted rather sniffily by those he left behind. 'It seems Mr Franks went to Berlin with the intention of seeing more of the world, but what has become of him is one of those mysteries which we would be glad to see cleared up.'[36]

Unimpressed with Berlin, he decided on a pilgrimage to Königsberg, the home of Immanuel Kant. Königsberg (now Kaliningrad) is on the Baltic Sea coast, east of Danzig (now Gdańsk). Franks travelled by slow train, fourth class, up the 'Polish Corridor' that separated Poland and East Prussia. The journey was broken by his arrest for climbing out of the train window at one of the many stops. All efforts at direct communication with his Polish guards proved fruitless. It transpired, however, that they did have one thing in common: bridge. Franks made an incongruous fourth. The guards were fanatics. They played for a solid twenty-three hours. At the end of this marathon, exhausted, he was put on the next train, and eventually reached his destination.[37] In Königsberg he walked the streets that Kant had walked on his proverbial daily constitutional. The great man would always go alone, from the conviction that conversation, since it causes a person to breathe through the mouth, should not take place in the open air; and with such regularity, it was said, that the townsfolk used to set their clocks by the time of his passing. On the shore Franks saw an even stranger sight. The waves of the Baltic were frozen in mid-air, the water trapped for a season. To avoid the same fate he fled to Vienna, where he watched the bewitching Josephine Baker tickle the ears of an enraptured nightclub audience. Franks was clearly enjoying his travels. 'My weight is 13.5 at the moment', he wrote to his parents. 'I am informed that I look like a Glaxo baby. Anyhow I am very fit.'[38]

After Vienna, he 'behaved like Goethe's young man' and went over the Brenner Pass into Italy.[39] There he was arrested again, in possession of Plato's *Republic*, by Mussolini's police. After brief detention he made his way at last to the captivating city of Florence, where he grew older gracefully for a while before returning home to Bristol. Appropriately enough, it is in the timeless dialogue of *The Republic* that Socrates makes the argument that 'there will be no end to the troubles of states, or indeed . . . of humanity itself, till philoso- phers become kings in this world, or till those we now call kings and rulers really and truly become philosophers'. The arrest of the tyro philosopher by the shirt-sleeved myrmidons of *Il Duce* is a fine thing to contemplate.[40]

What kind of philosopher, then, did this tyro turn out to be? Stuart Hampshire has written that 'the whole of human life and of human history is open for inspection and evaluation under the title of moral philosophy'.[41] Franks was a moral philosopher in this spirit. He believed that philosophy could provide real answers to real questions about life. 'Philosophy is not an expertise, it is an attitude of mind', as one of his former students expressed it:

Franks made us see philosophy as a way of life: it was not a body of knowledge to be learned, but an essential weapon in the armoury with which to cope with living and working: he did not teach us stuff, book-lore that we might peddle, he made us philo- sophic rather than soi-disant philosophers. . . . We were trained not as academics, would-be professional researchers, but rather as Socratics to ask questions about Life, to analyse and unravel them, and to work out in and for ourselves the answers.[42]

Challenged to say what these questions are—philosophically, something of an impertinence—Franks would make a short answer. God, freedom, and immor- tality: the great unanswerable questions that have bothered people in every century of recorded history. Pressed to elaborate, he would frame them so: Is there a general purpose to the universe? Can we choose, or are we compelled? What sense is there in talking of an afterlife? Asked if progress had been made in answering them, he would say, firmly, no. 'Metaphysics is like pictures painted upon air' (a favourite phrase from Anselm).[43]

In addition to the sheer intellectual (or conceptual) difficulty of these ques- tions, we are bound to analyse them in the language that we have available: there is no other. But it is inadequate to the metaphysical task. To take an example much discussed in Oxford philosophical circles at the time, the hero of Kafka's story *Metamorphosis*, a commercial traveller called Gregor Samsa, wakes up one morning to find that he has turned into a cockroach, although he retains clear memories of his life as a human being. How are we to speak of him—as a man with the body of a cockroach, or as a cockroach with the consciousness of a man? 'Neither', declared the pre-eminent and unsparing J. L. Austin. 'In such cases we should not know what to say. This is when we say "words fail us" and mean this literally. We should need new words. The old ones just would not fit.'[44]

Franks would probably have agreed with this judgement, insofar as it high-lighted the obstacles in the philosopher's path, but he would not have thought it very helpful or very interesting. As a professional craftsman, he used language with precision, and on occasion with subtlety; but he never had any sympathy with what he called the linguistic school, or with its many ingenious offshoots.[45] If philosophy was to be merely talk about talk, as Gilbert Ryle suggested, then Franks would keep his silence. Plato himself had wondered whether language is naturally rooted in reality or is merely arbitrary: crudely, whether there are true words and false, whether it makes any sense to say, as a seventeenth-century theorist said, 'the French call it *pain*, the Germans call it *Brot* and we call it *bread*, and we are right, because it *is* bread'. Like Socrates in Plato's dialogue, Franks was elusive on the question; philosophically, it was a matter of indifference to him.[46] Similarly, the problems of perception which so excited Oxford philosophers in the 1930s left him profoundly unmoved. J. L. Austin could turn to his friend and colleague Isaiah Berlin and enquire, 'If there are three vermilion patches on this piece of paper how many vermilions are there?' 'One', said Berlin. 'I say there are three', rejoined Austin with relish, and they spent the rest of the term on the issue. It is hard to imagine Franks engaging with them, or with the brilliant little group that assembled around them.[47]

Intellectually, Franks preferred to walk by himself. His early philosophical guru was Gilbert Ryle. That did not last. When he first became a don he was induced to join with Ryle in founding another little group, the 'Wee Teas', an informal dining club of six junior philosophers who met once a fortnight during term, with the host of the evening providing a discussion-opening paper after dinner. As Ryle remembered it,

The club was not, either academically or philosophically, a cabal or a crusade. We never aimed at unanimity or achieved it; but we could try out anything on one another without anyone being shocked or rude or polite. Each of us had five friends and no allies. Without our noticing it at the time, hustings-words ending in 'ism' or 'ist' faded out of our use. In this and in other ways we were outgrowing some then prevalent attitudes towards philosophical issues. We discovered that it was possible to be at once earnest and happy.[48]

This proved congenial for a while; then Franks's involvement diminished. Constant to the end, however, was his affinity for John Locke.[49] Weeding the garden of philosophy (to use Berlin's phrase), the task to which so many of his colleagues dedicated their working lives, was not at all to Franks's taste. He much preferred to cultivate his own. As student and teacher he had drunk deep of the indomitable Lockean belief that philosophy was the study of the foundations of human knowledge. For Franks, human beings are so constructed that they *must* ask certain questions—the unanswerable questions—and it was to these that he had to address himself.

Famously, he chose to lecture on 'God' (in a series by divers hands on 'Metaphysical Problems'). The lectures were remembered as a critique of traditional arguments for the existence of God, followed by a strong case for the reality of religious experience.[50] Following in the footsteps of Prichard and Ryle, most of Franks's lecturing was done on 'The History of the Theory of Knowledge', or more simply 'The History of Philosophy', from Descartes to Hume, a two-term tour of the horizon for students of Greats and of the new School of Modern Greats: Philosophy, Politics, and Economics (PPE). This appealingly contemporary combination was a daring innovation in Oxford, where the classical virtues of *Literae Humaniores* had reigned supreme for so long. (In 1924, after a year's post-Greats preparation, Ryle had been invited to sit the final examination in PPE in order to set a standard for first-class performance in it. This he successfully did.) In the early 1930s, when Greats was still king and Modern Greats the young pretender, Franks played a leading part in making the new degree intellectually respectable. His contribution was happily central to the conception of its founders, for whom it was indeed a contemporary analogue to the classical original. As Franks wrote at the time:

By virtue of his studying philosophy, politics, and economics, a student is led to weigh evidence and judge coolly in matters affecting his social environment. He should be able to think strictly but be saved by his knowledge of the facts from shallow dogmatism. A liberal attitude of mind is insensibly formed which does not inhibit action because it makes it less prejudiced and more reflective. If a man has got what modern greats has to offer, he should be a more intelligent companion and a better citizen.[51]

The emphasis here was at once moral and practical—a distinctive blend which for want of a better word one might call Franksian.

Franks's lectures were exceptionally popular. He would develop an argument of magisterial lucidity, step by step, in the plainest possible language. There were no embellishments and no histrionics. Unlike Austin or Berlin, or his own favourite Joachim, Franks was not a performer. He impressed, but he did not excite. His lectures were unremarkable; that is to say, they were remarkable only for their clarity and economy, and for the ease with which one could take copious, shapely notes.[52] These are the things that matter more to students than to posterity.

He was an outstandingly successful college tutor. Properly speaking, the tutorial system—'the private hour'—lies at the heart of an Oxford education. By now Franks had formed very clear views about how that system should operate. These views were expounded to some effect thirty years later when their author headed an inquiry into the workings of the whole university. Of the tutorial system Franks wrote:

At its heart is a theory of teaching young men and women to think for themselves. The undergraduate is sent off to forage for himself among a long list of books and journals and to produce a coherent exposition of his ideas on the subject set. The essay or prepared work is then read by its author and criticized by the tutor. In this discussion the undergraduate should benefit by struggling to defend the positions he has taken up, by realizing the implications of the argument, and by glimpsing the context in which a more experienced scholar sees his problem. This process can succeed only when the tutor takes undergraduates singly, or in pairs. To be a tutorial, in the full sense, each pupil must have written his essay and his particular view of the matter must be fully explored. . . . If in any group one pupil has written an essay and one or two others merely listen and perhaps throw in an occasional opinion, they are not experiencing a tutorial but merely attending a class.

His conclusion was a neat (and very Franksian) formulation: 'For the tutorial means that the undergraduate has to try his hand at creation under correction.'[53]

This exposition promised a rigorous regime. Franks was convinced that, so taught, philosophy offered an excellent training in conceptual analysis; in seeking the interconnectedness of things; above all, in *reflection*. It is no coincidence that these were the very habits of mind he identified in himself. 'To reflect' was both a favourite verb and a necessary process.[54] Of course, philosophy also offered intellectual enjoyment; but the enjoyment should be taken seriously. This was the thrust of his celebrated comments on students' progress. ('Mr Ross has been walking out with philosophy rather than making her his wedded wife.'[55]) Tutorials with Oliver Franks were not for the chuckle-headed. 'I think that it is true to say that we stood in awe of Franks in a way that was not the case with our other tutors. No one would have dreamt of calling Franks by his Christian name [as happened with some of the other young tutors at Queen's]. No one took liberties with him, and therefore we did our task without question—or any attempt to excuse lateness with our work.'

He was a wonderful tutor: his aim was to teach us to think; he would sit in his armchair and listen to us reading our essays, and with never a pencilled note or aide-mémoire immediately come back with an, often quantified, judgement: 'You have made four points, one . . ., two . . ., three . . ., four . . .; and you have missed out three other considerations . . .'. Even as a very ordinary student one was introduced to logic in action, and to the fundamental difference between δοξχ [opinion] and ἐπιστήμη [knowledge]. His powerful mind could take up a feeble contribution and make it the basis for a lead into the real deep problem; he could use the time with splendid economy, and one went out feeling that the hour had been well filled and one's mind had been truly stretched.

As the *Oxford Magazine* remarked at the time, 'few men have got so much work so willingly from their pupils'.[56]

The academic and administrative burden on a conscientious college tutor is not to be underestimated. Nevertheless, throughout his period as a full-time philosopher, 1928–39, it has to be said that Franks did remarkably little philosophy, if by 'doing philosophy' is meant writing and publishing original or quasi-original work. He wrote no books (which was not unusual). He delivered a single, substantial paper, on 'Choice', to the hallowed Aristotelian Society on 25 June 1934, which duly appeared in the Society's *Proceedings*. The paper is a minute dissection of the process of rational deliberation. It has nothing to say about impulse or intuition. Characteristic of its author, it is couched as a kind of sustained excogitation. When it was written it stood alone, or virtually alone, in the field; and that is exactly where it remained. It had no noticeable impact on philosophical debate in Oxford, or elsewhere, or indeed on the subsequent development of philosopher Franks. In short, it led nowhere.[57] Some four years later, at a joint session of the Aristotelian Society and the Mind Association, Franks participated in a symposium chaired by H. A. Prichard on 'What is Action?', but his contribution was no more than an extended critique of the other two papers (by John Macmurray and A. C. Ewing)—in effect, an august tutorial.[58] And that appears to be the sum total of Oliver Franks's published work as a philosopher: even by the attenuated standards of the time and the subject, not a significant output.

A general explanation for this paucity has been offered by Isaiah Berlin, apropos Oxford philosophy in that period. 'We were excessively self-centred,' he writes.

The only persons whom we wished to convince were our own admired colleagues. There was no pressure upon us to publish. Consequently, when we succeeded in gaining from one of our philosophical peers acceptance or even understanding of some point which we regarded as original or important, . . . this satisfied us completely, too completely. We felt no need to publish our ideas, for the only audience which was worth satisfying was the handful of our contemporaries who lived near us, and whom we met with agreeable regularity. I don't think that . . . any of us thought that no one before us had discovered the truth about the nature of knowledge or anything else; but . . . we did think that no one outside the magic circle—in our case Oxford, Cambridge, Vienna—had much to teach us. This was vain and foolish and, I have no doubt, irritating to others. But I suspect that those who have never been under the spell of this kind of illusion, even for a short while, have not known true intellectual happiness.[59]

Another and more personal explanation is that Franks was politically engaged in the early 1930s—in a way that he never was again—and that this too made inroads on his time. In later life he was given to describing himself as 'an unreconstructed Gladstonian Liberal'; in playful mood he might even suggest that by the early 1990s he and Lord Gladwyn (the former Gladwyn Jebb) were the only ones left—a conceit in which the latter was happy to share.[60] What exactly he meant by this plangent phrase (to adopt the approach of his tutor Paton) was never made entirely clear. By accident or design its very utterance had the effect of stifling further enquiry. At a minimum it seems that he always voted Liberal, consorted with Liberals, and thought of himself as one of their number. At the same time, like William Beveridge, he was reluctant to be publicly identified with any single political party or faction. The declaration made by Beveridge was rather a Franksian one: 'I am as nearly non-political as anyone can be, but when I have any politics I am a Liberal.'[61] His friends in Oxford over the years were all of a Left-Liberal coloration: the pioneer psephologist R. B. McCallum, who would doff his hat whenever he drove through a Liberal constituency; the philosopher William Maclagan, a fellow member of the Wee Teas; the influential James Meade, who described himself a Liberal-Socialist economist, and his Quaker wife, Margaret Wilson; the labour economist Henry Phelps Brown, a softly spoken Baptist, at length perhaps the closest to Franks; and the versatile Geoffrey Wilson (brother of Margaret), also a Quaker, with whom he holidayed in old age.

During the 1940s and 1950s Franks attended meetings of XYZ, a clandestine dining club of Labour supporters and sympathizers in the City, founded by Vaughan Berry, an assistant manager of the Union Discount Company, in 1932. The early XYZ had an intellectual, Fabian flavour, with a strong dose of economic sophistication. Stalwarts included Hugh Dalton, Evan Durbin, Hugh Gaitskell, Douglas Jay, and Francis Williams. James Meade was recruited a little later. During the war years they met more hurriedly at the Griffin public house in Villiers Street, near to the Ministry of Supply, where Franks worked closely with Jay. In the 1950s he became moderately friendly with Gaitskell, in many respects a compatible character, who sometimes saw him as a future Governor of the Bank of England under a new, reinvigorated Labour Administration—an intriguing possibility never to be realized, not least because of Gaitskell's untimely death in 1963.[62] There was, indeed, something of the Fabian about Oliver Franks. He would build a new Jerusalem; and he would repine for its soul.[63] Typically, he was not an XYZ member as such, more 'a sort of benevolent assessor'.[64] When ennobled in 1962 he accepted the Liberal whip, as expected, though in unmistakable cross-bench fashion his sponsors were Lord Bridges (a Civil Servant) and Lord Evershed (a judge). To the disappointment of some, he took no part in debates; it was five years before he made his maiden speech, on the economy. After 1962 he did permit himself an occasional foray into national politics, chairing election meetings of the Oxford Liberals in 1963 and 1964, and addressing a Liberal Party rally at the Oxford Union in favour of a decisive vote to remain in the EEC in the referendum of 1975. Just how Liberal (or liberal) he was, or became, is a moot point. Unquestionably, party meant little to him. Party politics was too much a game, too often trivial or reprehensible—not serious. There was a touch of disdain in Franks's contemplation of the political stew. During the intervals of his Falklands inquiry in 1983 he would sit back and listen as 'the parliamentarians cracked their silly parliamentary jokes'. It was an attitude reminiscent of Demodocus on the Milesians:

> Milesians are not stupid, I aver;
> But they behave the same as if they were.[65]

He was equally resistant to the lure of ideology, even in the 1930s, when ideologies ran rampant. Franks had beliefs, not systems; precepts, not constructs. Unlike a number of his contemporaries, he never flirted with communism. Flirting of any kind was not a Franksian thing to do, neither with ideology nor with women, and certainly not with men—another common peccadillo among the intelligentsia of the liberal Left. The Spanish Civil War did not obsess him, as it did so many of 'our age'.

> We are left alone with our day, and the time is short, and
> History to the defeated
> May say Alas but cannot help or pardon.[66]

Father Franks was not interested in Auden. He had no urge to man the barricades, no repentance to seek. He was not lightly inspired or disillusioned. What really captured his imagination was the destinies of the world, and the material life which shaped them. He was a believer in the *longue durée*. The terminology is that of his favourite historian, Fernand Braudel.[67] For Franks the fascination lay in the fate of nations, and civilizations, over time. This was politics on a grand scale. Like John Maud (later Lord Redcliffe-Maud), Franks was a mugwump.[68] He disliked labels, but it may be appropriate to adapt the one he gave himself. He was, if anything, an unreconstructed liberal internationalist.

The beginnings of this were evident in the early 1930s. Franks joined with McCallum, Maclagan, Meade, and another young don at Queen's, L. M. Fraser, in what they called the Oxford Movement for the Propagation of Peace. At the time of the Disarmament Conference in 1932 they held public meetings in the city and issued a broadsheet urging that pressure be brought to bear on the Government to promote a more effective disarmament policy. The broadsheet attracted some fleeting attention. The movement did not.[69] In 1934, anticipating the debates over Abyssinia and the Rhineland, the group issued another broadsheet on the nature and use of economic sanctions. They sent it to Gilbert Murray at the League of Nations Union, with a covering statement and a plea for help.

The changes in the international situation during the past few years have made hopes of permanent peace uncertain. No one can today view the future and hold the danger of war unreal.

We believe that the only alternative to drifting into war lies in the intelligent understanding, preparation and application of Economic Sanctions between nations. In the past, too little attention has been given in this country to the subject; and we ask you to assist in the work of convincing the Government and the nation of the need for action in this respect.

The broadsheet was considered by the Economic Committee of the LNU and may well have reinforced its own line of thinking. Murray himself was appreciative yet sceptical: 'I think we have to admit that economic pressure must have the possibility of military pressure behind it. Otherwise what are we to do if, for example, your embargo really damages Germany and Germany retorts by an air-attack on London?'[70] To this the Oxford Movement for the Propagation of Peace had no answer.

More prosaically, Franks's writing arm was badly broken in a motoring accident in 1931. Only after two operations and a painful two-year recovery period did he regain the full use of it.[71] This was surely trying and inconvenient, yet one may ask whether it was fundamental to philosophizing. In retrospect it is clear that, accidents or no, Franks was *always* reluctant to put pen to paper. All his life he was a magnificent reader but a meagre writer. He disliked writing and did everything he could to avoid it, in public life as in academe. Throughout his career he drafted little and published less. There is no completely satisfying explanation for this rather curious phenomenon, unless it is the simple fact that he thought he was bad at it.[72] It is possible, however, that Isaiah Berlin's metaphysical speculations cut close to a deeper truth.

Did Franks know 'true intellectual happiness' as a philosopher? His pupil and successor at Queen's, Tony Woozley, took leave to doubt it. 'I'm sure I learned a lot from him, but, although I have always liked him, and have had that feeling of awe towards him that pupils tend to retain towards their teachers, I have never had a very high opinion of him as a philosopher. I didn't believe, and I still don't believe, that he was really committed to the subject.' The admiring Ronald Lunt, paired with Woozley for tutorials, voiced somewhat similar reservations. 'He was interested in philosophic problems more than in any particular philosopher, in method rather than any -ism. . . . I find it hard to imagine the learned tomes that might have come from the Press over his name; for I do not honestly think that he is a gifted writer—he is a wonderful problem solver, but he needs the problem to be given him to untangle.' Gilbert Ryle liked to tell of how he had wrestled for his friend's philosophical soul, and lost.[73] The heavyweight contest probably took place in Heidelberg, Ryle's defeat signalled by the departure of Father Franks for the flesh-pots of Berlin. Notwithstanding the excursion to Königsberg, Franks's Continental travels were not notably philosophical. In Vienna, for example, he made no mention of the hive of philosophers active there—the nascent Vienna circle—or the seminal text they were already discussing, Wittgenstein's *Tractatus Logico-Philosophicus*, first published in German in 1921 and available in a parallel German/English edition the following year. During the 1930s, to his credit, Franks twice passed beyond the Oxford orbit evoked so felicitously by Isaiah Berlin; but in each case the doubts about his philosophical commitment remain.

In 1935 he was invited to teach for a semester at the University of Chicago.

He took an apartment on the top floor of the Plaisance Hotel, with a grand view over Lake Michigan, and adopted an appropriately New World policy of 'refusing nothing the first time it offers'.[74] Franks had not been to America before but he had encountered Americans at close quarters in Heidelberg. It was an instructive experience, conveyed to his parents with almost lyrical intensity.

I have been learning a great deal from the Americans here recently. They are not the Americans one meets in England: that is people from the East Coast or high in the Academical world. They are principally from the Middle West. . . . They don't know what it means to think, except in terms of dollars. One chap here says that out of thirty-five chaps who got their BA at the same time as him at Wisconsin State University he would be prepared to swear that none or at most one had ever opened the covers of a book since. Yet in spite of this incredible lack of culture of any and every kind, one feels that the breeze of youth and optimism blows very strong and clear in the Middle West: no cloud even the size of a man's hand has yet been seen on the horizon. It is a feeling which can only be envied but not attained by us who carry the shackles of many centuries on our backs. I can see what people mean when they say that Chicago is already the real capital of America and that the real driving force is coming more and more and will finally almost exclusively come from the Middle West. The place so long as we think of its advantages ie its negation of the evils of European civilization—no slums—all the modern comforts in every working man's home—every man his motor—heating supplies to the whole town from one centre—is almost like the Never Never Land come true: but when we reflect on the absence therefore of our advantages—the utter absence of anything approaching a sense of vocation or meaning in their lives and the total lack of spirituality in the broadest sense—they have not really gained very much: they have all the riches of the world but have not yet found their soul.[75]

At Chicago he lectured most mornings and conducted a weekly seminar. 'The lectures are going off very peacefully at present', he reported to his parents. 'The students talk more than at Oxford but with less point, and are terribly prone to think that everything is settled by the use of labels: for example if you can label a doctrine idealist, that is as good as saying it is false or true, according as you feel.' The basic issue was succinctly stated: 'they do not think enough'—the charge foreshadowed at Heidelberg. He returned to it a few weeks later: 'My greatest difficulty here is to make people think as opposed to merely absorbing someone's views. They often look quite hurt if you suggest or hint that they have not thought out and accepted or rejected the various consequences of a view they have embraced.'[76]

Franks had been installed at Chicago for barely a month when he had an interview with the legendary Robert Maynard Hutchins. Hutchins was the boy wonder of American higher education—Dean of the Yale Law School at 28, President of the University of Chicago at 30. He was also a Presbyterian, a scholar, a seer, an apostle of Socrates, fired by the vaulting Socratic axiom that no unexamined life is worth living. 'What Hutchins communicated was the necessary miracle of personal dialogue with the master spirits past and present. He made the university a house of live reading, in which voices sprang at you from the printed page.'[77] If all of this suggests a natural affinity between President Hutchins and Professor Franks, the suggestion would not be totally out of place. Hutchins was in many ways like a charismatic Franks. Hutchins may have sensed this. Franks did not. Their first meeting was brief but dramatic. To Franks's amazement, he was invited to become Chairman of the Department of Philosophy, and to name his own salary. He could return to Queen's in five years' time if he so wished. A little later, Dean of the Faculty of Humanities was added to the package.[78]

Franks again sought time for reflection. His first reaction was cautiously negative. 'It is in its way a flattering offer, with great opportunities and much scope, but I think it highly probable that I shall refuse.' After two weeks he was arguing, as yet inconclusively, 'that there is no sufficient reason for leaving Oxford and coming to live here. So I think the matter is deciding itself.' It took a further two weeks for his position to become clear. 'I agree both with Father when he says that to come here with or without a five years agreement in all probability entails the choice between being English and being American, and also with Mother that I don't want to be an American.'[79] After one deliberative month, the matter had been settled. Hutchins was refused. It would be thirteen years before Franks was tempted by another and very different opportunity 'to be an American': a temptation he did not then feel able to resist.

The process of reflection is as interesting for what it conceals as for what it reveals. One would not guess from any of Franks's contemporary comments that Chicago under Hutchins was one of the finest centres of scholarship and instruction in the Western world, the cradle of the 'Great Books' programme devised by Hutchins and Mortimer Adler as a liberal education and a declaration of faith, the Mecca for ambitious students of every stripe, the generator of a tremendous, competitive thirst for intellectual gratification. There is no hint of the 'hammering excitement' stirred in the young George Steiner a decade later, as he sat through whole nights 'arguing Marx or Dewey, analysing, word for word, a paragraph out of Joyce's "Dubliners" or Tarski's logic'. Steiner wrote in 1989:

To this distant day I tingle at the recollection of OII—Observation, Information, and Integration, the crowning course in the college. Here an often inspired teaching staff introduced us to the attempt, from Plato to Carnap, to discover a general principle of human understanding, to find logic and meaning in both the world and the thought in which we incorporate the world. Hutchins' vision was radically historical: a mathematical theorem, a literary form, a philosophical idea, even history itself had a history. Nothing could be truly grasped out of its intellectual context. The work was often exhausting, and we undoubtedly fell short. But Hutchins' sovereign ruling that it was the highest of privileges to be in an OII section . . . rang true. Plato's Academy,

Galileo's dialogues, Hegel's Berlin lectures reborn—one felt it in one's bones. And the best jazz and Caesar salads just off campus, on 63rd Street. And the steel mills in Gary and White City flashing their lights, making their ovens redder when the news came through from Newark that Tony Zale, his hand broken, beat Rocky Graziano (a quite mad occasion and hosanna I can't separate from the memory of a wretched paper I did on Mill's social theories) . . .[80]

Franks made no mention of any of this. In his letters home the University of Chicago sounds for all the world like Wisconsin State. 'Refusing nothing' took him to Stravinsky conducting the Chicago Symphony Orchestra in a programme of his own music, to an unappreciated lecture on 'An English View of What is Important in Education' at the Chicago Women's Club, and no further. He appears studiously disengaged. The top floor of the Plaisance Hotel, three short blocks from the jazz and the Caesar salads, might have been as far away as Oxford itself. Perhaps he was not equipped to enjoy it. At 30, he had been magisterial for some time. The electric current of popular culture failed to connect with Oliver Franks. High culture was not a high priority. He liked ballet but saw little. His aesthetic pulse was weak. Fervid intellectualism was not his style. A whole night spent analysing Marx or Dewey was not his idea of a good time. Whole nights were for sleeping. With friends he was good company. With acquaintances he was neither comfortable nor congenial. He was never one for joining things; he was not often asked. Had he been a Cambridge man, one could scarcely imagine him a member of the Apostles (though stranger things have happened—Wittgenstein was an Apostle).[81] At Oxford he was never invited to join The Club. It was felt, rightly, that he would not have fitted in. The Club, like so many clubs, was for fat men. Franks was a thin man. He was too puritan: 'a walking moral imperative'.[82] He administered a silent rebuke. It was the same in the New World. Chicago, that toddlin' town, struck no chord with Father Franks.

But the decision to return to Oxford was not his alone. In 1926 a young woman called Barbara Tanner came up to Lady Margaret Hall to read PPE. The following year two changes could be observed in Oliver Franks's lifestyle. 'He is buried in the obscurity of North Oxford, emerging occasionally, no longer on a bicycle but in a car, no longer alone, but tête-à-tête.'[83] The relationship developed, as it were, philosophically. Mr Franks became Barbara's tutor. Happily, he noted, the thrice repeated 'a' in her name echoed the first syllogism of Aristotle.[84] Apocryphally, the fierce intellectual exchange reduced her to tears, but all was not lost because he had a towel to hand for this very purpose. They married at the Redland Friends Meeting House in Bristol on 3 July 1931. It was an appropriate ceremony, much like the regular Quaker meeting for worship.

History and memory are not celebrated in the Quaker meeting house, as they are in all the churches in Rome. The grave individual conscience, alone with its own spontaneous and troubled thoughts and its own hesitations, is here the centre of religion and ethics. Each soul must strain towards an entirely authentic self, an entirely true witness, purged of all pretence and all inherited conventions and authorities. The singleness of each person is essential, though not the separateness.[85]

Quakers have always disapproved of 'hireling priests'. Early in the course of the meeting the bride and groom stood up, took each other by the hand, and made their solemn declaration of marriage. Oliver was resplendent in morning suit and top hat. Prudently placed in the top hat were his words:

Friends, I take this friend, Barbara Tanner, to be my wife, promising, with God's help, to be unto her a loving and faithful husband, so long as we both on earth shall live.

Barbara, clutching a bunch of sweet peas, declared similarly. The Quaker marriage certificate was signed by the couple and by two witnesses. The meeting continued as it began with a period of Quakerly silence, broken by anyone who felt moved to speak. Traditionally, this is the time when the man and women concerned gain inspiration and a continuing source of strength for their married life; the opportunity for those who attend the meeting to ask God's blessing on the marriage and commit themselves to support the couple in whatever way they can. Franks thought of his parents' marriage at the Meeting House in Redcar thirty years before, when someone spoke from the text, 'Woe is me, for I am undone!'[86] No such sentiments were expressed that day in Bristol. The meeting closed, as normal, after the elders had shaken hands. They signed the civil marriage certificate, and the pact was sealed. He was 26; she was 23.

Aristotle says that the only perfect friendship is between adults of virtuous character. This one turned out to be a marital friendship of appropriately Aristotelian cast. Barbara Mary Tanner was born in Glasgow on 19 September 1907, the oldest child and only daughter of Herbert George Tanner (1882–1974) and Agatha Mary Gales (1877–1957).[87] The Scottish connection was only temporary—a recurring phenomenon in her life. Her father was from Bath, a West Countryman from a long line of West Countrymen. He worked, man and boy, for the Bristol-based paper-manufacturers E. S. and A. Robinson, joining them at 14 in 1897, becoming a Director in 1918, Managing Director in 1929, and retiring voluntarily in 1945 to a further thirty years of civic duty zestfully discharged.[88] He had grown up in a high-minded household of teetotallers, vegetarians, non-smokers, pacifists, Nonconformists, and Liberals. The Tanners' was a stern and self-improving morality. Women's Total Abstinence Union meetings, peace meetings, board meetings, church meetings, school meetings, political meetings: Herbert was weaned on good organization and good causes. He embraced them all, fiercely, and led a life of shrewd philanthropy. He was a strict, not to say severe, teetotaller; a militant pacifist, protecting the interests of Glasgow's conscientious objectors in the Great War and later refusing to wear the ceremonial sword as Sheriff of Bristol; a Quaker by convincement after the war, and thereafter a thoroughgoing Friend; an evangelistic Liberal, pressed several times to stand for Parliament. In retirement from Robinson's he became chairman of a whole host of organizations, among them Friends Provident and Century Insurance (in which capacity he was succeeded by his son-in-law), the South-West Regional Hospital Board, and the Bristol bench of magistrates. He was a long-serving Treasurer and latterly Pro-Chancellor of Bristol University. His favourite book was Morley's life of Gladstone, his favourite passage the Gladstonian precept which concludes that monumental work. Herbert Tanner read it regularly to his children and grandchildren, and used it to close his own *Recollections and Reflections*, published privately and circulated in the family for their information and edification:

Be inspired with the belief that life is a great and noble calling; not a mean and grovelling thing, that we are to shuffle through as we can, but an elevated and lofty destiny.[89]

This was a formidable patrimony, but there was more. Barbara's mother Agatha talked little and prevailed often. A Quaker by upbringing, the daughter of a Liberal electoral agent and peace activist, she was a kind, quiet, delightful woman of artistic bent and domestic avocation. Entirely unassuming, she yet conveyed great firmity of purpose. Her writ ran unchallenged in the Tanner household, where there were very clear rules about what one could and could not do (clearer, they found, than in the Franks household). Punctuality at mealtimes was an absolute and indispensable requirement. So too was cleanliness, of dress and person. Kitty Franks was not always so scrupulous, but Agatha Tanner brooked no argument. The rules were understood and obeyed.

Barbara and Oliver first met whilst they were still at school. The Tanners' house in Bristol had two particular advantages: it had fruit trees and a tennis court in the garden. The two families knew each slightly, at the Meeting House and elsewhere. In traditional fashion the older Franks children, Oliver and Rosalind, would be invited round for a game of tennis. There was no hint of romance; the two did not pay much attention to each other. At this time Barbara went to Sidcot, the coeducational Quaker school in Winscombe, Somerset, where her grandfather Gales had been a pupil in the 1850s (and where Robert and Kitty Franks settled in retirement from the Western College). At Sidcot she was shy but happy, a competent scholar and a first-rate netball player. Before going up to Oxford she spent a few months with a French family in Avignon and a German family in Frankfurt, a miniature Grand Tour in plain Quaker style. She emerged at Lady Margaret Hall an attractive young woman with light brown curly hair and a well-developed dress sense, at once responsible and adventurous, Captain of Boats, a lively dancer, often the leader in such enterprises as finding the best way on to the roof to sleep out under the stars. In youth as in maturity, she had both sense and sensibility. She also had a keen social conscience, and an impulse to act.

Her vigorous commitment to public service antedated that of her future husband: in this respect, as perhaps in others, it was he who learned from her.

Already in the 1930s Barbara was serving on the committee of the Eye Hospital in Oxford, and organizing the Plantation Club for poor girls in the Gorbals—her first, horrifying glimpse of extreme poverty at home. She also acted from time to time as research assistant to Sir George Clark, the historian.[90] During the Second World War she worked first for the Press Research Department of the Foreign Office, evacuated to the playing fields of Balliol, on the humble task of reading and digesting German newspapers. In 1943 she transferred to the Women's Voluntary Service and turned her attention to the practical matters of evacuees, meals on wheels, and the maintenance of the motor pool. After the war the family's movements enforced a break in such activities, but no sooner were they re-established in Oxford in the 1950s than she began an intensive and continuing involvement in the social provision of the city. Signally, she was a magistrate for twenty-two years (1955–77), by common consent an outstanding chairman of the city bench, compassionate, expeditious, and fair. She served as a member of the board of governors of Aylesbury and Oxford Prisons, Huntercombe Borstal, Campsfield Detention Centre, and a local probation hostel; she took a particular interest in the Juvenile Panel. In addition she was at various times chairman of the local Citizens' Advice Bureau and of Age Concern; a long-serving trustee of Oxfam; an independent member of two wages councils; and a member and then chairman of the management committee of the Nuffield Orthopaedic Hospital.[91]

Oliver Franks and Barbara Tanner were fundamentally compatible people. They shared the same values in life and the same belief in religion as relevant to the living of it. For Franks, that was what was most important in the marriage. 'It is more important to make the same prayers than eat the same food', as Herbert Tanner used to say.[92] At the heart of this was a certain simplicity, evident in the pastimes they shared: gardening, reading, walking, shrimping (in the Isles of Scilly). Franks was proud of his wife's distinction on the bench, proud that she held the same office as her father and grandfather before her. It appealed to his sense of the fitness of things. They both took great pleasure in the generational continuity—and in the more equal opportunity it betokened. Quietly, they were each concerned about 'the subjection of women'. John Stuart Mill's famous case for equal treatment was made in precisely the terms Franks found most persuasive—'the nerve and spring which it gives to all the faculties, the larger and higher objects which it presents to the intellect and feelings, the more unselfish public spirit, and calmer and broader views of duty, that it engenders, and the generally loftier platform on which it elevates the individual as a moral, spiritual, and social being'—this was just the sort of thing Mr Franks might have underlined to Miss Tanner in tutorial.[93]

There was a mutual respect between them. If she was not his intellectual equal, in human terms he was if anything overmatched. In general she ranged further than he. Her Quaker sympathies were deeper, her pacifist leanings stronger. She was rash or enthusiastic enough to join the breakaway Social Democrats in the early 1980s. She followed her father in her vegetarianism and her faith in homoeopathic medicine (but came round to accepting a glass of sherry or wine). In middle age she lost her shyness but retained her modesty. She practised yoga and tai chi. She liked to meditate. At 75 she learned to stand on her head. She was her own woman, an expression she would probably have deplored. At the same time she supported Oliver in everything he did, just as he supported her. This was not a matter of form, but a grave moral obligation. In the last ten years of her life Barbara took up painting, with amazing success. She sought technical instruction and went on painting holidays in the south of France, revelling in the warmth and colour of the late summer. Oliver supported her in that, making tea and chatting amiably to the assorted amateur artists who appeared in the house or set up their easels in the garden, before resuming his reading—Braudel, perhaps, or Gibbon, or Philip Guedalla, leavened with Le Carré and, on holiday, a steady diet of detective stories (a shared taste). In adult life he was not much taken with the essential confidence trick of the novel. When the great German historian Leopold von Ranke compared the portrait of Louis XI in Walter Scott's *Quentin Durward* with the portrait of the same king in the memoirs of Philippe de Comines, Louis's minister, he found 'the truth more interesting and beautiful than the romance'. Notwithstanding the delights of his father's library, Franks came to believe the same.[94] After the Caliph Vathek there was no more fantasy. In this way a thin man could easily become a colourless one. Literally and figuratively, Barbara supplied the lack.

Franks consulted her on anything of consequence. 'You'll want to discuss it with your wife', he once admonished a startled Nicholas Henderson. 'One does, doesn't one.'[95] For her part Barbara was certainly happy to spurn Chicago and return to Oxford in 1935. She was not happy, however, for him to become Oxford-bound. They had not been back long before it was determined that he should apply for the first available (and interesting) philosophical post in the UK. This happened to be the Chair of Moral Philosophy at Glasgow University, a chair previously held by none other than Adam Smith, and more recently by A. D. Lindsay, the Master of Balliol. Unlike Barbara, Franks had never been to Glasgow. He duly applied. It was the only job for which he made an unsolicited application in his entire career. He was successful. The plan, such as it was, had worked. They left Oxford in 1937. The new Professor of Moral Philosophy was 32. At Glasgow he met an impressive young economist called Alec Cairncross. In conversation one day Cairncross asked him what he thought he would do next. 'Set course for sixty', replied Father Franks sagely.[96]

3 *The Ministry of Supply*

FRANKS had been at Glasgow barely a year when he received a fateful communication from London. 'In September 1938 we all had a bit of paper from the Ministry of Labour.' On the bit of paper was a terse enquiry: 'Do you undertake to go wherever you are sent in the event of a national emergency?'[1] This contingent call-up was not entirely unpremeditated. Mobilizing 'men of the professor type' for war had been stealthily discussed between Civil Servants and representatives of the universities for some months. Now, galvanized by the Munich crisis, Whitehall broke cover. Much to his surprise, Franks found himself on a roster of 'personnel with scientific and technical and professional qualifications, and persons qualified for higher administrative posts'. He would have been even more surprised to learn that his 'general administrative experience' was deemed 'readily capable of adapting itself to the needs of the Civil Service machine'.[2] The sum total of that administrative experience to date was membership of the governing body of an Oxford college, and a little committee work on air-raid precautions in Glasgow.

Franks responded promptly and affirmatively. The Ministry's enquiry occasioned some reflection, certainly, but no crisis of conscience. Perhaps this should not be cause for remark. And yet, 'some of us wondered very much what Oliver would feel it right to do when war came—would he feel morally bound to take the strictly pacifist line? There must have been a mighty moral think-tank at work in him to reach a decision.'[3] It was typical of him that his attitude towards the war was not simple and unquestioning. By heredity and temperament and training he was disposed to reject solutions by violence rather than by reason. He was after all a disciple of Locke. 'Some Trust one in another' was necessary for society to function. As he himself wrote of the Anglo-American war effort, 'it depended upon men . . . making a general agreement to agree in face of all difficulties and then submitting their problems and difficulties to rational examination and accepting the results'.[4] He may have continued to harbour private doubts—Douglas Jay, a neighbour and colleague, thought as much—but it was also typical that he should in the end reach the plain man's conclusion about this particular war: 'Hitler had to be squashed.'[5] Franks's clarity of mind had a pronounced stoic quality to it; in a sense he may have been prepared for this moment for some time. In April 1935, commenting on the march of events in Europe, he wrote to his parents:

The news does not appear very good; but it has at least one merit: it has shown people where they really are. We have all known for two years that Germany was rearming morally and physically very fast and have at some time turned a blind eye to it. Now we can't and we have to deal with the actual state of affairs.[6]

'I think what you must do is see things as they are', he would say.[7] He strove to do the same. To Oliver Franks the Second World War was not a good war, but it was a necessary one. If conscripted, he would have served.[8]

War was declared on 3 September 1939. Men of the professor type received their marching orders by telegram the following day. Franks's read, cryptically, 'Go to the Ministry of Supply.' He went. It was a long, long war: he remained in the Ministry of Supply until June 1946. After that, as he later remarked, life was not the same.

He had been picked out as one of 100 principal secretaries 'required on the outbreak of war' by various Government departments. His summons to the Ministry of Supply—as if from the Community Chest in a game of Monopoly, as Peter Hennessy has said—arose in the first instance because that ministry, desperate for additional manpower, had indented for 'six dons' from the Central Register of the Ministry of Labour.[9] Five of these came from Oxford; Franks was the sixth. His selection may not have been purely a matter of chance. Among those originally involved in making dispositions for war were two who had been able to observe Franks at close quarters, A. D. Lindsay, the Master of Balliol, and Sir Hector Hetherington, the Principal of Glasgow. Hetherington had already introduced Franks to his old friend Lord Woolton, who became the first Director-General of the Ministry of Supply. The businesslike Woolton was much impressed with this moral philosopher, and immediately recommended his recruitment to the Minister, Dr Leslie Burgin. Whether Burgin took action is another matter: well described by Franks as 'an embarrassed phantom', the Minister was not known for his powers of decision.[10]

Franks got off the night train and proceeded with all due speed to the ministry's headquarters in the Adelphi building near the Strand. It was rumoured that he did not know the way from Piccadilly Circus to Trafalgar Square. Certainly he had never set foot in a Government building. He had never even seen a file before, as he was fond of saying. 'My filing system had consisted of two pockets in my jacket and a drawer in my desk.' In short, he was a complete amateur, a status he shared with the great majority of his colleagues.[11] Franks and fellow auxiliaries outnumbered the regular Civil Servants by twelve to one—an extreme instance of a general trend.[12] On arrival he found that jobs had already been allocated to the other five dons, who had started work the previous day, 'but when I appeared they had run out of ideas'. For want of anything better he was put in the Establishments Division, which had responsibility for all personnel matters in the ministry.

I was given a room and for three days no person or piece of paper entered it. I was bored: I went out into the corridor, found a messenger and said I wanted to see the Director of Establishments. 'You can't,' he said, 'he is a very important person.' I made a fuss and was finally admitted to the presence. I told him my sad little tale. 'You mean,' he said, just like P. G. Wodehouse, 'you mean you have nothing to do?' 'Yes,' I replied, and asked if I could have my lecture notes sent down from Glasgow to occupy me. 'Go back to your room,' said the Director of Establishments, 'and wait half an hour.' I went back and within twenty minutes four feet thick of files arrived and were dumped in my in-tray. . . . I opened the first file: it was a War Office file with all the minutes on one side and all the supporting paper on the other. I read it with astonishment.[13]

Franks's induction into the mysteries of the Civil Service was about to begin. He discovered that the Ministry of Supply had many outstations in every part of the country, ranging from a radar station at Malvern to a proving-ground for guns at Shoeburyness. These outstations, it appeared, were inhabited by three categories of personnel: military, scientific, and administrative. The issue raised in the file was the appropriate ration of petrol for all of these people in their various grades. This was evidently a matter of some delicacy, but the newest principal secretary in the ministry was not dismayed. He addressed the problem in quintessentially Franksian fashion. He read the file through, reflected, and wrote a minute, 'setting out in the light of pure reason what seemed to be appropriate allowances for each and all'. He put this minute with the other minutes on the left-hand side of the file, put the file in the out-tray, and went home.

Next morning it had gone: the day after, my telephone became red hot. I had committed the most fearful of crimes, equating the petrol allowance of a naval captain with that of a senior scientific officer and so on. Dignity, rank, and intrinsic worth, I was informed, had been savagely attacked by me. I learned a lot about the Ministry and the Government that week. In the end I discovered a volume called Civil Service Regulations: if I had had it earlier it would have saved a lot of bother.[14]

Franks devoured not only the Civil Service Regulations but also the twelve-volume official history of the Ministry of Munitions, of which the Ministry of Supply was the lineal descendant, 'in order to find out how to write the rule-book of their association'.[15] His book-reading then abruptly ceased. In September 1946, approached by the BBC as one of those 'fortunate enough to be set aside to think and read and write', for a contribution to the series 'What is Man?', he replied with magnificent restraint: 'I have not read or thought for seven years and I must reflect a little before I presume to ask other people to listen to me.'[16] The fact was that life in the ministry was all-consuming, especially during the protracted and disastrous opening period of the war, a period which came to an end only in November 1942 with Montgomery's much-needed victory at El Alamein and the coincident success of the Allied landings in north-west Africa.[17] Work went on all the time. Office hours were from 9.30

to 7.30 on weekdays, 9.30 to 4.00 on Saturdays and every other Sunday. Franks frequently put in two or three more hours after dinner on papers he had taken home. He shared a flat in Hampstead with Stephen Wilson and James Meade. They would pore over maps of the latest campaign together, with Douglas Jay and Herbert Hart who lived nearby.[18]

For days on end Franks did not leave his own building at all. When he was not working, he was eating (in the canteen), sleeping (in the basement), or fire-watching (on the roof). He rarely left London except on Sundays, and often not then. In consequence he saw little of Barbara or their first-born, Caroline, both of whom spent the war in Oxford. Separation was part of the prevailing ethos. Alec Cairncross, summoned to the neighbouring Ministry of Aircraft Production, captured it well:

We were a close-knit group, although each of us was very busy with our own affairs. We were all young, high-spirited, and not lacking in a sense of our own collective self-importance. The Ministry was our oyster to which we provided the necessary intellectual grit for the cultivation of those pearls of the higher logic—the production process. We could observe other departments with the amused detachment of a visitor to a zoo and report to each other on the latest absurdity. Life was frantic, nonsensical, but above all hilarious. We were endlessly occupied with complex and important issues and yet endlessly entertained by paradoxes and trivialities. . . . We lived for the job and could rarely get away except on Sundays when (until I married in 1943) I made a point of cycling out of London or walking in the Chilterns. But there were some who managed to keep a link with peacetime duties. Richard Pares, then in the Board of Trade, could be seen in the evening in the canteen editing the *English Historical Review*. And early in 1943 I found time somehow to complete the last two chapters of my textbook on economics and get it off to the printer.[19]

Franks did none of these things. What he did do, with remarkable speed, was acculturate.

The Ministry of Supply when Franks entered it was more of an idea than a reality. It had been improvised in July 1939 by joining the production side of the War Office with the imports side of the Board of Trade. 'Still as Saxon slow at starting, still as weirdly wont to win.' Lloyd George remembered starting the Ministry of Munitions in 1915 with 'two tables and a chair', which the Office of Works promptly attempted to remove.[20] Allowing for the hyperbole, the situation was a good deal better in 1939—if only because of the institutional memory of that earlier experience—but muddle was in its way a more formidable opponent than Hitler, and the battle had hardly yet begun. The work of the ministry was split into two departments, according to its origins. Within each department there were a number of functional divisions. The main responsibility of the Production Department was to supply all munitions and stores required by the War Office and certain items common to all three fighting services (small-arms ammunition, wheeled vehicles, machine tools, and the like), and to act as the general planning authority for all war-related manufacturing activity in the British economy. The main responsibility of the Raw Materials Department was the acquisition and distribution of a sufficient supply of raw materials for the war effort and for essential civilian needs. Such materials were often scarce and usually imported, raising the controversial question of available shipping—in itself a scarce commodity—and imposing the requirement to co-ordinate policy with the Americans. Many raw materials had to be processed before they could be used by the finishing industries. The ministry ran a number of regional Raw Materials Controls, manned by the relevant industry, for this purpose. Thus the Iron and Steel Control at Leamington Spa juggled not only with iron ore, coal, and limestone, but also with the production of iron and steel up to the point at which it was cut or shaped.

As the task evolved, so the monster grew. At its greatest expansion the staff of the Ministry of Supply numbered over 414,000. Of these, some 346,000 were industrial employees, the majority in the Royal Ordnance Factories, 'producing only weapons which were of use in the Crimean War', as Franks was heard to remark in a rare moment of exasperation.[21] The remainder were Civil Servants, temporary (63,000) and permanent (5,000). Most were not based in London. The headquarters staff was 17,000 strong, with no more than about 200 administrative Civil Servants among them. Franks was one of these. His time at the ministry, he recalled, 'consisted of being set to do successively a number of things'. In the controlled anarchy of the day, everything was possible. He was conscious of power for the first time. 'I said go, and they went.'[22] For most people this was apt to be either alarming or exhilarating. For Father Franks it was a pleasant surprise. He discovered an unusual talent for operating under conditions of uncertainty, when organization was lacking, and opinion divided or unformed. 'Everything was malleable by a few men who knew what they wanted to do', he observed of the period immediately after the war. That was a perception born of his formative experience in what some called the Ministry of Mules.[23]

In particular, it was during the war that Franks established his unimpeachable reputation as an adjudicator, his most natural and effective role on the public stage. In a number of different guises, this was the role for which his name would be invoked for almost fifty years. As Stuart Hampshire has written, 'The work of practical reason is never finished, never final and secure.'

Surveying any tract of history, and looking into our own minds, we see the ebb and flow of contrary passions and interests needing to be reconciled; in the mind by that form of inner adjudication which is called reflection, and in the state by the literal and visible adjudication of parliaments and law courts . . .

. . . and, we may add, Oliver Franks.[24] Douglas Jay has pictured him in this period moving on every few months to a higher bureaucratic rank, which is scarcely an exaggeration. Predictably enough, he did not stay long in the

Establishments Division. Briefly Director of Special Enquiries as an Assistant Secretary, in 1940 he became Director of Labour Supply as a Principal Assistant (now Under-Secretary). By 1943 he was Second Secretary in charge of the Raw Materials Department. His opposite number on the production side, the redoubtable George Turner, was a study in contrast: he had joined the War Office before 1914 as a messenger boy and risen steadily through the ranks. Turner was reputed to know everything that went on in the ministry; his approval, or disapproval, counted for (almost) everything. Fortunately he approved very much of Mr Franks, who heartily reciprocated the feeling.[25] The final stage of this inexorable ascent came in 1945, when Franks became Permanent Secretary, and the whole gigantic enterprise was his.

Director of Labour Supply was already an important post, in which the scale of the responsibilities was easily matched by the urgency of the problems. By early 1941 probably the most urgent was the First Drop-Forging Crisis. The root of the crisis was an acute shortage of skilled labour in the drop-forging shops of the Midlands.[26] As a consequence, they were rapidly falling behind the output expected of them. Douglas Jay had just arrived in the Labour Directorate from the *Daily Herald*. He was immediately dispatched to Birmingham to exhort the recalcitrant drop-forging employers to take on large numbers of additional workers, including the extremely scarce die-sinkers; to pay much higher wages; and to man up their plants very rapidly on double shifts. These were unwelcome demands. Jay carried with him a special appeal from the Minister which explained that aircraft-engine production, tank production, and much else was threatened by the appalling bottle-neck in drop-forgings, and that the whole war effort was at risk. The employers were unmoved. Jay was considerably shaken. 'Some appeared not merely threatening but still unaware there was a war on.' He returned to London empty-handed.

Near-panic ensued at the Ministry of Supply. Finally, 'the inevitable decision was reached: the drop-forgers must be invited to the Adelphi and addressed in person by Mr Franks'. As Jay remembered it:

They came and—one is tempted to say—saw Mr Franks, and he conquered. He addressed them for fifteen minutes, after which they unanimously agreed to carry out all the requests of the government, including the outrageous proposal nearly to double there and then the rate of pay of die-sinkers. At the end of this meeting, which took barely one hour, several of the drop-forgers present approached me quietly and asked whether I could introduce them to Mr Franks, because they would be only too glad to do anything in their power which he wished.[27]

The First Drop-Forging Crisis had been resolved.

By the winter of 1942–3 a Second Drop-Forging Crisis loomed. This time it appeared that suitable labour for the Midlands could be secured only by closing down a number of iron foundries elsewhere, in advance of the official 'concentration' scheme. But the Iron and Steel Control resisted all pressure for closures. The struggle reached the Controller himself, Sir Charles Wright, Controller also in the First World War. He flatly refused to budge. Every avenue seemed to be closed. Recourse was had to Mr Franks. Sir Charles Wright was invited with his second, George Briggs, to Franks's office. Douglas Jay witnessed the final trial of strength.

> To all entreaties he [Wright] answered: 'It can't be done,' duly echoed by Briggs. After forty minutes I noticed beads of perspiration on Franks's forehead; and as I had never seen such a thing before, I feared he was at last going to fail.[28] But no. Raising his lofty brow to its full moral altitude, as if from a pulpit, Franks directed to Sir Charles a stirring appeal to his personal patriotism, and then instantly broke into one of the most charming and disarming smiles I have seen: 'Don't you think so, Sir Charles?' The double shaft was invincible. 'All right,' said Sir Charles: and the Second Drop-Forging Crisis was overcome.[29]

In a labour crisis of a different sort, trivial but embarrassing, Franks was not quite so effectual. At the end of 1940 Jay was allocated a new assistant, one Monica Felton, 'a young woman of marked ability, unhappily half-crippled by polio. Her disability naturally excited the sympathy of all of us; and when I was told most confidentially that she was the mistress of the chairman of the House of Commons Select Committee on National Expenditure, I ignored this as wholly irrelevant.' However, as time went on it became apparent that Miss Felton was 'inexcusably ignoring her job'. She was transferred elsewhere, but the habit persisted. Jay consulted Franks. Together they dismissed her. Some weeks later they were surprised to find that she had been appointed clerk to that same Select Committee, and even more surprised when the committee published a report on the Ministry of Supply Filling Factories. Next they learned that there was to be a secret debate in the House of Commons in which the Minister of Supply (then Sir Andrew Duncan) and the Minister of Labour (Ernest Bevin) would speak for the Government. Clearly Duncan should be told of 'the curious relationship' involved. What about Bevin? The matter was taken up with the Permanent Secretary, Sir William Douglas, who ruled that Bevin must be told. But who should tell him? There was only one possible choice. 'With much careful stage-management, it was contrived that Franks should meet Bevin absolutely alone in the latter's personal office, and confide in him, with due solemnity, in the greatest privacy, the terrible secret.' On hearing it, Bevin remained wonderfully impassive. "Undreds of people have told me that', he said.[30]

Franks's relationship with Bevin, however, waxed rather than waned. It was the most important political connection he ever made. On labour-supply issues it helped that he was able to work harmoniously with Bevin's trusted Director-General of Manpower, Godfrey Ince; on occasion the two together would consult their respective political masters. This became especially

important when Lord Beaverbrook replaced Duncan as Minister of Supply—
the fourth since the beginning of the war—from 1941 to 1942. Beaverbrook's
motto was 'urgency to the uttermost'. He had made a sensational impact at the
Ministry of Aircraft Production for a few meteoric months in 1940, and he
dearly hoped to repeat the trick at the Ministry of Supply in 1941. On taking
office, he wrote to the Prime Minister with his characteristic huff and puff:

The sense of urgency must be in all we do. It must be raised to a degree of tension
greater than anything that has gone before. It must become a passion in the minds of
men everywhere, so that energy in the factories does no more than reflect a universal
consciousness that emergency is upon us. . . .

Providence has been bountiful to the Ministry of Supply. Providence has heaped
many gifts upon it. For if there had been heavy fighting during the past year, much
abuse would have been directed against this Ministry. . . .

We thrive on unrest.[31]

Mischievously, Beaverbrook's first day at the ministry was a Sunday. He
arrived early and asked which of his senior officials were already on duty. Mr
Franks, he was informed, was already on duty. Franks and Beaverbrook had a
lengthy conference. Beaverbrook's confidence in this resourceful official was
initially high. But it was not mutual. Mr Franks regarded the new Minister
with well-concealed distaste—well concealed, that is, until a 1949 *Time* magazine profile plausibly attributed to him the presentiment that Beaverbrook,
'that awful little man', would wreck the organization.[32] The Beaverbrook press
did not forget that public slight.

   In spite of Franks's sabbath prescience, relations with the new Minister did
not run smooth. Beaverbrook was 'essentially a privateer who did not in the
least mind a little piracy if it served some immediate need at the expense of
another department'.[33] His arch-rival was the formidable Minister of Labour.
One day, completely unadvised, Beaverbrook confronted Bevin in a Cabinet
committee with some figures for labour requirements in the Filling Factories,
which the Ministry of Labour had allegedly failed to meet. Bevin said bluntly
that he did not believe that the figures were genuine, adding for good measure
that he would accept figures from Mr Franks but not from Lord Beaverbrook.
The exchanges became acrid and the meeting was terminated.[34] Franks had
been fire-watching on the roof of the Adelphi, unaware of the greater danger
below. When the all-clear sounded about 2 a.m. he went to bed in the basement. He did not get much sleep.

An hour later I was awakened by a figure saying that the Prime Minister wished to see
me immediately at Chequers. I put on some clothes: there was a car, and I was driven
to Chequers. There I found the Prime Minister pacing up and down the room in his
baby blue rompers. He addressed me and said that he would not have his ministers
quarrelling over figures in the Cabinet. We meet there, he said, to take decisions on
policy, not to discuss figures. You, he said to me, must produce a set of figures to
which both ministers have agreed. He went on for about an hour in the same vein and

I was dismissed. What was I to do? I could not make ministers agree with my assessment of the figures, and yet I had to do exactly that.[35]

Early that morning Franks asked his statisticians whether any sense could be made of Beaverbrook's pirated figures. Some sort of justification was offered. 'That', said Franks, 'is what I would call chicanery. Now let's get the real figures.'[36]

Once armed with a credible set of figures, the question was how to proceed. Wisely, Franks chose to start with Bevin, 'the more rational of the two ministers'.

I saw him: the grapevine had already told him that the Prime Minister had sent for me. He said, 'Oliver, what do you want?' I explained that I had figures on labour supply on the matters in dispute and that I thought his department would broadly agree with them. Godfrey Ince confirmed this and I had Bevin's agreement. The next thing was my Minister, a man of moods. I was lucky. I saw him late at night on the same day. He was asthmatic: the kettle full of Friar's Balsam was steaming on the hob. He felt low and talked about his symptoms. I explained about the Prime Minister and the figures and he was not interested: he just said I agree with what you have. I cheerfully got the agreed figures off to the Prime Minister's Principal Private Secretary and heard no more.[37]

The dispute was settled. With a classical combination of fortune and sapience, Franks's adjudication had proved successful.

This episode was perhaps his first close encounter with Winston Churchill. Later he would become more familiar with the Prime Minister's highly individual manners and methods. Later still, in 1957, his considered opinion of the old man was sought by Churchill's doctor Lord Moran—for the interesting reason that 'none of his opinions is borrowed from other people'. Moran recorded or reconstructed their conversation at fascinating length in his Boswellian diary. The diary itself is a controversial source of some notoriety. It raises ethical questions—it is odd to have a Boswell as a doctor—as well as evidentiary ones: can the diarist possibly have remembered, word for word, such extensive dialogue? Did he not interpolate his own opinions, *post facto*? In general there is good reason for scepticism on all counts. In this instance, however, Franks's views as conveyed by Moran appear to be absolutely authentic, in expression, allusion, and intellectual formation. If that is so, then they are not only vivid and acute—and remarkably uninhibited—but also self-revealing. We eavesdrop at a private feast: Oliver Franks free-wheeling.

Moran began by asking Franks if he found it difficult to reconcile the legend of Churchill with some of his faults.

FRANKS: 'Winston has, of course, many excellencies and many deficiencies. And if you are going to measure him with that foot-rule, I should be as baffled as you are. But surely it is the size of the man and the way history met him, giving him an opportunity which multiplied his size, that sweeps away, for me at any rate, all difficulties of that kind. Luck you may call it. But even greater men need luck. Calvin had it; Luther too.'

MORAN: 'What do you mean by size?'

FRANKS (musing): 'Well, that is difficult. Winston embodied the soul of the nation. He succeeded in being the nation, for that is what he was. In the simplified conditions of war he could be that, whereas in the more complex days of peace he never was, never could be, that. Asquith, on the other hand, as war minister [in the First World War], was only the chairman of a committee trying to make wise decisions.'

MORAN: 'Joan of Arc, I suppose, played that role, and Chatham [William Pitt] perhaps [in the Seven Years War].'

FRANKS: 'Yes. And Elizabeth to be sure, at the time of the Spanish [armada] crisis and the speech at Tilbury [in 1588]. Winston became a prophet. We can't explain him, any more than we can understand Isaiah or Elijah. I remember early in the war attending a meeting on the roof of the Ministry of Supply when Winston addressed us. I came away more happy about things. He dispelled our misgivings and set at rest our fears; he spoke of his aim and his purpose, so that we knew that somehow it would be achieved. He gave us faith. There was in him a demonic element, as in Calvin and Luther. He was a spiritual force.'[38]

Attitudes to Churchill often depended upon the amount of direct exposure to him. Franks was never one of the great man's 'Secret Circle', that close-knit, trusted, troglodytic band familiar to Churchill, 'who were called upon to provide him with help and services of various kinds'.[39] This was the privileged yet parasitic existence that so overwhelmed the critical faculties of the talented young men who were chosen to sample it. Nor was he one of those, like the Beaver or the Prof., who were part of the daily circus of the Prime Minister's social and political life (categories frequently inseparable where Churchill was concerned). Franks did not yield a nickname in this company.[40] As they had discovered at Oxford, he was not 'a man with whom it was agreeable to dine'—the traditional mark of Churchillian favour. In Washington he was more consul than satrap. He tendered advice from time to time, from the outside. He did have a famous bout of intense exposure there in January 1952, when Churchill came to visit; but by then it was late in the day, and Churchillian history was repeating itself as farce. Thus Franks's attitude to the phenomenon he described to Moran was mostly the outcome of prolonged reflection on a man and a moment worthy of any great tragedy: the Churchill of the few, the beaches, the hour,

the famous public image, which is no longer distinguishable from the inner essence and the true nature of . . . a man larger than life, composed of bigger and simpler elements than ordinary men, a gigantic, historical figure during his own lifetime, superhumanly bold, strong, and imaginative, one of the two greatest men of action his nation has produced, an orator of prodigious powers, the saviour of his country, a mythical hero who belongs to legend as much as to reality, the largest human being of our time.

This was Isaiah Berlin's portrait of 'Mr Churchill in 1940', which immortalized for the Atlantic generation a wartime perspective on Churchill as colossus—not merely prophet but even messiah. Berlin's *éloge* first appeared in 1949, fittingly, as a review of the second volume of his subject's war memoirs, *Their Finest Hour*. It was instantly taken to heart by the attentive public, and much reprinted.[41] Franks read it then and was still quoting from it forty years later.[42] No doubt everyone who examines Britain's recent past, and especially what Correlli Barnett has called the audit of war, must sooner or later confront Winston Churchill in 1940. Nevertheless, it is interesting to encounter two of the finest intellects of the time grappling with the Churchillian colossus. They were, of course, very different. Isaiah Berlin was fascinated by ideas, but also by the human beings who embodied them. Character and personality captivated him: historically, he had a long attention span. 'Some men', he said simply, 'occupy one's imagination for many years.' Berlin had a glorious style of expression, uniquely his, well described by Churchill himself as perfervid. As Noel Annan has remarked, 'he will always use two words where one will not do'.[43]

None of this was true of Oliver Franks. Franks was a purposive thinker. He thought for a purpose. (The very word was one of the guiding stars in his moral firmament. To demonstrate firmness of purpose—*constantia*, a key Stoic concept—was for Franks a great virtue. To lack a sense of purpose was an equally serious flaw. Unity of purpose was not only efficient but good.) There was a limit to his intellectual curiosity. He said of himself that by the early 1950s he was 'spoiled as a scholar', after many years away from the university.[44] This was perfectly true, but there was something missing. William Beveridge's biographer observes in a suggestive passage that 'no one who rejected the opportunity of a life of pure scholarship so frequently . . . can be seen as having a vocation in that direction. He was always much happier when directly involved in practical problems'.[45] Franks too had a predilection for problem-solving. The character of the individual was incidental, or at best instrumental, in this endeavour. In Fernand Braudel's great work, *The Mediterranean in the Age of Philip II*, the Spanish king makes his appearance well into the second volume; neither he nor his fellows bulk large in the story. Franks had a somewhat similar outlook. He believed with Braudel that *mentalités* outweighed personalities. He had no doubt of achieving a North Atlantic Treaty in 1948–9, for example, because of the climate of the time—a debatable proposition then and since.[46] Franks lacked nothing in acuity when taking the measure of a man; but he was rarely tempted to dwell on the results.

It is no surprise, then, that Berlin's anatomy of the Churchillian colossus is the more elegant and the more sustained of the two. Yet there is also a certain correspondence. Moran was right—Franks's opinions were his own. But he did have a remarkable capacity for retaining and reordering what he read. In this case Berlin's analysis, and in particular his stirring peroration, may well have provided the necessary fructification. Two years before the appearance of 'Mr Churchill', Franks had distilled his wartime experience into an influential series of lectures at the London School of Economics. Their theme was 'Central Planning and Control in War and Peace', a matter of some consequence in the tightly rationed time of 1947. Together with his widely read Sidney Ball Lecture, 'The Experience of a University Teacher in the Civil Service', they constituted a kind of *De Officiis* for the modern age, offering moral and political instruction for members of the governing class on their duties to their fellow citizens in public life.[47] Franks argued that it was a mistake to think (as many did) that things could return to normal again now that the war was over; no such prelapsarian state still existed. There was 'a new normal'—'some form of central planning and control is inevitable for the foreseeable future'. The Government 'has gone into business management and become general manager of the national economy', with far-reaching implications for both governors and governed, or in Franks's words, 'a real revolution in traditional habits of thought'.

How the quantitative, abstract and generalized expressions which represent the goal to which the economy is directed are to be given flesh and blood so that they live as the hope and desire of the people I do not know. It is at once the task and the miracle of statesmanship to translate them into terms which have meaning and inspiration to ordinary men in ordinary circumstances.

I am aware that such leadership has to effect a revolution in men's minds: that it has to change their conception of the role of the state in industry and commerce and therefore alter their idea of their own parts. That is the measure of its necessity in a democracy. It is comparable to what was done by Winston Churchill amid the events of 1940. It may be compared, too, to a very different task, undertaken in a different context with very different methods by Stalin in the Five Year Plan. Yet there is no alternative if central planning and control in the economic field is inevitable. It is a condition of that unity of purpose without which men cannot be organized together to do the work. As in war so in peace that unity is necessary to overcome the difficulties of the scale of the total operation. It is the first stage in the prevention of woolliness.[48]

As this passage begins to suggest, Franks drew a distinction between politicians on the one hand and statesmen on the other. Politicians respond to events; statesmen transcend them. Fundamentally, the statesmen has a *theme*.[49] By luck and genius Churchill found an inspirational one: 'Winston became a prophet.' Thus he met his moment. In Franks's words to Moran, 'he was a spiritual force'. It was a very characteristic compliment, perhaps the highest he could bestow. Berlin advanced the same argument with splendid rhetorical flourish:

Bismarck once said that there was no such thing as political intuition: political genius consisted in the ability to hear the distant hoof beat of the horse of history—and then by superhuman effort to leap and catch the horseman by the coat-tails. No man has ever listened for this fateful sound more eagerly than Winston Churchill, and in 1940 he made the heroic leap. . . . His prose records the tension which rises and swells to the culminating moment, the Battle of Britain—'a time when it was equally good to live or die'. This bright, heroic vision of the mortal danger and the will to conquer, born in the hour when defeat seemed not merely possible but probable, is the product of a burning historical imagination, feeding not upon the data of the outer but of the inner eye: the picture has a shape and simplicity which future historians will find it hard to reproduce when they seek to assess and interpret the facts soberly in the grey light of common day.[50]

For his part, Franks was stimulated to such reflections by the transitional tasks he was asked to perform as Permanent Secretary in 1945–6. The largest of these was the amalgamation of the Ministry of Supply and the Ministry of Aircraft Production, a task eventually accomplished in March 1946 in collaboration with Edwin Plowden, Chief Executive of the MAP. The administrative difficulty of amalgamating two huge, differently structured, and often competitive organizations was considerable. It was dwarfed, however, by the psychological one. As Franks recalled, 'everybody knew that the government had decided on amalgamation: the lion and the lamb had to lie down together. But the real problem was reconciling human temperaments. People from the one ministry did not want to be with, or work under, people from the other ministry.'[51] Suddenly it was no longer possible to maintain the amused detachment of Alec Cairncross's visitor to the departmental zoo. Position and pride were at stake. Franks was given a practical lesson in the art of management. 'It could not be done by simple fiat.' On the contrary, it required patience, empathy, and what he subsequently called 'rational persuasion'.

If the civil servant is successfully to use the methods of reason he must use his imagination as well. His explanations must make explicit and communicable what is implicit in his thoughts and he must gauge the extent to which he must carry the description of background if he is to secure intelligent agreement. He must be able to put himself into his hearer's position and not take for granted what otherwise he would take for granted himself. Rational persuasion depends on this process. . . . I venture to think that a good deal turns on the point. . . . It must often depend on how they expound the policy behind a particular proposal to a member of the public whether he goes away conscious of what 'They' have ordained rather than of what 'We' are committed to carry through.[52]

The gift of persuasion may be the greatest of all gifts in practical affairs. The Ministry of Supply showed that Oliver Franks possessed it in full measure.

Franks pursued similar concerns on the Steering Committee on Economic Development, an interdepartmental group of high officials and advisers, chaired by Sir Edward Bridges (Permanent Secretary at the Treasury), and including his old friend James Meade (now directing the Economic Section of the Cabinet Office), which met periodically to plan and peer into the future.[53] One meeting gave rise to a heated discussion on what publicity should be given to the Government's draft Economic Plan for 1946 (forerunner of the annual Economic Surveys). The basic issue was whether to publish the national income and expenditure figures upon which the plan was based. The general mood was timorous. It was argued that the figures derived from assumptions about such uncertain quantities as productivity, prices, and wages which might prove wrong or, equally undesirable, self-fulfilling. In effect they would be announcing a boom or a slump. Why accept the risk? Franks listened, chose his moment, and dissented—strongly—making 'a very moving appeal for publication. He stated that in the sort of democratic community in which we were operating we should have to publish in the end, and the desired results would be obtained only by frankly disclosing objectives and inviting co-operation to meet them.'[54] The mood of the meeting began to change. Meade adduced copious econometric arguments in support of Franks. Eventually it was decided to go ahead and publish, and soon.

Franks, however, was growing weary of the fray. Agreement to publish the income and expenditure figures represented no more than a tactical success. What had become of the strategy? It seemed that the demands on the governmental machine were increasing, without any fundamental reassessment of how they were to be met.[55] At supper with the Meades 'he spent most of the time arguing about the efficacy of all the work which we were doing on the Steering Committee'.

Would ministers when the time came really have the will to act quickly and extensively enough in stimulating total demand so as effectively to avoid a major depression? Were they not more likely to do too little and too late and then to deal with the trouble piecemeal, by particular 'planning' interventions for each industry and region, so that our hopes of anything 'liberal' in the solution were slender?[56]

One minister at least was exempt from these gloomy thoughts. For Franks (though not for Isaiah Berlin) the war had thrown up another home-grown hero: Ernest Bevin.[57] The tall, spare don and the short, squat docker made an ill-assorted pair, as Bevin himself pointed out. 'You, Oliver, 'ad a university experience. My experience is in the 'edgerows of life.' They had apparently nothing in common, save a Bristol connection about which Berlin might reminisce, and some shreds of Nonconformity. ('Bevin in his youth had preached in Methodist and Baptist chapels. But as the years passed his God had become less and less distinguishable from Social Reform.'[58]) Yet their utter dissimilarity mattered not at all. 'I am broadminded', Bevin declared. 'I have been to Eton one night, Harrow one afternoon. I have the DCL [Doctorate of Civil Law] of Bristol. I have been elected a Fellow of Magdalen [College, Oxford]. And I left school when I was eleven!'[59] If there is often a certain insidious condescension about the terms in which Ernie Bevin is discussed, Franks would have no part of it. Asked by Alan Bullock what allowance he made for Bevin, Franks was very clear—none. Bevin had enormous natural intelligence;

what he lacked was the power of generalization. That was why he resorted to anecdote. As Bullock has written, 'he required time to let a considered judgement precipitate from a mixture of reasoning, intuition and experience which he neither fully understood nor could explain . . . but which he trusted far more than any powers of logical argument'. Franks aptly termed this process 'visceral' and came to place his faith in it too.[60]

Bevin may have been broadminded, as he said, but he also bore grudges. One of his private secretaries noted perceptively that it was difficult for Bevin to believe in disinterestedness on the part of others. Reared as a fighting trade unionist, he never completely dispensed with what was once described as his 'Corsican concept of public business'. He was not strictly a docker but rather a carter—'a carter all his life, with no manners or ideas', as a former ministerial colleague commented maliciously after his death. The vendetta never ends. In these circumstances, the fact that Franks had no 'history', as he said of himself, was a positive advantage.[61] In Bevin's experience he was at once judicious and resourceful: a masterly adviser, able and willing if necessary to controvert ministerial arguments.[62] Ideology did not obtrude between them. If Bevin read Franks's post-war reflections on central planning, he was untroubled by what he found. He liked this sure-footed philosopher, who could be of such help to him. One could rely on Oliver Franks, without obligation. For Bevin—for any major politician—that was an extremely attractive proposition. On Franks's side the chemistry was simple. He approved of Ernest Bevin, and of what he was trying to do. He even joked about him, an unusual public sign of affection. ('The Secretary of State', he once informed the waiting Dean Acheson, 'is doing his own version of hurrying to the meeting.'[63]) Superficially, Bevin looked an unlikely statesman. In fact he too had a theme, as Franks was soon to discover.

Once he had seen through the amalgamation with the Ministry of Aircraft Production, Franks felt he could at last leave the Ministry of Supply, after nearly seven years' service as a Whitehall irregular. It had been a liberating experience. These were not the best years of his life, as they were for so many of his coevals, but they were the determining ones. Franks did not have fun in the war, like his friend Henry Phelps Brown, serving gallantly in an anti-aircraft battery and 'bathing in the waters of Carthage'.[64] He did have success. In spite of his amateur status he had risen to the top of a thriving and important ministry, a feat equalled only by his fellow don and classics scholar, John Maud, at the Ministry of Food.[65] Success brought recognition; even, in official circles, renown. Franks had been thrust into a new subculture. If this subculture operates according to a system of reputations, as has been proposed, then Oliver Franks's reputation was made in the Ministry of Supply.

The elements of the system are the holders of top official positions. The counters by which reputations are measured and traded are *units of esteem*. . . . Esteem is measured in terms of intellect (is he bright?), influence (can he carry along his colleagues and masters?), and especially in terms of trust (is he reliable?). All three factors combine to affect the participants' sense of mutual confidence.[66]

Intellect, influence, and trust: by 1945 probably no one in Whitehall was trading at a higher level of esteem. 'I suppose Franks is not available . . .?' was a constant refrain whenever a new appointment was discussed. Franks was coveted by the Board of Trade and the Ministry of Works; he was beseeched to remain at the Ministry of Supply; he was offered the National Coal Board, the proud flagship of the nationalized fleet.[67]

In 1946 he wanted none of these. Approached with some trepidation, the new world of Whitehall had proved compelling—more compelling than the New World of Chicago—and in many ways congenial. His kinship, however, was in some measure provisional. He had always felt that he was in it but not of it—a characteristic position. He was a temporary Permanent Secretary, as he liked to say. Now he was in need of a restorative. The nationalized industries failed to 'light a spark'. More than once after the war Franks considered the possibility of working 'at the grindstones of politics and administration', in various guises, only to reject it (after some hesitation) every time.[68] About nationalization he seems to have had reservations from the outset. He remembered only one serious disagreement with the Minister, John Wilmot, during the transition to peace. It concerned the steel industry, and took an instructive form:

He wanted me to put forward a paper proposing its nationalization. I refused on the ground that there were no good administrative reasons, for or against. It was a purely political matter. He did not like this and put pressure on me. In the end I said I should have to send him a formal minute of dissent. After that he could only give me an order. By good fortune he did not do so and the episode ended.[69]

Luckily, Franks was also offered a position he did want—the only one, he said, that he ever really wanted. It was a position for which he was apparently predestined, if not actually pre-elected, since before the war: Provost of Queen's College, Oxford.[70] All entreaty to remain in Government service was set at nought. With a light heart, the prodigal son returned to his old college, briefly 'careless of the sharp, harsh, exigent realities of the outer world'.

PART II

The Partner and the Queue

4 *The Marshall Plan*

'OXFORD, that lotus land, saps the will-power, the power of action.' So wrote Max Beerbohm of those who stay. Oliver Franks rarely courted that danger. Free at last, he spent a year at Queen's 'frisking like a lamb in green pastures'.[1] On 30 June 1947 he was given leave of absence by the Governing Body of the college in order 'to prepare a scheme for the comprehensive restoration of the economy of Europe on the lines adumbrated by Mr Marshall, the United States Secretary of State'.[2] The scheme was to be submitted by 1 September 1947. It was surely the largest long-vacation task ever undertaken.

Cloistered at Harvard some three weeks earlier, on 5 June 1947, Marshall had spoken with characteristically austere eloquence of the 'hunger, poverty, desperation and chaos' then rife in Europe, and of the need to find 'a cure rather than a mere palliative' for this grave condition. He went on to make the famous proposition that is automatically associated with his name. In conception it had a deceptive simplicity. As his deputy and successor Dean Acheson later pointed out, the original Marshall Plan consisted of six sentences, only one of which dealt with what the Americans themselves might do. The firm emphasis was on European organization rather than American cash. Marshall said:

It is already evident that, before the United States Government can proceed much further in its efforts to alleviate the situation and help start the European world on its way to recovery, there must be some agreement among the countries of Europe as to the requirements of the situation and the part those countries themselves will take in order to give proper effect to whatever action might be undertaken by this Government.

It would be neither fitting nor efficacious for this Government to undertake to draw up unilaterally a programme designed to place Europe on its feet economically.

This is the business of the Europeans.

The initiative, I think, must come from Europe. The programme should be a joint one, agreed to by a number of, if not all, European nations.

The role of this country should consist of friendly aid in the drafting of a European programme and of later support of such a programme so far as it may be practical for us to do so.[3]

The following morning witnessed one of the great myth-making moments of British statesmanship. Ernest Bevin, now Foreign Secretary, woke up, groped for the news on his small bedside radio, happened to catch the BBC's regular 'American Commentary', heard for the first time of Marshall's speech, and immediately shouted the hedgerow equivalent of eureka![4] This was Bevin's finest hour. Fittingly, like Churchill, he himself supplied the shape and colour of the story. 'I assure you, gentlemen,' he recalled for the hard-bitten National Press Club in Washington, 'it was like a lifeline to sinking men. It seemed to bring hope where there was none. The generosity of it was beyond our belief. It expressed a mutual thing. It said: "Try and help yourselves, and we will try to see what we can do. Try and do the thing collectively, and we will see what we can put into the pool." I think you understand why, therefore, we responded with such alacrity, and why we grabbed the lifeline with both hands.'[5]

Bevin's apperception galvanized Whitehall. A lifeline had been extended. The pressing questions were how and where to grab, and with whom. Initial thinking in London focused on the need to establish a small international task force as soon as possible, even before the end of June, in order to assemble a coherent response by September. This body would be tractable, pragmatic, and expert. Its members would be drawn from a representative group of European countries led by Britain and France, including for example Poland, Czechoslovakia, Belgium or The Netherlands, and Denmark, but excluding the Soviet Union. Bevin subsequently expressed a preference for a group of five—he mentioned France, Czechoslovakia, and Italy—and insisted that any Benelux representative be Dutch.[6] American, British, and French officials from the respective occupation zones would speak for Germany. The Soviet zone was not considered. It was anticipated that Oliver Franks would lead the British team and Jean Monnet, no less, the French. Bevin actually spoke of something resembling an Anglo-French Monnet Plan at this time. The task force would concentrate their attention on cereals (already known to be in desperately short supply), coal, and transport. Together they would construct the programme for which Marshall had called, a programme which would 'fire the imagination of the American people and the Congress', emphasizing self-help, mutual aid, and joint planning. They would speak for Europe (or at least for some of it). Their watchwords were well chosen: the programme should be 'simple, striking, and concrete'. Immediacy was all. 'In the long run its form may be more important than its content'—a canny speculation.[7]

Behind this thinking lay a whole concatenation of vexatious issues, of which two were fundamental. First, to borrow a phrase from Hugh Seton-Watson, 'what is Europe, where is Europe?'[8] The issue is unresolved to this day. It is, perhaps, unresolvable. Charles Péguy said: 'Tout commence par la mystique, et finit par la politique.' Now seems to be the time for *la politique*. After the Second World War it was *la mystique*. Everything was malleable then, as Franks himself remarked. In 1947 the European jelly had not set. 'There was this vast vacuum of what had been Germany, and the occupation forces looking at each other across the middle . . . Nobody knew what the shape of things was going to be. It was worked out step by step and these great adventures in policy were taken one by one against perceived need.'[9] But the shape of the mould could not be determined wholly from within, for in the aftermath of the Second World War the countries of Western Europe were freakishly dependent upon the benevolent disposition of good old Uncle Sam, whose wealth was as great as his appetite.

To frame the question more concretely, was it to be an all-European or a Western European programme? Marshall had addressed himself to 'any government' willing to assist in the task of recovery. Was Washington really as disinterested as this studiously open invitation seemed to suggest? For their part, the British already had decided preferences on the appropriate participants. (Asked whether he expected the Russians to accept Marshall's invitation, Bevin made the gnomic reply: 'The Tsar Alexander still hasn't answered Castlereagh's questions.'[10]) What they did not yet know was whether those preferences were acceptable to Washington. Bluntly put, was American funding to be contingent on Soviet participation?

The Americans were not the only ones who had to be squared. If a well-formed 'Western bloc' was to emerge from the process of recovery planning—an idea that was already taking shape in Bevin's mind—then French preferences, too, would have to be accommodated. Accordingly, Bevin conferred with his opposite number, Georges Bidault, in Paris from 17 to 19 June. From Bidault he learned that French enthusiasm for Soviet participation matched his own; that the French also were thinking in terms of an international task force, sectoral specialization, and maximum speed; and that they would insist upon Paris rather than London as the venue for meetings because they thought (rightly) that London had an 'anti-Soviet flavour'.[11] Bidault was anxious to avoid the blame for any rupture—rather too anxious, as it seemed to Bevin. Nevertheless, after some disputation, the two Foreign Ministers agreed to proceed on this basis. They would formally invite the Soviets to preliminary, tripartite discussions of Marshall's proposals. In so doing they would at once clarify the issue and place themselves beyond reproach. They took the precaution of informing the US Ambassador in Paris, Jefferson Caffery, that they were prepared 'to go ahead full steam even if the Soviets refuse to do so'.[12]

The second fundamental issue for the British tended selfishly to cut across this display of Anglo-French cordiality. To what extent would Britain's 'special position' *vis-à-vis* the United States enable her to secure more influence, or for that matter more money? This was not only a question of 'more cash with less strings', as it was put to Franks by the Foreign Office, a trifle inelegantly.[13] It was also a question of national pride and power politics: a potent mixture. The issue arose out of the strong integrationist thrust of Marshall's proposals. Marshall planners tended naturally to assume that the countries of

Europe could, and should, unite to save themselves. The putative outcome of this process, a United States of Europe, was for many Americans merely a rational analogue of their own historical experience. The harvest of that experience had been a remarkable prosperity. Self-evidently, unity was the path to plenty. Why should the Europeans not take it?[14]

This was the integrationist refrain. The firmest response came from the British. Their general objection was liable to take the form of a short history lecture. The prevalent tone was one of disdain.

The fact that most of the countries concerned had in different ways, but all to the limit of their means, spent four years fighting against integration imposed by a foreign power, the fact that to work together in this way meant at least a resumption of the internal governmental controls which they and the Americans themselves so strongly disliked, and which they regarded as an evil only to be endured in time of war; the fact that the quotas and exchange restrictions complained of were the consequence and not the cause of their difficulties; the fact that trade could scarcely be done with Germany because of the financial and commercial policies followed by the occupying powers, among which powers the Americans were perhaps the most important; the fact that behind state boundaries were differences of race, language, religion, forms of government, standards of living, and degrees of distress; the fact that some states were continental nations only, whilst others were centres of a world-wide union of nations; in short, that the momentum of a thousand years of history went to account for the existing national boundaries and differences of national psychology; all this, it was assumed, could be overcome by a six weeks' conference convened at a week's notice to suit the legislative timetable of the American Congress. It was a large assumption. It was made, and it was not fulfilled.[15]

These were general arguments, with a 'world-wide' (that is, British Commonwealth) subtext. The particular British objection to integration had to do with the nature of her relationship with the United States. By 1947, British policy-makers had managed to secure a relationship best described as covertly special.[16] With this they were by no means content. What they wanted was something more avowedly exclusive. Ernest Bevin's greatest foreign policy project was the negotiation of a satisfactory 'basis of partnership' with Washington. Central to this project was explicit American recognition of the fundamental British belief that they were not 'just another European country', as Bevin put it to the imperious Under-Secretary of State for Economic Affairs, William L. Clayton, who arrived in London for some preliminary consultations in late June.[17] The Foreign Secretary's argument was that Britain's position was a singular one, demanding singular treatment. She was not meant to stand with the others in what Franks called 'the European queue'. The metaphor haunts the official correspondence of the period. The European queue, like any dole queue, carried a dreadful stigma. British *grands décision-aires* wished for nothing more than to escape it, with Washington's full connivance.[18] The stated Foreign Office principle was 'one foot in and one foot out' of Europe's affairs. As the British delegation in Paris were reminded, 'we are not economically a part of Europe (less than twenty-five percent of our trade is with Europe); the recovery of continental Europe would not itself solve our problem; we depend upon the rest of the world getting dollars (UK and Europe's deficits with USA are only half the world dollar shortage)'.[19]

The conviction was absolute: Britain was a Great Power, fallen upon hard times. She knew what it was to have international responsibilities. Bevin made the point in a parable. 'The US was in the position today where Britain was at the end of the Napoleonic wars. When those wars ended Britain held about 30 percent of the world's wealth. The US today holds about 50 percent. Britain for 18 years after Waterloo "practically gave away her exports" but this resulted in stability and a hundred years of peace.'[20] Britain still possessed the combined imperial attributes of moral authority, organizational capacity, and global influence. It was essential to make use of these attributes, for nowhere else in the cockpit of Europe were they deployed to such powerful effect. The best guarantee of European recovery and a new period of stability, Bevin contended, was an Anglo-American financial partnership. In the words of his private secretary: 'Europe under American water[ing] cans handled by British gardeners blossoms into a happy Western Garden of Eden.'[21] But this Arcadian vision would not be realized if Britain was simply 'lumped into the problem of Europe' and reduced to the status of Yugoslavia *vis-à-vis* the Soviet Union—the stark parallel suggested to Clayton. To endure such a fate, said Bevin sorrowfully, would be to sacrifice 'the little bit of dignity we have left'.[22] Britain had much to contribute. She would play her part—and jump the queue—if only the Americans would let her.

Awkwardly for Bevin, financial Dunkirks undermined financial alliances. 'Fancy the Socialist Government in England keeping themselves alive, economically and politically, by these large annual dollops of dollars from capitalist America', crowed Churchill in the 1950 general election campaign. 'They seek the dollars, they beg the dollars, they bluster for the dollars, they gobble the dollars, but in the whole of their 8,000-word manifesto they cannot say "thank you" for the dollars.'[23] The unpalatable truth behind the electioneering was that Britain had no option but to subsist on dollars. In this case the victor was also the debtor—by 1945, the biggest in the world. One-quarter of her total wealth had been consumed in the war. A $3.75 billion American loan negotiated in 1945 and authorized in 1946 was used up by 1947. Gold and dollar reserves ebbed away, unstoppable as the tide. According to the terms of the loan, sterling was made fully convertible into dollars in July 1947. There was an instant flight from the pound. The following month the arrangement was suspended, though not before Bevin had sounded the US Ambassador in London about the possibility of immediate relief 'to the tune of a billion dollars . . . to carry them over the hump'.[24] The Ambassador, Lew Douglas, was a trusted friend, and the approach was a personal and informal one. But what was Washington to think? The sterling crisis was becoming a regular feature of transatlantic life. The fiasco of convertibility may have helped to dramatize the mutual benefits of a financially able ally—this was the perennial British contention—but in so doing it served to expose something rather shocking. Here, truly, was a poor relation.

A Poor Relation is the most irrelevant thing in nature, a piece of impertinent correspondency, an odious approximation, a haunting conscience, a preposterous shadow, lengthening in the noontide of your prosperity, an unwelcome remembrancer, a perpetually recurring mortification, a drain on your purse, a more intolerable dun on your pride, a drawback upon success, a rebuke to your rising, a stain in your blood, a blot on your scutcheon, a rent in your garment, a death's head at your banquet, Agathocles' pot, a Mordecai in your gate, a Lazarus at your door, a lion in your path, a frog in your chamber, a fly in your ointment, a mote in your eye, a triumph to your enemy, an apology to your friends, the one thing not needful, the hail in harvest, the ounce of sour in a pound of sweet, the bore par excellence.[25]

To be always poor and always special was to ask the impossible. The State Department was adamant that, as a matter of principle, the Marshall Plan should conform to a 'continental' rather than a 'country' approach. It should be a work of synthesis rather than a collection of disaggregated demands. Special difficulties tended to be dismissed as special pleading. In such a climate, when neediness continually threatened to outbid closeness, the rhetoric of cousinhood would not suffice. After the war was over, official America was found to be as unmoved by Winston Churchill's grandiloquent appeals to 'the fraternal association of the English-speaking peoples' as by the Pilgrim Society's maudlin annual chorus of 'hands across the sea'. To invoke the common heritage—'blood, class and nostalgia', in one acerbic formulation—was profoundly unconvincing. As Dean Acheson tersely observed, 'We know all that.'[26] Instead, superior statecraft was required. This called for persuasiveness, a living sense of what was possible, and high international esteem. Oliver Franks's domestic reputation was about to be traded in a wider market.

The next stage in what Franks called 'the practical dialectic' to save Europe was a corrosive series of tripartite Anglo-French-Soviet meetings held in Paris between the respective Foreign Ministers, Bevin, Bidault, and Molotov.[27] During the preceding weeks it had been made abundantly clear that the Soviets had no wish to 'barter their independence for American dollars' or to acquiesce in the 'conversion of all Europe into [the] colony of [a] dollar empire'.[28] Molotov was obviously suspicious of the exclusive Anglo-French and Anglo-American consultations that had already taken place, and with good reason, for Bevin now had the priceless advantage of knowing that the French were staunch and the Americans permissive on the key question of Soviet participation. Formally, the American position as adumbrated by Clayton was that, 'while it is hoped that the scheme will cover Europe as a whole, the US Administration would be satisfied if it could be started with the Western countries of Europe as a nucleus, on the understanding that the scheme would be open to other countries if they so desired'.[29] Informally, there were indications of a heartening convergence of official thinking in Washington and London. Even Soviet opposition, it was whispered, would have the merit of solidifying congressional support for the plan.[30]

It was apparent that the Soviets faced an intolerable situation. If they would not agree to the conditions laid down by the Western powers, the Western powers would proceed without them. Agreement was never seriously sought by either side. The meetings opened on 27 June and closed on 2 July with Molotov's acrimonious departure. ''e walked out, uttering threats', Bevin reported to Attlee. For the first time, there was an open breach. The Foreign Secretary was quite content. 'I am glad that the cards have been laid on the table and that the responsibility will be laid at Moscow's door', he told Ambassador Caffery.[31] Even at the time, they sensed a climacteric. For Franks as for others, it was Soviet non-participation in the Marshall Plan that determined the Cold War.[32]

'When the cat was away the mice could work.'[33] Bevin and Bidault lost no more time. An Anglo-French communiqué was promptly issued to twenty-two European countries inviting them to send representatives to Paris by 12 July. 'The task to be undertaken will be to draw up a European reconstruction programme in which the resources and needs of each state will be co-ordinated as each of the European countries freely decides. . . . A temporary organization must be set up to collect the data on which such a programme will be based.' An explicit reassurance was offered to the invitees that this organization would take no action 'which could be regarded as a violation of their sovereignty'.[34] It was proposed to hold a procedural conference to agree and establish the necessary machinery. The real work could then begin.

The invitation embraced a broad definition of Europe. East and West, allied and neutral: all were included. Apart from the Soviet Union, only Fascist Spain was (for the moment) beyond the pale. There was provision for Germany to be represented by the Western occupying powers. As expected, however, eight of those who were invited—all within the Soviet sphere of influence—felt compelled to refuse. Czechoslovakia and Poland, at least, would have accepted but for direct pressure from Stalin, who made it ominously plain that their participation in the programme would be regarded as 'an act specifically aimed against the USSR'.[35] Thus the conference which convened in the airless splendour of the Grand Palais on the Champs-Élysées, perplexed and perspiring in the overpowering heat of that extraordinary summer, consisted of representatives from sixteen nations: Austria, Belgium, Denmark, France, Greece, Iceland, Ireland, Italy, Luxemburg, The Netherlands, Norway, Portugal, Sweden, Switzerland, Turkey, and the United Kingdom. Bevin was elected chairman. Politically, this was a foregone conclusion. In effect Britain had traded the venue for the chair.[36] Yet, clearly the Foreign

Secretary could not spend the whole summer in Paris. Anticipating the problem, he had selected a trustworthy substitute. Bevin oversaw the inauguration, celebrated the storming of the Bastille in fine style on 14 July, and withdrew across the Channel the following day. He was certainly 'present at the creation'; he gave a number of useful hints. But he left the arrangements in the capable hands of Oliver Franks.[37]

On 15 July 1947, therefore, Franks found himself chairman of the working conference, now reconstituted as the Committee of European Economic Co-operation (CEEC), and leader of the British delegation. He had been given plenipotentiary powers and remarkably few instructions. He was to go to Paris and do his best. Bevin simply told him to get on with it. He had been left in no doubt of the priority accorded to this endeavour.[38] Whitehall, apparently, stood ready to supply his every need. Any minister or official would be flown over at once, on request. When a member of the delegation sent an exasperated telegram to London asking how they could be expected to make bricks without straw, he received the immediate reply: 'Goldman, expert strawless brickmaker, is on the way.'[39]

In lieu of a brief from the Foreign Office, Franks reread Marshall's speech. His cardinal perception was that this was a European problem which should be looked at through American eyes—through the eyes of those to whom it would eventually be presented.[40] Unlike some of his compatriots, he took seriously the promise of 'friendly aid' in drawing up the programme. Franks always tended his American relationships with loving care. He made a point of involving and informing, but never condescending. Before he left London he talked to Ambassador Douglas. When he got to Paris he sought out Ambassador Caffery. Through a contact man in the American Embassy he kept in touch with the wandering William Clayton, who was also negotiating what became the General Agreement on Tariffs and Trade (GATT) in Geneva. These men he called the triumvirs. Their presence was felt more or less continuously throughout the summer.[41] Douglas was a born intermediary, one of the very few who could outcharm Franklin Roosevelt. He could 'talk longer, say less, and make more people like him, than anyone else'. Caffery was by virtue of his ambassadorial position the channel for interesting international gossip. Otherwise he had little to recommend him. 'If anything went on in Caffery's head you'd never know what it was, all he does is nod acquiescence'. Clayton was the one to reckon with—a wealthy Texas cotton broker and militant free trader whose missionary work among the Europeans was an important influence on the out-turn of events in that crowded year.[42]

From the triumvirs Franks learned the guilty secret of the State Department. Weeks after Marshall had spoken, the Marshall Plan resembled nothing so much as a flying saucer—'nobody knows what it looks like, how big it is, in what direction it is moving, or whether it really exists'.[43] At about

the time the CEEC began its work, the position was accurately and tren-
chantly summarized in an internal memorandum by George Kennan:

We have no plan. The Europeans must be made to take responsibility. We would consider [a] European plan only if it were a good one and promised to do the whole job.
Our main object: to render [the] principal European countries able to exist without
outside charity. Necessity of this:
   (a) So that they can buy from us;
   (b) So that they will have enough self-confidence to withstand outside pressures.[44]

'Outside pressures' allowed of differing interpretations. In the opinion of one
CEEC delegate, 'this conference is the turning point of European history.
Failure to reach agreement would mean a Red tide might sweep over Europe.'
This was an apocalyptic expression of a pervasive fear. None of the principals
in London or Washington expected Soviet tanks to roll in 1947—in Berlin and
Paris they could not afford to be quite so sanguine—but there was genuine
uncertainty about 'whether the political and economic structures of Western
European countries would hold together', as Franks recalled soberly, and
uncertainty too about American intentions in the event of a collapse.[45] The
central administration in many of those countries was in chronic disarray or
lacking altogether. Strong Communist Parties were licking their lips in the
wings. The malaise had spread to the very gates of Paris. At the end of August
the French Government announced the suspension of all dollar imports except
cereals, coal, and a few other essentials. At the beginning of September the
Italian Government suspended purchases of even these. It was not too far-
fetched to see the proud French Fourth Republic as another rotten apple in a
bottomless barrel.[46]

   Here, then, was a difficult combination of opacity and urgency. It was the
latter that bore most heavily on Franks personally. The procedural conference
had determined that the CEEC should submit a report to the United States on
'European availabilities and requirements' for the four years 1948–51 by 1
September 1947.[47] These were his terms of reference. He had six weeks.

   In later years Franks made sure of discussing the terms of reference carefully in advance. In this instance he had neither the opportunity nor the
temerity to attempt any of that, but resolved the task to his own satisfaction
into a single, simplifying objective—the search for a European antithesis to the
American thesis. In plain language, what was the response to Marshall going
to be? For Oliver Franks, 'the purpose of the exercise was being European'. It
was a collective endeavour or it was nothing. His first problem was the chairman's problem of how to bring all the sheep into one fold. As he later wrote:
'the sixteen nations were being asked to do something unprecedented. They
were confronted with something that was not part of their previous experience. They had to create a map and use it simultaneously.'[48]

   As Franks quickly discovered, some of these sheep were goats.

Five had colonial empires, two had less than one million inhabitants. Two were important powers with large armed forces, one was occupied by two of the others, and two had been neutral powers for more than a century. Two had per capita national incomes clearly exceeded only by that of the United States, four were still underdeveloped economies. Some had based their recovery on planning and stringent controls, others had been ardent advocates of decontrol and a *laissez-faire* economy. Some had a worldwide pattern of trade and investment, for others their international economic connections were overwhelmingly with the European continent. The one country whose affairs more than any other had been responsible for the conference and which was the most important Western European economy was not represented there at all.[49]

Several were present with reservations. Switzerland, 'intent on preserving the seamless robe of neutrality in all directions', had accepted the invitation on the understanding that the conference would not deal with political matters.[50] The Scandinavians were concerned lest the conference bypass the United Nations, or interfere with their trade in Eastern Europe, or compromise their neutrality. Sweden in particular (represented by the young Dag Hammarskjöld) fretted about the hostility of her bearish neighbour to the east. Negotiating with Hammarskjöld was reminiscent of the medieval philosophers' disputations about the number of angels dancing on the head of a pin. It was intellectually demanding, but neither politically nor philosophically very satisfying.[51] Ireland—that is to say, the Irish Republic—was delighted to be part of a European Recovery Programme but anxious not to be drawn too close to the jackboot authority of the British. Greece and Turkey were already receiving substantial aid from the United States under separate legislation, a commitment reinforced by the enunciation of the Truman Doctrine in March 1947. Quite apart from being south-eastern rather than north-western in orientation, and agricultural rather than industrial in organization—'preoccupied with figs and raisins', as Franks said unkindly—both countries had an infuriating propensity to object to anything which could conceivably jeopardize their own dollops of dollars. At this stage, 'being European' appeared to do just that.[52]

Also manifest at the conference table were the deep-seated insecurities and resentments that are the normal currency of international relations. Notably, the smaller nations on the CEEC were automatically suspicious of Anglo-French dictation.[53] The French in particular aroused strong feelings among the weak and mixed feelings among the strong. It was symptomatic that in his capacity as spokesman for the CEEC the French representative was soon criticized for giving a French slant to the information released; alternative arrangements were quickly made.[54] The representative in question turned out to be, not Jean Monnet, but Hervé Alphand. Committed as he was to *le plan*, Monnet continued to do what he did best: operate guerrilla-fashion behind the lines, free of diplomatic encumbrance. Franks consulted him informally and often, and found him an invaluable resource for his technical expertise (especially on food and agriculture), and for his political connections. To get a quick answer out of the French Government—otherwise unobtainable—one had only to ask Jean Monnet.[55] Hervé Alphand, on the other hand, was cast in a more traditional mould. Monnet was for something that transcended the nation-state. Alphand, a consummate professional, was for France.[56] 'I have known many worthy French diplomats,' wrote that great Belgian European, Paul-Henri Spaak, 'and the best of them were sometimes the most difficult.'

But one thing is certain: it is easier to get a sympathetic hearing at the British Foreign Office (and even more so at the American State Department) than at the Quai d'Orsay. At the Foreign Office you are more likely to be given a friendly reception and not be left with the impression that you are merely being tolerated. I remember Bech, for so long the Premier and Foreign Minister of Luxembourg, saying to me in Geneva when I was just a novice: 'To be well thought of in Paris one must love France and France alone.' I have always loved France, and still do. But I confess that I have loved other countries as well. Sometimes I have had the impression that this is the one thing the Quai d'Orsay cannot forgive.[57]

Spaak thought that the mistrust between Belgium and France stemmed from soon after the Great War. Franks had reason to believe otherwise:

In the early stages of the work of the Committee I found the French at odds with the Dutch, the Belgians, and the Luxemburgers. The French wanted the recovery programme to be for four years: the Benelux countries thought two would do—enough time, they argued, to repair the damages of war. Neither side would budge. I could not understand why the parties were so unyielding. So one night I had the Dutch and Belgian leaders [Dr H. M. Hirschfeld and Baron Guillaume] to dinner and we talked till late into the night, until finally the root of the difference was exposed. With the power vacuum that had been Germany, now ruled by the generals commanding the four zones, the only country in a position of power was France. If the recovery programme lasted for four years and enabled full reconstruction, the fear was that France might use its power and attempt to do what Louis XIV had done, dominate the Low Countries. Memories of 250 years ago were alive, but as is often the case, once the ghost had been exhumed and seen for what it was, the affair was over and we all settled for four years.[58]

It was a typical encounter. Franks's success as a negotiator was in large part due to his ability to listen. He listened well—that is, openly and constructively—and he listened long. If so inclined, he could outlast the most indefatigable talker. He was also a penetrating inquisitor. The key question for Franks was not '*what* do you believe?' but '*why* do you believe it?' It was the premiss and not the argument that really interested him. Churchill called Harry Hopkins, Roosevelt's wartime go-between, Lord Root of the Matter. The title would have done as well for Oliver Franks.

The French for their part were suspicious of American dictation—'chewing-gum imperialism'—in all things, but most acutely in any aspect of French security, military or economic.[59] Their immediate and atavistic concern was

Germany, which subsumed both elements. The French attitude towards German recovery was an emotional one, as Franks told Clayton—competitive, if not actively hostile. They favoured the partition of Germany into smaller states, the annexation of the Saarland, and the internationalization of the Ruhr. If there was going to be an integrated Western European system, then Germany should be subordinate to France as its political and economic centre. Upward revision of the permitted levels of industry in the Anglo-American 'Bizone' was described by Bidault as tantamount to giving German reconstruction priority over French reconstruction. Progressive measures towards rehabilitation were stigmatized as 'Germany first'. If the CEEC proposed an increase in German output beyond the 'level of security', Alphand declared at its second meeting, France would take 'an entirely negative position'.[60] When the French delegation flatly refused to accept new estimates of Bizonal steel, coke, and coal production, the CEEC's work on these vital commodities was effectively paralysed. Under American and British pressure, French intransigence moderated somewhat over the following weeks. Propitiated by a round of tripartite talks, they were induced to acquiesce in the promulgation of the revised level of industry agreement for the Bizone. They signed, 'with serious hesitation', but did not cease to snipe.[61] In general it was apparent that Alphand had spoken no more than the truth. His riposte was delivered with unaccustomed pungency, as late as 1954: 'If you British want us to get into bed with the Germans, then you British must be the bolster!'[62] It might be said that, for the French, the purpose of the European Recovery Programme was to keep the Germans down, the Soviets out, and the Anglo-Saxons away.

The bolster in the Grand Palais was Oliver Franks. Whether or not 'the German problem' was the mainspring of American or British foreign policy is a matter for scholarly debate.[63] In the pell-mell proceedings of the CEEC it was something of a distraction. From the beginning, the assumption had been that data on the 'availabilities and requirements' of each country would have to be collated by experts in the field. In conformity with early British and French planning, four Technical Committees were originally proposed for this purpose: Food and Agriculture, Fuel and Power, Iron and Steel, and Transport. As the work got under way, these four were soon elaborated into nine: Food and Agriculture, Coal, Electricity, Petroleum Products, Iron and Steel, Timber, Inland Transport, Maritime Transport, and Manpower. A small Balance of Payments Committee was added a little later. (And finally a Committee of Financial Experts, an unwieldy body whose membership was synonymous with membership of the CEEC as a whole, to examine the means of removing financial obstacles to intra-European trade. This committee did not work to the same timetable as the others.)

Each Technical Committee designed a questionnaire to elicit the information that seemed to be required. With the approval of the CEEC, the questionnaires were then sent out for completion by the central governments of the participating countries, guided as necessary by their representatives in Paris. Germany was not forgotten. Optimistically, the questionnaires were also sent to the Commanders-in-Chief of all four occupation zones. They were duly completed by the American, British, and French; and duly ignored by the Soviets. Data on 'Western Germany' therefore constituted an integral part of the information published and analysed in the CEEC's report.[64] Broader reflections on the German problem were relegated to an appendix consisting of a 'note agreed by those participating countries which were at war with Germany'. The rubric signalled the accommodations that had to be reached. To appease the French: 'The German economy must not be allowed to develop to the detriment of other European countries, as it has done in the past.' To reassure the Benelux: 'But, if European co-operation is to be effective, the German economy must be fitted into the European economy so that it may contribute to a general improvement in the standard of living.' To satisfy everyone: 'In particular, the output of the Ruhr coalfield, which is essential to the European economy as a whole, must not again be used by Germany in such a way as to constitute a threat to European security, but must contribute to the rehabilitation and economic stability of the whole of Europe, including Germany herself.'[65] It is idle to complain of these tergiversations. Franks and his colleagues were dealing with 'intimate figures in an infinitesimal period of time'.[66] The situation was worsening almost daily. Washington was waiting. This report, like other Franks reports, was at once expeditious and unanimous. In both respects, the instincts of the chairman matched the needs of the hour. To deliver as much, Franks recalled, he had to be 'a sort of flaming angel waving a sword'.[67] Angels, it seems, understand very well how to compromise.

The crying need for a sound statistical base was a lesson learned from the war.[68] Many of those involved in the CEEC and its subsequent reincarnations, the OEEC and OECD, had direct or indirect experience of the plethora of wartime combined boards—food, raw materials, shipping, production, and the like—which accustomed a generation of civilian and military officials to the habits of working-level international co-operation. The combined boards were strictly Anglo-American, but the shared experience included such key players as Jean Monnet and his brilliant young associate Robert Marjolin.[69] Franks himself had dealt regularly with the combined boards during his time in the Ministry of Supply. He had also been involved in a further seed-bed of international co-operation, the United Nations Relief and Rehabilitation Administration (UNRRA), one of several international agencies which sprang up under the umbrella of the nascent UN in the latter years of the war. Alphand and Marjolin, among others, were present at the creation of another, the Food and Agricultural Organization (FAO), in 1943.

Franks's deputy on the CEEC, the estimable A. D. (Denny) Marris, was specially recruited from Lazard Brothers, the merchant bank, of which he was a Director (and later Managing Director). Not the least of his recommendations was an extensive experience of the combined boards in Washington during the war, followed by a stint as Secretary-General of the short-lived Emergency Economic Committee for Europe in 1945–6.[70] Marris was already house-trained, as Franks put it, to both the Americans and the Foreign Office. In Paris he mediated between the chairman and the British delegation on the one hand, and the various committees on the other. Unobtrusively he cleared space for Franks to think. He was interlocutor and adviser, candid, independent, and informed: a true *amicus principis*.[71]

In spite of this background, the need was easier to identify than to remedy. Gathering and standardizing statistics across Western Europe posed tremendous problems. For some Europeans, the Technical Committees were a dangerous innovation and their questionnaires a baffling intrusion. The coal questionnaire, for example, called for disaggregated production, consumption, import, and export figures for 1929, 1935–8 (the averages), 1945, and 1946; estimates for 1947; projections for 1948, 1949, and 1950, based upon gradually increasing supplies; and targets for 1951, given a number of specified assumptions. The questions were formulated with the help of 'technical advice' from an American officer on the staff of the European Coal Organization.[72] They were approved by the CEEC on 25 July. Participating countries were expected to furnish the answers by 4 August.

And coal was only the first. Other questionnaires, on similar lines, soon followed. Soon, the capitals of Europe were inundated with the beastly things. To complete them all was a formidable undertaking for any government. For some it was a virtual impossibility. Late one night in the Grand Palais, Robert Marjolin and Eric Roll found the Greek representative in his office, the questionnaires arrayed in front of him, busily filling them in himself. Indignant, they remonstrated with him. Did he not understand that this was supposed to be done in Athens? How could he possibly know what figures to record? The Greek was unembarrassed in the face of this Franco-British assault. Certainly he understood that the questionnaires should be sent home. Of course he was inventing a good deal. Did they suppose that Athens knew any better?[73] On another occasion, the Turkish representative had to be dissuaded from recording a deliberate underestimate of his country's growing balance of payments deficit. It was carefully explained that there would be no reward for virtuous austerity—rather the reverse, if dollar aid was to be calculated on the basis of projected deficits.[74] The use of questionnaires for this purpose was novel and very influential; but the perils of the technique were manifold. As one CEEC delegate exclaimed with feeling, 'On fera de la poésie.'[75]

Miraculously, most of the questionnaires had been completed by the end of the first week in August. Now the returns had to be collated, and as like as not revised. It appeared, for instance, that the aggregate steel production target for 1951 would require coke supplies far in excess of even the best year before the war.[76] Meanwhile, the chairman had indeed been doing some thinking, in an effort to clarify the policy issues which the CEEC ought now to be addressing. Policy was first of all the business of an Executive Committee of five: France (Alphand), Italy (Campilli), The Netherlands (Hirschfeld), Norway (Colbjornsen), and the UK (Franks). Franks gave them all a brisk tutorial on Marshall's speech—demonstrating the Greats man's proper respect for the text—which he interpreted as posing three major problems for them all:

1. The immediate increase in European production of essential commodities.
2. The financial problem, subdivided into (a) external balance of payments, and (b) internal financial stabilization in European countries.
3. The problem of freeing trade movements within the European community.[77]

Franks had also been thinking pragmatically about the end-product: the report itself. The items he enumerated for the Executive Committee were all sub-stantive macroeconomic problems. They related to real-world issues. Yet in a sense the real world was beside the point. As William Diebold has written, 'the main job in Paris was finding some numbers that would pass muster in Washington'.[78] This is appropriately down to earth. The elementary problem facing the CEEC was not economic but diplomatic. It was the problem of palatability.

In recapitulating the proceedings of the Executive Committee for Clayton, Franks floated the idea of 'obtaining [the] services [of] some American so that [the] report could be drafted in such a manner that it would be attractively presented to the United States'. This was received unenthusiastically. Clayton offered some encouragement but preferred consultation as required, on a 'within the family' basis.[79] It was clear that the American imprimatur would not be given lightly, or unofficially. Franks returned to London for consulta-tions in early August more than ever convinced that, as he explained to a high-level group of British officials, 'in order to make the Paris Conference a success and to ensure anything like adequate American financial response it will be necessary to put in one or two "plums" to make the mass of figures and claims palatable'. The possible plums were, in order of succulence:

1. A European Customs Union.
2. Internationalization of the Ruhr.
3. Integration of European production.
4. European monetary co-operation.
5. European trade co-operation.[80]

The biggest and juiciest plum of all was a customs union, as London had re-cognized for some time. Among those tendering friendly aid, the strongest proponent of such an arrangement was Clayton, who was prone to lay down the law of integration as if from Mount Sinai. In Washington too, no doubt, a customs union would be a very acceptable sign that the Europeans meant business. For their part, the Benelux countries had already taken action. The Scandinavians were making preliminary moves. The French were ardent for negotiations to begin; the Italians likewise. The Greeks and the Turks made encouraging noises.[81] For the British, however, a customs union presented 'very special difficulties'. It was a familiar refrain.[82] On this occasion it fell to Franks to explain the difficulties to the other Europeans, and so, once again, to the Americans. On 15 August 1947 he delivered a carefully prepared statement to the Executive Committee:

These difficulties arise from our links (both economic and political) outside Europe and especially with the Commonwealth. It is, we think, in the long term interest of Europe, as well as of the United Kingdom, that these links with the Commonwealth should be maintained, and it is a fact to be recognized that they have the effect of making the United Kingdom an extra-European as well as an intra-European power. Before the United Kingdom could enter a customs union with one or more European powers, it would be necessary to decide such difficult questions as the conditions under which Commonwealth products should in future enter the United Kingdom and the territories of the other members of the customs union, and the conditions under which the products of other members of the customs union should enter the Commonwealth. There is the further question as to whether it would be possible for the Commonwealth itself to participate wholly or in part in a European customs union. I will not elaborate these points, but I would also recall that the Commonwealth includes one important industrial and trading nation which is a neighbour of the USA itself. These are all problems which we have to consider and which would involve negotiations before a customs union could become a practical proposition for the United Kingdom.

'For these reasons', Franks concluded brutally, 'there can be no question for the UK of entering into any hard and fast commitment in the next few weeks; it would be dishonest to do so because frankly we do not know whether we shall be able to fulfil it or not.'[83] Thus the project was lost. As the British intended, a study group was formed. A customs union was not.[84] The immovable object of palatability had met the irresistible force of national sovereignty.

If Franks had personal views on this seminal issue, he did not press them. Enumerating the plums for the 'London Committee' of officials monitoring the activities in Paris, he went so far as to suggest that by joining a customs union now Britain might be able to retain empire trade preferences, even against American wishes. Yet faced with the proposition that preserving the sterling area was incompatible with full membership of a customs union, he did not dissent.[85] Never to offer gratuitous advice was an article of faith with Oliver Franks. He held to it in personal as in official life. It meant that he was most unlikely to pursue an argument on what might be called the grand strategy of foreign policy unless someone specifically asked him to. Perhaps no one did. In any event, an opportunity was missed, and the fault lay with Franks. When it came to advice on policy, self-abnegation could be carried to excess.

There was a further difficulty. Insofar as the merit of a customs union was a question for the economist to answer, Franks was conscious of his own formal limitations. Throughout his career he took care to seek professional advice from economists of a similarly practical bent—in the early days at Oxford, James Meade; later on, two of the ablest men in Government service, R. W. B. ('Otto') Clarke and Robert Hall, both of whom Franks had encountered in the Ministry of Supply. In this particular instance it is possible that he was influenced by Denny Marris, who was decidedly and eloquently opposed:

When the United Kingdom's standard of life is still above that of the Continent; when her trade unions and some of her industries still follow restrictive practices; when her steel industry is built upon protection; and when it is from the outside world rather than from Western Europe she has to draw her foodstuffs and raw materials; when the whole nexus of her relations with the British Dominions has to be taken into account, the difficulty of the choice and the hazards of the decision are plain to see. It may be the solution, but I suspect it is the last that the United Kingdom will have the temerity to try.[86]

On the other hand, Franks's chief interlocutor on the issue, as on all CEEC policy matters, was his friend and fellow in Bevin's inner circle, Edmund Hall-Patch. According to legend, when Bevin heard that a member of his staff was optimistic of finding a solution for a certain problem, he snorted: 'Optimistic, is he? Send for 'all-Patch. 'E'll chill 'is bones.'[87] Hall-Patch was something of a maverick mandarin. No lover of Americans, he believed that the British prejudice against a customs union was unjustified and outmoded. He addressed his argument directly to the Foreign Secretary. It was a forceful one.

There is a well-established prejudice in Whitehall against a European Customs Union. It goes back a long way and is rooted in the old days of Free Trade. It is a relic of a world which has disappeared, probably never to return. The Board of Trade is overstating the case against it. One of their most potent arguments is that we have to *choose* between a European Customs Union and the Commonwealth. However that may be, the Board of Trade have successfully blocked for two years our efforts to look at these proposals objectively. As a result of Marshall's proposals European imaginations have been fired. It may be possible to integrate in some measure comparable with the vast industrial integration and potential of the United States, which the Russians are trying to emulate. If some such integration does *not* take place Europe will gradually decline in the face of pressure from the United States on the one hand and the USSR on the other.

This trenchant submission may well be the best proxy statement of Franks's views that we have. Significantly, Hall-Patch himself added, 'I have discussed these issues with Oliver Franks exhaustively.'[88] In fact Franks was not entirely convinced that European imaginations had been fired. From loose talk in Paris he had gleaned that the other countries, especially the Benelux group, would not be enthusiastic about a customs union if the UK stood aside. That knowledge probably reinforced his inclination to think that the European echo of support for the idea was not truly serious—that it was so much 'political straw'. But the thrust of Hall-Patch's argument was that the typical either/or approach to Europe exemplified by the Board of Trade was misconceived: that the 'choice' between Commonwealth (or sterling area) and customs union was a bogus one. The British could, and should, grasp both. In the development of this basic point there is good reason to suppose that Franks was in cahoots with Hall-Patch—who was, after all, 'a very prescient man'.[89]

The suggestive picture of Franks as a premature if undemonstrative integrationist is corroborated by two further pieces of evidence. (To say nothing of the fact that Bevin himself was even more premature. As leader of the Transport and General Workers' Union he had argued the case for a European customs union as early as 1927; as Foreign Secretary he had twice resurrected the idea, in October 1946 and January 1947.[90]) First, Franks's conversion is attested by another of the 'Friendly Aid Boys' of the State Department, Paul Nitze, later the silver fox of nuclear diplomacy. In late July 1947 Nitze went to Paris, took a room near Franks in the Hotel Crillon, and did his level best to talk him round over a series of working breakfasts. He claimed complete success.[91]

More circumstantially, in 1950 the French Foreign Minister, Robert Schuman—'a man from the Carolingian Middle Kingdom', as Franks noted—proposed a plan for a European Coal and Steel Community (ECSC). Behind these prosaic words lay a breathtaking idea, developed by Jean Monnet. The ECSC was to provide the structure for a lasting Franco-German reconciliation. As Schuman said, 'on a tout refusé aux allemands quand on aurait dû leur donner quelque chose et on leur a tout donné quand on aurait dû tout leur refuser: je voudrais, moi, faire autre chose'.[92] Invited to join this historic enterprise, the nucleus of a new Europe, the British begged to refuse. In the immortal words of Herbert Morrison: 'It's no good, we can't do it, the Durham miners won't wear it.'[93] In diplomatic language, the Foreign Office made the same response. Franks was then Ambassador in Washington. Again his advice was not sought. Forty years later Peter Hennessy asked him what he would have said. Franks was not given to sweeping speculation. He would caution interviewers repeatedly on the difficulties of finding the truthful answer among the wrecks of memory and the tricks of hindsight. On the Schuman Plan, however, he was most emphatic.

I should have said that the idea of . . . persuading Adenauer [the German Chancellor] to bring France and Germany together, as Schuman described it to me, 'in an embrace so close that neither could draw back far enough to hit the other' . . . was *worth everything for the peace of Europe* . . . No, I think we ought to have gone in.

That was not simply a retrospective judgement, though Franks's memory had betrayed him. In fact he did overcome his reluctance sufficiently to write a personal and 'most unofficial epistle' to Roger Makins in the Foreign Office. It was an expression of disquiet about the timidity of government policy. 'I know that this is none of my business but I cannot help wondering whether we are on the right lines . . . I should have thought that if there is a real chance of bringing off the Schuman Plan with its high authority there is also a chance of securing an anchor man over 90 million [people] strong in Western Europe. This is putting the stakes very high but I think the play is or might be for these stakes.'[94] The clear implication was that the British would have to raise their game. On this occasion the message went unheard.

In later years Franks liked to quote Dean Acheson, who wrote of the British decision to opt out of the ECSC: 'Some decisions are critical. This . . . was one. It was not the last clear chance for Britain to enter Europe, but it was the first wrong choice.' With this Franks was in full agreement. He appended a single, poignant observation—that 'the decision cost us the leadership of Europe which we had enjoyed from the end of the war until May 1950'.[95]

In August 1947 the immediate outcome of the internal British debate over European integration was that Franks returned to Paris with no plums to put in the pie. At the same time it was increasingly apparent that the CEEC's analysis of European requirements for dollar assistance would be sure to make Congress choke. The problem of palatability was sharpening nicely. On 19 August Franks had a lengthy meeting with the triumvirs to prepare them for the worst eventuality. The figures, he warned, might need 'pruning down'. He also tried to ascertain the Americans' minimum demands with regard to commitments on future integration, and on what became known as the continuing organization—whether the CEEC or something like it should remain in being, and if so for how long, after making its report.[96] In London on 21 August, very privately, he broke the news of the CEEC's preliminary findings to Douglas. In Geneva on 23 August he went over them in some detail with Clayton. For the sixteen countries plus Western Germany they showed an accumulated balance of payments deficit of $29.2 billion over the four-year period 1948–51. The grand total of $29.2 billion therefore became the headline figure of dollar aid required, in the CEEC's estimation, for a sustainable European recovery programme. Of this cumulative global deficit, no less than $28.2 billion was with the American continent: $8.1 billion in 1948 reducing annually to $5.8 billion in 1951.

To the Americans these figures were doubly shocking, first because of their order of magnitude, and secondly because of their pessimistic outlook.[97] $29.2 billion was a colossal figure, far exceeding Britain's aggregate international lending throughout the nineteenth century. For the United States it was 'out of the question', as Clayton immediately told Franks. Marshall planners might not know the size of the Marshall Plan, but they knew it had to be smaller than this. Clayton had always thought in terms of $16–18 billion; that was his own calculation, but the range was indicative.[98] Even more disturbing was the clear intimation that the aid programme would not be sufficient to restore equilibrium at the end of the four years, as Washington had hoped and expected. A deficit would remain after 1951, and with it the prospect of further importunings. When would the Europeans finally be able to stand on their own feet?

The figures also tended to confirm instinctive American doubts about Western Europe's collective resolve. According to Clayton, Franks was candid in admitting that the work 'represented primarily an assembly of individual country estimates although some "shaking down" had been accomplished in cases where combined estimates were obviously greatly in excess of available supplies'. To the Friendly Aid Boys this smacked of the 'Molotov approach' to recovery planning. When pressed on the lack of scrutiny of individual requirements, Franks's first recourse was to the terms of reference of the original plenary conference, which made it clear that there would be no diminution of national sovereignty; coupled with the plea that comprehensive scrutiny was simply impossible in the time available.[99] Were the Europeans only mouthing the words of self-help and mutual aid, or were their difficulties genuine? George Kennan, in the middle of a brief reign as the uncrowned philosopher-king of the State Department, was sent to Paris to find out the facts. Not for the first time, he penned a lengthy dispatch, magisterial, insightful, and politically astute. 'The representatives of the sixteen European nations assembled in Paris have had the character of their work prescribed for them with considerable rigidity by the background of their meeting and the atmosphere in which it is taking place', he began, in a statement which Franks would have feelingly endorsed.

By way of reaction to Soviet charges, there has been strong emphasis on national sovereignty (perhaps the only triumph of Molotov's visit to Paris). None of the delegates is a strong political figure domestically. There is no one who could take any extensive liberties with the anxious reservations of the home governments. Finally, in the absence of the Russians the gathering has reverted, with a certain sense of emotional release, to the pattern of old-world courtesy and cordiality in which many of the participants were reared and for which they have instinctively longed throughout the rigours of a post-war diplomacy dominated by the Russian presence. This has practically ruled out any critical examination of the other fellow's figures—particularly as most of the delegates must have lively doubts as to the entire validity of some of their own, and cannot be eager to enter a name-calling contest between pot and kettle.

It would be wrong to laugh at this gingerly approach or to put it all down to short-sighted timidity in the persons concerned. It reflects serious European realities which must be taken into account. Many of these governments are operating under formidable strains, internal and external. Some of them have internal economic problems with which they are politically too weak to cope. They do not want these problems spotlighted and made critical issues by the Paris conference. Others, particularly the Scandinavians, are pathologically timorous about the Russians. Finding themselves somewhat unexpectedly in a gathering denounced by Molotov as politically wicked, they have the jumpy uncertainty of one who walks in pleasing but unaccustomed paths of sin. All of them are inhibited, I think, by the consciousness of what seem to them Herculean differences among the great powers over Germany and by the consequent feeling that the necessary centre of any real European planning is beyond the effective scope of their activity. This conference reflects, in short, all the weakness, the escapism, the paralysis of a region caught by war in the midst of serious problems of long-term adjustment, and sadly torn by hardship, confusion and outside pressure.

'In these circumstances', Kennan observed, 'we must not look to the people in Paris to accomplish the impossible.' This was an analysis at once sensitive and dispassionate. From it the author distilled policy recommendations of impressive realism:

We can make efforts to have the report presented in such a way as to avoid any impression of finality; let it come to us on the understanding that it will be used only as a basis of further discussion; try to whittle it down as much as possible by negotiation; then give it final consideration in the executive branch of our government and decide unilaterally what we finally wish to present to Congress.

'This would mean that we would listen to all the Europeans had to say,' he concluded, 'but in the end we would not *ask* them, we would just *tell* them what they would get.'[100]

In disposing of the palatability problem, Kennan's conclusion pointed a way out of the developing impasse over the report. He had been led to it by his exchanges in Paris with 'the more far-sighted' of the CEEC representatives, including the chairman, whom he liked and admired for his high seriousness as a diplomatist. These men, Kennan found, 'recognize that their report will inevitably be padded. They know that they themselves cannot pare it as it should be pared.' He was especially struck by one particular admonition made to him: 'You people go ahead and cut it down. We will squawk over every cut. Never mind that. Most of your cuts will be justified, and we will squawk anyway. If any of your cuts are really unjustified, we will set up such a genuine and unmistakable howl that you will know that you have made a mistake and you can then correct it.'[101] Kennan quoted this in his dispatch, naturally without attribution. It was certainly a very Franksian formulation.

Nothing better illustrated the job of finding some numbers than Franks's approach to the troublesome total of $29.2 billion. No sooner had he revealed it to Clayton than he went on to say that 'a quick examination of the supporting documents indicated that the total could be trimmed by probably 5 billion dollars'. Some of the requirements, it transpired, included imports of capital equipment for reconstruction purposes, which might be more appropriately financed by the International Bank for Reconstruction and Development (the World Bank). In other cases, requirements clearly exceeded available supplies; obviously these would have to be re-examined. Ultimately, however, as Clayton reported to Acting Secretary of State Robert Lovett, 'if the total had to be reduced, say to 15 billion, he [Franks] was sure *this could only be done if we told them it had to be done*.[102] This was just the kind of plain speaking to appeal to the moral pragmatists who inhabited the US Department of State.

Robert Lovett was the supreme pragmatist, and Marshall's *alter ego*, but he was not yet ready to settle for 'sixteen shopping lists' instead of 'a constructive programme' without a final, concerted effort to exert American diplomatic leverage.[103] Such a programme would have to satisfy a number of stringent conditions—Washington's famous 'essentials'—communicated by the triumvirs to the Executive Committee on 27 August. First, it must provide the basis of a self-sustaining Western European economy after four years. Secondly, as a corollary to this, the need for outside aid must be completely eliminated by the end of that period. Thirdly, production goals for essential commodities (food, coal) must be regularly monitored. Fourthly, long-term capital projects must not crowd out short-term plant renewal; the former must be financed separately. Fifthly, internal monetary and financial stability must be restored. Sixthly, steps must be taken to establish a multilateral trade and payments system, in conformity with the charter of the International Trade Organization. Lastly, provision must be made for a continuing multilateral organization, which would periodically assess the performance of the participating countries.[104]

The theme here was what Clayton called mutuality of interest. The subtext was integration. The tone was minatory, in spite of some feeble protestation to the contrary. The language of recovery, evidently, had been corrupted. In June, Marshall had issued an *invitation*. His agents now spoke of *conditions*. Conditions were there to be imposed. Friendly aid seemed suddenly less friendly.

There followed three weeks of intense American pressure on the Executive Committee to bow to these conditions. Progress was excruciatingly slow. In desperation, the original deadline of 1 September was extended to 15 September. Argument centred on viability after 1951 and the multilateral organization (the first and last of the essentials). The former stuck fast on Franks's principled objection to wishing away the likelihood of a continuing deficit, and therefore perhaps a continuing need for aid.[105] The latter proved to be the CEEC's King Charles's head. The Americans insisted absolutely on a firm undertaking on a continuing organization, multilateral, preferably permanent, and autonomous—a blow to the heart of national sovereignty. The Europeans, every one of whom had strong feelings on the subject, were chronically unable to agree a response. Until they could, there was nothing more to be done.

On 10 September the triumvirs reconvened with the Executive Committee. As the extended deadline approached, tempers began to fray. Clayton brusquely suggested a further postponement of one month to allow time for the report to be extensively reworked. As one man, the committee refused. A heated discussion ensued. Clayton intimated that in its present form the report would be unacceptable to the United States. When a member of the committee remarked that European countries were not in the habit of looking over the back fence of their neighbours to see what they were doing, Clayton lost his temper. With the parting shot that 'perhaps we were all pursuing a will-o'-the-wisp and might as well forget about it', he abruptly left the meeting.[106]

The crisis of the conference had arrived. The Europeans were variously bewildered and offended at the turn of events. 'It was really a very strange performance', Hirschfeld commented. Colbjornsen reported to Oslo that 'the American demand means we should write a new report at American dictation'. Alphand told Hammarskjöld that it would be impossible for the French Government to accept all the American conditions because of the internal political situation in France. Bidault in particular found it 'quite intolerable'; most assuredly, 'he would not yield to pressure of this nature'.[107] For Bevin, Clayton's tantrum only added insult to injury. Always irked by enforced delay—especially if enforced from Washington—he had already given his opinion to Douglas that Franks had carried the participating countries as far towards co-operation as this conference was ever likely to go. Now he was moved to address Marshall himself. 'I fully understand and appreciate the intentions of the United States government in making this intervention, but the impression has been created that the work of the conference has been unsatisfactory and is now having to be done again under American pressure. This is, of course, not the case.' The gravamen of this cool politeness was 'external pressure'. Ernie Bevin did not take kindly to being bullied.[108]

Franks for his part was in search of a workable compromise. The day after the Executive Committee meeting broke up in disarray, reinforced by Hall-Patch, he huddled privately with the triumvirs. Together they agreed on a six-point package of emergency repairs to the report:

1. Statement that individual countries should obligate themselves to the group to attain the production targets they had set for key commodities.
2. Revision of financial section [chapter iv] to remove thread of thought that effective stabilization measures could only be adopted after external aid commenced and production substantially increased.
3. Greater emphasis on and sharpening of principles, including commitment to reduce and eventually eliminate trade barriers among the participating countries.
4. Segregation of capital equipment items (agricultural and mining machinery excepted), with clear indication that conference will look to International Bank and other lending agencies for financing these items.
5. a. Agreement to 'recess' rather than 'adjourn' the conference.
   b. Postponement of formal conference [closing] session to September 20 [amended later to 22].
6. Firm commitment by participating countries that, if assistance is assured, they would form a multilateral organization with powers to review performance of each country.[109]

Subsequent consultation with Hirschfeld yielded the additional proposal that the report should be issued as a 'first' report, skilfully accommodating and diverting repeated American demands for it to be labelled 'provisional' or, worse still, 'tentative'.[110] The implicit trade-off was symptomatic. These points retained only vestiges of the much-vaunted essentials. Their general thrust was quite different. Where the essentials were matters of substance, the six points were matters of presentation. They were salient, but they were also cosmetic. The partial exception was the last one, on continuing organization, which contrived to offer an undertaking that was at the same time firm *and* contingent. Translating this awkward compromise into a mutually acceptable form of words for the report was a triumph of British backstairs diplomacy.[111] The outcome was probably the trickiest paragraph in the entire report, finally redrafted in the nick of time by that most reluctant of draftsmen, Oliver Franks himself. It read:

The Committee believes that if means for carrying out the programme are made available, a joint organization to review progress achieved in the execution of the programme will be necessary. The participating governments declare themselves ready in this event to set up such an organization by mutual agreement. This organization will ensure, to the full extent possible by joint action, the realization of the economic conditions necessary to enable the general objectives to which each country has pledged itself to be effectively achieved. The organization will make periodical reports to the various European governments on the extent to which the programme is being realized. The governments will supply the organization with all information required for this purpose. The organization will be of a temporary character and will cease to exist when the special aid necessary for the recovery of Europe comes to an end.[112]

The driest draft often conceals the bloodiest battles. Therein lies the skill.

The first great transatlantic bargain of the post-war period now lay on the table. Would anyone pick it up? On the European side, friendly aid, however benign, was a touchy subject. Franks's cosiness with the Americans was not universally admired, even among his own delegation—by common consent the most powerful and effective in Paris. The British provided the mechanics, as Marris said; they had to. They were a motley bunch, in the words of one of their number, drawn from across Whitehall, with a lively apprehension of their own, disparate, departmental interests.[113] If at any given moment the Treasury suspected a sell-out to the Americans, the Board of Trade to the Europeans, and the Ministry of Food to the Foreign Office, it would not have been at all surprising. As Eric Roll remembered, 'those of us who were concerned with specific areas of planning . . . tended to be suspicious of the diplomatic members, from the Foreign Office or elsewhere, whom we regarded, unjustly I am sure, as more concerned with pleasing political masters at home'.

Our group was soon known in the delegation as the 'resistance movement', and one of our members developed a particular talent for warning the rest of us at delegation meetings when he thought that some particular bit of trickery was afoot. He would draw a corkscrew on a piece of paper which he managed to display to us without those who were under suspicion being aware of it.[114]

Franks, we can be sure, was one of the prime suspects. Nevertheless, as he had forecast, the Executive Committee were found willing to commend the compromise package to their colleagues and Governments, subject only to a few minor modifications. The CEEC as a whole took it well. Bidault, arraigned in private by Monnet, was persuaded to recant. With heavy reassurance from Franks and Hall-Patch, Bevin pronounced himself content.

In Washington meanwhile, Kennan had been read with profit. Lovett's ingenuity was already focused on the details of the congressional timetable. Freshly spurred, the triumvirs were now eager to demonstrate how much they had secured. 'We have checked over the draft of the first report. Assuming that most of our suggestions are adopted, the final draft should appear to the public as neither black nor white but rather as a shade of grey.' Will Clayton was no Mark Antony, but his message was the same.

> . . . Therefore let our alliance be combin'd
> Our best friends made and our best means stretched out
> And let us presently go sit in Council,
> How covert matters may be best disclos'd
> And open perils surest answered.[115]

The drafting of the report caused problems of its own. Originally the French were to do it. Illness prevented that, and the task fell to the British. Franks was clear that it could not be done by committee—it should come from one pen—and that it should be understandable to the educated layman, not only in Washington, but also in Kansas City. This was a tall order. Putative draftsmen were produced from London and found wanting in Paris. Precious time elapsed. Isaiah Berlin had the misfortune to be passing through, as he imagined, on his first post-war holiday. Franks called him in. 'I felt I was being summoned by God. I could not refuse, though I knew it was a mistake. When the prophet Jonah was summoned by God he refused. Everybody realized in a day or two I was hopeless.'[116] To his intense relief, Berlin wriggled free. Eventually Franks turned to Otto Clarke, a prodigious draftsman, who had the double advantage of a journalistic training and an intimate knowledge of the CEEC's work from his chairmanship of the London Committee. With astonishing speed—and a shift system of shorthand typists—Clarke dictated the best part of a 25,000 word report, known to the British delegation as 'the torso'.[117] It remained only to repaint it an appealing shade of grey.

The desired effect was achieved primarily by giving the torso a head. A 'preamble' was added, whose twelve paragraphs contained most of the trigger words in the vocabulary of friendly aid.[118] 'The circumstances in which the report has been drawn up give it the character of an initial report', it declared obediently. (The Foreign Office had balked at a 'first' report but acquiesced in an 'initial' one which alluded to the possibility of further amendments and supplements.) 'So far as possible however the replies to the questionnaires, which were sent to each of the participating governments, have been subjected by the Committee to a critical examination.' Borrowing shamelessly from Lovett, the report was '*in no sense a "shopping list"* of the goods which the participating countries and Western Germany need from the United States'. Rather it was 'an examination of what the participating countries can do *for themselves and for each other* to work towards a lasting solution'. There was a rousing conclusion:

In presenting this report in response to Mr Marshall's suggestion, the participating countries believe that the programme of concerted action, which it sets forth, marks the advent of *a new stage of European economic co-operation.* Through the achievement of this programme, by their own efforts and with such support as the United States may feel it proper to supply, the participating countries can march forward towards the attainment of that essential economic well-being which is the best assurance of peace and happiness.[119]

As to numbers, the report was marvellously murky. The Marshall planner and economist Charles Kindleberger said that he 'felt like hell' about some of the things he had to do with 'all these damn numbers' for the congressional hearings which followed.[120] Oliver Franks might well have felt the same. The preamble gave an explicit warning: 'The amount of aid which each country needs in order to make its full contribution to this European recovery programme is not specified in this report.' The report dealt with dollar deficits. Dollar aid was a matter for the United States. The 'tentatively estimated deficit' with the American continent had shrunk to an accumulated total of $22.4 billion over the four-year period: $8 billion in 1948 reducing to $3.4 billion in 1951. If capital equipment other than agricultural and mining machinery were shown (and financed) separately, as agreed, then the numbers became $19.3 billion, $7.1 billion, and $2.8 billion respectively. Moreover there was a 'tentatively estimated surplus' with the rest of the world of $2.8 billion over the same period: a marginal deficit of $240 million in 1948 turning into a surplus of $1.8 billion in 1951. For technical reasons to do with dollar liquidity, the report doubted the possibility of offsetting this surplus against the dollar deficit. Merely to mention it, however, was enough for enticingly small net figures to swim before the eyes.[121]

These numbers passed muster on at least two counts, notwithstanding the stinging comment in one newspaper that they could prove 'as meaningless as they turned out to be in the case of the British loan'.[122] First and foremost, their order of magnitude was no longer scary. In a nutshell, the European antithesis to Marshall's thesis was $19.3 billion. A bid of that magnitude could certainly be reconciled, not only with Clayton's back-of-the-envelope calculations, but more importantly with the actual outcome. The Administration's synthesis was $17 billion. The ERP bill for that sum, over four years, was presented for congressional approval in December 1947. In April 1948 Congress made available a first tranche of $5 billion for an initial twelve-month period. Of this, the British received no less than $1.24 billion, an unexpected satisfaction owing something to the calming presence of Oliver Franks. (If the Marshall Plan was indeed a 'pork barrel', as the Friendly Aid Boys sometimes feared, then it was the British who were most adept at pork barrel politics. In time the UK became the biggest beneficiary of the whole programme, receiving some $2.7 billion of the $12 billion disbursed between April 1948 and December 1950, when the appropriations ceased.) Secondly, the CEEC's numbers provided at least a fig-leaf of cover for the private parts of viability. The report concluded with the positive assurance for which the Americans had so insistently called: 'Certainly the deficit after the end of 1951, on these assumptions, should be of dimensions which will be manageable without special aid.'[123] On this occasion, perhaps, Franks's principles had been overborne.

A frenzied marathon of roneoed duplication meant that everything was now ready for the ministerial signing ceremony on 22 September in the Grand Palais, where it had all begun. Bevin came over the day before, accompanied by Sir Stafford Cripps, the Chancellor of the Exchequer, who immediately dropped a small bombshell by announcing that he would not sign the report: it involved an infraction of sovereignty. At the eleventh hour it seemed that Franks would have to persuade him otherwise. The two men squared up for a gladiatorial contest. There were some similarities between them. They shared a love of the Scilly Isles and an invincible moral authority. They also knew each other of old. Franks knew that Cripp's lawyerly reasoning would be exceedingly difficult to fault. His premiss, however, might be vulnerable. Franks decided to attack there. If he could dislodge one premiss (sovereignty) and replace it with another (co-operation), then the Chancellor would be forced to yield. The point to establish was a practical one. Now was not the time to worry about sovereignty; or at least not to the extent of scuttling the whole enterprise. It took two hours of hard pounding for this strategy to work. At last Cripps surrendered. He would sign with the rest. The flaming angel had vanquished the high priest of austerity. The caravanserai could continue.[124]

After the signing and the speechifying, 'that frigid gathering of statesmen and economists', as the Italian Foreign Minister later described them, went home.[125] The following morning, feeling completely drained, Franks ate a solitary breakfast in the Hotel Crillon. Suddenly, he began to weep. He was still weeping when Edmund Hall-Patch came upon him. Prescience was not Hall-Patch's only quality: he also had insight. He loped off, found a car, collected Franks, and drove to Chartres. They went to the cathedral. Hall-Patch told Franks to sit there by himself for one hour. When he returned they had lunch—a very good lunch. After that Franks passed another hour in the cathedral. Then they drove back to the hotel. The next day Franks too went home, quite restored.[126]

5 *The North Atlantic Treaty*

FRANKS returned to Oxford to recoup. The report had been prepared in the long vacation after all; but now there was to be a coda. An integral part of the transatlantic bargain was that a deputation from the CEEC should go to Washington and explain themselves to official America. After some haggling, Franks took a moderately representative team of six: Alphand (France), Boland (Ireland), Campilli (Italy), Colbjornsen (Norway), Hirschfeld (Netherlands), and Verdelis (Greece). They were accompanied by a 'co-ordinating group' consisting of van der Beugel (Netherlands), Colonna (Italy), Marjolin (France), Marris (UK), and Serreules (France); and attended by a small posse of technical experts conversant with the esoterica of the questionnaires. They arrived on 9 October and stayed for almost a month, chiefly occupied with the profusion of interdepartmental and investigatory bodies (the Harriman Committee, the Krug Committee, the Nourse Committee) established to scrutinize and legitimize the Marshall bounty. Elements of these bodies were already clamouring for the very thing that Franks dreaded most—reconvening the Paris conference. Redoing the work at the command of the United States, with full publicity, was not an appealing prospect for any European, as Bevin had already made plain.[1] 'The process of revision and refinement', however, was another matter. That activity continued apace, ungrudgingly for the most part, propelled by a shirt-sleeved confederacy of experts: 'une complicité tacite', as Marjolin wrote, to make a convincing pitch to Congress. Behind closed doors, friendly aid had evolved a stage further.[2]

At bottom, the Administration required reassurance about European competence and commitment. In more personal terms, Lovett required reassurance about Oliver Franks. Washington politics were by nature intensely personal. Robert Lovett or his friend Dean Acheson rarely referred to anyone working for the State Department or for some other agency. They would say, 'He worked for Mr Stettinius', or, 'He worked for Mr Morgenthau.'[3] Lovett himself was more fortunate than these. He worked for General Marshall, and before that for Colonel Stimson, the Guardians of the twentieth-century republic.[4] Like Stimson, he was a Republican who served Democratic presidents. Party and ideology are of no concern to the true Guardian. Out of office, Lovett also worked for the banking concern of Brown Brothers Harriman and Company, thus achieving an impeccable pedigree. He was in every way a well-tailored man, 'experienced, sensible, respected, popular, informed, smart, gentle, tough, mean, and considerate', in the words of an early profile, accustomed by habit and temperament to avoiding the limelight. 'Always the bridesmaid, never the bride', he remarked of himself without rancour. In history he stands, as he stood in his own lifetime, in the giant shadow of the two men with whom he was most closely associated, Marshall and Acheson. While it was impossible to match the unimpeachable authority of the former or the conspicuous brilliance of the latter, it was Lovett who was the most completely equipped.[5]

Subtle and effectual, Robert Lovett made a sympathetic shepherd. It was he who brought the Marshall Plan to fruition, and it was he who supervised the negotiations for the North Atlantic Treaty. His European partner in both enterprises was Oliver Franks. In October 1947 the two shepherds met for the first time. They liked what they saw. Lovett cross-examined Franks expertly on the work of the CEEC. Both men rather enjoyed the intellectual exercise. Franks enlarged on the psychological significance of the programme: for a recovery of confidence as well as crops. The key word in this analysis was *hope*.

I cannot too much stress that the programme which is before you now is important in its political as much as in its economic aspect. The Paris Conference, following so closely on Mr Marshall's speech, created a new hope in men's minds in Europe. . . . If this hope is to be preserved and the new spirit of a common purpose which was such a feature of our work in Paris is to be kept alive, it is essential not only that our present discussions should succeed, but that from them there should emerge a programme which the people of Western Europe believe is likely to lead to a full measure of recovery in a relatively short time. Hopes are fresh and it is vital they should not be disappointed or deferred.

For Washington this was an interesting reversal. *European* rather than *American* expectations were what counted. Franks made a fluent transition to the job of finding the right numbers for Congress:

The programme is a *recovery* programme and not a programme of temporary relief. It has therefore to be a large programme and the amounts available under it have to be sufficient to do the job. Otherwise it loses its character, becomes a further instalment of relief, and at its end the people of Western Europe will be on your doorstep again. . . . I do not at all suggest that the Administration should accept the precise amounts mentioned in the Report, but I do venture to suggest that the size of what is recommended should not greatly differ from what the sixteen countries have stated that they will need. A few billions of dollars (and I am not suggesting a billion dollars is a small sum) may make all the difference between success and failure.[6]

If Lovett and his colleagues were not wholly persuaded by these arguments, they were mightily impressed with Oliver Franks.[7] The Administration did not cease to whittle away at the estimates in the report, but the Europeans were spared the humiliation of reconvening the Paris conference. The CEEC's mission had not been in vain.[8]

Franks also found himself lifted out of the Washington maw in order to address 'the Town Meeting of the United States'.

I was sent out all over the United States explaining. I talked on the radio. I talked to school teachers. I talked to committees of young businessmen . . . I had a generally friendly reception, but a great many people simply didn't understand what it was about. I spent a lot of time in that vast Middle West area between the Rockies and the Alleghenies, all the way from the Great Lakes down to the Texas Gulf and New Orleans, explaining to wheat farmers, for example, in Kansas that a Frenchman who wants a loaf of bread has to buy flour: 'it's no good him approaching a man in Kansas City with French francs—what will he use it for in the shop? He wants a dollar bill. There's a problem about the exchanges: the mere fact that he has the wheat and the Frenchman needs it doesn't solve it. That is what the Marshall Plan is about: it's putting dollars in the hands of the Europeans so that they can buy your wheat and you can sell it.'[9]

The whole visit is perhaps best seen as an educational experience for all con-cerned, not least for Franks himself. He gained a vivid impression of the American political process—'the phenomenon of many voices', all raised in cacophonous debate; the loosely woven texture of government; the grandiose position of the press; the power of the congressional bogey. Franks learned a lot about Americans. He also learned to like them better. Soon he was quoting a felicitous passage from 'that wise and eclectic philosopher', Santayana:

If it were given to me to look into the depths of a man's heart and I did not find good will at the bottom I would say without hesitating, you are not American. But as the American is an individualist, his good will is not officious. His instinct is to think well of everybody and to wish everybody well. But in a spirit of rough comradeship he expects every man to stand upon his own legs and to be helpful in his turn. When he has given his neighbour a chance he has done enough for him. He figures it an absolute duty to do that.[10]

Franks's new appreciation stood him in good stead. On his return to England he went to visit his parents in Bristol. One evening the telephone rang. His mother answered, then summoned her son. 'Oliver, a man called Attlee wishes to speak to you.' In fact the Prime Minister wished to offer him the embassy in Washington, Britain's premier diplomatic post. Once again, Franks was sur-prised. As usual he asked for time to think it over.[11]

Attlee's offer did not come as a surprise to everyone in Whitehall. The idea seems to have originated with Robert Hall, Director of the Economic Section of the Cabinet Office. Hall had chanced to meet Franks in Oxford in late September, after his return from Paris and before he took the delegation to Washington. The two men were friends. Franks liked Hall and respected his judgement; with Franks the two often went together. He tended deliberately to use Hall as a sounding-board, and therefore spoke very openly to him. He might not have done so had he known that Hall kept a diary, since published, a practice of which Franks was inclined to disapprove. Hall recorded:

He looked tired but seemed in good form; he talked about what he had to do in Washington in presenting the 'Marshall Plan' scheme. He is very gloomy about the prospects for the UK until we realise how bad everything is [economically]. I think that he is very anxious to get back into public life if he can (a) square Queen's, (b) time his reappearance so that he can pull us out of our troubles. He thought that the 40s should replace the 60s—at least the former had some ideas and some knowledge of how to carry these out.

A few weeks later Hall saw the well-connected Edwin Plowden, now Chief Planning Officer on the Central Economic Planning Staff, and suggested Franks for the ambassadorship. 'He could be just the man to keep the conditions for the loan [that is, Marshall aid] tolerable.' Plowden liked the idea and undertook to 'float it'.[12] Apparently it floated well. As Franks implied and C. P. Snow imagined, the time was ripe for new men. As early as July 1945, at the Young Victors Party given by Hugh Dalton for the new Labour MPs, the irrepressible Oxford don Richard Crossman had held forth on Labour's stance towards the superpowers. 'The Russians', he thought, 'could not be properly handled unless we remained strong. They were expecting the Labour Government to be easy to squeeze, and we should have to make it clear that that was not so.' 'In the case of the USA the position was quite different. To handle them it was necessary to appeal to sentiment. A Labour Ambassador should be appointed in place of [Lord] Halifax and he should be a non-professional with a background somewhat similar to that of the Master of Balliol [A. D. Lindsay].'[13] There were many who agreed with this diagnosis without endorsing the cure. Bevin, however, was in no hurry to make a revolution. The lordly but strangely effective Halifax served on until May 1946, only to be replaced by a dyed-in-the-wool professional, the amiably erratic Lord Inverchapel (Archibald Clark Kerr), an inscrutable selection matched by Bevin's inscrutable remark: 'Ah, Archie, I know you want the job, but you needn't think you're the best man for it. What you are is a member of the Union and I'm the General Secretary. So you're going to get it.'[14]

If 'the General Secretary' was inscrutable, the Prime Minister was monosyllabic. Clement Attlee was not given to self-explanation. His future biographer Kenneth Harris once asked him, 'Who is the ablest man you met outside politics?' 'Franks.' 'Is he a Labour sympathiser?' 'Don't know.' 'Well why did you send him as Ambassador to Washington?' 'He was the best man for the job.'[15] Franks represented an obvious break from Halifax and Inverchapel—on grounds of age alone—but he was evidently not a Labour ambassador in the Crossman sense, or the harbinger of a socialist foreign policy. In fact that was one of the most reassuring things about him. He could explain the welfare state to Washington in straightforward humanitarian terms. Labour's programme of nationalization (or socialization in American parlance), about which the Americans nurtured deep suspicions, was made to appear perfectly innocuous; Labour Ministers who seemed doctrinaire or even dangerous (Emanuel

Shinwell, for example) were put in their proper, harmless, perspective. As an exercise in damage limitation this was remarkably successful. In the United States the damage potential of the Labour Party's ideological baggage has always been very great. The actual damage done has depended mainly on performance. Practical heroism beats doctrinaire socialism every time. 'In the Anglo-American relationship,' Oliver Franks observed wisely, 'British policy has to pass the test: can the British deliver?'[16]

It has been said that Franks was a great hesitater. Yet Cicero himself counselled caution. 'If we do change our way of life, every care must be taken so that we appear to have done so with good judgement.'

It is, however, an extremely rare type of person who is endowed with outstanding intellectual ability or a splendidly learned education, or both, and who has also had time to deliberate over which course of life he wants above all to follow. In such deliberation all counsel ought to be referred to the individual's own nature. For just as in each specific thing that we do we seek what is seemly according to what and how each of us has been born . . ., we must exercise much more care when establishing our whole way of life, so that we can be constant to ourselves for the whole length of our life, not wavering in any of our duties.[17]

Franks certainly deliberated or hesitated for some time over the Washington embassy. Despite its glittering promise, there were a number of things that told against it. Personally, he already was where he had long hoped to be. 'Squaring Queen's' would not be easy. To leave again might mean never to return. Moreover he was an honest man. Did he want to lie abroad for the good of his country? In particular, did he want to lie in the United States? Twelve years ago in Chicago he had decided that he was not cut out to be an American. What had changed? There were also family responsibilities to consider, as well as *res publica*. He now had two young daughters, aged 3 and 8, who would have to be transplanted to the New World. How would they fare as Americans? And what of that other half of himself, Barbara?[18]

Barbara Franks's reaction to the offer was not at all that of Nancy Mitford's inspired creation, Fanny, wife of Sir Alfred Wincham, who held the Chair of Pastoral Theology and who was 'detached from all human emotions'. When *he* was offered an embassy, wrote Fanny,

In the first place, of course, I was happy to think that my dear Alfred's merits should have been publicly recognized at last, that he should receive a dazzling prize (as it seemed to me) to reward him for being so good and clever. Surely he was wasted in a chair of Pastoral Theology, even though his lectures on the pastoral theme made a lasting impression on those who heard them. During the war he had filled a post of national importance; after that I had expected to see him take his place in the arena. But (whether from lack of ambition or lack of opportunity I never really knew) he had returned quietly to Oxford when his war work came to an end and seemed fated to remain there for the rest of his days.[19]

On the contrary, Barbara's first reaction was clearly negative. She was most reluctant to leave Oxford. It was the place where her husband had found his niche, where the children were happy, where she herself wanted to live. She had no desire to be an ambassador's wife, and no appetite for Washington. She cried in Plowden's office.[20]

And yet Franks at length accepted. His own explanation was perfectly in character. 'In the end, the obvious dawned. Unless there is a proper objection of conscience, there are things it is not appropriate to refuse.'[21] The Stoic technical term for this is *kathekon*, or appropriate action. To the philosopher's question, 'What is the end of life?', the Stoics returned a one-word answer: virtue. Virtue was the only thing that was good, and to live well was to live virtuously. In these terms, Franks's choice was a virtuous one. He did what he thought right; that is to say, *honourable* and (as Cicero advised) *seemly*.[22] Perhaps also there was another consideration. Franks did not mention it—that would not have been seemly—though it was quite consistent with honour. It is conjectural, but it is important. It had to do with practical effect. Cicero once suggested to his brother that his consulship was the realization of Plato's dream of the philosopher-ruler; he celebrated his own achievement, 'not without cause, but without end', as Seneca later remarked. Franks became Ambassador at the same age of 43 and did not venture such a boast. But he did believe that he could make a difference.

The announcement in February 1948 that Oliver Franks had been appointed British Ambassador in Washington and would no longer have any direct involvement with what became the OEEC in Paris caused a considerable stir.[23] Four months later he set sail in the *Queen Elizabeth*. 'I find it difficult to believe that it will be so', wrote Franks to his parents on the eve of departure, but the party included, besides four Frankses, Nannie, Ruby (Barbara's maid), a butler, a footman, a housemaid, and an assistant private secretary, not to mention Lulu, the unfortunate family cat (lost at sea): an unaccustomed ambassadorial retinue. In June, Franks's strikingly accomplished début before the National Press Club only fuelled speculation about the transatlantic switch. In the United States he was welcomed with acclaim, and an audible sigh of relief. The *Washington Post* found him refreshingly 'free from prepossessions'. *Time* magazine hailed him as 'the most unneurotic man in Britain'.[24] But there was also regret that he would not be in a position to 'galvanize' the OEEC as he had its predecessor. Franks himself reported:

Whereas it was at one time confidently expected that we [the British] should take the lead in setting Europe on the road towards a fully integrated economy—and eventual political federation—we are now not only accused of failing to live up to these expectations, but of actually discouraging any substantial move in this direction.

In fact they were accused of something more. The suspicion was that Franks's arrival in the US capital betokened a British wish 'to deal unilaterally with Washington, more or less bypassing the permanent organization in Paris'—shutting out the babel that was Europe in order to succour the proverbial special relationship.[25]

There was some substance to this, and a strong element of calculation in Treasury circles, as Robert Hall's original suggestion made clear; but a fuller explanation must comprehend Franks's mid-life career as the special agent of Ernest Bevin. It was Bevin who had recalled him to the colours in Paris; and it was Bevin who had a specific purpose in dispatching him to Washington, a purpose reiterated in a personal message sent to Franks amid the euphoria of Truman's surprise win in the presidential election of November 1948. The message was relayed through a trusted Foreign Office official, who was careful to preserve Bevin's authentic figures of speech:

When discussing the question of the Atlantic Pact, he asked me to write on his behalf and say that he regarded this as probably the most important task of your Ambassadorship; and he relied on you to push this through with the same resolution and speed as you showed over ERP. He feels that if we can get this Atlantic Pact buttoned up, the prospects of world peace will be so improved as to enable us to sleep quietly in our beds. So we must take advantage of the present honeymoon period and clinch the thing.[26]

Here lay the secret of Franks's appointment to Washington. Quite apart from any preference of his own, there was never any prospect of his returning to Paris. If the European Recovery Programme materialized, the economic security of Western Europe was assured. By December 1947 the British priority, above all Bevin's priority, was the containment of the Soviet Union. This meant some form of collective defence. Exactly what form took time to discern. 'A sort of spiritual federation of the West' was Bevin's first, famous airing of the idea, on 17 December 1947. Within days he was speaking the harder language of treaty engagements and security systems. On 8 January 1948 he presented a paper to the Cabinet entitled 'The First Aim of British Foreign Policy' which argued that 'we should seek to form with the backing of the Americas and the Dominions a Western democratic system comprising Scandinavia, the Low Countries, France, Italy, Greece, and possibly Portugal. As soon as circumstances permit we should of course wish also to include Spain and Germany, without whom no Western system can be complete.' Bevin still thought this system might be an informal one, 'though we have an alliance with France and may conclude one with other countries'.[27]

Bevin was thinking aloud. The idea was becoming more concrete, but there was more mixing to be done. It set finally on 11 March 1948. Addressing Marshall with a new degree of urgency, he proposed an Atlantic Approaches Pact of Mutual Assistance, 'in which all the countries directly threatened by a Russian move to the Atlantic could participate, for example the US, the UK, Canada, Eire, Iceland, Norway, Denmark, Portugal, France (and Spain, when it has a democratic regime)'.[28] Bevin realized well enough that this arrangement would not work—that is, would not reassure the West and deter the East—without a clear undertaking from the United States. The Brussels Treaty, signed the same month between the UK, France, and the Benelux countries, was an earnest of intent but not a viable system of security.[29] In the military sphere, too, Western Europe needed help. The Atlantic Pact required an American commitment, ultimately a commitment to use force. For the heirs of George Washington to make such a commitment it was axiomatic that a dose of moral stiffening would be needed. Who better than Father Franks to administer it?

The first round of negotiations preceded Franks's arrival in Washington. Formally known as the United States–United Kingdom–Canada Security Conversations, or more simply the Pentagon Talks of March 1948, they were held in such secrecy that the meeting-place in the labyrinthine Pentagon was almost impossible to find.[30] If this was reminiscent of a Borgesian fiction, the reality trumped even Borges. These conversations were concealed from the French until long after a North Atlantic Treaty came into being, but promptly revealed to the Soviets by a quietly efficient member of the British delegation, Donald Maclean. It is a splendid irony that the pretext for this elaborate deception was the porous nature of French security. In fact there was a good deal of Anglo-Saxon superiority involved. Only recently Bevin and Cripps had warned their Cabinet colleagues that 'we shall be associating ourselves with partners in Western Europe whose political condition is unstable and whose actions may be embarrassing to us'. As Franks later remarked, 'We behaved very badly to the French then.'[31] Subsequent evasions and embarrassments may account for the curious blanks in official and semi-official accounts of NATO's origins, which tend either to omit the Pentagon Talks altogether or fail to acknowledge Maclean's singular contribution to them.[32] One has only to imagine the tables turned to take the measure of 'Sir Donald's' success in so rudely unhorsing the Anglo-American intelligence establishment. A fully convincing damage assessment has yet to appear. When it does, it may well have more to say about the psychological blow than the diplomatic reverse.[33]

The Pentagon Talks astonish in one other respect. Neither military nor Soviet experts made any substantive contribution to them. The US Secretary of Defense was represented by the Director of the Joint Staff (and future Supreme Allied Commander Europe), Major General Alfred M. Gruenther, who made only one intervention of note, to emphasize the need for flexibility as to *where* action should be taken against any aggressor. If Belgium were threatened, for example, the United States might increase its forces in the United Kingdom. Assistance need not be given locally.[34] The point was well taken, though much later in the negotiations Gruenther's formulation was found wanting. After all, as the Belgian Ambassador modestly observed, 'If I should walk up to [the boxer] Joe Louis and say, "I'm going to smack you on the jaw", he would be threatened but he would not be in danger.' The logic was irrefutable, and the relevant clause in the treaty was altered accordingly.[35]

The typical military attitude to the Pentagon Talks was clearly indicated by Gruenther himself in a letter to the President's long-serving Chief of Staff, Admiral William D. Leahy. 'Thus far I have managed to say practically nothing', he wrote after the first two sessions. 'I consider my role to be that of observer.' Gruenther's passivity was matched by Leahy's indifference. The Admiral's diary, that lugubrious chronicle of life in the Oval Office ante-room, makes no mention of either the negotiations or the issues at stake.[36] Thereafter, the American military establishment was effectively excluded from the negotiating process. The Secretary of Defence, James Forrestal, had no say. The National Security Council, barely a year old, cut no ice. There was some informal liaison with the Joint Chiefs of Staff, but not much. The hurried JCS submission on the draft treaty of December 1948 was scarcely discussed. The British Chiefs of Staff fared little better.[37] For all its tremendous ramifications for national security and defence policy, this particular entanglement was the province of the striped pants brigade.

The Pentagon Talks constituted a kind of secret prologue to the negotiating process—secret, that is, from everyone except the Soviets. Before the main performance could begin, a long intermission was imposed by the State Department, pleading a combination of public unreadiness, congressional disquiet, internal opposition, and the exigencies of the electoral timetable. This was a serviceable list, but the constraints were real, as Bevin understood. He told Attlee: 'We shall be lucky if the President and the American Senatorial leaders pronounce in favour of a treaty binding the US for the first time in history to accept positive obligations in the way of the defence of her natural associates and friends.'[38] Bevin fretted impotently in the doldrums. Meanwhile, Robert Lovett gradually obtained some freedom of manœuvre. Working surreptitiously with John Foster Dulles—a prime candidate for the office of Secretary of State if the Republicans should win in November—Lovett held a series of private consultations with the chairman of the powerful Senate Foreign Relations Committee, Arthur H. Vandenberg, a Republican from Michigan.[39] Vandenberg held the key to a bipartisan foreign policy. His personal advice and consent was a matter of great moment, and no one was more aware of this than Vandenberg himself. He was the very personification of senatorial authority, a man of genuine stature and monumental self-importance. Lovett courted him with marvellous dexterity. Gently, almost tenderly, he led Vandenberg to the enunciation of his famous Senate Resolution of 19 May 1948, the enabling act of any Atlantic Pact.

The Vandenberg Resolution advised the Government of the United States to pursue a number of objectives within the terms of the United Nations Charter (which Vandenberg himself had helped to draft some three years earlier). Among them was this: 'Contributing to the maintenance of peace by making clear its determination to exercise the right of individual or collective self-defence under Article 51 should any armed attack occur affecting its national security'.[40] The Senate passed the resolution by an overwhelming majority on 11 June. Lovett immediately telephoned the newly arrived British Ambassador. 'Oliver, why are you so slow? Why don't we get talking at once?'[41] Three months had passed since the Pentagon Talks. Now, at last, they were out of the doldrums. Franks spoke officially to Marshall on 14 June, to re-emphasize Bevin's sense of urgency. On 23 June the State Department invited the Governments of Belgium, Canada, France, Luxemburg, The Netherlands, and the UK to 'top secret exploratory talks pursuant to the Vandenberg Resolution', starting within the week.[42] To the British and the Canadians, at least, it was apparent that serious negotiations for an Atlantic Pact were about to commence. The curtain went up on 6 July 1948.

It turned out to be a marathon event. The coyly named Washington Exploratory Talks on Security continued intermittently, it sometimes seemed interminably, until the North Atlantic Treaty was eventually signed on 4 April 1949. Despite their exhausting length, the negotiations were remarkably good-humoured. The participants evidently enjoyed themselves. They told stories; they made jokes; with one exception, they became friends. This did not stop them quarrelling and intriguing among themselves, but that was only to be expected. Quarrel and intrigue, the very stuff of international relations, were not to be suspended over the issue of national security.

The transcripts of the Washington Security Talks are preserved in the archives. They purport to be unedited even as they mark, straight-faced, the regular interludes in which the participants go literally 'off the record'. The fundamental American concern about the nature of the US commitment to a collective defence is rendered, rather presciently one might think, as 'atomic' rather than 'automatic'. The mysterious 'Mr Cannon' at some of the early sessions turns out to be that well-known contortionist George Kennan, who proceeded, as if in defiance of this sobriquet, to dispute the relevance of a military alliance and dissent from full US membership of it.[43] Apart from these diversions, the transcripts also provide important clues to the atmosphere of each meeting, the personalities of the negotiators, and the spirit of the negotiating process, all of which influenced the outcome in ways that are still not well understood. The atmosphere of a meeting is especially difficult to reconstruct and interpret; the participants themselves often found it hard to fathom at the time.[44] It is here that the transcripts are most revealing. They allow us to peep behind the curtain of the minutes, and eavesdrop on the actors' actual words. (The minutes were full but 'agreed', that is, offered in draft form to each participant for scrutiny and correction—the kiss of death for documentary frankness.[45]) Everyone knew the Cabinet Office ditty:

> And so when the great ones repair to their dinner
> The secretary stays getting thinner and thinner
> Wracking his brains to record and report
> What he thinks they will think that they ought to have thought.

Much of the jocularity relates to the mock-serious diplomatic quadrille danced around the negotiating table by the Ambassadors of the six nations, according to their appointed hour on some imaginary clock. At twelve o'clock went the sagacious Dutchman, Eelco van Kleffens, who was always invited to speak first. Next, at one, came the exasperating Frenchman, Henri Bonnet; at two, the upright Oliver Franks; at three, the incisive Canadian, Hume Wrong, or on occasion the equally incisive Lester Pearson; at four, the somnolent Luxemburger, Hugues Le Gallais; at five, the emollient Belgian, Baron Silvercruys.[46] The clock was devised by Robert Lovett in his role as chairman—or, as he preferred, master of ceremonies—and it is clear that the Ambassadors were much taken with it. At one meeting van Kleffens apologized for intervening again, 'although it is five minutes past twelve now'. At another, Bonnet made the subversive suggestion that the discussion should start at 12.30. When Dean Acheson took over from Lovett in February 1949 there was no more accurate index of his failure to grasp the intangibles of the process than his upsetting habit of turning first to Franks, who promptly corrected him:

> 'Eelco, I believe.'
> 'Oh, not at all', van Kleffens demurred impeccably.
> 'Please, I am sure we must follow custom.'
> 'Well, we won't haggle about it.'[47]

On the American side of the negotiations, the 'pick and shovel' work (to use his own favourite expression) was done by the much-admired Director of the Office of European Affairs, John D. Hickerson, probably the earliest and canniest exponent of some kind of Atlantic Pact in the State Department.[48] Hickerson was a Texan and an internationalist, and a shrewd bureaucratic operator of considerable experience. He had served throughout the war on the US-Canadian Permanent Joint Board of Defense. Subsequently he had been an adviser to the US delegation at the Conference on International Organization in San Francisco in 1945, and to the ill-fated Council of Foreign Ministers in London in 1947. Like Lovett, he was already familiar with several of the other key players in the negotiations, including all of the Canadian principals, whom he had known for some twenty years.

Hickerson usually attended the meetings of the Ambassadors' Committee, as it came to be known, but his primary function was to steer the international Working Party constituted in mid-July 1948 to do precisely the pick-and-shovel work to which he was so committed. Whereas the Ambassadors convened only irregularly, the Working Party met every few days from July to

September 1948 to compile the first, sprawling report of the Exploratory Talks, the so-called Washington Paper of 9 September 1948.[49] In mid-December, after an interval dictated largely by the presidential election, the members of the Working Party were directed to pick up their tools once again and produce a draft treaty as quickly as possible. This was achieved, rather to everyone's surprise, on Christmas Eve 1948.

Unlike the Ambassadors' Committee, the proceedings of the Working Party were not constrained by the normal conventions of diplomatic discourse. There were no transcripts of these meetings, indeed no formal record at all, save a few severely abridged memoranda.[50] In consequence, the members of the Working Party, especially the Americans, the British, and the Canadians, who dominated every forum of the negotiations, shed their inhibitions to a remarkable degree. Constructive indiscipline was the order of the day, and it is evident that this free-thinking atmosphere, so reminiscent of the great days of the wartime combined committees, was both liberating and efficient. In this way a bond was formed. At the end of the year Hickerson proposed that a monument should be erected to the Ambassadors' Committee, bearing the inscription:

> IN MEMORY OF
> THE SEVEN DEPARTED
> IN SPITE OF WHOM
> THE PACT WAS DRAFTED[51]

Hickerson was aided and abetted by another true believer, Theodore C. Achilles, head of the Western European Division, who became perhaps the most convinced Atlanticist of them all.[52] Achilles was proud of the 'rather unorthodox diplomatic habits' he had picked up in his long experience of Anglo-American relations in London and Washington. 'I trusted people I dealt with, shared highly classified information with them freely, and was never let down.' Like many other Anglo-Saxons, he was leery of the French in general—'a cynical, difficult and untrustworthy people'—and of their diplomatic representatives in particular. These prejudices were to be reinforced as the negotiations progressed.[53]

Both Achilles and Hickerson were good committee-men, Hickerson exceptionally so. His approach was a nice blend of efficiency and accommodation. 'Perched forward on the edge of his chair, he would dispose of difficulties, drastically, like a man swatting flies, and when confronted with new suggestions he would welcome them eagerly in the manner of an auctioneer receiving bids.'[54] Procedural skill was a vital element in the negotiating process, not only internationally but also intramurally. No other member of the State Department was as closely or consistently involved, partly because of their multifarious responsibilities and frequent absences from Washington, but partly because of Hickerson's resourcefulness in monitoring different points of view.

The two foremost Soviet experts in the department, Charles Bohlen, the Counsellor, and George Kennan, the Director of the Policy Planning Staff, had no influence on the negotiations in their specialist capacity and little enough as senior members of the small circle of advisers around the Secretary of State. Bohlen, whose purview extended to Congressional relations, impinged on the process only in the high-rolling months of February and March 1949 when he was used in that capacity by the incoming Acheson.[55] Kennan's contribution has been the subject of some controversy, fuelled by his own copious writings. In practical terms it amounted to the identification of a single, significant phrase in the drafting of the treaty.[56] The circumscribed role of these two men is all the more interesting because each voiced grave doubts about the wisdom, and in Bohlen's case the feasibility, of American adherence to such a treaty—the tip of a potentially large iceberg. As the seismic shock of the Berlin blockade began to register in June, as Truman won against all expectation in November, as the negotiations gathered pace in December, such doubts came to seem increasingly misplaced, politically unrealistic if not actually wrong-headed. In truth, the high salience of George Kennan's ideas in Washington was no more. By mid 1948, the creeping marginalization that led from appointed seer to court jester to internal exile at the Institute for Advanced Study at Princeton had already begun.[57]

The British fielded a strong team, as usual. Here too, as in the CEEC, they provided the mechanics. Their procedural skill completely outclassed that of every other delegation except the Canadians, with whom they worked hand in glove. Franks was supported by the experienced Minister at the Embassy, Derick Hoyer Millar, and by a young Second Secretary, Nicholas Henderson. Donald Maclean attended the first few meetings but luckily left Washington for Cairo in September 1948, still unsuspected. Hoyer Millar (later, in one of those transformations peculiar to the British aristocracy, Lord Inchyra), was the mandarin *par excellence*, Permanent Secretary of the Foreign Office by 1957. In classic mandarin style he concealed a rapier-like mind beneath an exterior of absolute detachment. 'In the schoolroom of the Working Party he was that rare but recognizable character who, seemingly without effort or desire and sometimes with apparent indifference, always seemed to know all the answers and come out top in exams. It was all very easy, if at times rather a bore.'[58] This was just the sort of demeanour to alienate the Americans, as it often did in the case of Gladwyn Jebb, who had led for the British at the Pentagon Talks.[59] Yet somehow in Hoyer Millar's case it did not. He knew Washington, having served there for most of the war. He knew how to appeal to the Americans in the Working Party. He also possessed a cautionary sense of humour, delighting the French representatives by repeating every so often his favourite maxim: 'Le mieux est l'ennemi du bien' (Voltaire). Nicholas Henderson, too, was a brilliant diplomat in the making, as his triumphantly dishevelled ambassadorial appearances on prime-time television during the

Falklands War of 1982 were later to show. Moreover he performed a significant additional service by writing a detailed contemporary account of the negotiations for the Foreign Office, now published, noteworthy alike for its elegant indiscretion and a certain native condescension.[60]

The British could be relied upon to take a broad view. They appeared to be eminently reasonable. Achilles liked to quote an example from the Working Party. One day, Hoyer Millar 'made a proposal which was obvious nonsense. Several of us told him so in no uncertain terms and a much better formulation emerged from the discussion. Derick said: "Those were my instructions. All right. I'll tell the Foreign Office I made my pitch and was shot down, and try to get them changed."'[61] This was a possibilist approach, requiring careful co-ordination. British positions—even their fall-back positions—were invariably well prepared, the relevant documents always to hand, a new proposal snug and ready. Failing that, all of the British representatives had an unnerving facility for extemporaneous drafting. They prospered accordingly.

The French, by contrast, were surprisingly maladroit. They appeared profoundly unreasonable and not a little disorganized.[62] They harped constantly on their own immediate security needs. They wanted military equipment and they wanted it now. This was a crass misjudgement of both the purpose of the negotiations and the mood of the US Administration, in part attributable to French ignorance of the frame of reference provided by the Pentagon Talks. But it was the way in which the demands were couched that really gave offence. Henderson provided a brilliant sketch of the chief offender, the importunate Henri Bonnet.

Bonnet, of course, was not inhibited by any Anglo-Saxon notions of team spirit. He was there to state the French case, the whole of the French case, and nothing but it. This he did with remarkable tenacity and tactlessness from the beginning to the end of the negotiations. Not conspicious for his lucidity of thought or expression, he nevertheless brought with him to the table an array of arresting qualities: an excellent temper, a Maurice Chevalier accent, a gift for generous and irrelevant gesture, and superb pipe-manship. As he wielded all these in weary repetition of the French point of view, he appeared quite unconscious of the effect he was having on the others.[63]

Bonnet soon became the *bête noire* of the Ambassadors' Committee. The extremity of feeling he aroused is well attested by a magisterial rebuke delivered late in the proceedings by Oliver Franks, provoked finally by Bonnet's heedless effort to lay down conditions for French participation in the alliance. 'When Mr Bonnet spoke of conditions,' the minutes record,

Sir Oliver was not happy because it was not the way in which the negotiations had been conducted. . . . He would appreciate it if the French position could be put, not in the language of conditions, but in the language of views strongly held by the French Government. He did not think that it was really a question of conditions but of a joint effort to achieve a right result under difficult circumstances.

Franks objected to a pistol being put at his head. The impenitent Bonnet replied that he felt the same when 'he was engaged in a negotiation and had the impression of talking to a wall'.[64] No one was much amused that day.

Franks's intervention was unexpected, though not uncharacteristic. As his reproof of Bonnet served to dramatize, 'He, more than any of the other representatives, imparted a sense of collectivity to the negotiations.' He had been a European in Paris; he was an Atlanticist in Washington. 'He sought to lift the discussions from a series of statements of national viewpoints to a plane where all were endeavouring to reconcile minor disparities for the achievement of an aim of great importance to them all.'[65] This was the constant theme of his contributions to the formless early meetings of the Ambassadors' Committee in July 1948, contributions clearly designed to give shape and substance to objectives as yet alarmingly amorphous: to promote the fundamental notion of 'mutuality of interest' (borrowing imaginatively from the lexicon of friendly aid); to postulate a meaningful 'North Atlantic area'; and to press for a new 'Atlantic' pact rather than an enlarged Brussels one.[66]

A position taken by Oliver Franks could not easily by controverted. Although fully ten years younger than his fellow Ambassadors, he swiftly attained a unique position in the negotiations. This was initially a consequence of the manner of the man. What first impressed Washington was the authority of his presence. As Henderson noted, Franks 'possessed capacities of intellect and exposition which none of his colleagues could equal or ignore'. But it was not simply a question of mental acuity. The highly esteemed Canadian Ambassador Hume Wrong, Robert Lovett, Dean Acheson, and Franks were all well matched in this regard. They consorted together in a kind of playful intellectuality that entirely excluded the more ponderous Henri Bonnet, whose capacities they tended privately to disparage.[67] Franks did display an extraordinary ability to resolve the most complicated discussion into, say, six main points and summarize them with breathtaking clarity (and if need be, when he had finished the summary with the fifth point, quite shamelessly to make up a sixth). This distinctive blend of extreme clarity of mind with what has been called 'heavy moral purpose' seemed to elevate him above the heads of lesser men.[68]

Franks could easily appear awe-inspiring, but he took some care to add a redeeming tincture of fun, all the more attractive for its habitual understatement. One of his greatest virtues lay in knowing how much he impressed without letting the knowledge dehumanize him. Chasing final agreement on the contentious economic and social article 2, sponsored principally by the Canadians, he offered the gently compelling argument

that we could leave this matter, so far as any recommendations to our government goes, simply as something to be settled, really, with the Canadians as prime movers, because they have this difficulty, you see, and that the rest of us should go along with what can be achieved by not trying to get further alterations. I am quite sure that pretty considerable efforts have been made on the American side to get where we have gotten, and therefore I had rather hoped that despite the advantages of the intellectual life that we all once knew, we shall be content with stating a preference.

The transcript marks the Ambassadors' amusement and the successful curtailment of a protracted debate.[69]

In this way Franks became the unofficial moderator of the Ambassadors' Committee. He guided and persuaded. Almost as a matter of habit, he clarified. He advanced business with great dispatch. He was after all a committee-man of unbeatable experience. He had chaired not only the sixteen-nation CEEC, but also the Governing Body of Queen's College, Oxford, compared to which, he observed, the Europeans were child's play.[70] He was interested in procedure, and above all in speed. 'It seemed hopeless to try to get agreement on texts [the articles of a draft treaty] in the full meeting of ambassadors,' he explained to Bevin in December, 'and on my suggestion the detailed work has been left to a working party. The seven countries are represented on this and the working party has been at it fairly continuously, referring from time to time to the ambassadors. This way of proceeding has speeded things up a lot.'[71] It was Franks who pressed for the transmission of a complete text, however tentative or imperfect, to the respective Governments before Christmas; Franks who appealed for candour in the Ambassadors' Committee; Franks who most persistently sought an end. 'I think there seems to me to be one overriding consideration at the present time,' he interjected at a meeting in late February 1949, 'and that is the need, within reason and subject to the satisfaction of all our governments, for speed.'

I also think, insofar as it is possible for any of us to make some kind of guess based on experience and past transactions about how our governments are likely to feel about changes of elements in the present text, that so far as we can do that this morning it is of very great advantage to the other governments because when we send it home one of the things that we want to be able to say is how far something seems likely to be cause for serious consideration, how far it seems likely to be acceptable generally, if one's own government can take it. It seems to me that provided we all had in mind the limitations and safeguards on the expression of our views it can speed things up a bit if we talk quite freely this morning.[72]

Franks's ultimate goal, however, was the pledge.

The pledge was the crux of the treaty, the provision for collective defence against armed attack. The clause embodying this provision was described in various ways, all more or less euphemistic. It was called the solemn engagement, the obligation, the commitment, and the guarantee (or even *garantie*). The implication that a 'guarantee' would be invoked automatically meant that this term was taboo in Washington, in spite of its usage elsewhere. The other terms, less pithy and less pointed, were more acceptable. Not surprisingly, the language of the pledge was the most intractable issue of the negotiations. It was finally resolved in March 1949, after a severe crisis the previous month. Until the very end, there was no certainty about the nature of the North Atlantic Treaty. The basic elements of the problem have been well stated by the Canadian diplomat Escott Reid, who followed the negotiations from Ottawa. 'The firmer the pledge, the greater the effect the treaty might be expected to have in deterring the Soviet Union and in restoring in Western Europe the confidence necessary for its recovery. The weaker the pledge, the less reluctant the Senate would be to ratify the treaty.'[73] The Europeans emphasized the importance of the first consideration. The Americans emphasized the importance of the second. The Canadians usually favoured the Europeans.

The pledge eventually embodied in the North Atlantic Treaty evolved through a number of sinuous but significant compromises. An early prototype was contained in the so-called Pentagon Paper that emerged from the secret tripartite talks of March 1948:

Provision that each Party shall regard any action in the area covered by the agreement, which it considers an armed attack against any other Party, as an armed attack against itself and that each Party accordingly undertakes to assist in meeting the attack in the exercise of the inherent right of individual or collective self-defence recognized by Article 51 of the [UN] Charter.[74]

This was a weak pledge. It was modelled on article 3 of the Rio Pact (the Inter-American Treaty of Reciprocal Assistance) of September 1947, which had already been ratified by the Senate.[75] The operative phrase, 'assist in meeting the attack', was a bland and unspecific undertaking, though something of a new departure when it was first made. Its reappearance in the Pentagon Talks testified to the intimidatory power of Vandenberg and his friends. It also represented a considerable retreat from a previous version, which spoke of each nation meeting an attack with 'all military, economic, and other aid and assistance in its power'—a much more explicit formulation that followed a draft by Escott Reid, who borrowed in turn from the main alternative model for Atlantic treaty-makers, article 4 of the recently concluded Brussels Pact.[76]

The Pentagon Paper was an exclusively Anglo–American–Canadian document. The first round of the expanded Exploratory Talks yielded the Washington Paper of September 1948, and a much-strengthened pledge:

Provision that each Party should agree that any act which, in its opinion, constituted an armed attack against any other Party in the area covered by the treaty be considered an attack against itself, and should consequently, in accordance with its constitutional processes, assist in repelling the attack by all military, economic and other means in its power in the exercise of the right of individual or collective self-defence recognized by Article 51 of the Charter.[77]

This wording—'repelling the attack by all military, economic and other means in its power'—was suggested by Hoyer Millar in the schoolroom of the

Working Party. It was presented in the Washington Paper as an explicit compromise between the American preference for the Rio model ('assist in meeting the attack') and the European preference for the Brussels model ('afford
the Party so attacked all the military and other aid and assistance in their
power').[78] Its unexpected adoption, even in this left-handed manner, clearly
represented a very satisfactory compromise from the point of view of the
Europeans, and one which was also supported by the Canadians; but it was
equally clear that the Americans found it wanting. The tension between the
two sides of the table remained real.

The renewed burst of activity at the end of the year produced the draft
treaty of December 1948, and a recast pledge:

> The Parties agree that an armed attack against one or more of them within the area
> defined below shall be considered an attack against them all; and consequently that, if
> such an armed attack occurs, each of them, in exercise of the right of individual or col-
> lective self-defence recognized by Article 51 of the Charter of the United Nations, will
> assist the party or parties so attacked by taking forthwith such military or other action,
> individually and in concert with other parties, as may be necessary to restore and
> assure the security of the North Atlantic area.[79]

This pledge, article 5 of the draft treaty, still erred on the European side.
'Forthwith' emphasized resolve and underlined the need to avoid procrastination if the pledge was to meet the essential criteria of being credible to
aggressors and reassuring to allies. There was explicit reference to military
action, albeit as a possible alternative to some other action; and 'military' was
mentioned first (a drafting point of some subtlety, but one quickly spotted by
Vandenberg as reversing the sequence embodied in the UN Charter).[80] The
basic formulation—'taking . . . such . . . action . . . as may be necessary to
restore and assure . . . security'—was George Kennan's contribution to the
proceedings, patterned on article 42 of the Charter.[81] As a whole, the draft
article appeared to please both sides of the table. 'It seems to me', Franks
wrote reassuringly to Bevin, 'to give us everything we really want.'[82]

The pledge contained in the draft treaty survived more or less intact until
early February 1949. As a mark of approbation, it was not even discussed at
the 14 January meeting of the Ambassadors' Committee, Lovett's swansong.
Acheson took office on 21 January 1949, initially distracted by other things.
On 3 February and again on 5 February he discussed the text of the draft
treaty privately with the two key figures on the Senate Foreign Relations
Committee: the new chairman, Tom Connally, a Democrat from Texas, and
the senior Republican, Vandenberg. All three men were quite unfamiliar with
the detailed history of the negotiations. Acheson had been hastily briefed by
Lovett, but had not had enough time to master the intricacies; Vandenberg
had been kept informed in a general way, but had not been shown the various
papers; Connally had only just assumed the chairmanship, and had never

received the attention paid to his Republican colleague, a fact of which he was uncomfortably aware.

Both Connally and Vandenberg now saw the draft article for the first time. Both were considerably shaken. Connally immediately fastened on the 'automatic aspect' of the pledge. 'In his opinion it was far too broad and it did, in effect, commit the United States to go to war through military action in certain circumstances.' Vandenberg's objections were less thoroughgoing but still fundamental. He was chiefly concerned to make absolutely clear that each party to the treaty had the right to determine for itself what action it was 'necessary' to take. He observed that 'the word "military" was like a red rag to a bull and would condition the [congressional] attitude towards the entire article'. He therefore suggested that 'action' should be left unqualified; and that 'forthwith' should be struck out. The emasculated pledge would then commit the signatory to 'assist the party or parties so attacked by taking action . . . to restore and assure the security of the North Atlantic area'.[83]

We can only speculate on whether the Senators would have reacted as badly if coaxed through the text by the dexterous Lovett. Hume Wrong for one (a close friend) thought that Acheson's indelicate handling of the meetings only exacerbated the difficulties.[84] Certainly he fared no better when he met the Ambassadors' Committee on 8 February to report on the latest developments. Acheson was reluctant to disclose to the Ambassadors the full extent of the Senators' unease. About article 5 he said relatively little; but that was more than enough. He blithely dismissed 'military or other' action and 'forthwith' as 'unnecessary embellishments', even as he claimed that there was no intention of weakening the language of the treaty.[85] The Ambassadors were dismayed by this senseless act of linguistic vandalism. Acheson appeared ready to dismantle the painstakingly constructed edifice that was the draft pledge, without any real appreciation of the consequences. Long ago Thucydides had warned of the disintegration that followed when 'the agreed upon currency of words for things was subjected to random barter'. A similar theme was developed in a commanding intervention by Oliver Franks:

In a sense, the substance of the treaty was what mattered and the words were of secondary importance. But there was another angle to this. It was not just a matter . . . of what would in fact happen if one of the Parties to the treaty were attacked. There was also the question of the effect which the articles of the treaty would produce themselves.

If this North Atlantic Pact came into being, there would be established a set of arrangements between the countries of North America and the West of Europe which might ensure peace for a lifetime. One of the conditions of this was that the words of the Pact, while sober in tone, should make it plain beyond misunderstanding what would happen in the event of trouble occurring. . . . It was therefore necessary to balance what opinion in North America might be prepared to accept with what those on the eastern shores of the Atlantic would regard as necessary. Wording which erred on the side of understatement might make the Pact look weaker than it really was and thereby detract from its value in maintaining peace.[86]

This was as close as Franks ever came to linguistic philosophy.

The February crisis was reaching its peak. On 12 February it was reported that Acheson had told the Norwegian Foreign Minister that the pledge 'would be interpreted as a moral commitment to fight', though Congress alone could declare war. This allegation provoked a display of virulent isolationist sentiment on the floor of the Senate, in the course of which Tom Connally, 'on his best *opéra bouffe* behaviour', announced that he did not believe in giving '*carte blanche* assurance' to the nations of Europe—'do anything you want to do, you need not worry, as soon as anything happens we will come over and fight your quarrel for you', and a good deal more in the same vein.[87] Immediately afterwards Connally and Vandenberg conferred again with Acheson about the wording of the pledge. Predictably, the two Senators proved most recalcitrant. Connally even attacked the hitherto inviolate opening declaration, suggesting merely 'an attack on one would be regarded as a threat to the peace of all'.[88] Harried from all sides, Acheson retired in disarray.

There followed two days of intensive discussion within the State Department to reassess the situation. It seems clear that by this stage all Acheson's principal advisers were prepared to capitulate to senatorial opinion in order to secure a treaty. After a meeting with Hickerson, Achilles, and Dean Rusk, Bohlen presented their agreed 'minimum' draft to the Secretary of State on the morning of 16 February. They retained the word 'forthwith', but conceded everything else. Their version of the operative phrase met the objection originally voiced by Vandenberg by incorporating two suggestions of Connally's: to take 'measures', rather than 'action' or 'military action'; and only the measures individually 'deemed' necessary. Thus each signatory would 'take, forthwith, individually and in concert with the other Parties, the measures it deems necessary to restore and maintain the security of the North Atlantic area'.[89]

As to how to proceed with the negotiations, Bohlen and his colleagues made a revealing recommendation:

That I [Bohlen] be authorized, in a private and informal manner, to discuss it with Sir Oliver Franks in order to ascertain his personal opinion as to the probable effect of this new draft on the other countries involved in the discussions. I would, of course, explain to the British Ambassador that I was seeking his judgement before the subject was discussed by the Secretary [Acheson] with the Senate Foreign Relations Committee.

That if Sir Oliver Franks believes that this draft would not seriously impair the objectives of the Pact and would therefore be generally acceptable to the other countries, the President and the Secretary should see Senator Connally alone in an endeavour to enlist his support for the draft.[90]

The moderator of the Ambassadors' Committee had become the guarantor of the treaty on the European side.

Meanwhile Acheson was taking the matter into his own hands. On the afternoon of the same day, 16 February, he conferred alone with Franks. It was the beginning of four years of almost conspiratorial confraternity. Franks and Acheson had first met during the war, for the inaugural council sessions of the United Nations Relief and Rehabilitation Administration in Atlantic City in November 1943 and Montreal in September 1944.[91] Much taken with each other then, they were able to develop their friendship in the salons of Georgetown during the latter part of 1948, before Acheson returned to office. Lovett must also have reported favourably on Franks's mastery of the CEEC negotiations and the early meetings of the Ambassadors' Committee. So it was that 'not long after becoming Secretary of State' Acheson made Franks his famous 'unorthodox proposal'.

On an experimental basis I suggested that we talk regularly, and in complete personal confidence, about any international problems we saw arising. Neither would report or quote the other unless, thinking it would be useful in promoting action, he got the other's consent and agreement on the terms of a reporting memorandum or cable. . . . We met alone, usually at his residence or mine, at the end of the day before or after dinner. No one was informed even of the fact of the meeting. We discussed situations already emerging or likely to do so, the attitudes that various people in both countries would be likely to take, what courses of action were possible and their merits, the chief problems that could arise. If either thought that his department should be alerted to the other's apprehensions and thoughts, we would work out an acceptable text setting out the problem and suggesting approaches.[92]

In this spirit Franks and Acheson re-examined the pledge from first principles. Initially they considered the changes suggested by the Senators. Fortified by prior discussion with the judicious Hume Wrong, Franks thought the original formulation 'as may be necessary' preferable to 'as it deems necessary', but did not consider it crucial as long as no obstacles were raised to staff talks and joint military planning between the parties to the treaty. He was even prepared if necessary to dispense with the trusty 'forthwith'. He was adamant on two points only: the cardinal principle of an attack on one being regarded as an attack on all, and the explicit provision for a military response. The two men disassembled all the pieces and together constructed a new form of words—'a bit of redrafting to ease the constitutional sensibilities of the Congress', as Franks put it later.[93] Acheson then returned to the State Department. The minimum draft was set aside. Three new versions of the pledge were prepared, in order of priority, representing 'more preferable drafts in the light of the British Ambassador's observations'. The first two of these reinstated the words 'such military or other action'; the third spoke only of 'action'. All jettisoned 'forthwith'.[94]

The next day, again unaccompanied, Acheson met President Truman to go over the various drafts of the pledge, gain his approval of the best of them, and enlist his help in the forthcoming campaign of persuasion—confidently expected to be a difficult one.[95] Acheson naturally had with him the three State Department drafts. But there was a surprise in store. He also produced for the President's inspection a different version, almost certainly a Franks-Acheson version, concocted in secret the previous afternoon. It read:

The Parties agree that an armed attack against one or more of them in Europe and North America shall be considered an armed attack against them all; and consequently that, if such an armed attack occurs, each of them, in exercise of the right of individual or collective self-defence recognized by Article 51 of the Charter of the United Nations, will assist the Party or Parties so attacked by taking forthwith such action including the use of armed force, individually and in concert with the other parties, as it deems necessary to restore and assure the security of the North Atlantic area.[96]

With the appealing innovation, 'including the use of armed force', carefully inserted *after* the word 'action'—to conform with the UN Charter, and assuage Senator Vandenberg—this version was unquestionably the most sophisticated compromise package yet developed. It persuaded Truman, who undertook to 'impress upon' Senator Connally that very evening his own backing for the Franks–Acheson pledge. As a poor second, the State Department's minimum draft might be possible, the President thought, but only 'if it was absolutely necessary after a stout fight'.[97]

The following day, 18 February, Acheson, flanked by Bohlen and Achilles, appeared before the full Senate Foreign Relations Committee in executive session. The Secretary of State endured a prolonged interrogation without misstep. The Senators did not finally commit themselves, but they did go some way towards provisional approval of the new draft.[98] For the first time Acheson felt that he knew 'where we were all going'. Bohlen told Franks that he thought 'a solid basis had been established'.[99] On 19 February Acheson called an informal meeting of the Ambassadors to report a cautious optimism and to permit the new text to be relayed to their respective Governments. On 24 February Ernest Gross, Assistant Secretary of State for Congressional Relations, reviewed the latest revisions with Connally and Vandenberg, who pronounced themselves satisfied.[100] On 25 February the Ambassadors' Committee formally reconvened in order to gauge European reaction to all of the proposed changes in the draft treaty—now two months old—and to gauge, also, how well Oliver Franks would serve as guarantor.

The same day James Forrestal reminded Acheson of the Defense Department's interest in discussing 'the question of bases and other *quid pro quo*' which the US could obtain 'in return for our military aid to Western European countries'. A similar thought had crossed his mind (and Vandenberg's) apropos Marshall aid. Acheson prevaricated, and nothing came of this particular overture.[101] Mercifully, the Ambassadors did not get to hear of it. Seeking a *quid pro quo* for American largess squared poorly with genuine mutuality of interest. Only recently, riled by the hullabaloo in the Senate, Bevin had written to Acheson demanding to know 'whether or not the US government accepted the conception of the Atlantic Community as one fundamental unit which has got to be defended together for the sake of all of the parts'. It behoved the United States to remember who took the greatest risks in signing any pact. 'I thought the principle had been accepted and there was no difference of status between the various parties in such a unity (except indeed that we, the European members, were in the front line and would probably take the first knock in any emergency).'[102] Forrestal's suggestion, it is safe to say, would not have been well received in February 1949.

Would Franks do as a guarantor? He had been thrust into the role by the February crisis and by his admirers in the State Department. Acheson's small circle of self-made philosopher-kings—men like Philip Jessup, Paul Nitze, and Dean Rusk—regarded Franks very much as one of themselves, 'a useful member of the central team of the US government', as Nitze put it.[103] His acceptability to the Europeans was now to be put to the test. On the basis of the CEEC experience there was every reason to be confident. The unanimity of testimony on Franks's chairmanship in Paris is very striking. According to H. M. Hirschfeld, the capable Benelux representative on the Executive Committee, 'the highest tribute should be paid to Franks. If constructive work was done on the European side, it was to a considerable degree the result of Franks's objectivity, great knowledge, fairness, etc.' These were the recurring themes. Denny Marris summed it up: 'Franks was amazingly good where fairness and integrity were absolutely essential.'[104]

When they met on 25 February the Ambassadors were properly anxious to discuss the draft treaty thoroughly, article by article; there was a feeling that this might be their only chance. Franks let them talk. As the passion subsided, he offered his colleagues a blueprint for their evaluation of the pledge that was at the same time a candid appraisal of the negotiating process, and a personal declaration of faith in the outcome. He began with the reflection that 'the text that we have in front of us now is more nearly what we have had in mind for some months', a result which 'didn't seem at all likely two or three weeks ago'.

The general instructions which I think on this side of the table we have all had, as I understand them, are in terms of preference. That is to say, and I want to be quite open about this, we would prefer that the original wording '[such action] as may be necessary' remain and that the importation ['as it deems necessary'] had not taken its place. But . . . there had got to be a give and take inevitably, [and] speaking for myself only, I think we have got as well as given. I do attach very considerable importance to the reference to armed forces, I think it makes a very great deal of difference to the article; I attach very great importance to the start of the article; and when you take the whole thing together, . . . I rather hope that, unless anyone has different feelings, we can feel that, if not the best, a good job has been made of a difficult situation.

'I don't know', he ended encouragingly, 'whether that is going much beyond what some of my colleagues feel.' It was not. Franks effectively carried the meeting. There was no dissent from the gracious response of Baron Silvercruys. 'I am impressed, as we all are, by the personal opinion which is expressed by Sir Oliver, that I think should bear great weight with every one of us and, naturally, with our governments.' It was left only for the grace-less Henri Bonnet to add, 'Well, I think we should go to another article now.'[105]

The marathon performance was almost over. Acheson, accompanied by Gross, appeared again before the Senators in informal session on 8 March. During the session Gross had the inspiration of transposing the key phrases at the end of the article so that it ran, in even greater conformity with Vandenbergian principles, 'such action as it deems necessary, including the use of armed force, to restore and maintain the security of the North Atlantic area'. The transposition was embraced with enthusiasm by Acheson, who used it cleverly to forestall any attempt by the ultras on the committee to barter with the currency of the language. Senator Bourke Hickenlooper's artful sug-gestion, 'which *may* include the use of armed force', was rejected. No substant-ive changes were made.[106] In essence, the bit of redrafting undertaken by Franks and Acheson in February became article 5 of the North Atlantic Treaty in April. It has remained in place ever since.

The treaty was signed at a ceremony in Washington on 4 April 1949 by twelve Governments: Canada, the United Kingdom, and the United States, the three in the Pentagon basement; Belgium, France, Luxemburg, and The Netherlands, the four other Brussels powers; Norway, which joined the negoti-ations (at six o'clock) in March 1949 at its own request; and Denmark, Iceland, Italy, and Portugal, invited to become original signatories in the same month, after much wrangling among the first seven. This time there were no eleventh-hour apostates. In the background, the US Marine Band played a catchy selection of tunes from Gershwin's *Porgy and Bess*, including 'I've got plenty of nothin'', and 'It ain't necessarily so'.[107] Nothing could detract from the extraordinary nature of the deed itself. An entangling alliance was being created, against the weight of history. As Bevin reported to the Cabinet, American readiness 'to enter into a commitment to defend Europe in time of peace marked a revolutionary step in their policy'. Appropriately enough, it was Bevin and Franks who signed for the UK. Bevin was exuberant—his bio-grapher hazards that these were the greatest ten days of his life. Without ques-tion the North Atlantic Treaty was the crowning achievement of his foreign secretaryship.[108]

The American commitment was formally expressed in the pledge they made in article 5 of the Treaty. How should we assess this bone of con-tention? It was a strong pledge (not as strong, perhaps, as the Brussels one), but its strength lay ultimately in the glorious fact of its agreement.[109] It was a temperate pledge, but its temperance was a product of creative transatlantic tension. It was an unlikely pledge, in doubt until the very end.[110] Finally, it was a negotiated pledge—the best available—the heart of the second great transatlantic bargain of the post-war era. And it was delivered by Oliver Franks.

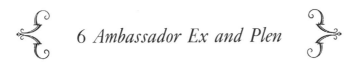

6 *Ambassador Ex and Plen*

FRANKS was an amateur ambassador. 'Amateur diplomatists', reflected Harold Nicolson, sage-like, in a classic work on the subject, '. . . are prone to prove unreliable.'[1]

It is not merely that their lack of knowledge and experience may be of disadvantage to their governments, it is that the amateur diplomatist is apt out of vanity and owing to the shortness of his tenure to seek for rapid success; that he tends, owing to diffidence, to be over-suspicious; that he is inclined to be far too zealous and to have bright ideas; that he has not acquired the humane and tolerant disbelief which is the product of a long diplomatic career, and is often assailed by convictions, sympathies and even impulses; that he may arrive with a righteous contempt for the formalities of diplomacy and with some impatience of its conventions; that he may cause offence when he wishes only to inspire geniality; and that in his reports and despatches he may seek rather to display his own acumen and literary brilliance than to provide his government with a careful and sensible balance-sheet of the facts.

The conclusion to be drawn from this dismal catalogue of callowness was only too clear. 'It will always be desirable that the foreign policy of any great country'—Nicolson was writing in 1939—'should be carried out by professionals trained in their business.'[2]

In Washington, however, it is not so. 'Anglo-American relations are too important to be left to the diplomats', as David Reynolds has observed. Franks himself quoted to the National Press Club (who had probably heard it before) the proverbial response of the candidate for the nineteenth-century Foreign Office, when asked what were the most important things in life. The young man promptly replied: 'God, love, and Anglo-American relations.' Naturally his application was successful.[3] In more serious vein Max Beloff has written magisterially of 'the alternation between the professional diplomat and the statesman or man of affairs, which began with the appointment of Bryce [in 1907] and has remained characteristic of Britain's handling of the Washington embassy down to the present day': a practice indicative of the prevailing uncertainty 'as to whether Washington is a foreign capital like any other, or the second centre of an English-speaking world linked to London by ties much more significant than those of traditional diplomacy'.[4]

James Bryce, historian and politician, the renowned author of *The American Commonwealth* (1888), served from 1907 to 1913. He was succeeded by Sir Cecil Spring-Rice, a professional (1913–18); Lord Reading, a financier and

Lord Chief Justice (1918–19); Sir Auckland Geddes, a businessman turned wartime administrator (1919–24); Sir Esmé Howard, a professional (1924–30); Sir Ronald Lindsay, another professional (1930–9); Lord Lothian, a Liberal Atlanticist out of Lord Milner's kindergarten and Lady Astor's Cliveden Set (1939–40); Lord Halifax, the deposed Foreign Secretary and Holy Fox run to ground (1941–6); and Lord Inverchapel, a professional (1946–8).[5] After Franks came two professionals, Sir Roger Makins (1953–6) and Sir Harold Caccia (1956–61), followed by Sir David Ormsby Gore (Lord Harlech), a Conservative MP and friend of the President (1961–5); Sir Patrick Dean, a professional (1965–9); John Freeman, a Labour MP and editor (1969–71); Lord Cromer, a Baring and therefore a banker (1971–4); Sir Peter Ramsbotham, a professional (1974–7); and Peter Jay, an economic journalist and son-in-law of the Prime Minister (1977–9). The Thatcher era ushered in an unprecedented run of four professionals: Sir Nicholas Henderson (1979–82), Sir Oliver Wright (1982–6), Sir Antony Acland (1986–91), and Sir Robin Renwick (since 1991). Ostensibly, a remarkable tradition is dying. But the picture is cloudier than it first appears, for Margaret Thatcher was thwarted in her original purpose. Her first offer was apparently made to her skulking predecessor, the former Conservative Prime Minister Edward Heath, who rejected it. Both Nicholas Henderson (veteran of the North Atlantic Treaty negotiations) and Oliver Wright were eminently suitable; but both had to be specially recalled from retirement, as their respective entries in *Who's Who* do not fail to mention. Beneath the calm surface of ambassadorial exchange, the old uncertainty lingers on.

Who, then, was the best man for the job, in the Attlee vernacular? Comparisons are odious and difficult. Tenure of varying lengths, at different times, in changing circumstances (war and peace, rise and decline), over almost a century, serve to complicate any comparative assessment. Nevertheless, it is not obvious that the amateurs were outclassed by the professionals. Perhaps posterity will be kind to Henderson. If so, that will be a consequence of the rare opportunity provided by the Falklands War, a passage of arms at once anachronistic and spectacular. Henderson mastered both aspects with conspicuous skill. His reward was television coverage unrivalled since the great days of Gladwyn Jebb's operatic performances at the UN during the Korean War.[6] Stardom, however, is evanescent. In their time, Bryce, Lothian, Halifax (somewhat controversially), Franks, Ormsby Gore, and Freeman won the highest acclaim. None has yet suffered any serious debunking, but only the first two have been properly investigated. In the small mountain of literature on Halifax his embassy is either afterthought or anticlimax. Ormsby Gore was famous, for a while, for his intimate connection with Kennedy's Camelot; now he is forgotten. Of John Freeman virtually nothing is now known.[7]

It is tempting to suggest that the recipe for ambassadorial success in

Washington is an amateur diplomatist of intellectual bent, compromising temperament, proconsular virtue, and strong religious belief. Henderson himself has written of Franks that 'he did not have the back-slapping bonhomie that helps popularity in some American circles; but the United States also has a heart for the good, the high-minded, the liberal and the serious'.[8] The compromiser often stands condemned. In diplomacy compromise is a notoriously difficult art. Once, it might well have been labelled differently. 'The English are really indifferent,' says the French Foreign Minister in Nancy Mitford's tale of Alfred, the Professor of Pastoral Theology turned Ambassador, 'they don't care, but whenever they can please the Americans without it costing anything they like to do so.' This is a good working definition of appeasement; but in the twentieth century the meaning of the word has been corrupted, perhaps irredeemably.[9] For Bryce to practise appeasement was unexceptionable. For Franks to do so—openly—was unthinkable. What used to be positively desirable had become thoroughly despicable because of its automatic association with Hitler. Remarkably, both Lothian and Halifax had what is commonly called the stench of appeasement about them when they arrived in Washington. Yet whatever difficulties of adjustment they experienced (and Halifax's were severe), in neither case did the noxious past cause much trouble. Their compromising temperaments overcame their compromising histories.

According to Carlyle, 'it has been well said, in every sense, that a man's religion is the chief fact with regard to him'—by which he meant not 'the church-creed which he professes', but 'the thing a man does practically lay to heart, and know for certain, concerning his vital relations to this mysterious Universe, and his duty and destiny there'.[10] For the British Ambassador, it seems, the denomination is immaterial. Bryce, like Abraham Lincoln, was a Presbyterian. When he attended the Old Presbyterian Church in Washington he was always escorted to Lincoln's pew. Lothian, famously and in a sense tragically, was a Christian Scientist. He died early of uraemic poisoning, having refused medical treatment in accordance with his beliefs. Halifax, equally famously, was a High Church Anglican. His friend and confessor Fr. Ted Talbot described his view of religion as 'completely transcendental like Job's'.

He expects nothing from God, he hopes nothing material, he would not understand 'guidance' or 'being charged' in Dr [Frank] Buchman's sense. The idea that . . . 'I have left it all to God' would . . . strike him as incomprehensible. His religion is one in which the soul is consistently paying tribute to its creator; worship, giving, paying homage, rendering oneself in perfect fullness back to the Divine Life is his philosophy. Whether or not that happens to make you a better man would strike him as quite irrelevant . . . he is a little inhuman.[11]

The first and last sentences of this description could probably be applied as well to Oliver Franks; though he was not so much concerned with paying homage or rendering an account, except to his own stern conscience. Franks was a lifelong attender at Quaker meeting, but not strictly a Quaker. Unlike his mother and his wife, he never joined the Society of Friends. 'You must allow for my unsatisfactory nature', he would say, and summon St Augustine to his defence: man is in *this* world; it is necessary to be happy *here*. Religious beliefs were relevant to living. Franks bound himself to live properly.[12] 'Be faithful', the Quakers advised; and he was. There were paths of faith down which he could not go ('maintaining our witness against all war as inconsistent with the spirit and teaching of Christ'), but not for want of moral seriousness. In any final reckoning, it was true of Franks as it was of Wittgenstein: 'in a way that is centrally important but difficult to define, he had lived a devoutly religious life.'[13]

Of course, whatever the congruities, the six amateur Ambassadors were individuals with differing personal styles. Bryce, Lothian, and Ormsby Gore, for example, each had an appreciable public following in the United States, to which they gave considerable attention. 'Old man Bryce is all right', was the reputed verdict of one Nevada miner. It is highly unlikely that the miner's descendants felt moved to say anything of the sort about old man Franks, even if they knew of his existence—and the gossip in the Beaverbook press was that they did not.[14] Lothian, it was said, loved nothing better than speech-making and Southern fried chicken. Franks did not share either of these enthusiasms, and found it hard to pretend that he did. (He might have sympathized with John Pope-Hennessy's feeling that 'nothing makes one feel so unclean as simulating enthusiasm'.) For Franks the ambassadorship was something of a mystery tour, by turns magical and oppressive. 'We live very strangely but so far have had no opportunity or moment to reflect on it', Barbara wrote home, Franksian fashion. 'We have acquired a cheap American car: the theory being that we can go out in it and escape notice rather more easily than in the Rolls', Franks reported to his parents after a year in office. 'It was very pleasant,' he wrote of one ambassadorial visit, 'except that yesterday from 9.30 to 8.30 we were not alone for a moment but always talking to, or being talked to, by people.' And that was at Princeton.[15]

Franks was certainly keen to visit every state—the pins in the map on his office wall told of his progress—but he was not good at tickling pigs. On the other hand, by 1948 he was not to be accused of any of the besetting sins of British representatives in the United States: sheer ignorance, bland indifference, or 'our maddening *superbia Britannorum*', in Sir John Wheeler-Bennett's magnificent phrase.[16] And he did unbend further than Halifax. Wheeler-Bennett recalled an exquisite moment during the war when he and his colleague Aubrey Morgan were summoned to the Embassy in Washington from their office in the British Information Services in New York 'to explain America' to the newly installed Lord Halifax:

1. *The Franks and the Shewells c.1908* (Franks family)
Standing (L–R): Eleanor Shewell, Albert Shewell, Gertrude Shewell, Robert Franks, Thomas Shewell, Katharine Franks, Wilfred Shewell. Sitting (L–R): Bernard Shewell, Miriam Shewell, Caroline Shewell, Joseph Shewell (Rosalind Franks on his lap), Theodore Shewell, Helena Shewell. In pride of place: Oliver Shewell Franks, aged three.

2. *The offspring on holiday at Aberdovey, 1920* (Franks family)
L–R: Oliver Franks, Rosalind Franks, Mary Shewell, Martin Franks, Joanna Franks, John Shewell, Millicent Shewell, Edmund Shewell, Geoffrey Shewell, Michael Shewell, Constance Shewell.

3. *Beames House Rugby XV, Bristol Grammar School, 1922–3* (BGS)
Standing (L–R): R. Hogden, G. R. Fells, R. E. Hopper, R. D. G. Organ,
[?] Coomer, S. C. Wake, R. G. Gell.
Sitting (L–R): E. J. L. Rengert, G. Burkinshaw, O. S. Franks (Captain),
F. Beames Esq, M. J. M. Tapp, J. R. Rossiter, T. L. Robertson.
Akimbo (L–R): R. E. Moore, A. R. Pirie.

4. *Wedding day, 3 July 1931* (Franks family)
L–R: Margaret Thomas, Oliver, Barbara, Gilbert Ryle.

5. *En route to Paris, 1947*
(Times Picture Library)

6. *'New envoy to United States'* (Associated Press)
In the quad at Queen's, 1948.

7. *With Barbara, Oxford, 1962* (Times Picture Library)

8. *At home, in a favourite chair, 1983* (Times Picture Library)

We lunched *à quatre* with him and Charles Peake, his Personal Assistant, essentially a European, and developed [the] theory of a continent composed of regions. Aubrey, like many Welshmen, can speak with tongues of men and angels, his affection for America is as great as mine and his knowledge considerably greater. On this occasion he was in excellent voice, limpid and lapidary. Under his graceful yet vigorous prose the pageant and romance of America were unrolled before his audience. I, myself, was spellbound but I was even more fascinated by the look of utter bewilderment which gradually crept across the faces of his other two listeners. When Aubrey finally checked, perhaps a trifle breathless, there was a silence, then Lord Halifax remarked: 'Thank you, Mr Morgan. How very interesting.' Neither Aubrey nor I was ever asked to expound on any subject on any other occasion during Lord Halifax's embassage.[17]

It is hard to imagine Franks behaving in the same way. He listened, or he did not. He was strikingly free of that pernicious tendency to sieve people and information through the fine mesh of English snobberies about background, education, culture, and value, which so often redounded to the disadvantage of one's rich country cousins. For too many ambassadors of whatever stripe, the Americans merely 'confused civilization with plumbing'.[18] In this respect Franks proved as refreshing as his early publicity had promised. 'The world looks different viewed from Kansas City outwards', he remarked to a British audience, quoting by way of explanation from that great paean of praise to the New World, *Oklahoma*:

> I got to Kansas City on a Frid'y
> By Satidy I larned a thing or two
> For up to then I didn't have an idy
> Of what the modern world was comin' to
>   Ev'rythin's up to date in Kansas City
>   They've gone about as fur as they c'n go![19]

Such enlightenment on Franks's part had something to do with the aforementioned Aubrey Morgan, who succeeded Denny Marris as *amicus principis* throughout Franks's time as ambassador. The silver-tongued Morgan may have been beyond the pale for Lord Halifax, but he was just the man for Oliver Franks. Characteristically, it was Franks himself who saw the need and seized the opportunity of a walk round John Wheeler-Bennett's garden to overcome Morgan's initial reluctance, and persuaded him to return to Washington. His special remit was public relations broadly conceived: humanizing Franks for popular consumption, as the Ambassador's private secretary put it.[20] This was exactly as it should be, as both men must have appreciated. Seneca did the same for Nero. 'One role of the *amicus* was to advise the *Princeps* on his public behaviour and to intervene in his personal affairs where they touch politics; in their frank advice lay the only hope of sane government.'[21] In Franks's case this was something of a risky enterprise, but Aubrey Morgan was an absolute master of his craft. Wealthy and well connected, he knew America, he knew the press, he knew the form. He was also, as his friend Wheeler-Bennett said, 'a splendid person', an irreverent Welsh Liberal out of Charterhouse and Cambridge, with a deep contempt for pomposity of any kind. As an *amicus* he was well-nigh perfect—'utterly fearless, full of initiative and imagination, ruthless when necessary and having essentially "the power to mould the manifold of experience into new unities"'. His new *Princeps* came to like him and rely upon him in equal measure.[22]

Perhaps the nature of the job discloses something of the nature of the man. The ambassador's letter of appointment from His Majesty the King spoke of

giving and granting to him in that character all power and authority to do and perform all proper acts, matters and things which may be desirable or necessary for the promotion of relations of friendship, good understanding and harmonious intercourse between our realm and the United States of America . . .

Not for nothing were the two nations divided by a common language. The ceremonial English was translated by *Time* magazine to mean, 'Oliver, we're getting along all right with the Americans, but the situation is ticklish and might come unstuck. Go over there and keep a sharp eye on things, keep in touch with the right people, keep selling the good old Empire'—to which we can now add, in the authentic voice of Ernest Bevin, 'get this Atlantic Pact buttoned up', and mind our dollar lifeline!'[23]

By appointment, therefore, Franks had to be at the same time petitioner, interpreter, and conciliator. These roles were diverse, if not actually divergent. To reconcile them was not easy. The 'power and authority' vested in him by the King was impressive chiefly for proclamatory purposes. Brute reality was rather different. 'An ambassador is the lowest form of animal life', Franks's opposite number in London told the boys of Bristol Grammar School, with pardonable exaggeration.[24] Stripped of regal rhetoric, an ambassador is a go-between, not a principal. He may recommend, but he may not decide. He is both prism and heliograph, dependent in the first instance upon the receptiveness of others: those whom he represents, and those to whom he is accredited. Lacking power, he traffics in influence. Happily for Oliver Franks, it is the condition of the ambassador to follow the maxim accepted by Immanuel Kant: 'Be ye therefore wise as serpents, and harmless as doves.'[25]

Given what Franks once described as 'the special ambivalent emotional relationship' between Britain and America, what influence could a British ambassador hope to exert?[26] In the twentieth century two alternative models are available: house friend and functionary. The functionary is a prisoner of circumstance. He counts for no more than his country. He may be a familiar figure on Capitol Hill, he may dine occasionally with the Secretary of State, he may even play tennis with the President; but his personal clout is minimal. He is agreeable rather than influential. In the language of partnership and the queue, if a partner is sought for a certain enterprise, then so is the functionary.

If it is merely a question of maintaining first position in the queue—'chief mendicant', in Otto Clarke's biting phrase—then he must wait in line with the rest.[27] The typical functionary is safe, diplomatically speaking, but not creative. Most professionals fall into this category; many amateurs too.

The house friend plays for higher stakes, with a corresponding increase in diplomatic risk, *à la* Harold Nicolson.[28] He has ideas, and is liable to expound them compellingly. These ideas may not always correspond exactly to the ideas of HM Government. Indeed the former might well be couched as a critique of the latter. Characteristically, he is close to the Administration, and especially close to one particular figure in it—a powerful figure. Here lies the key to the house friend's influence. He has found 'a possible America'.[29] This is a great discovery, perhaps the greatest an ambassador can make; but it means that his sympathies are engaged. To *like* Americans is essential for a British ambassador in Washington. To like them too well, however, is to 'go native', in the practised idiom of empire. Morally, this is thought to be a dreadful sin. Professionally, it is a mortal one, for if the perception cannot be shaken, the unfortunate ambassador gains the confidence of those to whom he is accredited but forfeits the confidence of those whom he represents; an intolerable situation for all concerned. To avoid embarrassment to either party, therefore, friendly relations are often half-concealed from the official gaze of both London and Washington. They draw strength from the penumbra. Furthermore, these relations are most unlikely to be confined solely to bilateral Anglo-American issues. Constitutionally, the house friend ranges widely. That is part of his appeal.

Only amateurs make good house friends. Of the six already mentioned, all but Halifax may be considered from this perspective. Those who best fit the model are, anti-chronologically, Freeman, Ormsby Gore, and Franks. Freeman's possible American was Henry Kissinger, then the power-hungry National Security Adviser.[30] Ormsby Gore's was the President himself, John F. Kennedy, with whom he had been on first-name terms since their student days—making Ormsby Gore a special case. Harold Macmillan, who appointed him, explained slyly:

You see, the President had three lives: he had his smart life, dancing with people not in the political world at all, smart people, till four in the morning; then he had his highbrow life, which meant going to some great pundit (like Professor Ayer), and discussing his philosophy; and then he had his political life. And David belonged to all three . . . that was unusual in an Ambassador (well, what is diplomacy?) . . .[31]

Franks was the original, in more ways than one. There was a time when it was almost as natural to do business in London as in Washington. Pearl Harbor put paid to that. Once the United States was a full belligerent, there was no argument about the location of the Combined Chiefs of Staff and the multitudinous combined boards: Washington was axiomatic. Seldom has the passage of power been so concretely or swiftly defined. The more astute British representatives realized what was happening at the time. Sir Arthur Salter, a veteran of British shipping missions to the United States in two world wars, wrote in early 1942:

> It must be accepted that policy will be increasingly decided in Washington. To proceed as if it can be made in London and 'put over' in Washington, or as if British policy can in the main develop independently and be only 'co-ordinated' with American, is merely to kick against the pricks. Policy will thus be increasingly Washington-made policy. But it need not therefore be American. It may be Anglo-American.[32]

These were wise words, but the process of adjustment was slow. As Alistair Buchan pointed out, the American Ambassadors John Winant, Averell Harriman, and Lew Douglas were nearly as important links in the chain of diplomatic interchange as Lothian, Halifax, and Inverchapel, their counterparts in Washington during and immediately after the war. It was only with Oliver Franks, in 1948, that Washington became unambigiously 'the place where serious business must be transacted'.[33]

Franks's possible American was the consummate Dean Acheson. The quality and scope of the relationship between Franks and Acheson, as Ambassador and Secretary of State, is unparalleled in American history, and likely to remain so. If the first requirement for the influential ambassador is *access*—ready and early—then Acheson's proposal to Franks, to 'talk regularly, and in complete personal confidence, about any international problems we saw arising', may be read as a textbook demonstration of how it can be achieved. Their arrangement was unorthodox and open-ended, as Acheson underlined. 'I consult Oliver on problems that have nothing to do with Anglo-American relations,' he confided to the well-liked *Sunday Times* correspondent Henry Brandon, 'and if you write this, I'll cut your throat.'[34]

Acheson was once accused by the poisonous Senator Joseph McCarthy of being a 'stuffy, striped-pants, stuffed-shirt, pseudo-Englishman'. Much has been made of this last attribute. It carried the implication that Acheson could be swayed; that where Anglo-American relations were concerned he was more susceptible than possible; that in the McCarthyite demonology he too was guilty of appeasement, not only of the Reds, but also of the Brits. Nothing could be further from the truth. The Secretary of State did have an undeniable weakness for English (and Scottish) commodities, such as hand-bound books, moustache wax, crust-free cucumber sandwiches, and a superior malt; but to accuse him of pseudo-Englishness (or its evil twin Anglophilia) was to confuse style with substance, not at all an Achesonian thing to do. Whatever else he was, Dean Acheson was no push-over. Even in stylistic terms, the accusation neatly misses the point. 'Contrary to the myth, few Englishmen dress well, and when they do they look like tailors' dummies because they lack that suppressed spontaneity that struck one on meeting Mr Acheson'—

who looked, in fact, 'every inch an American', as Noel Annan observed.[35] A much more intelligent assessment—and some sense of the largeness of the man—was conveyed to the readers of the *Manchester Guardian* by Alistair Cooke:

Mr Dean Acheson, the new Secretary of State, is a 55-year-old, six-foot-two Velasquez grandee who has submitted, with a twinkling eye, to his present reincarnation in fine tweeds as a Connecticut Yankee, distinguished corporation laywer, and a Democratic statesmen with one of the most creative political minds of his time . . . His vivacity, his smiling irony, his sleek tailoring are readily admired by snobs and by homesick Europeans who like to have their diplomats look that way. They have probably cost him the tiresome attentions of people who never knew his enormous industry and the genuine democratic passion which explains his long forbearance with Congressmen who think as hounds do, by padding off in the direction of suspicious smells. Among senators who instinctively distrust the brilliant professional, he is the only intellectual they have learned to like and admire. He is in a way the pioneer of what must soon become a new type of American statesmen . . .[36]

Dean Acheson is one of the very few individuals on whom Franks dwelt publicly at any length. Franks's recollections fill out Cooke's sketch of the Velasquez grandee, and at the same time hold up a fascinating mirror to their author. As he dilates on this 'remarkable creature . . . the most remarkable man I have known intimately' it is impossible to suppress the thought that this is displaced autobiography. Just possibly, Franks on Acheson may be the most candid reflection on record of Franks on Franks.

Acheson, he thought, was not a complex character. Unlike, for example, Ernest Bevin and his bastardy or Winston Churchill and his melancholy, Dean Acheson had no incommunicable emotional depths.[37]

He combines an 18th-century style of personal taste with the moral conscience and austerity of a 17th-century puritan. I don't mean that he doesn't drink and enjoy good living, but his life is austere. His life at home in Georgetown is far from ostentatious, and life on the Sandy Springs farm [in Maryland] is downright austere. He takes pride in doing hard, pioneering things; his cabinet making and gardening. You never allow yourself to forget the New England roots out of which it is all done. He is profoundly American in this regard.

Two qualities are at war in Acheson. The historical sense which he shares with Truman, and the lawyer's skill at creating the case he must argue. His sheer lucidness could be overwhelming and could take him out of the context in which he was arguing.

Acheson is incapable of entertaining intellectual shoddiness with patience. He lacks the indispensable political gift (for a long-run political career) of believing that every argument has an equally legitimate intellectual background. That gift just wasn't given to Acheson. He could not tolerate entertaining trivial ideas or reasoning, however well meant, as worthy of respect. And when he chose to say what he was thinking, the words wounded and were neither forgotten nor forgiven. His unwillingness to show deference to every piece of nonsense a Senator or Congressman chose to utter was complete.

[Justice Oliver Wendell] Holmes is his intellectual mentor with his pragmatism and scepticism. At the same time, he is imbued with a sense of obligation to moral imperatives.

Acheson is quite a remarkable creature. One of the most remarkable types of his time.

'Being a gentleman', Franks reflected, 'is not a matter of who you are born, or of how much money or what class, but of the style in which you conduct your living. Of the kind of tastes and principles you live by. In this sense he [Acheson] had few comrades, really.'[38]

Unquestionably, Oliver Franks was one of the few.[39] But how efficacious was comradeship? 'Great democracies are not deflected from their national policies by personal friendships', Max Beloff has contended. 'Individuals might help to dissipate genuine ignorance or genuine misunderstanding—a Lothian, a Halifax might make relations easier . . . But the great issues were decided as a result of factors outside their control.'[40] A Franks, however, could do better than that. So long as he maintained the absolute confidence of Bevin and Attlee, he could, if he chose, intervene in British foreign policy making. The effectiveness of the intervention depended in large part on its timing. The best chance for 'deflecting' policy, in either capital, was to catch it in confusion. But effectiveness also depended on his standing with the Americans, possible and impossible alike. Credibility abroad enhanced credibility at home. Secondly and perhaps more importantly, he could become 'a participant in internal American deliberations', as Henry Kissinger has said. Paul Nitze had vivid memories of Franks in this sought-after role.

Oliver had a capacity for lucid exposition greater than anyone else I've ever worked with. We'd have a big meeting with people from the Pentagon, the generals, the defence people and so forth and so on and those of us from the State Department who were involved with the matter and he'd hear the debate between us and there'd be, you know, ten or fifteen different views expressed and then when the argument had settled down so he could see what all the parts, all the elements in the argument were all about, he would summarise the discussion in a way which was so much clearer than anything anybody else had said that we were all entranced with the lucidity of his analysis. And this included the generals and the defence people and everybody else so that we rather looked at Oliver as being the preceptor, the professor of the class. So that everybody valued Oliver. He was much more influential than . . . he wasn't representing his country; he was, in effect, doing that but he did it in a way in which he became a US leader. He really captured the US Government. It was beyond belief.[41]

Crystallization is the house friend's stock-in-trade. Conclusiveness was a speciality of Oliver Franks.

Such a role was in the strict sense a privilege, not to be taken for granted. Over the period 1949–52 Acheson spent more time with Franks than with all other ambassadors combined. No doubt this was mostly because Franks was useful to him. He was dispassionate; he met Acheson's demand for intellectual rigour. He acted as stimulant and sounding-board, adviser and confessor. 'His was a non-State Department view, a non-State Department approach to problems.' Theirs was a non-official relationship, and that was part of the bond between them. For all his professionalism, Acheson too was an amateur diplomatist.[42] Additionally, however, they saw a lot of each other because Franks made no attempt to insist upon it. Franks may have read Castlereagh's advice to the new British Minister in Washington in 1819: 'The first precept which I will recommend is to transact your business with the American government as far as possible by personal intercourse with the Secretary of State rather than by writing notes.'[43] If so, he did not take it too literally. By contrast, Acheson found that the French Ambassador (the egregious Henri Bonnet) 'always felt he had to see me'; he had the distinct impression that Bonnet wanted to be able to report to his masters in Paris that he had seen the Secretary of State, and thereby discharge himself of responsibility. The Secretary of State was not amused by these tactics. 'Oliver', on the other hand, 'was perfectly willing to see the person who was effective in it [whatever it was], and no prestige matters entered into it.' Thus Franks often dealt directly and unfussily with the relevant Assistant Secretary of State, or simply transacted business through Acheson's trusted Special Assistant Luke Battle. This method of working suited everyone, and Franks duly conquered a whole new echelon of State Department officials.[44]

In general he was appreciated for the qualities discussed in a *New York Times* profile by the perceptive but pseudonymous 'Academicus', who forecast correctly: 'Franks will study America and Americans seriously. He will answer questions clearly and without diplomatic platitudes. He will try to understand and explain misunderstandings. I think the American people will find him the most interesting, the least dull, Ambassador sent by Britain within living memory.'[45] By temperament and training Franks was averse to platitudes. He once informed the Secretary of State that 'when his people [British officials] feel they do not have something sensible to say, they don't say anything; our people [American officials] tend to have something to say, and say it. This causes a degree of irritation in the UK.' On the other hand, he firmly believed that 'what is left to be understood is misunderstood', and consequently took great pains to encourage candour. 'The condition of finding agreement in Anglo-American relations', he said, 'is that the tacit assumptions are made explicit, the different perspectives recognized.'[46] Franks himself was habitually explicit. Within the family circle of the State Department he was remarkably free, however much he may have felt unfree in the magnificent confines of Sir Edwin Lutyens's Embassy. In April 1951, for example, he called on Acheson after a brief trip home, to explain 'the general temper of London' to the Secretary of State. To set the scene, he said that it had been a terrible winter, the wettest winter in eighty years; there had been the bad flu epidemic; the Government had been under unceasing fire and had had to cope with crises about once a week, which they had barely pulled through; everyone was tired; the Foreign Office had been practically leaderless, with the Prime Minister, Mr Bevin [who was fatally ill], Mr Younger [the Minister of State], Mr Strang [the Permanent Under-Secretary], all contributing a little, with Dixon and Makins [the Deputy Under-Secretaries] contributing most of the leadership.

After an extensive discussion of matters to do with the Far East, Acheson asked him whether there were any 'procedures' that were bothering him. Franks indicated that the problem was one of inertia and exhaustion in London, and lack of leadership, rather than any specific complaint. 'He thought we [the United States] definitely had to take the leadership in this period.' Acheson asked him specifically whether the Attlee Government was being 'blackmailed' by the left wing. Franks 'doubted whether that was the case'. He then turned to Europe:

he said that he found the Foreign Office adhering to rather partial and wholly inadequate conclusions, such as the idea that a revitalized Germany offered no solution, but great danger [which was one part of London's difficulty with the Schuman Plan]. They had no idea what they wanted to do. He had explained both to the Prime Minister and Morrison [Bevin's successor] that thinking along this line was Morrison's major job for the next three months. He said that continually the visceral feeling became articulate. The rearming of the Germans was a very painful subject and there was a general desire to escape from this problem in ways which those who followed it knew were inadequate. He said that this was not a policy, or intellectual reaction, but was just a deep-seated feeling.

One imagines Acheson nodding, sympathetically, throughout this analysis. 'As a result of the talk,' he said, 'he had been reassured that there was no fundamental rift or misunderstanding between Washington and London.' In his opinion, 'what should be done, beginning tomorrow, is to have a series of specific talks about specific points, looking to the State Department's coming out with clear proposals, which Sir Oliver could then get behind and put across to London'. Sir Oliver cordially agreed.[47]

This was just the sort of exchange which Acheson valued so much. Franks's analysis was notably unrestrained; but that was quite normal. Acheson responded in kind. Franks was usually prepared to do a little judicious freelancing. 'Putting himself in Attlee's place,' he would say, 'he thought . . .'. Or, 'he was without instructions from London, and his observations were purely personal . . .'. The crucial redrafting of article 5 of the North Atlantic Treaty was done on precisely that basis.[48] Such an informal *modus operandi* demanded candour, but also confidentiality. Rather like the treaty negotiations themselves, these talks were 'off the record', that is, off the *official* record. A commitment to explicitness meant being explicit about what, if anything, was officially repeatable. Acheson and his associates spoke freely to Franks because they found that he was trustworthy. 'He could respect confidences without reporting them', as Freeman Matthews put it. In diplomacy, as in other walks of life, 'a man is ultimately judged, not by his brilliance, but by his rectitude'.[49]

Franks was good at 'not reporting'. Unofficially, however, the substance of these talks was usually made known to those who needed to know, on both sides of the Atlantic. They were in fact the hard currency of the special relationship. Franks reflected later on his own experience: 'The special relationship was not a mystique of the shared inheritance of the English-speaking peoples. It arose out of common aims and mutual need of each other; it was rooted in strong habits of working together on which there were supervened the sentiments of mutual trust.'[50] Franks had no time for the game played endlessly by so many of his countrymen—the game of Greeks and Romans. The rules of the game were codified by that modern master of anachronism, Harold Macmillan, who never tired of playing it. During the latter part of the war Macmillan was Minister Resident in the Mediterranean, billeted on Eisenhower's roving Allied Force Headquarters (AFHQ). In 1943 the young Richard Crossman was sent out to join him. By way of induction, Macmillan told him this:

We, my dear Crossman, are Greeks in this American empire. You will find the Americans much as the Greeks found the Romans—great big, vulgar, bustling people, more vigorous than we are and also more idle, with more unspoiled virtues but also more corrupt. We must run AFHQ as the Greek slaves ran the operations of the Emperor Claudius.

In another variant from the same period: 'These Americans represent the new Roman Empire and we Britons, like the Greeks of old, must teach them how to make it go.' And in the fraught circumstances of 1956–7: 'We are the Greeks of the Hellenistic age: the power has passed from us to Rome's equivalent, the United States of America, and we can at most aspire to civilise and occasionally to influence them.'[51]

If ever there was a Greek, it was surely Oliver Franks. No better proving-ground for the games of empire suggests itself than the Middle East. What is known to the West as the Iranian oil crisis of 1950–1 was triggered by the Iranian threat to nationalize the Anglo-Iranian Oil Company (AIOC), popularly known as 'Anglo-Persian', the forerunner of British Petroleum (BP). Half a century earlier Lord Curzon had written prophetically that, once British rule in India was ended, 'your ports and your coaling stations, your fortresses and dockyards, your Crown Colonies and protectorates will go too. For either they will be unnecessary, as the toll-gates and barbicans of an Empire that has vanished, or they will be taken by an enemy more powerful than yourselves.'[52] Anglo-Persian was a toll-gate of Empire. For the British, the Iranian oil concession was economically vital (as a source of foreign exchange as well as oil), though not indispensable, as Roger Louis has noted. For the Americans, locked in the Cold War, Iran itself was a strategic asset. The Iranians for their part wanted the maximum benefit from their own bounty. The issue had all the makings of a test case. Helpfully or unhelpfully, depending on one's point of view, there were a number of American precedents. In Mexico the oil concession has been expropriated in 1938, with small compensation. In Venezuela a fifty-fifty profit-sharing arrangement had been in compulsory and successful operation since 1943. Momentously, in Saudi Arabia a similar arrangement had been negotiated by the mighty Arabian-American Oil Company (ARAMCO) as recently as December 1950.[53] Which self-respecting Arab nationalist would now settle for less?

In April 1951, at a relatively late stage in the protracted crisis, a series of Anglo-American talks were held in Washington in an effort to find a common platform and a decent way out. Franks, whose involvement thus far had been only peripheral, led for the British. The American side was led by George McGhee, the Assistant Secretary of State for the Near East, South Asia, and Africa, a domain he called the Middle World. To all outward appearances, the dauntless McGhee was perfect for the part of the new Roman. Just 39, oil-savvy and oil-rich himself, the Assistant Secretary's impregnable self-assurance and sharp tongue were enough to give British officials convulsions. In the privacy of their correspondence they called him, scathingly, 'that infant prodigy'.[54] A later generation might have had recourse to 'Indiana Jones'. Like the film hero, however, there was more to George McGhee, D.Phil., than met the eye. A former Rhodes Scholar, he had spent three years as a graduate student at Queen's College, Oxford, completing his doctorate in 1937. After Dallas, Texas, the Southern Methodist University, and the University of Oklahoma, this Oxford experience had a profound effect on him, as it did on the many Rhodes Scholars propelled into Government service during the Democratic cycles of the 1940s and 1960s—Philip Kaiser and Dean Rusk, to name but two. In McGhee's case, one aspect in particular left its mark. At Queen's, as at most Oxford colleges, each student has a 'moral tutor' whom he would see regularly, if infrequently, and to whom he could go in case of need, moral or otherwise. McGhee was allocated to an energetic philosophy don hardly older than himself, and yet, as it seemed, infinitely knowledgeable and infinitely wise. This paragon was Father Franks.[55]

So the stage was set for a classical confrontation. Who better to tame the new barbarian? Was this not the very essence of Greeks and Romans: confronting one's moral tutor—a philosopher, no less—across the negotiating table? Alas, it was not to be. The game of Greeks and Romans is the purest escapism. Macmillan's persistently seductive analogy was, and is, an illusion. Historically, it makes no sense. As Robin Edmonds reminds us—one Greats man reproving another—'not only did they speak different languages. The Romans acquired their eastern provinces by defeating the Greeks in war; and they went on to pillage the immense riches of the Greek world on a vast scale.'[56] Moreover, the analogy is inescapably patronizing. It assumes that the Greeks (that is, the British) know best. No sooner is the assumption made explicit, Franksian fashion, than the fallacy is exposed. The central point about the re-encounter between Franks and McGhee over Anglo-Persian was that, of the two, it was McGhee who knew better. In reality McGhee matched none of the stereotypes for which he was so eagerly fitted in London: he was not anti-British, he was not a simple-minded anti-colonialist, and he was not (as Sir William Strang charged) an 'appeaser' of Iran.[57] He was merely the expert. Perhaps the Americans could be Greeks to their own Romans after all.[58]

The re-encounter demonstrated something else, equally chastening for the British. By April 1951, after many months of havering by Anglo-Persian—characterized as 'confused, hidebound, small-minded and blind' by their Labour Adviser, Sir Frederick Leggett—there was no decent way out.[59] After the Anglo-American talks were over Franks held a post-mortem with Acheson and his senior colleagues:

Sir Oliver said he thought none of us have the answer to the Middle Eastern problem. The break-up of the Turkish empire left a power vacuum. This happened so recently in history that *the Kipling type of technique was not then appropriate*. The influence of the universities has offset the economic benefits which have been brought to the area. The US talks about more and more money which just disappears in the sand. No one has found out how one exercises the necessary degree of control in the power vacuum which exists. The universities are the acid in the situation. These chaps now have ideas. The same problem exists in Cairo.[60]

Anglo-Persian was formally nationalized the following month. The crisis rumbled on. Tempers were frayed. Sabres were rattled. But no precipitate action was taken in 1951 (unlike in 1956, over the nationalization of the Suez Canal—Franks's remark about Cairo was a prescient one). Such restraint testified to no special solicitude for the Iranians. Indeed, in one sense Iran was not the issue at all. The Cabinet minutes are categoric: 'It was . . . the general view of the Cabinet that, in the light of the United States attitude, . . . force could not be used to hold the refinery and maintain the British employees of the Anglo-Iranian Oil Company in Abadan. *We could not afford to break with the United States on an issue of this kind.*'[61] If that is appeasement, it is not automatically to be condemned.

Franks concurred, but took no active part, in the decision on Iran. In an earlier case of breaking or not breaking with the United States, however, a case which had far greater salience for the Americans themselves, his intervention was decisive. This was Korea. Setting aside the tangled question of causation, the Korean War broke out on 25 June 1950, when South Korea was invaded by the North. Taken by surprise, and suspecting the red hand of

Stalin, the United States decided immediately to 'let the world know that we mean business', as Truman said, and deploy naval and air forces in support of the beleaguered South Koreans. A few days later, the harder decision was taken to commit ground forces to the Korean peninsula in order to expel the invaders. Like the crisis over the Iraqi invasion of Kuwait in 1990, all of this was done under the umbrella of the UN Security Council. On 7 July 1950 a United Nations Command (UNC) was established under General Douglas MacArthur, the living totem of American invincibility in the Far East. Insofar as he took orders at all, MacArthur took his orders from the President and the Joint Chiefs of Staff in Washington. From the outset the UNC was more fig-leaf than umbrella.

Equally surprised, and equally suspicious, London at once released naval forces from Hong Kong to assist the Americans. The Foreign Office informed Franks that 'there would not be a more useful demonstration of the United Kingdom's capacity to act as a world power with the support of the Commonwealth, and of its quickness to move when action rather than words are necessary'—both dubious assertions. With this Britannic gesture went the tenuous hope that Washington would not reduce Marshall aid to Britain because of 'certain preconceived and ill-founded notions about European integration'.[62] The Attlee Government did not hesitate to back the United States in the Security Council and at sea; but they did hesitate to go any further. On 6 July Attlee himself wrote to Truman proposing immediate, secret, high-level staff talks in Washington on both the political and the military implications of the crisis. 'No one can attempt to provide precisely for every eventuality. But I hope you will agree with me that we should look ahead as far as we can and reach some agreement as to our common policy in these areas in the event of further outbreaks.' From the British point of view the talks would be useful, certainly, but they would also be *special*. 'Other governments, in particular the French, may be concerned, but it will suffice if they are informed as and when the situation demands.' Gratifyingly, Truman readily agreed.[63] The same day, the Defence Committee of the Cabinet decided that 'no land or air forces should be made available for operations in Korea'. The decision was reached without much difficulty. British defence capabilities were already overstretched in Western Europe, Hong Kong, Singapore, and Malaya (where they had to cope with a large-scale Communist insurgency). The Chiefs of Staff swung the full weight of their professional opinion against even a token contribution of British land forces, declaring that, 'whilst they recognize and fully sympathize with the political arguments for this, they are technically opposed to it on military grounds'. The Prime Minister argued that the situation in Korea should not blind the West to dangers nearer home. The Minister of Defence (Emanuel Shinwell) welcomed evidence that 'the Korean affair was not distracting American attention from the vital European theatre'.[64]

As a dry calculation of the national interest, this stance had much to recommend it. As an imaginative response to the emergency at hand, it was soon found wanting. The world did indeed look different from Kansas City outwards. From there, and from Washington too, it looked extremely bleak. In the early phase of the war the North Koreans proved unstoppable. Throughout July they swept down the peninsula carrying all before them—now including three American divisions. 'What happens', Sir John Slessor dared to ask, very quietly, in London on 14 July, 'if the Americans have a disaster in Korea and have to stage a Dunkirk'?[65]

It was natural for Slessor, as Chief of the Air Staff, to advocate a cross between strategic bombing and air policing as the solution for the UNC in Korea. His military colleagues were enamoured of these ideas, but the Foreign Office was not. 'I do not presume to discuss the merits of strategic bombing,' wrote Sir Pierson Dixon coolly,

but I am inclined to think that at this moment it might have a bad effect on our relations with the Americans if we broached with them a plan based on the assumption that they would be driven out of Korea. We do not want to seem defeatist, nor to interfere with MacArthur; nor of course would we like it if the Americans thought we were seeking an excuse not to make a contribution on the ground.[66]

The last point in particular was a shrewd one. It had been anticipated by Oliver Franks, who took the highly unusual step of writing personally to the Prime Minister on 15 July. 'Now that it is evident that the ground operations in Korea will be difficult and prolonged,' he cautioned, 'the importance of the token ground forces comes to the front.'

For some ten days now there has been a steady increase in interest, questioning and criticism in Washington on this subject. It spreads through all branches of the government and press. In the last two days it has spread outside Washington and has reached editorial columns in out of town newspapers. On this I wish to make one comment. Too often in the past we have taken our time to make a decision with the result that often, when we have done what was in line with American ideas, we have got no credit or approval for it; the decision has followed upon and seemed to be extracted from us by the massive discussion, criticism and pressure that has been built up in the US . . .[67]

It was a constant theme of Franks's advice to London that 'the initial British reaction to any major question is the most important from the American point of view'. If the initial reaction seemed negative, 'then we are "against it" no matter what happens afterwards. The reverse applies.'[68] His advice to Attlee echoed Horace: 'Dare to be wise! Begin now.' Franks disclaimed any attempt to suggest what the outcome should be ('that lies outside my province'), but his letter was magisterial enough. As a philosopher he had been concerned with the problem of choice. Over Korea a choice had to be made about a token. It was a token of low military value, comparatively speaking, but high international esteem. In effect it represented the British stake in the global poker game that was the deep Cold War. Franks was in no doubt that Britain could and should be playing at the table. As he put it a few weeks later, reflecting on this conjuncture: 'We no longer had to rest content with the knowledge that we were a great power. We could behave like one.'[69] To Attlee he wrote again of partnership and the queue. In one frequently quoted passage:

Three or even two years ago . . . we were one of the queue of European countries. Now with new strength and vitality in our associations with the Commonwealth, a reviving, more flexible and much stronger domestic economy, and great improvement in our overseas payments, we are effectively out of the queue, one of two world powers outside Russia.[70]

This token, then, was also a token of friendship. As Franks emphasized to the Prime Minister, 'the Americans will to some exent—I know this to be true of the Defense Department—test the quality of the partnership by our attitude to the notion of a token ground force'. The old question had been posed anew: could the British deliver?

'There is only one argument for doing something,' said F. M. Cornford; 'the rest are arguments for doing nothing. The argument for doing something is that it is the right thing to do.'[71] Franks might have differed. He certainly thought that 'resistance to aggression in Korea' was right. He also thought that for the British to 'stand with [the Americans] on the ground' was necessary.[72] But in this there was a strong element of expediency, reflected in his tactics of intervention. Franks's misgivings about the vigour of the British response to the Korean War coincided almost exactly with his misgivings about the vigour of the British response to the Schuman Plan. In both instances he felt strongly that the penalty for being niggardly far exceeded the risk of being venturesome. On the Schuman Plan, as we have seen, he registered his misgivings with Sir Roger Makins, the Deputy Under-Secretary immediately concerned. On the Korean War he petitioned the Prime Minister.[73]

In fact he did more. He dispatched the Economic Minister in the Embassy (Sir Leslie Rowan) to London with instructions to impress upon Whitehall that 'we had a good chance to be treated as partners if we did our stuff', and in particular '*now was our chance to earn a lot of dollars*'—the highest expedient of all.[74] Meanwhile the staff talks requested by Attlee opened in Washington. Following his suggestion, they were of a 'politico-military' character, and ranged all over the globe. Oliver Franks and the chairman of the British Joint Services Mission in Washington (Marshal of the RAF Lord Tedder) led for the British; Philip Jessup, Ambassador at Large and confidant of Dean Acheson, and the chairman of the Joint Chiefs of Staff (General Omar Bradley) for the Americans. On the very first day Bradley made a carefully calculated pitch for reinforcements from other UN countries, 'even though they might not be able to arrive in Korea for some time. But an early public announcement of the intention to send such reinforcements would be of immense political value.' The message was clear, and Franks studiously underlined it in his report to the Foreign Office.[75]

Franks was now asked for a formal expression of his views. He retired to his bath to think, and on 23 July produced a memorable answer. It took the form of a long, forceful, and one might almost say impassioned telegram, arguing an American reliance on their partnership with Britain: a paradoxical case of the stronger power relying on the weaker.[76] Forty years later Franks remembered:

I felt a weight of responsibility because I knew that what I was dealing with was other men's lives, but I decided in the end I'd got to put that from me, and say what I thought, and I think I said two things really. The first one was that the Americans regarded us as their dependable ally. They would not understand it if we did not stand with them on the ground in Korea and I thought that the damage would be deep and long-lasting. Secondly, I said something quite different. That there's something in the psychological make-up of the American nation which makes them like to have company when they're in trouble, and from this point of view they wanted, under the United Nations' flag, allies to help them and they turned to Britain as the key. If we helped, others would also. And this went back and the Cabinet decided to send the Gloucesters. That's how it happened.[77]

The argument was as conclusive as Franks suggested. Attlee put it to his colleagues that they could not expect to maintain a special relationship with the Americans purely on the strength of disinterested advice. Greek wisdom, superior or otherwise, was not enough. Even the ancients had to get their hands dirty. At the next meeting of the Defence Committee the Chiefs of Staff announced that they had reconsidered the question, and 'although in their view it was still militarily unsound', they were now prepared to send a brigade group of British troops to fight alongside their muscular American cousins. Nothing less would do. The committee found in favour of this recommendation. The following day, 25 July 1950, on Attlee's prompting and Franks's argument, the full Cabinet endorsed the decision as 'a valuable contribution to Anglo-American solidarity'. One month after the outbreak of war, a token force was on its way.[78]

Franks was very convincing in 1950. The need for a close Anglo-American relationship was clear. It was the world's best hope for peace, as he once said, and Britain's best hope for prosperity and power—power by proxy. The winds were favourable then—America, after all, is proverbially where the weather comes from—but the Slough of Despond in British political and official circles about the deployment of ground troops in Korea was a deep one. There was a real possibility that London, like Neighbour Pliable, would turn back. When the time for hesitation was over, Oliver Franks guided them firmly across. *The Pilgrim's Progress* affirms that 'the Gate will be opened to broken-hearted sinners'. After the Cabinet meeting on 25 July 1950 the corridors of Whitehall were teeming with broken-hearted sinners. There is no clearer demonstration of ambassadorial influence than the commitment, albeit the token commitment, to war.

Franks's vision of Anglo-American relations was a working partnership of unequals. That was the limit of his aspiration for the special relationship—an expression forbidden to him, as it was to Acheson, who famously suppressed a State Department paper which attempted rashly to define it.[79] Given Britain's persistent economic dependency, this was still an optimistic vision. Some would call it an illusion. Franks continually emphasized the debilitating effect of 'the giver–receiver relationship' on both sides, not least because, 'as all recent American observers have reported, Britain is the only Western European country which dislikes having to receive aid'.[80] He accepted inequality. Yet he proclaimed partnership often enough to raise false hopes. Perhaps the wish was father to the thought: in Franks's case, most uncharacteristic behaviour.[81] The generalized power of the wish, however, cannot be doubted. Partnership—equal partnership—was the vision which animated British policy-makers for a generation. Many could not accept what Franks accepted. No sooner had the decision for ground troops been taken than the Foreign Office instructed:

We are anxious, during the period which is now beginning, to get away from the conceptions of aid and the procedures which have been developed under ERP. These have always made for an uneasy relationship between the UK and the USA and we are anxious to substitute for it the Atlantic Pact relationship where we can sit at the table on a basis of equality.

Some months later, after a celebrated series of talks with Truman, Attlee borrowed Franksian language to report to Bevin, 'throughout these talks the UK was lifted out of the "European queue" and were treated as partners unequal no doubt in power but still equal in counsel'. What a world of meaning is compressed in those two small words, 'no doubt'.[82]

Curiously, Franks has remained convincing. The case he made for Anglo-American solidarity in 1950 rested on a combination of passive and active measures to be adopted by the British in their dealings with the Americans. First of all, they should be dependable. If there is a touchstone of British foreign policy in the post-war period, this is it. Secondly, they should be companionable. America's peculiar psychological need for international 'company' was a theme to which Franks returned several times during his ambassadorship.[83] It is interesting to find that an idea which might easily have been dismissed as sentimental is now incorporated in the literature of the special relationship. As two distinguished American scholars have written: 'It is not the old saw about Britain playing Greece to America's Rome: rather, it is a sense of company in a confusing, unfriendly, world.'[84] If dependability and companionability were both essentially passive, Franks hinted at a more active role *vis-à-vis* other countries. 'If we helped, others would also.' The British would set an example. More than that, they would actively encourage the others to help the United States (and incidentally themselves). Britain would be the mobilizer, the whipper-in, the prefect.[85]

It is but a short step from executant to abasement, or, in the slightly hysterical words of *The Economist*, 'being driven into a corner by a complex of American actions and insistencies, which, in combination, are quite intolerable'.[86] Some self-protection therefore seemed advisable. There was another active measure, not mentioned by Franks, which purported to meet the need. Britain would mobilize; but she would also moderate. This already involved a certain concession. 'If we cannot entirely change American policy,' wrote Pierson Dixon, 'then we must, it seems to me, resign ourselves to a role of counsellor and moderator.' How it grated.

We have already had considerable effect in this role. But we should accept the disagreeable conclusion, in the end, that we must allow the United States to take the lead and follow or at least not break with them. It is difficult for us, after centuries of leading others, to resign ourselves to the position of allowing another and greater power to lead us.[87]

The advantage of being implicated in American actions would be the privileged opportunity to exercise some restraint—a quasi-Greek function. That most unlikely Greek, Ernest Bevin, told the Indian Prime Minister that 'the United States is a young country and the Administration was too apt to take unreflecting plunges. We had made it our business to try to restrain them.' In other words, the Mad Haberdasher in the White House would not be permitted to run amok.[88]

But that is exactly what he proceeded to do—or so it appeared. After an interlude of spectacular successes, the war in Korea had turned sour once more. MacArthur's advance northwards to the Yalu River led him straight into what Robert O'Neill has described as the largest ambush in history: over 300,000 Chinese troops. The advance became a withdrawal, the withdrawal a headlong flight. All thoughts of 'Home by Christmas' were forgotten. This was indeed an entirely new war, with a vengeance: 'the wrong war, at the wrong place, at the wrong time and with the wrong enemy', as Omar Bradley described it in the following year. At a press conference on 30 November 1950, the President told reporters that he would take 'whatever steps are necessary' to deal with the situation, and gave the impression that the use of nuclear weapons had 'always been [under] active consideration'. In any such eventuality, he added, the person 'in charge' would be the military commander in the field—presumably the megalomaniac MacArthur. Despite a swift 'clarification' from the White House, these ill-judged remarks caused consternation everywhere, not least within the American Administration.[89] In London there was uproar. For over three months Attlee had wanted a 'parley at the summit', in Churchill's phrase, but had been determinedly put off by Franks and Acheson.[90] Now he could be put off no longer. On 3 December, after an emergency Cabinet meeting and rapid consultations with the French (who came to London at their own suggestion), the Australians, the Canadians, and the Indians, Little Clem flew to Washington, the eyes of the world upon him, to prise the Mad Haberdasher's finger from the nuclear trigger. Never again would the British Prime Minister cross the Atlantic with the transparent purpose of restraining the President of the United States from the escalation of a major war. Never again would anyone expect that he could. The Truman–Attlee talks of December 1950 were the last, vestigial, public appearance of the 'Big Two'.

The talks took five days and covered many subjects. In spite of the sensational prelude and the heightened expectations—and unlike many 'summits'—the talks were actually an intensive working conference.[91] In this they contrasted sharply with the Truman–Churchill talks which followed in January 1952, when almost no work was done other than the arduous business of socializing without adequate supplies of alcohol (as Churchill was wont to complain, *sotto voce*).[92] Truman and Attlee were naturally much concerned with the fortunes of war in Korea, and with the cardinal issue of China policy, but the talks also dealt with European defence matters and a thicket of economic questions concerning the pricing and allocation of scarce raw materials. Not surprisingly, the principals were edgy at first. Helped by the soothing ministrations of Father Franks, however, the atmosphere progressively relaxed, especially after a dinner at the British Embassy on the third night. The Prime Minister and President had met before, in 1945, but Franks made a point of reintroducing Major Attlee to Captain Truman, and the shared memories of an earlier and more terrible war may have done something to ease the passage between those two proud old soldiers. Captain Truman hammered out some Great War standards on the much-abused Embassy piano. Major Attlee sang along with tuneless gusto. For a brief moment all was well with the world.[93]

Attlee, meanwhile, bided his time. On the fourth day, after the singing, he struck. In the course of a rather ramshackle plenary meeting, the two leaders had a brief *tête-à-tête*. When the session resumed the President announced cheerfully that they had been discussing the atomic bomb. He had told the Prime Minister 'that the governments of the United Kingdom and the United States had always been partners in this matter and that he would not consider the use of the bomb without consulting with the United Kingdom'. This was music to British ears. Attlee enquired shrewdly whether their agreement should be put in writing. Truman made a response typical of the man and the relationship: 'if a man's word wasn't any good it wasn't made any better by writing it down.'[94]

With this informal exchange the British had to rest content. Acheson promptly remonstrated with his chief for going so far. The President's words were deleted from the American record of the talks, though they stayed in the British version. London maintained that an undertaking had been given—a partnership undertaking. Washington was adamant that whatever had passed between Truman and Attlee in private was an irrelevance. What mattered was the official communiqué, sanctioned by all. The final work on the communiqué was done by a small cabal in the President's office: Truman, Attlee, Franks, and Acheson. 'We began drafting a suitable paragraph,' as Acheson remembered it, 'Oliver Franks acting as scribe. The President pulled out the slide at the left of his desk. Oliver left his chair and knelt between mine and Attlee's to write on it. "I think that this is the first time," said the President, "that a British Ambassador has knelt before an American President."'[95] On the bomb, the solution offered by Franks was mute:

The President stated that it was his hope that world conditions would never call for the use of the atomic bomb. The President told the Prime Minister that it was also his desire to keep the Prime Minister at all times informed of developments which might bring about a change in the situation.

This wording was inserted without comment in the lengthy Joint Communiqué.[96] Its innocent appearance masks the extreme delicacy of atomic consultation, even among friends. Behind the scenes, reports of Truman's largess rocked the American delegation, among whom there was dark muttering about being 'raped' by the British. 'I don't [know] which is worse,' scrawled a White House *apparatchik*, 'to have it in the communiqué, or to have Attlee tell the Commons about it, and make everybody think that Truman and Attlee made secret deals at which Truman lost his shirt. It will be like Yalta—a pretty and sweet communiqué, and then all the sordid details coming to light later.'[97]

To general relief, these forebodings were never realized. Once the talks were concluded the Prime Minister gave no hint of dissatisfaction with the assurances he had received. Neither did he attempt to exploit the ambiguities of his dealings with the President.[98] Simply by meeting, Attlee had achieved some purpose. His mercy dash had been therapeutic, if not cathartic, for both sides. They had reached the point at which mutual self-explanation was mutually beneficial. The reckless use of the atomic bomb was, in truth, a non-issue, as Franks always assumed and Attlee quickly discovered. Truman was unusually forthright; like Attlee himself, he took great pride in his dispatch ('polishing off', as Attlee called it); but he was no Mad Haberdasher. On the contrary, he was eminently cautious and responsible. Nevertheless what he said at his notorious press conference was broadly true. The possible use of the bomb *was* under consideration, and had been ever since the outbreak of the war. We now know that it was not considered favourably. There is no doubt that it was considered seriously.[99] Attlee's appearance in Washington, the need to articulate, the whole tenor of the discussion: all worked to sensitize the

Americans to the British point of view, and to reinforce a natural caution. To this intangible extent the talks were a success.[100]

Attlee may therefore have come to the view that carping was not cricket (a game of which he was inordinately fond). He must also have appreciated that it was not practical. In his statement to the House of Commons he argued with a beguiling mixture of casuistry and candour that it was not even prudent. 'I should like to pay tribute to the really admirable work which is being done by our representatives in Washington,' he said, 'both by Lord Tedder on the military side and by . . . Sir Oliver Franks on the political side.'

Many of their contacts are, of course, informal. They depend for their success very largely on the friendly relations these men and their colleagues can establish with their American opposite numbers. I have high hopes that these valuable interchanges will continue, and indeed, that the relationships they have fostered will grow ever closer; but it would, to my mind, be a mistake to try to formalise these arrangements. Anything more formal might very well be misunderstood, and it would, I think, destroy some of the essential features on which their present success depends. . . . Direct discussion across the table will always do more to clear up misunderstandings than the exchange of formal communications. The close working relationships which grow up in this way will do far more to harmonise our policy and actions than any written agreements about consultation.[101]

Whatever the Prime Minister might tell the Commons, the fact remained that there was still no satisfactory arrangement for Anglo-American consultation about the bomb. The Truman–Attlee talks had yielded nebulous expressions of hope and well-meaning declarations of intent, but no commitment. *L'appétit vient en mangeant.*

London sought prior consultation with Washington not only on the use (or threatened use) of atomic weapons world-wide—in Korea, for instance—but also on the use to be made of US bases in the United Kingdom. British interest was unpalatably plain: no annihilation without representation. Once upon a time, they recalled, there had been a marvellous collaborative enterprise. British science and British scientists had fertilized the wartime Manhattan Project to build a bomb before the Germans did so. At Quebec in 1943 Churchill and Roosevelt had signed an agreement not to use it against third parties without each other's consent (ostensibly, an absolute veto), and at Hyde Park, New York, in 1944 an *aide-mémoire* on full collaboration for both military and commercial purposes after the war. But the fairy-tale promise of these agreements never materialized. The perfunctory way in which British consent was sought for the dropping of the bomb in 1945 bespoke the letter rather than the spirit of the Quebec Agreement. The Washington conference of November 1945, the first post-war meeting between Truman and Attlee, did not augur well. Barely a year after the end of the war Congress passed the infamous McMahon Act which formally severed the main arteries of atomic information exchange, the vital source for any genuine consultation. Numb with shock, London lurched on alone.

Out of this packed history grew two fundamental beliefs, deeply at odds with each other. To the British, atomic consultation was a right, to be reclaimed as a matter of natural justice and shared risk. Under the draconian regime of the McMahon Act, Washington was practising nothing less than atomic extortion. Compensation was deserved and overdue, just as it was in the matter of economic recovery. To the Americans, on the other hand, atomic consultation was a privilege, to be granted or withheld according to the dictates of Washington politics and national security. After Hiroshima, the constitutional authority of the President and Commander-in-Chief with regard to the absolute weapon was not to be compromised by written agreements with allies, however special the relationship. In 1948 the Anglo-American *Modus Vivendi* summarily removed the requirement for consent, made no offer to consult, and restored only limited technical atomic information in return: a very weak position from which to extract any fresh concessions.

For difficult extraction work in Washington the obvious candidate was Ambassador Franks. The Truman–Attlee talks had greatly enhanced Franks's already high standing. His crystalline summaries of the rambling debate in the plenary sessions captivated everyone.[102] Bevin's absence through illness meant that he carried an especially heavy load. With Acheson, he ran a kind of shadow conference of officials and advisers, meeting in the interstices of the main event, and helping to make it go.[103] Most fundamentally, the talks served to bring his interpretative function into perfect focus. The Americans were cast as trigger-happy and the British as complaisant. These were powerful images ('the risk of war v. the risk of appeasement', as Joseph Alsop put it), difficult to break. Since Franks's motives were above suspicion—in a significant phrase, Truman wrote of his 'friendly approach to the questions before us'—his interventions were reassuring to all.[104]

Franks had tried at intervals throughout his ambassadorship to address the question of atomic consultation, without much success. Now he redoubled his efforts, but met only procrastination—largely from the Defense Department—until September 1951.[105] In that month, with election fever mounting in London, a new round of politico-military talks began in Washington at the earnest entreaty of the British. What was the Prime Minister to say if questioned on the subject of atomic consultation during the campaign? What was he to tell the incoming Churchill if Labour should lose? Franks and Air Marshal Sir William Elliot (successor to Tedder) sat down with Freeman Matthews, Paul Nitze, and Omar Bradley. An exhaustive discussion conducted with remarkable candour revealed that, though the Americans were prepared to meet the British position with regard to US bases in the UK, they were not prepared to make any concession whatsoever on the wider issue.[106] The internal summary prepared by Matthews and Nitze concluded:

On the question of whether we proposed to use UK bases without their consent, we stated, and General Bradley concurred, that prior consultation and agreement with them would obviously be required. . . .

On the more general question of consultation . . . our position was that we wanted to talk to them as frankly and in as broad an area as possible, but that we could not enter into any agreement or commitment or procedure that would imply a commitment, even a commitment to continue to talk or to follow any given procedure.[107]

Franks held out for more, but no more was forthcoming. Another month went by. Election day loomed. Finally, following an earlier suggestion of Nitze's, he produced the Delphic formula which has become part of the essential grammar of post-war Anglo-American relations. With regard to US bases in the UK:

The use of these bases in an emergency would be a matter for joint decision by His Majesty's Government and the United States Government in the light of the circumstances prevailing at the time.

This formula was immediately accepted by the Americans. In addition it was agreed that, if pressed on the issue of the bases, British Ministers would reply, 'there is naturally no question of their use in an emergency without our consent'—but only if pressed. Both Governments also approved, but did not release, a statement drafted in Washington on 'Consultations on Atomic Warfare', which embroidered vacuously on the joint communiqué of the Truman–Attlee talks.[108]

These miscellaneous transactions appear to constitute the celebrated but semi-secret Truman–Attlee Understandings of 1951. Confirmed by Churchill during his own talks with Truman the following year, they have been regularly reaffirmed by successive Governments ever since. From the British point of view they surely leave a lot to be desired. Yet no one, not even Winston Churchill, has been able to improve upon them. Harold Macmillan's claim to have initialled a 'regular' agreement with President Eisenhower in 1958 has not been substantiated.[109] Unequal partnership has its price. Churchill was propitiated with the public announcement of the 'joint decision' formula—an early indication of its excellent political serviceability for both sides—but the old man of war was offered nothing new.[110] The formula itself is easy to criticize, but its apparent weakness conceals its real strength: it is open to interpretation. As Luke Battle has observed, with Machiavellian clarity, 'the agreement was as precise as anyone could make it—as precise as we wanted it to be—but there was still . . . ambiguity there that served everybody's interests . . . and needs'.[111]

As for the author of the formula, Nicholas Henderson has noted Franks's 'realism, his political awareness, and his focus on the end-result'.[112] The Truman–Attlee Understandings in general, and the joint-decision formula in particular, speak eloquently of all three qualities. It is noteworthy that Franks was not much exercised by the issue most troubling to future generations, the issue of national sovereignty. At one stage during the politico-military talks Nitze remarked that, 'if it were necessary publicly to make the point that the UK maintains control over its own bases, it might be wise concurrently to make the other point that the West must stand together or run [the] grave risk of being defeated piecemeal'. The record shows that Franks for his part 'agreed that the basic problem was of a much wider nature and that the problem of UK control over its own bases was essentially illusory'. More surprisingly, perhaps, he said much the same in public. In a speech to the Foreign Policy Association of St Paul, Minnesota, on the question of an allied base in Egypt—in retrospect, a question charged with interest—he argued as follows:

To give an ally facilities on your own soil was not necessarily derogatory to your own sovereignty. If it were, Britain was doing precisely that now by permitting the United States to maintain bases in Great Britain. The Four Powers [Britain, France, Turkey, and the US] ask no more of Egypt in the base which they wish to maintain there than has been asked of us in Britain and freely given.[113]

This was a convenient argument, no doubt, and now seems an inadequate one. But September 1951 was not the time to stand on principle. For the British, it was late in the day, in more senses than one. They had to close a deal. The Truman–Attlee Understandings, of which Oliver Franks was the principal agent, ratified another transatlantic bargain. The bargain was weapons for bases. It had a classic progenitor. In 1940 the weapons were superannuated destroyers, and the bases were in the West Indies. After the war it was atomic bombers in East Anglia. Later still it was nuclear submarines in Holy Loch. In the Anglo-American relationship, comparative advantage has been exploited almost as ruthlessly as fellow-feeling. Trading in these dangerous commodities was peculiarly dependent on personal trust. Trustworthiness is hard to specify, but it so happens that the British have an expression for it. In 1937 a middle-aged spinster called Hilda Chamberlain wrote to her elder brother Neville that the Americans were 'hardly a people to go tiger shooting with'. Neville, we can be certain, knew exactly what she meant; as Prime Minister, he felt just the same. So too did many of his Cabinet colleagues.[114] The Truman–Attlee Understandings, on the other hand, mark the willingness of the policy-making élite in both countries to go tiger-shooting together with few qualms, something they were never prepared to do before the Second World War. One of the most important reasons for this new confidence resided in the British Embassy in Washington. As Dean Acheson would testify, tiger-shooting with Oliver Franks was a wonderfully liberating experience.

PART III

The Pillar and the State

7 Oxford Regained

EVEN tiger-shooting can pall. 'Personal relations are the important thing for ever and ever, and not this outer life of telegrams and anger', wrote E. M. Forster. Despite an invitation to stay on, Franks chose to depart the outer life in December 1952. In Forster's terms the decision was readily explicable. Franks had no use for anger and no love of telegrams, believing, with A. J. P. Taylor, that 90 per cent of what they contain can be found in the newspapers.[1] He had visited every state in the union. Was he to go round again? Barbara—his most important personal relationship—urged a return to England, for the sake of the children, and perhaps for their own sake too. And so he abandoned the Embassy. But for what? 'I have made little acquaintance, and kept little company, in a house where so much came', John Locke had written. 'My unmeddling temper . . . always sought quiet, and inspired me with no other desires, no other aims, than to pass silently through this world with the company of a few good friends and books.' Oliver Franks might well have said the same. He had no firm plans and no 'positive and directed ambition'.[2] In fact, he did not know what to do. On his return to England, as if to symbolize his indecision, he lodged with his father-in-law, Herbert Tanner, now retired and living in Somerset.

On a visit to London he laid out the possibilities heuristically for Robert Hall:

(a) He didn't want to teach but would not mind an academic job such as Head of a House [that is, an Oxford college], or Vice-Chancellor. The most promising thing now was the Chairmanship of the UGC [University Grants Committee].[3]

(b) He wouldn't mind a business job if it were exactly right—not otherwise. He didn't want a nationalized industry.

(c) He *did* on the whole want something in Government service, either FO or Treasury. But neither William Strang nor E[dward] B[ridges] [the respective Permanent Under-Secretaries] were capable of saying 'Here is a man with such and such qualities, what can we use him for?'! They just offered him whatever was next on the list. He wanted my views on the offer from the Chancellor [of the Exchequer, R. A. Butler] of the (or a) Treasury job.

(d) Finally, if it were better to wait, he could get a reasonable competence for several years as a Research Fellow, without conditions, from the Rockefeller Foundation.[4]

To Robert Hall's surprise, it was 'the Treasury job' that seemed to interest him most: a half-baked scheme of Butler's to make Franks a kind of Second

Permanent Secretary, in order to bring some greater cohesion to that large and fissiparous department. Hall was off-putting. 'I told him I thought that the main difficulty was that neither the Chancellor nor EB were capable of making up their minds, RAB by constitution and Edward by exhaustion.' Franks eventually took the cue, concluding that the double harness would not work, much as he admired Edward Bridges.[5] The chairmanship of British Railways, or British Petroleum, or (later) the Atomic Energy Authority met a similar response to the earlier offer of the chairmanship of the National Coal Board. The director-generalship of the BBC, a nationalized industry of a different sort, went the same way, in spite of Churchill's pressing. So did the headmastership of Harrow. The editorship of *The Times* gave him pause, momentarily, but he decided that he was not temperamentally suited to the act of creating something new every day. By such a quintessential piece of Franksian reasoning that spark too was soon extinguished.[6]

All this passed in review before him. 'He was a philosopher, however, and such men are not moved to happiness or unhappiness by Fortune's favours or her slights; for them greatness and power are accidents of an almost trivial nature.'[7] None the less, it is interesting that he dallied with the idea of further Government service. His unmeddling temper was genuine, and one of the most important things about him, but he did not always seek quiet. John Locke's professed desire to tiptoe through the world in complete silence is scarcely more convincing in the case of Oliver Franks. 'Wonderfully quick and effective as an expository talker and writer, a genius in the calm clarity with which he could see the shape of complicated things, he was not a man who could lose himself in the act of political doing, or even of intellectual creation. His was an effectiveness at one remove, a power to fascinate the men of action, and in his last years he enjoyed to the full the directive influence it gave him.'[8] Franks was a powerful fascinator, wherever he went. In British political circles he fascinated the makers of the Butskellite consensus, including the eponymous politicians themselves. On his return from Washington, Butler actually told him that he would have to choose: he could either be Chancellor of the Exchequer or Governor of the Bank of England. No doubt Franks was less status-conscious than Locke—one cannot imagine him cancelling the title-page of a book, as Locke did, because it styled him Esq. rather than Gent.—and he may have exercised a stricter moral conscience, but it is difficult to believe that in the still, small hours of the night he, too, did not enjoy the directive influence he had gained. Throughout his time in the United States he had made a point of checking 'how his stock was' in Whitehall.[9] Franks understood the market in esteem as well as anyone. It was as inappropriate for him to undervalue as to overvalue himself. A proper sense of his own worth was an integral part of his moral authority. But he would not sell himself, as the politician must. Roman senators competed for *dignitas*; Oliver Franks did not. In the final year of his ambassadorship he was offered the chance to become the first Secretary-General of NATO. It would have meant more telegrams, and another sojourn abroad, but this was a position for which he was singularly well fitted, as everyone recognized at the time. Here too he could have made a difference. Fresh from Washington, he would have had the stature and the scope to galvanize another new organization—in effect, to put the 'O' in NATO. In other circumstances these arguments might have appealed to him, not least because Dean Acheson was the keenest appellant. And yet, by a curious though not untypical chain of events, the opportunity was missed. The new Foreign Secretary, Anthony Eden, fumbled the pass.

The appointment of a Secretary-General and the establishment of a political headquarters for the North Atlantic Treaty powers had been mooted for some time. Matters came to a head at the NATO Council meeting in Lisbon in February 1952. The points of contention were all too familiar—the nationality and personal standing of the appointee, and his subsequent location. At least three Foreign Ministers were known to be interested: Halvard Lange of Norway, Lester Pearson of Canada, and Dirk Stikker of The Netherlands. Of these, Pearson considered himself to be, and probably was, the front runner; but he was not the universal favourite. At length a CEEC-type trade-off was made. The headquarters would be in Paris, but the Secretary-General would be British. It was up to the Foreign Secretary to make a nomination at the Council meeting. Eden's strong preference was for Sir Ivone Kirkpatrick, then British High Commissioner in Germany. This was an unhappy choice, for good and predictable reasons. Kirkpatrick was not renowned for his independence of mind; it was his dual misfortune to be at the same time a Municheer by association and an Eden acolyte by conviction. During the Suez fiasco in 1956 he told a colleague that 'the PM was the only man in England who wanted the nation to survive, that all the rest of us have lost the will to live; that in two years time Nasser will have deprived us of all our oil, the sterling area fallen apart, no European defence possible, unemployment and unrest in the UK, and our standard of living reduced to that of the Yugoslavs or Egyptians'.[10] For the American king-makers such a man was probably unworthy and certainly unacceptable. Faced with this *non placet* Eden pressed Kirkpatrick's candidature just long enough to irritate his colleagues and exacerbate the difficulties of selection. Finally the name of Oliver Franks was mentioned, and promptly endorsed by Acheson. No objection to Franks could be found. Pearson, however, remarked that Acheson's endorsement 'had let the cat out of the bag, but the only difficulty was that it left several more cats in the bag and perhaps we'd better let them out too'. This sally cost him the nomination. Suddenly, Franks was all but elected. No one—certainly not Anthony Eden—had thought to ask if he would serve.[11]

Awkwardly, it fell to Eden and Pearson (the current chairman of the Council) to telephone Washington to see. Franks was suffering from a bad cold, and according to Acheson 'was in a very cantankerous and difficult state of mind'. Franks had been reading the public speculation about his new appointment for the past few days. Asked now whether he would be Secretary-General of NATO, he replied directly, no. Pressed to think it over, he reluctantly agreed to do so for forty-eight hours. It was clear that his mind was made up. Acheson was prevailed upon to essay a personal approach, but even he got no further. 'I said, "Oliver, I hesitate to raise again this question of the Secretary-General of NATO." He said, "Dean, I wholly commend your hesitation. I'll continue to think about it." I said, "All right, just so you think about it." And that ended that.'[12] Franks thought, and declined. He was not to be moved by such frivolity. In his response to his friend Dean Acheson we catch the icy blast of stern disapproval. Ethically 'thick concepts'—scrupulousness, for instance—had real meaning for Oliver Franks.[13] They related to the way he lived his life, and the way he believed life should be lived. Plainly, the secretary-generalship of NATO was a *gravis* matter, weighty and important. Franks was a *gravis* man. He was serious, exhibited seriousness of purpose, and was to be taken seriously. Against the moral ideal of *gravitas*, the NATO Council met its match.

Perhaps it was not all high-mindedness. Franks surely knew that he was not Eden's favourite. The feeling was mutual. The regimes he found most admirable were melting away. On the American side, in the presidential election of November 1952 the wide grin and war record of General Dwight D. Eisenhower proved unstoppable. Harry Truman went back to Independence, Missouri. Asked what he did on his first day home, he replied: 'I took the suitcases up to the attic.' Franks thought Truman a great President (a verdict much more common now than it was when Franks first recorded it). Often we admire in others what we aspire to ourselves. Quoting the suitcase remark, Franks commented: 'One gets an impression of simplicity of manner, directness of speech, a practical man who when he has finished one thing gets on with the next.'[14] Eisenhower's Secretary of State was to be John Foster Dulles. Franks knew Dulles of old, and he knew the contemporary declension: 'dull, duller, Dulles'. If Dean Acheson was a pragmatist, Foster Dulles was a moralist. Something would be lost in the exchange.

On the British side, the incomparable Ernie Bevin was already dead. That prideful provincial Herbert Morrison was no substitute. (When Morrison mispronounced 'Euphrates', giving it two syllables instead of three, it was said that neither Bevin nor Morrison could pronounce the names—the difference was that Bevin knew where they were.[15]) When Attlee lost the general election of October 1951 Churchill and Eden returned to office. The war-winning combination was not what it was. Both Prime Minister and Foreign Secretary seemed dismayingly out of touch. During their visit to Washington in January 1952 Acheson went so far as to tell Eden, apropos Iran, that 'the business of foreign minister today was very different from what it was when Lord Palmerston was handling things like this'. Eden, he recorded, 'sort of withdrew from the conversation'.[16] For an Oriental linguist and amateur of Persian poetry this was hurtful indeed; but it was no more than the truth. To represent a Foreign Secretary so expert yet so unprofessional was a duty to tax even Cicero, and one that Franks may not have wished to prolong. His interpretation of Eden to Acheson was a *tour de force*: a marvellous exposition of Eden's essential irrationality, a characteristic which two such rational beings as Franks and Acheson were bound to find deeply disturbing. The latter remembered:

Oliver came down the next day and said he [Eden] was wounded about this and I had to go out of my way to fix this up, which I proceeded to do. And then Oliver made some observations about Anthony's mind, which I think were very good indeed. He said that he had one great asset and that was political instinct. He was not trained in any kind of rational processes. He knew that he was now at point A, which was an uncomfortable point to be at and he didn't want to be there, and he saw point B over here and he would like to be there. If you start to examine him on how to get from point A to point B, you were just trying to do the impossible, that wasn't something he was capable of doing. If you said why would you rather be at point B than point C, he couldn't explain that either. He just had a good strong 'feel' that where he was wasn't where he wanted to stay, and that over here was where he wanted to get. Now, he [Franks] said, you've got to work around, and if you have differences and you think you ought to be somewhere else, you have to do it other than as though you were arguing a case. He said all you do is baffle and confuse him and rather humiliate him because you show him that he oughtn't to want to do what he wants to do, and that upsets him. So I said I was sorry about it and . . . he came to my house and we spent an evening together and everybody got to love one another and it was fine.[17]

There was also the matter of style. For Franks, as for Acheson, Ernie's untutored ways were infinitely preferable to Anthony's foppery. 'Oliver, me lad' was perfectly acceptable. 'Oliver, dear', on the other hand, seemed entirely inappropriate.[18]

At length, Franks accepted a much more unexpected offer, mediated by the ubiquitous Lord Brand: the chairmanship of Lloyds Bank, the largest of the London clearing-houses. Why? Franks's answers were perhaps a shade defensive. First of all, it was a proper and not an improper thing to do. His own father-in-law was proof of that, and the Cadburys and Rowntrees—'the chocolate conscience'—ample confirmation.[19] He was not trained in economics: nor were many professional bankers. In the international sphere he already had a good deal of experience. Domestically he saw no reason why he could not pick it up. Running a large institution was not new. 'If you can run an Oxford college you can run anything.'[20]

Franks's perspective on running an Oxford college probably stood him in good stead at Lloyds:

I think it involves being interested, being about, being available, influencing opinion, giving a college a sense of direction and purpose, as far as you can. But it's *not* true that it takes 100 per cent of the activities of an active person. If it did, he'd be intolerable in the college, and therefore heads of houses tend to do other things. They may write books, they may go in for university administration, they may do external commissions, they may do all sorts of things. But I think that all these are conditional on the fact that the head of the college is believed to be about the place and be interested and available all the time, and I think in a college where this is *not* true, you find trouble developing fairly soon.[21]

At Worcester College, on the front door of the Provost's Lodgings where Franks resided from 1962 to 1976, there was a sign saying: 'Members of the College are requested to enter without ringing and to knock on the door of the Provost's study, which is the middle door on the left.' According to his predecessor, who put it there, it meant: 'The Provost Feels It His Duty To Be A Sitting Duck.' Against expectation, Franks did not remove it.[22]

Franks offered Lloyds his conscience—in Gordon Richardson's words, 'his moral eminence'—and his administrative gift. The bank in the mid 1950s was by no means a dynamic institution. As its historian records, with commendable restraint, 'when Franks became chairman Lloyds had been a going concern for approaching two hundred years and a corporate institution for nearly a century and, not so long ago, had struck a bad patch in the early 1930s. He sensed the cautious attitudes that lingered here and there, the conservatism sometimes evident.' Franks himself was more forthright. He said that it was like 'dragging a sleeping elephant to its feet with your own two hands'.[23] On the other side, Lloyds offered Franks a vantage point from which to observe the world. The chairmanship was a half-way house between the outer life and the inner. It paid handsomely—far more than any other position he ever held—and it allowed him to do many of the things canvassed above. He joined the Lloyds board in 1953 and took the chair in 1954. The same year he gave the BBC Reith Lectures, donating a substantial fee (£1,100) to Lady Margaret Hall, Oxford, his wife's college, and later his elder daughter's.[24] 'Britain and the Tide of World Affairs' is a conspectus much quoted but little read. The BBC producer of the lectures ('discourses written to be listened to', as Franks described them) was his former student, Ronald Lewin, the military historian. They lack fire, perhaps because Franks was keen to avoid 'sharp political controversy, as he attached importance to maintaining his non-party position'.[25] His central theme—his text, one might say—was what he identified as 'an accepted principle' of British political life. Simply stated, 'Britain is going to continue to be what she has been, a Great Power.' The capital letters blazoned the assumption. In hindsight, British acceptance of this principle has been justly excoriated. Commentary on Franks's articulation of it has taken on the character of rune-craft. In the first of the series he wrote:

A nation which is a Great Power has a certain range of choice and manoeuvre in world affairs and can take an effective part in the great decisions which affect the course of history. The action of a Great Power can decisively affect the fate of other

Great Powers in the world. It is in this sense that we assume that our future will be of one piece with our past and that we shall continue as a Great Power. What is noteworthy is the way that we take this for granted. It is not a belief arrived at after reflection by a conscious decision. It is part of the habit and furniture of our minds: a principle so much one with our outlook and character that it determines the way we act without emerging itself into clear consciousness. I think that almost all of us take this view of Britain for granted. I certainly have done so.[26]

This statement echoes and re-echoes down the decades of apparently inexorable relative decline. It was perfectly illustrated, in almost identical language, some twenty years later by the official historian of 'Britain and atomic energy', Margaret Gowing, in a celebrated passage explaining the origins of the British independent nuclear deterrent:

The British decision [in January 1947] to make an atomic bomb had 'emerged' from a body of general assumptions. It had not been a response to an immediate military threat but rather something fundamentalist and almost instinctive—a feeling that Britain must possess so climacteric a weapon in order to deter an atomically armed enemy, a feeling that Britain as a great power must acquire all major new weapons, a feeling that atomic weapons were a manifestation of the scientific and technological superiority on which Britain's strength, so deficient if measured in numbers of men, must depend.[27]

Franks was a great examiner of assumptions. Two years before Suez ('the lightning flash on a dark night'), what is noteworthy about his examination of the Great Power assumption is the contingent nature of that status. It depended upon the attitude of others. 'After the war we acted as a Great Power, though we had not the resources. A kind of confidence trick. It came off as long as the decisions we made were acceptable to the other Powers.'[28] Even more, it depended upon British attitudes. As Ronald Lewin wrote after one of their early discussions, Franks's purpose was to 'point rather firmly to other ways in which we *might* act as a great power if we thought about ourselves differently and conducted ourselves differently'. The last lecture of the series was entitled 'The Will to Greatness'. It concluded: 'Britain will continue a Great Power; she will be a leader among the nations and take her part in the great decisions; she will have the economic strength to sustain her role—if we make it our daily business. It is there that we become masters of our fate. Action begins in the workaday world, if we will to be great.' As so often with Franks, 'we therefore face a moral issue. By our choice we shall declare what sort of people we are.'[29]

Withal, Franks was optimistic. In the Reith Lectures the optimism is rather pedestrian; but in an 'oration' delivered at the London School of Economics, with some help from the novelist Joyce Cary, it is almost poetic. Franks, who knew Cary slightly through the Oxford publisher Dan Davin, had been reading *To be a Pilgrim*. At the end of the book an old Englishman muses allusively on the course his life has taken. From this soliloquy Franks extracted a finale to match his inspiriting purpose:

England took me with her on a few stages of her journey. Because she could not help it. She, poor thing, was born upon the road, and lives in such a dust of travel that she never knows where she is.

> Where away England, steersman answer me?
> We cannot tell. For we are all at sea.

She doesn't notice it because she looks forward to the road. Because she is free. She stands always before all possibility, and that is the youth of the spirit.

To which Franks himself was moved to add: 'As we look out on the world, we do not know what the future will bring. We do not know our destination. But we don't mind. We have confidence that from whatever quarter the winds blow and the rains come we shall get through. Old in story, we are young in spirit.'[30]

There was more to life than lecturing. In 1955 Franks succeeded his father-in-law as chairman of the Friends Provident and Century Insurance Office. In 1958 he became chairman of the board of governors of the United Oxford Hospitals, a role in which his Gladstonian principles of retrenchment and reform were both sorely tested. (Informed that their Government grant was inadequate, his first response was to remark, 'if you squeeze the cheese hard enough more water will always come out'. After some persuasion he relented, and pressed successfully for more.)[31] In 1960 he became chairman of the Committee of London Clearing Bankers, a body on which he subsequently held a small and more or less private inquiry.[32] In the same year he accepted a mission from the World Bank to make a reconnaissance of India and Pakistan, in order to clarify the role of Western aid in the development programmes of those two countries—a large and politically sensitive undertaking. India was considered to be the most important underdeveloped country in the world, and also one of the most advanced in terms of development planning. Franks was accompanied by Hermann Abs, chairman of the Deutsche Bank, and Allan Sproul, a former president of the Federal Reserve Bank of New York. After touring the subcontinent for a month the three men submitted a strongly worded report. They had found 'the familiar vicious circle of low income, low savings, and continuing low income, which cannot be broken effectively without an inflow of capital funds from abroad'. Their unambigious if unwelcome recommendation was for 'a very substantial increase in foreign assistance'.[33] The value of the exercise was assessed very candidly by the World Bank's vice-president:

This was not really a technical appraisal of the Indian programme, nor was it intended as such. The whole mission might be thought of as a very high level PR job to represent to India the interest being maintained in the West in their development problems . . . And on the other hand, the purpose of the mission was to educate these three outstanding citizens of the West, none of whom, as I recall, had ever been to India before, and who came back and have since been influential in public and private circles in forming opinion with regard to India.[34]

In Franks's case the education bore fruit in a number of addresses to well-heeled and influential audiences in the United States.[35] Paradoxically, however, his most interesting reflections on these issues were delivered shortly before he departed, at a meeting of the Trustees of the Committee for Economic Development in New York. In discussing changes in the political and strategic posture of the West, Franks remarked: 'Earlier the problems of East–West tension were dominant: now we have a *North–South* problem of equal importance.' This was a new coinage. He explained:

I mean the problems of the relationship of the industrialized nations of the North to the underdeveloped and developing countries to the south of them, whether in Central or South America, in Africa or the Middle East, in South Asia or in the great island archipelagos of the Pacific. If twelve years ago [in 1947] the balance of the world turned on the recovery of Western Europe, now it turns on a right relationship of the industrial North of the globe to the developing South.[36]

Western policy, therefore, had to succeed in two dimensions, North–South and East–West. It was a resonant idea.[37]

At home, meanwhile, Franks concentrated on macroeconomic policy. His formidable combination of intellectual potency, expository fluency, and personal authority gave him credence in financial counsels, in spite of the fact that he was an amateur in the Treasury and an interloper in the City. It was hard not to defer to Oliver Franks. The situation was well caught in a ditty composed by the Treasury official Edward Playfair in 1956 (when Harold Macmillan had succeeded R. A. Butler as Chancellor of the Exchequer, and C. F. Cobbold was Governor of the Bank of England).

> Sad little dinner for Mr Macmillan
>   Sadder still for Governor Cobbold
> Sitting still while Franks finds the villain
>   Who causes the woes by which we're troubled.
>
> Smiling blandly was Robert Hall
>   Discreetly silent was Tommy Brand
> Listening wisely to one and all
>   Listening while HMG is panned.
>
> R. A. Butler
>   Was far, far subtler
> No witnesses present when he talked to Franks
> No formal contact with commercial banks.[38]

The following year, when Lord Radcliffe was invited to conduct an inquiry into the working of the monetary and credit system, it was natural that Franks should be asked to be a member of his committee. The inquiry was an exhaustive affair; the committee reported in August 1959.[39] This was another educational experience. In his day Radcliffe was the *ne plus ultra* of public inquirers. His mind was as good as or better than Franks's own, his pen more fluent, his range more extensive, his reserve more impregnable. In a word, he was awesome. For Oliver Franks, jousting with Radcliffe was a rare treat.[40]

The days unenlivened by Radcliffe were not as absorbing as he might have hoped. Franks never found 'every atom of his being totally fulfilled' in any job he did. He would have been surprised if he had. He enjoyed the challenge of chairing Lloyds; but a challenge is apt to pale. It became increasingly clear to him that a banker's life was very comfortable, and occasionally very interesting, but it was not where his heart lay. By 1957 he was prepared to confide that he would give it all up tomorrow to go back to teach at Oxford.[41]

Franks's attachment to Oxford was a powerful thing. The Fellows of Queen's, doubting his rootedness, quite misjudged it in 1953. That was understandable, not only because of their recent experience of his prolonged absences, but also because the sentiment, strong as it was, seemed to elude definition. Franks, the inveterate clarifier, could not or would not clarify this. Perhaps he had some affinity with Clement Winter, the protagonist of a Brian Aldiss novel, who felt 'an almost mystical identification with the institutions around him: his College, the University, Oxford, or more particularly North Oxford—the Puginesque, Betjemanesque half-mile which contained so much diversity and snobbery—and, beyond that, England, the European idea, and the planet earth itself as a complex ecological unit'.[42] Franks was not given to analysing it. He chose to live in Oxford whilst he was at Lloyds—first at the top of Headington Hill, later in North Oxford quite near Clement Winter—and was often to be seen taking the early train home from Paddington. He liked the different ethos of the place. 'When you get to Didcot station you change your hat.' He liked being with passionately dispassionate people (a favourite phrase) actively in pursuit of the truth.[43] Uninterested in his own life, he was interested in the lives of others; or rather, in what interested *them*. Knowledgeable discourse, regardless of discipline, was his pleasure. The boardroom, he discovered, was no place for the passage of ideas.

In many ways he personified what Noel Annan has called 'the insufferable ideal'—the ideal of the English gentleman—a blend of practicality, stoic virtue, civic duty, understatement, and a deep respect for learning. In Annan's words: 'Every man's first loyalty should be to the country of his birth, and the institution in which he served. Loyalty to institutions came before loyalty to people. Individuals should sacrifice their careers, their family, and certainly their personal happiness or whims, to the regiment, the college, the school, the services, the ministry, the profession or the firm.'[44] But Franks did not swallow this whole. For the old firm of Attlee and Bevin he would have done almost anything. For the new firm of Eden and Selwyn Lloyd, for example, the same might not have held true—it is interesting to speculate on what Franks would have felt it right to do had he been in place in Washington during the Suez crisis, a venture of which he clearly disapproved. ('I regard Suez as a great aberration,' he said in a broadcast talk in 1958, 'a moment when we lost our touch with the realities. It was an old-fashioned act in a new-fashioned world.')[45] Annan's institutions, moreover, were incommensurable. As Franks remarked, 'It would be hard to have an intimate affection for Lloyds Bank.' He would be loyal to the bank but he would not sacrifice himself for it. Colleges, on the other hand, were more like clans, and clan loyalty was a different matter altogether. Even here he exercised a certain Franksian detachment, a compound of personal temperament and Nonconformist faith, reinforced by experience. He had seen too much of the world truly to love the learned pedant. Franks was not cut out to be 'a good college man' in the knowing, narrowing sense in which the expression is normally used. Noel Annan pricks and celebrates the post-war don in matchless fashion:

In his college meetings a don enjoyed the delectable illusion of being an architect or a farmer weighing the advantages of a dual-purpose shorthorn herd, bred for both milk and meat, over a herd bred by a cross of Aberdeen Angus on blue grey. He could develop a nose for the balance of a portfolio or of a young claret.[46]

This was not for Oliver Franks. The nose was not the organ by which he lived. In the realm of the senses he was comparatively undeveloped. He had no eye for painting, no ear for music, no taste for food (though his earlier passion for Pontefract cakes gave way to a weakness for dates at high-table dessert). It was as Montaigne said: 'Liberty consists, in great part, in a well-ordered stomach.' Franks was tolerant of donnish foible, but his loyalty was as much to the university as to any one college. His was an exceptional case: it was *Oxford* that claimed him, not Queen's, or Worcester, or (by marriage) Lady Margaret Hall. In the annals of Oxford, Father Franks has been compared to Archbishop Laud. The comparison is appropriate in one respect at least. For Franks, as for Laud, 'no place which had any connexion with him had ever cause to regret it: but no place had a closer connexion with him than Oxford, and his reward to it was memorable.'[47]

How was he to get from here to there? A peculiar conjunction of events forced another choice. The death of Lord Halifax in 1959 meant that the university had to find a new Chancellor, for the first time since 1933. The office of Chancellor was (and is) a curious one, prestigious, mysterious, and, according to some, superfluous. Indisputably it was the highest honour Oxford could bestow. Its duties were defined by ancient statute. They had been interpreted by Halifax to mean 'to exercise beneficent supervision of the University's life', and further interpreted by others to mean very little (in Paul Johnson's view, 'a free pass to dine at college high tables whenever he pleases'). Three centuries earlier Laud had kept a close eye on 'the formalities which are in a sort the outward and visible face of the University', not excluding the long hair of the students.[48] But Laud was unusually scrupulous. Most of his successors simply stayed away. Halifax's immediate predecessors included Curzon and Grey. For these men the Empire naturally took precedence over the University. This was only what was expected. In traditional conception the Chancellor was ornamental rather than useful. He (never yet she) added lustre, dignity, distinction. He was something akin to the monarch—constitutionally vital but politically insignificant. Like the monarch, the Chancellor reigned but did not rule. He reigned, moreover, for life: abdication was unthinkable. Like the monarch, he had an important representative function, but his chief preoccupation was ceremonial. He was, in short, a figure-head.

This tradition was not to be lightly overturned. In Oxford traditions live active lives. Nevertheless, when it came to a successor for Halifax there was some feeling within the university that now in this new age they needed what the philosopher Anthony Quinton called a 'functional' Chancellor, and no longer merely an ornamental one.[49] The idea was that the functional Chancellor would complement and not derogate from the Vice-Chancellor (or Prime Minister)—who did rule, but weakly, and for only a two-year term. The chosen mould-breaker was Oliver Franks.

Franks's name first emerged from a caucus of heads of houses organized with great dispatch in January 1960 by that quintessential Oxford don, Sir Maurice Bowra, Warden of Wadham and senior head, acting for the Vice-Chancellor (T. R. Boase), who was ill. After some discussion of possible candidates, it transpired that an overwhelming majority of those present favoured Franks (or could think of no one better). Only the Warden of All Souls (John Sparrow) and the Provost of Worcester (Sir John Masterman) explicitly reserved their position. Four others were absent from the meeting. Fatefully, they included the Master of Balliol (Sir David Lindsay Keir), adrift in the Sudan. In the light of their discussion Bowra undertook to ask Franks if he would accept the nomination.[50] He did so, without hesitation. At this stage the field was completely clear. No one else had declared, and there had been no time to cabal. Two other names were being canvassed: Harold Macmillan, who had a First in Greats from Balliol, and happened to be Prime Minister; and Lord Salisbury ('Bobbety' to his friends), whose studies at Christ Church had been mercifully interrupted by the Great War, and who had been a copper-bottomed member of numerous Conservative Governments, but was now in a rather uncomfortable state of aristocratic dissidence from the decolonizing trends in his own party. It was apparent that Salisbury would not stand against Macmillan. It was not apparent whether Macmillan would stand against Franks. (Or for that matter whether Franks would stand against Macmillan.) Again Bowra did not wait. As soon as he heard that Franks was willing to let his name go forward, he craftily informed the press that a contest was unlikely. Coming from Bowra, this prognostication was widely believed. The situation in early February 1960 gave every appearance of a successful pre-emptive strike.[51]

Meanwhile the Christ Church mafia were mobilizing. Their *capo* was Hugh Trevor-Roper (later Lord Dacre), the Regius Professor of Modern History, attended by the grey eminence of Robert Blake (later Lord Blake and himself an aspirant, notably unsuccessful). Trevor-Roper was a luxuriant High Tory, and something of a cavalier. His objection to Franks was predictably strong:

... he is not a traditional kind of Chancellor ... we do not want our Chancellor to be yet another official ... we consider the Chancellor always has been and still should be a great public man, who, though a member of the University, fond of it, and intellectu-ally distinguished (or at least appreciative of the intellectual world) is himself outside and above, not in the academic world, and intervenes only occasionally, and majestic-ally, in it and on its behalf.[52]

Trevor-Roper's hopes were pinned on Harold Macmillan, an authentic grandee. Not only did Macmillan have a respectable intellectual history. He had a good war—or rather two, for he was wounded on the Somme in 1916. He had played on the world stage. Above all, he had *style*. Hooded-eye panache would be his trump card. What could Franks offer in return? Mere austerity. Franks was colourless and unappealing. For any cavalier, a Chancellor with a puritan conscience was a grim prospect indeed.[53] There were political undercurrents too. Macmillan was, after all, the leader of the Conservative Party, if a somewhat raffish one. Franks had continued to main-tain his non-party position with some success, though few would have taken him for a Tory even if unaware of his Liberal sympathies. 'My own belief is that Maurice [Bowra], as a supporter of the Left, wants to avoid a Conservative Chancellor, and, since a Socialist candidate ... would never get in, has pitched on a safe non-political candidate to absorb both anti-Conservative and non-political votes.' Trevor-Roper's belief was plausible but insufficient. Isaiah Berlin was more nearly right when he suggested that Bowra identified Macmillan with pomposity and priggishness, both of which he found offensive. More positively, Bowra was already convinced of the need to ration-alize the university's byzantine central administration. Not for the first time, Franks was thought to be useful.[54] For Trevor-Roper, on the other hand, there was a debt to repay. As their name suggests, regius professorships are nomin-ally in the gift of the Crown. In fact the university proposes and the Prime Minister disposes. In 1957 Oxford had to make a new appointment in Modern History. There were two principal contenders. The outstanding one was the mischief-making, Tory-baiting iconoclast A. J. P. Taylor, a founder member of CND. The other was Hugh Trevor-Roper. Naturally Trevor-Roper was pre-ferred. The Prime Minister who made that preferment was Harold Macmillan.[55]

Trevor-Roper set about drafting Macmillan (who was then in Africa on his 'wind of change' tour). Bowra had bagged the heads of houses. He would bag the Professors. He organized in the common rooms, publicized abroad, and dispatched to the Prime Minister's office a steady stream of brilliant and enticing reports.

The Franks party has been built, like Mussolini's Italian army, for quick, bloodless victory against imaginary enemies, and although it looks sound on paper, it will melt away in real battle. Even the heads of houses are not sound. They have been kidnapped, and now they secretly resent their captivity. In fact (if I may change my metaphor), as Long John Bowra's pirate ship sails eastward to the Indian Ocean, I can see their anguished faces and desperate gestures at the port-holes, calling for rescue from that rotten hulk. When the firing begins, they will desert.[56]

Trevor-Roper had identified a significant weakness in Maurice Bowra's strategy. As an assembly, the heads of houses had obvious resonance but no official standing within the university. In this period, in fact, it was extraordinary for them to meet at all, and even more extraordinary for them to agree. In that sense their imprimatur on Franks's candidacy was always worthless. It gave him a certain impetus, but it also raised hackles. Oxford guards its democracy jealously. Constitutionally, the dons' parliament (Congregation) was sovereign. Actually, in the Unholy Roman Empire of the university the warring colleges were supreme. Six years later, this became a seminal theme of the Franks Commission's report on the university. The colleges, it said in a famous passage, 'have put their right to dissent too high among their privileges. This disjunction between the University and the colleges is dangerous to both, for so long as it persists the University must either remain ineffective or seek to bypass the colleges.' Then came the *coup de grâce*. 'It is possible that the colleges "will fall, one by one, an unpitied sacrifice in a contemptible struggle". The remedy, as Edmund Burke knew, is "association".'[57] It is a strange irony that if the commission's recommendations on 'association' had been followed in 1960, Bowra's caucus would have had legitimacy, discontent would have been muted, and the Frankophiles would have had a tremendous and perhaps decisive boost. In the event the Frankophobes fed on a gathering sense of resentment.[58] Opinion swiftly began to harden against Bowra's buccaneering. Trevor-Roper's ridiculing of the university Establishment—'those nameless, faceless, self-important Provosts of This, Masters of That, and Principals of the Other'—played on this cleverly. Very soon the pre-emptive strike looked disturbingly like an extra-parliamentary *coup*.[59]

'Things are beginning to move our way', Trevor-Roper reported roguishly:

The first thing to move was an object seen swimming towards us yesterday, from captain Bowra's pirate ship. At first we supposed it was some ordinary rat leaving the doomed vessel, but as it came nearer it seemed a particularly plump, peach coloured and port-fed rat; and when it scrambled aboard and dried out, we found that it was the Principal of Brasenose [Maurice Platnauer], one of the captive heads of houses. He is now safely with us. I am sure other captives would have followed in his dash for freedom, but of course Long John Bowra has quickly battened down the hatches. That is, he has sent their names to the printers, they can hardly do more than wriggle now. But others are moving . . .'[60]

In mid-February Macmillan agreed officially to stand. He could hardly resist it, in spite of the risk urged by senior members of his Cabinet. He wrote laconically in his memoirs: 'There was nothing at all to be gained in reputation if I was successful, and a good deal to be lost if I failed. But that, after all, is true of all field sports.'[61] As he declared, the outcome was uncertain. There were many who felt that 'Franks is the voice of the future; he is the new, oil-fired, centrally-heated sort of don', a curiously dated metaphor. Others had their doubts about the principle or the person. Macmillan himself put it very neatly. 'He [Franks] had every possible qualification for the task except one— he was still young and active and there was a possibility that he might actually "do" something, perhaps even do too much.' A few were actively hostile. Who was the 'very well-known don' who expostulated to Randolph Churchill, 'Oliver Franks—that bum-faced retailer of last year's platitudes'?[62] Macmillan for his part had the hope of Trevor-Roper's scintillating reports, and the whirlpools of intrigue that lay behind them. He had a gathering personal, political, and patronal loyalty. 'I rather enjoy patronage,' he told Alan Bullock afterwards; 'at least it makes all those years of reading Trollope worthwhile.' And—a signal point of honour—he had the solid support of his old college, Balliol, whose Governing Body met, decided in favour of Macmillan, and sent a telegram to the Sudan seeking the Master's agreement. The Master, 'a man of no great personality or views', acquiesced. It could easily have been different. Confronted by Bowra at the original caucus meeting, Trevor-Roper for one was in no doubt that 'he would have signed on the dotted line along with all the rest'.[63]

Franks now had to determine whether to withdraw: a more difficult decision than his original candidature. Not to do so would be to force a contest and a vote; for, unlike the monarchy, the chancellorship is an elective office. The franchise is an Oxford MA, yielding an electorate of some 30,000 world-wide (known collectively as Convocation). Turn-out, however, is low: 10 per cent would be regarded as a good poll. The explanation is largely a matter of logistics. It is necessary to vote in person, in Oxford, at the appointed hour or hours, wearing the appropriate academic dress. Only about 1,300 of those eligible to vote were resident in the city as senior members of the university; the rest had to make a special visit. For the great majority this was simply impossible. The candidates themselves take no part in the campaign. 'This would be far below the dignity of a prospective Chancellor.'[64] Nevertheless there would be a public trial of strength—Franks's first. The chairman of Lloyds Bank, a virgin, would be pitted against the Prime Minister of England,

Supermac himself, backed by the money and menace of the Christ Church mafia. Was this wise?

Franks consulted his friends, as the politicians say: no longer Maurice Bowra, now Acting Vice-Chancellor and officially neutral, but his old acquaintance R. B. McCallum (now Master of Pembroke, and in Trevor-Roper's estimation 'a sanctimonious Scottish ass'), aided by Sir William Hayter (Warden of New College and a former diplomat), and the faithful John Prestwich from Queen's. Their advice was firmly against withdrawal. Franks accepted it willingly. He was flattered. It was fitting. Most interestingly, the Prime Minister ought not to be given a clear run.[65] The election was on.

Polling days were fixed for 3 and 5 March—a day of fasting between two of Bacchanalia. The voting on the second of these, a Saturday, would decide the issue. The scattered distribution of the electorate scarcely curbed the exuberance of the electioneering in Oxford, which had all the trappings of a nineteenth-century rotten borough. The uncommitted seldom found a moment's peace; there was even lobbying at the Dean of Worcester's funeral. Scores were settled and favours called in. There was wooing, whispering, wheeling and dealing, bribery and coercion, even good old-fashioned smearing. Harold Macmillan was said to be personally responsible, as Minister of Housing, for tearing down the Clarendon Hotel in Cornmarket and replacing it with the largest Woolworths in England. On election Saturday, the voters were ferried to and from the hustings, plied with food and drink (the colleges were good at this), and subjected to a barrage of slogans and propaganda, some of it crude ('A vote for the Prime Minister is a vote against Lloyds Bank and *The Times*'); some more sophisticated:

> Summum apicem Haroldus
> ascendere dignus habetur:
>   Et praeese tibi, docte,
> peraeque decet.[66]

The animus against *The Times* stemmed from an eve of poll leading article supporting Oliver Franks, on the slightly eccentric grounds that 'high offices should be distributed. To be either Prime Minister of England or Chancellor of Oxford University is each sufficient for any one man without his being also the other. However skilfully affairs are managed, a single holder of two such posts may face a conflict of claims on time, on attention, on influence.' The article bore the self-important stamp of the editor, Sir William Haley ('Halier-than-Thou' to Macmillan), and was much resented—not just for its pontifical tone, but even more for its presumption. As Randolph Churchill informed the readers of the *News of the World*, 'Sir William Haley is not an Oxford man. He was educated at Victoria College in the island of Jersey and the only degree he holds is that of Hon. LL D (Cambridge).'[67] The chancellorship, like most Oxford business, was a family affair.

In keeping with the general tone of the campaign, there was no secret ballot, but a more or less open vote in the Divinity School, supervised in true seigneurial fashion by Maurice Bowra, and monitored by innumerable reporters, photographers, and television cameras. The tally could be kept with reasonable accuracy by watching Bowra's face. As each ballot paper was signed and handed to him, he beamed at the Franks voters and scowled at the Macmillan ones. At one point he spotted a black voting against the Prime Minister, and nudged Robert Blake. 'Ha, ha! The Winds of Change haven't blown all that far!'[68] Primed by all the publicity, feelings were running high. There was a record poll and a quick count. The results were announced (in Latin) soon after seven o'clock. They were:

Mr Macmillan	1,976
Sir Oliver Franks	1,697

Oliver Franks had lost his first and last election. The traditionalists had won. 'Those who voted for me were no doubt satisfied that as Prime Minister I should not be able to interfere,' wrote Macmillan, 'and that when I retired I should be too old to do so.' It had been a surprisingly close-run thing. Trevor-Roper, suddenly gracious, spoke of 'a great victory for Mr Macmillan, and not a great defeat for Sir Oliver Franks'. Now was the time for celebration. Later that evening in the roisterous streets of the city the cry was heard, 'Macmillan for king.'[69]

Some were disconsolate. Of Barbara's disappointment there is no doubt. 'I am sure we have an excellent Chancellor,' she told a sympathetic reporter, 'and it is very nice that they have elected the man they want.'[70] As for the gallant loser, it is hard to be sure. Physically, at least, Franks was far removed from the hurly-burly of the campaign. Coincidentally—and yet, one cannot help feeling, characteristically—he was in India and Pakistan throughout this period, on his mission for the World Bank. He returned only after it was all over. Of course it was impossible to escape from the election altogether, even in India. He was in regular telegraphic contact with McCallum; and Nehru (a Cambridge man, but mildly Frankophilic) wanted to talk of little else. Was the result a blow for Father Franks? Thirty years later, with a little hesitation— 'What is the truth?'—he was inclined to say no. His friends thought that he was disappointed for about a quarter of an hour.[71] Can it be that he and they were variously misled—that in 1960 he wanted to be Chancellor of his university almost as much as he had once wanted to be Provost of his college (an ambition to which he was happy to confess after he had achieved it)? If this is nearer to the truth, then failing to win that election was not the matter of small consequence it was subsequently made to seem. It was the greatest professional disappointment of a life uncommonly free of disappointments of that kind. Perhaps we should attend again to Edmund Burke: 'History consists, for the greater part, of the miseries brought upon the world by pride, ambition, avarice, revenge, lust, sedition, hypocrisy, ungoverned zeal, and all the train of disorderly appetites, which shake the public with the same "troublous storms that toss / The private state, and render life unsweet".[72] Consolingly, there were other possibilities for Franks to consider in that same year. Just before he was approached about the chancellorship he went to see Robert Hall, still Economic Adviser to the Government, and told him that he had been offered the headship of 'some Oxford college' (probably Brasenose). He was attracted by the offer, evidently, but undecided. He sought Hall's advice: 'did I think that he would be summoned before long to some great task'?[73]

He had one particular great task in mind—the governorship of the Bank of England. As Franks well knew, there had long been talk of the present incumbent, the much-maligned C. F. Cobbold, resigning (or being pushed) from the position he had held since 1949. By this time there was a widely felt need for a more powerful intellectual injection into the hardening arteries of the Old Lady of Threadneedle Street, a requirement demonstrated with embarrassing clarity by the forensic investigations of the Radcliffe Committee during the period from 1957 to 1959. Consulted about a possible successor for Cobbold in January 1958, Hall had recommended Franks as 'the only suitable person'. Not everyone agreed. For the reformists a highly regarded alternative was Edwin Plowden, who escaped the uncertainty by joining British Aluminium. The conformists, including the exalted Court of the Bank itself, favoured Lord Harcourt, Managing Director of Morgan Grenfell and recently Economic Minister and Head of the UK Treasury Delegation in Washington. In the event Cobbold sat tight, first until Radcliffe reported, then until the expected general election. If the Conservatives should win, the odds were on Harcourt; if Labour (led by Hugh Gaitskell), on Franks.[74]

In October 1959 the Conservatives secured an increased majority. But a change of some consequence did take place: Sir Frank Lee succeeded Sir Roger Makins as Permanent Secretary of the Treasury. Frank Lee was a formidable operator. He knew and esteemed Franks of old, in Paris and in Washington. In his view Harcourt was not up to the job. Slowly but surely, Franks's prospects revived. By September 1960 the new Chancellor of the Exchequer, Selwyn Lloyd, was convinced. Quietly, he saw Franks and told him so. Would he accept if asked? The final decision rested with the Prime Minister—Harold Macmillan once more—but Franks now knew that he was the candidate of the Economic Adviser to the Government, the Permanent Secretary of the Treasury, and the Chancellor of the Exchequer: a good combination. Macmillan's personal position was shrewdly appraised by Robert Hall. 'I still doubt if he likes Oliver but maybe he likes to be magnanimous after the Oxford election . . . it is also the case that he does not trust Cobbold and regards his attitude as out-dated and inimical to the government, and he probably gets a lot of pleasure at the thought of being able to tell him that he will appoint Oliver in spite of all the recommendations from the Bank to the contrary.'[75]

Franks deliberated and consulted for a full month. Apart from the merits or demerits of the governorship, there was a further consideration. Although he had declined the earlier invitation to be head of house, with some misgivings, he had now received another, this time from Worcester College. Franks had no special links with Worcester. He knew it to be a happy college, with a splendid house and garden; and he was impressed by the deputations he received.[76] He probably also knew that both A. J. P. Taylor and Isaiah Berlin had been sounded out, with a characteristic reaction in each case. Taylor rejected 'the offer' publicly, saying that he wanted to continue teaching and did not want to bring up his children 'in the antiquated environment of an Oxford college'. Berlin refused to discuss it any further unless they told him who else was being considered. When Franks's name was mentioned he said simply, 'Quite right', and withdrew.[77] The field was clear.

The Bank and the College: apples and oranges. As the weeks went by Franks juggled irresolutely with these very different fruit. Eventually he informed Frank Lee that he had decided *in principle* in favour of the Bank. From the slow motion of the past few months, the pace of events accelerated sharply. Macmillan saw a disgruntled Cobbold and told him that the matter was settled. His successor would be Oliver Franks. The appointment would be announced within the week. This was a Thursday. The next day Franks had discussions with Cobbold at the Bank. Over the weekend, reviewing the situation with Robert Hall, he made the startling admission that he felt 'sick, miserable, and uncertain' about his decision. The following Tuesday he told Selwyn Lloyd that he had made up his mind not to take the governorship after all. In view of what had gone before, this was an unwelcome surprise. At an interview with the Prime Minsiter that night Franks was induced to take a day to reconsider. The following morning he spoke to Lee. At Lee's instigation, Plowden spoke to Franks. A day turned into two. Still there was nothing conclusive. Hall was on tenterhooks. The previous December, reverting to an old theme, Franks had remarked to him that 'it was rather sad that the war had thrown up a small number of people like himself, Edwin [Plowden] and me, who were very good at public affairs. But now we were a dying race and no steps were being taken to see if there are any similar animals available.' If not now, when?[78]

Franks's dealings with Worcester were no less erratic. Having made their offer, the college heard nothing from him for six weeks. He then turned them down. Two young History dons were not prepared to take no for an answer. James Campbell and Harry Pitt went to see him again, and practically told him it was his duty to accept, not only in the interests of the college, but also in the interests of the university, which was assailed by criticism from within and without. Franks was needed 'to put a good face on a good case'—for Oxford's sake. This was an eloquent appeal, and a nicely judged one, but it failed to produce the desired effect. The answer was still no. Astonishingly,

Franks gave that answer on the very day that he saw the Chancellor of the Exchequer. He himself said that the most difficult thing was leaving Lloyds.[79] Pressed to choose between the apple and the orange, it was as if he had suddenly decided to give up juggling, throw them both away, and stay put.

The coda to these dramatic events was equally astonishing. On the third day of reconsideration the Prime Minister received a letter containing Franks's final refusal. The next day, a Saturday, Harry Pitt had a surprise visitor. It was Oliver Franks, as embarrassed as anyone had ever seen him, calling himself a bloody fool, and explaining that 'no' really meant 'yes' . . . if they still wanted him.

> How cold the vacancy
> When the phantoms are gone and the shaken realist
> First sees reality. The mortal no
> Has its emptiness and tragic expirations.
> The tragedy, however, may have begun,
> Again, in the imagination's new beginning,
> In the yes of the realist spoken because he must
> Say yes, spoken because under every no
> Lay a passion for yes that had never been broken.[80]

And so, by unanimous agreement, the Right Honourable Sir Oliver Franks was elected Provost of Worcester College, Oxford, as from 23 February 1962, at a fixed annual emolument of £2,000—a tenfold cut in salary—plus £550 allowance for entertainment and other necessary expenses. There was a ceremony of installation in the chapel; sherry in the Senior Common Room; dinner in Hall for Fellows and Lecturers, and in Mr Campbell's room for the ladies. Dinner-jackets were not worn. The occasion was domus; that is to say, the College paid.[81]

Franks settled down to a fourteen-year stretch at his new college, a period known among the older inhabitants, with more resignation than complaint, as the hair-shirt years. He was a second-time Provost (a record) and a first-time Garden Master, the latter a function absolutely essential to the seamless existence of an ancient foundation. Every afternoon he tended his own garden—at Worcester, a well-established and spacious enclosure with scope for judicious arboreal experiment. He interested himself in the myriad affairs of the college, which prospered in difficult times. He was amused, and occasionally exasperated, by his colleagues. He was not as forbidding as he had been at Queen's fifteen years earlier, when one remark could make the Common Room quail. ('If you reflect on what you have just said, you will realise how foolish it was'—this to the unfortunate Chaplain.)[82] He was treated with respect, tinged sometimes with affection. He had no real enemies and no close friends, except that he did, after a fashion, befriend his former suitors, James Campbell and Harry Pitt, browsing among their books and conversation in the evenings after dinner. Periodically he gave up pipe-smoking. On the whole he was content. Oxford life suited him, just as he had always thought it would. 'All academics', he observed benignly to Pitt, clearly excluding himself, 'think that they are experts on everything, have opinions on everything, and expect to get away with everything.'[83]

But it was not enough to be an under-labourer in the college garden.[84] Selwyn Lloyd bore no grudge, and suggested that he and his old friend Henry Phelps Brown become independent members of a newly constituted nod to corporatism, the National Economic Development Council (NEDC or Neddy). This he did for two years, 1962–4, to no noticeable effect.[85] His chief preoccupation during the early period of his provostship was, so to say, intra-mural. This was unexpected; though it had been accurately foretold by Campbell and Pitt. In February 1964 the university took the unusual step of appointing a three-man committee 'to consider the recommendations and criti-cisms in the Robbins Report and arising out of it which particularly affect Oxford; to establish how many of these are, or have recently been, the subject of investigation and the present state of such investigation; and to consider whether further investigations should be put in hand, and, if so, how they should be conducted'. This *petit comité* was chaired by Oliver Franks. The other members were the Rector of Exeter College and distinguished constitu-tionalist, Kenneth Wheare, who was about to become Vice-Chancellor; and the Waynflete Professor of Physiology, Sir Lindor Brown, a Fellow of Magdalen College. The three men wasted no time in recommending that the university take yet more drastic action, and appoint a full-scale Commission of Inquiry with the following terms of reference:

To inquire into and report upon the part which Oxford plays now and should play in the future in the system of higher education in the United Kingdom, having regard to its position as both a national and an international University.

Within this rubric the commission should pay particular attention to two fun-damental aspects of Oxford's character:

I. Whether the present powers, composition, procedure, and mutual relation of the central institutions of the University . . . are such as to ensure that the making of decisions upon future policy and the conduct or control of administration can be carried out with adequate speed and efficiency. . . .
V. Whether the present general relations between the autonomous colleges and the University require reconsideration. . . .

And much, much more, reaching into every corner of the establishment. Just in case anything had been forgotten, the two-page terms of reference con-cluded:

And to make recommendations on these matters and on such other matters as in the opinion of the Commission are relevant to this inquiry.[86]

All of this was promptly accepted, and in March 1964 Franks found himself chairman of a Commission of Inquiry into Oxford University, a task which consumed most of his energies for the next two years.[87] It was no small undertaking. The commission received about one million words of written evidence, published in fourteen volumes; and one and a half million words of oral evidence, all transcribed and made available on demand. They conducted two surveys of their domain and promulgated the results: 'Statistics on Teaching' and 'Emoluments'. In March 1966 their final report was published by Oxford University Press. It ran to two stout, hard-cover volumes, tastefully finished in blue and grey, the cost of which was substantially defrayed by a generous donation from the Delegates of the Press, a donation made on the polite insistence of Oliver Franks, always a prudent housekeeper.[88] The first volume was a closely reasoned and often trenchant statement of recommendations, complete with a draft set of new statutes; the second a statistical digest nearly 500 pages long. The commissioners themselves thought that the evidence they had amassed presented an unrivalled anatomy of the university organism. The claim was and remains an accurate one, endorsed twice over by the foremost commentator on the commission and its works, A. H. Halsey, whose recent verdict is as near to definitive as we are ever likely to get. In Halsey's judgement, 'the whole [report] constitutes perhaps the best sociological account of the working of a single university in this century'.[89]

The stimulus to this intensive activity was the publication in 1963 of the famous Robbins Report on higher education. Crudely, Robbins begat Franks. As the remit of the original committee of three indicated, Robbins's aspersions on Oxford (and Cambridge) cut to the quick. Franks later remarked that certain words of criticism in that report were engraved upon the heart of the commission much as 'Calais' was on the heart of Queen Mary. The ancient universities were portrayed as incoherent, involuted, and inert.[90] This portrayal was extremely damaging in itself (and these were precisely the tendencies to incur Franksian disapproval); but the report also acted as a remarkably efficient conductor of discontent, public and private. In Robbins's wake further opprobrium was heaped on Oxford, for its expensiveness, its backwardness, its exclusiveness, its richness, its smugness . . . in short, 'Oxford is terrible—why can't everyone go there?', as Max Beloff wrote in irritable rebuke.[91] The discontent spread to both major political parties. With a general election impending, there were awful intimations of the reforming zeal of Labour's Shadow Education Secretary, Richard Crossman (Winchester and New College), whose thuggish intellect and ill-sorted dynamism struck terror in the heart of many an Oxford don. Franks himself did not fear the Labour bogey: it was clear enough that the Tories had been similarly infected. The Chancellor alone remained majestically immune. 'What is the point', said Harold Macmillan, 'of having a commission? Everyone knows that Oxford is better than anywhere else.'[92] This was fighting talk—but the Macmillan of old was no more. Supermac had been laid low by scandal and illness. In 1964 the future belonged, improbably, to Alec Douglas-Home. In Oxford the omens looked bad. Much troubled, they sent for Father Franks.

Franks was joined by 'six knowledgeable local cosmopolitans', as Halsey wrote at the time: Lindor Brown from the *petit comité*; Jean Floud, sociologist and Fellow of Nuffield College, recently arrived from the London School of Economics; Robert Hall, confidant and now happily Principal Elect of Hertford College; Margery Ord, Fellow, Tutor, and Dean of Lady Margaret Hall, and University Lecturer in Biochemistry; Maurice Shock, Fellow, Politics Tutor, and Estates Bursar of University College; and Steven Watson, Student (that is, Fellow) and History Tutor of Christ Church. Brian Campbell, a Fellow of Merton College, was seconded from his post as Deputy Registrar to act as secretary and statutory draftsman. Seasoned in university administration, and not a little cynical, Campbell proved to be extremely useful. He was not a counsellor, as Franks explained with typical precision, but he was an expert. (Campbell likened their relationship to that between master and man.)[93] Except perhaps for Maurice Shock in the bursarial sphere, the commissioners themselves lacked expertise of that sort. But they did have help. They retained the services of professional statisticians and accountants from the Oxford Institute of Economics and Statistics and Messrs Price Waterhouse, to say nothing of a team of college bursars and a pool of secretaries.

The six commissioners were widely gathered, in the charitable phrase of a student reporter. The university 'seemed to be anxious to choose people who weren't eminent', one of them remarked, and there were many who would have agreed. Franks for his part had been anxious to achieve a balance, with regard to age, sex, experience, discipline, and college. The names had been settled in advance with the out-going Vice-Chancellor, Walter Oakeshott.[94] The commissioners did not necessarily know each other, and were somewhat intimidated when asked to give an account of themselves at their first meeting together. This was a favourite technique. Franks wanted a close-knit group, 'a team with a purpose', which is what they became. He knew them all to some degree, but Robert Hall was the only one of whose abilities he could be sure in advance. As it happened there were some surprises. Margery Ord had to be given extra tuition in the art of voice projection when taking evidence from witnesses. Steven Watson could draft like an angel—a vital attribute. In this instance the initial drafting was shared out by the chairman, but it was Watson as redactor who gave their report its striking, Augustan house style, pierced with occasional shafts of dry wit. On university administration as they found it: 'We are satisfied that, by heroic efforts, the machinery of Oxford has been made to move more quickly than it did twenty years ago; but it is a bizarre achievement to show great skill in avoiding obstacles of one's own creation.' On the effect of their reforms: 'We believe . . . that the mind of the academic community will be made up where it is at present often only pieced together.'

Watson also became a member of the Franks committee which examined section 2 of the Official Secrets Act a few years later.[95]

Unusually, the chairman drafted sizeable portions of the report himself: a chapter surveying Oxford's current administrative arrangements and their manifold shortcomings—which Franks regarded as central to his mission—and a stern appendix on All Souls, the only college singled out for individual treatment and, indeed, excoriation. All Souls had a considerable reputation (latterly besmirched by a facile identification with appeasement), an inflated endowment, and no students. Confronted by this strange phenomenon, wrote David Caute, 'Lord Franks reacted like a 19th-century factory inspector investigating conditions in an industrial slum; lucid and impartial, he recognized a scandal and proposed drastic reform without questioning the foundations of the system itself.' The report acknowledged that the college had mooted various schemes of its own, such as the admission of graduate students or Visiting Fellows. The schemes, however, were just that—none had come to fruition. 'When we reviewed the record of the years between the last Royal Commission and the present day,' ran the report's magisterial and much-quoted verdict, 'we were compelled to infer *infirmity of purpose*.'[96] It is difficult to conceive of a more characteristic condemnation. Like many of Franks's pronouncements, the phrase had a Shakespearian echo. This was picked up by Charles Wenden, Fellow and Bursar of All Souls in the post-Franks era: 'I like to think of Lord Franks, while contemplating the report he had to write, casting John Sparrow [the Warden] as Macbeth: "I'll go no more. I am afraid to think what I have done. Look on't again, I dare not." And Franks, as Lady Macbeth, replying: "Infirm of purpose. Give me the daggers."'[97]

Franks was not proud of his drafting, but he was proud of his *modus operandi*. Throughout the academic year 1964–5 the commission summoned witnesses twice weekly to the Examination Schools to give oral evidence. All of these hearings were held in public, a procedure regarded as bold in some quarters and quite scandalous in others, but a determination made by the chairman before ever he met his fellow commissioners. Franks was sure in his bones that as far as possible the whole inquiry had to be a participatory exercise, at once mirroring and substantiating the participatory democracy by which Oxford (and Franks himself) set so much store. He told Congregation at the outset:

No Commission of seven members of this University with our present terms of reference could profitably go away and, in isolation, write a report. The condition of our success is that Oxford, University and colleges alike, makes these two years the occasion of a reflective and constructive dialogue with itself.[98]

The public hearings were the most dramatic form of this dialogue. In conception they were collaborative, not adversarial. Franks explained it in Quaker parlance: he was trying to find 'the sense of the meeting', in committee and in the university at large. If he and his fellow commissioners could do that, and articulate it persuasively, their inquiry would be a success. Desirable change would follow. But people had to be prepared for change, in more senses than one. Their interest had to be engaged. They had to be encouraged to join the debate—as Franks said, to be 'implicated' in the inquiry. The actual value of the evidence was secondary. It was the *process* that mattered. In A. H. Halsey's words, 'Franks conceived of his task as an integrating process of collective reorientation.'[99] Quaker fashion, there would be no votes, and no compulsion. This commission differed from its predecessors in one material respect: it was not a Royal Commission but merely a baronial one. Its terms of reference were thoroughgoing, its proceedings were professional, but strictly speaking it was powerless. Unlike the monarch, Franks—now Baron Franks of Headington, a life peer, with the motto 'Esse quam Videre'—could only propose.[100]

In many inquiries, the inquirers tend to concentrate on the written evidence. For some, the extra yield of the oral evidence is marginal; for others, its collection is a time-consuming diversion or merely a nuisance. There were Oxford commissioners who succumbed to thoughts of this kind.[101] Franks himself did not think in these terms. He was generally in favour of open government. He had practised it before. The well-brought-up young Civil Servant who acted as secretary to his committee on Administrative Tribunals and Enquiries (1955–7) was 'somewhat taken aback' to discover at their preliminary meeting that the chairman had already made up his mind to take verbatim evidence in public—common practice for Royal Commissions but almost unheard of for Government-appointed committees. What was good for the state was good for Oxford. Franks also wanted to disarm the inevitable criticism of an internal investigation. Quite deliberately, he flouted the two cardinal principles of all official inquiries: no dirty linen in public; and outside critics are bores.[102] In Oxford's case a certain amount of dirty linen was a positive benefit. (Too much, of course, would be an acute embarrassment; but Lord Robbins had already attended to that.) The inquiry was first of all 'an exercise in exorcism', as the more enlightened members of the university noticed at the time. Apart from any consequent reforms, the commission was important for its very existence, and for the way in which it conducted itself. For Oxford, Franks fulfilled two essential functions. Internally he educated it. Externally he validated it. After Franks the climate of opinion was utterly different. Yet he himself knew that it was not possible to legislate for an indefinite future.[103] Parts of the work might last. After all, the Laudian statutes, completed in 1636, were still in place three centuries later. It sometimes seemed that the aversion to 'airy novellisms' in Oxford remained as strong as it had been in King James's day. On the whole, however, the validation lasted a generation. By the early 1990s the mistral of dissatisfaction was beginning to blow once again, this time more from within than without. The cry went up for another formal inquiry.[104] 'For a participant in the Commission of Inquiry to revisit his dead self is a strange experience', as Oliver Franks once said, but his own *obiter dictum* is perhaps the most interesting of all—'It gave them twenty-five years.'[105]

The suspicion lingers that Franks *enjoyed* taking oral evidence. Indisputably, he was good at it. With a difficult witness he was as patient as a mongoose with a snake. His forte was the long, late question, once the character of the evidence (and the witness) had begun to emerge. Often the question would be wrapped in a summary of the preceding discussion, a kind of re-presentation to the witness and the world of what he or she had just said, made miraculously coherent. The technique was well exemplified in the Official Secrets Act inquiry, during the interrogation of James Callaghan, as a former Home Secretary and Chancellor of the Exchequer.

THE CHAIRMAN: Would it be fair to ask you this question? You began by saying that you saw no reason in principle why in the whole sphere of government information there could not be cases where improper disclosure would merit a criminal sanction. Let us accept that. Now suppose we go on to stage two, and say that it might be reasonable that candidates for improper disclosure, and meriting criminal sanctions, might be found in the fields of defence and foreign policy and higher Treasury, for the sake of argument. Would it be true to infer from what you have been saying that, if you imagine these subjects that go to the safety and stability of the State are looked after in this way, the ordinary processes of government, up to and including the discussion of ministers in Cabinet, really ought to be looked after by means other than the Official Secrets Act, with its criminal sanctions? Civil servants look after themselves by their professional disciplinary code. Ministers look after themselves by, as it were, the laws of their political being, and in neither case does the existence of an Official Secrets Act or the possibility of criminal sanctions being applied really affect the situation, they will behave as they behave whether it is there or not. This is borne out, to an extent anyhow, by the fact that I think no minister and, I suspect, no really senior civil servant, has ever been brought under the Act for prosecution. Would that be a fair representation of your thought, or not?
[CALLAGHAN]: Yes, I think it would be, expressed much better than I have expressed it. . . .[106]

In especially tricky cases the question could be posed pre-emptively at the start of the hearing. In an earlier inquiry, into Administrative Tribunals, the principal official witness was the Permanent Secretary of the Ministry of Housing and Local Government, Dame Evelyn Sharp, a Whitehall warrior of truly Boudiccan ferocity and cunning, later famous as 'the Dame' in the Crossman diaries. Franks opened with a question so long and intricate that it occupied almost three pages of printed transcript. It was delivered without notes, eyes fixed on the witness and her bearers. But the Dame's reputation had not been lightly won. She replied immediately and sweetly that it was rather a long question to take in, and perhaps the chairman could repeat it? 'Certainly', said Franks, and did so. When the transcript was examined later by the curious secretaries they found that the repetition was identical to the original, save for some half a dozen words here and there.[107]

For some witnesses in the Oxford inquiry the proceedings were eerily reminiscent of an earlier ordeal. 'The air of the viva was unmistakable', wrote one:

I had sat in when a friend was done, to spot the form; it was the same room, which I
had not been into since my own viva in Greats many years ago, the same table, the
lonely candidate on one side, the sombre Inquisitors on the other, courteous, considerate, anxious that the candidate should acquit himself well, but sure to notice every fallacy or error. Others, too, had sensed the likeness. 'Yes, I think the candidate passed'
one tutor said meditatively, of an ennobled Vice-Chancellor; 'I think the Examiners
passed too; very fair, very fair—but very searching. You had better look out.'[108]

Remarkably, the current Vice-Chancellor, Kenneth Wheare, relived exactly
this experience. As a Rhodes Scholar reading Modern Greats he had been
done by Father Franks in 1932, when he got a First. More recently, he had
served with Franks on the Tribunals inquiry. His performance before the
commission, spread over several days, was 'masterly': the verdict of his chief
Inquisitor. Admiral Sir Kenneth Wheare—as Chancellor of Liverpool
University he was enrolled as Honorary Admiral of the Isle of Man Herring
Fishery Fleet, which gave him much pleasure and a box of kippers each
year—had a supple mind and an inventive wit. In committee his interventions
were shrewdly timed and memorably phrased. 'Over my dead body, Mr Vice-
Chancellor,' he was heard to say to one of his predecessors, of some proposal
that displeased him, 'if I may take up a moderate position in this matter.'[109]
His fencing with Franks on the finer points of Oxonian administration was
greatly relished, drawing large crowds to the Examination Schools. In 1964 the
vice-chancellorship was still a matter of Buggins's turn. Heads of houses were
rotated into it for a whirlwind two years. The time they devoted to the job;
their competence in it; the extent to which they would or could 'speak for
Oxford': all these remained open questions. Franks's reference to 'the
grasshopper succession' of Vice-Chancellors provoked from Wheare the comment that he was not familiar with the habits of grasshoppers. When Franks
asked him whether he considered that his post was a full-time occupation, he
replied that, on the contrary, it was a full-time *pre*occupation.[110]

It was not all knockabout. In general Wheare found himself in a delicate
position. He knew full well that there was a huge discrepancy between the
way in which Oxford was formally supposed to operate and the way in which
he and a few senior colleagues actually functioned. To most of the university
the nature and extent of the discrepancy came as a considerable surprise. Here
was the very thing that Franks was bent on exposing, and then regularizing.
In any organization Franks's attention habitually fastened on the machinery
of government, and the efficiency with which it worked. He had become
convinced that the machinery in Oxford was badly in need of a thorough
overhaul; he was determined that the proceedings of the inquiry would
demonstrate the proof of that theorem. Wheare was broadly sympathetic to

this enterprise, but disinclined to say so explicitly in public. He had no wish to alienate the demos, his masters in Congregation. As the sitting Vice-Chancellor he was most reluctant to pronounce on what should be done in the future: that was the job of the commission. Franks could lead him to the water of reform, but could he make him drink? Not without a fight—conducted, of course, with the utmost civility:

THE CHAIRMAN: The root issue here is whether there is any reason for going on with what appear to be rather attenuated fragments of an older system which means that the University does not have, officially, a unitary administration. . . . Would any member of [the Hebdomadal] Council wish to take that view?

SIR MAURICE BOWRA: I very much agree with you. I will say quite clearly that I have thought that for some years, and the fact that it works at all is a miracle of good temper, goodwill and all that. . . .

THE CHAIRMAN: I feel that one of the problems we are confronted with is that through the very great efforts of a relatively small body of people in the University over the last ten years, it has been possible to make the University, as a whole, and its central machinery do all almost anything. It has achieved quite remarkable success but I think it has done it in spite of the organization rather than because of it. If one is confronted with the need of looking at the organization for what it is and we consider the difference between statute and practice, then, you see, these questions do come up. We, I suppose, in the end, have to try to find an unambiguous recommendation. Therefore, I am pressing this point because if it was seriously thought that a unified administration . . . was undesirable, we ought to be told.

THE VICE-CHANCELLOR: I think you will find that there is a body of opinion which is against centralization and against saying that so-and-so is top and that the others come underneath. You will find that it is just a fact of our community here.

THE CHAIRMAN: We appreciate that.

THE VICE-CHANCELLOR: When we think of what we are going to try and do we have to bear that in mind. . . . As for the rest, I would have thought that we would be content for the Commission to decide on this matter and make the recommendation that they think fit.

THE CHAIRMAN: But it is proper, is it not, for us to inquire whether Council has any suggestion, advice or opinion which it would wish to offer?

THE VICE-CHANCELLOR: Yes. I was thinking that if in due course you recommended something and said 'We were glad to find the Hebdomadal Council agreed' on this suggestion, I would feel a bit awkward. Therefore, I hope you will not press us to agree with what you said. But you did ask us just now whether anybody disagreed and not a soul said anything. As you know, this is very often the other side of being overlapping members of various bodies: you have a lot of loyalties. But your analysis of the situation struck me as very clear, if I may say so, and certainly pointing in one direction.

Here was a substantial concession. Franks pocketed it immediately, and published the exchange in the report.

THE CHAIRMAN: We will leave it at that.[111]

8 *Grand Inquisitor*

By the mid 1960s Oliver Franks had become the Grand Inquisitor of Our Age. He had chaired two major inquiries and taken a leading part in a third. He seemed to have been in session almost continuously for over a decade: on Administrative Tribunals and Inquiries (1955–7), on the Working of the Monetary System (1957–9), and on Oxford University (1964–6). His progeny were multiplying steadily. There were already two fat Franks Reports, both bursting with recommendations (ninety-five on Tribunals, no fewer than 170 on Oxford), to say nothing of the seminal CEEC Report on European Economic Co-operation. Two more were on their way. In 1971–2, at the request of the Home Secretary, Franks inquired into the controversial catch-all section 2 of the Official Secrets Act of 1911; and in 1982–3, at the request of the Prime Minister, into the Government's handling of the Falklands conflict. In between, Franks kept his hand in with a number of smaller and essentially solo productions on the economic development of India and Pakistan (1960), British Business Schools (1963), the Committee of London Clearing Banks (1974), and a register of immigrants' dependants (1976). In 1975 he was briefly but happily reunited with Radcliffe on a Committee of Privy Counsellors inquiring into the publication of Ministerial Memoirs.

Franks did not write these Franks Reports, and yet he was their author.[1] Once he had his commission, he would reflect on the nature of the task. The period of reflection was fundamental. From it would emerge the shape and direction of the inquiry. It involved deep meditation on a sacred text: the terms of reference. For the Oxford inquiry Franks had the opportunity in the *petit comité* virtually to write his own. Normally, the terms of reference were given to him. His disposition, reinforced by the experience of the CEEC, was first to interrogate and preferably to vet them; and then to navigate by them, scrupulously. If he was not satisfied, he would refuse the commission. He turned down the once powerful ideologue of the free market, Keith Joseph, who wanted him to report on the state of British universities, because he believed the terms of reference were slanted. No second Robbins he. Franks hated getting lost or diverted. 'We could have gone into all these questions [of monetary policy]', he said of his earlier experience with Radcliffe, 'but, if we had produced answers to all of them, we would have been more than a committee. We would have been divinely inspired. We therefore stuck to our terms of reference.'[2]

Before he convened a committee, then, Franks sought to discover by means of excogitation what exactly they should inquire into, and how they should proceed—'how to lay the whole thing on'. This did not mean that his colleagues were deprived of the pleasure of thinking it through for themselves. After each one had given an account of himself, as like as not they would find that their first task was to go through the terms of reference, line by line, 'clearing the ground a little, and removing some of the rubbish that lies in the way of knowledge'.[3]

Secondly, Franks's predilection for public hearings (or at least published evidence), and his complete mastery of the form, progressively augmented his personal authority as each inquiry ran its course.[4] A similar progression could be observed, cumulatively, from one inquiry to the next. This phenomenon may have had the effect of humbling some witnesses—though senior politicians and, it may be thought, Oxford dons are extraordinarily difficult to humble—but it also meant that the process of the inquiry was effectively controlled by the chairman. In camera or out, there was no monkeying with Oliver Franks. 'Of one thing I am certain', said Wittgenstein. 'We are not here in order to have a good time.'[5] That was often how it seemed, though Franks himself might not have gone so far. Unmistakably, however, his inquiries were not for sport.

The reports which followed were imbued with his presence. They excelled in exposition and analysis. They exhibited a drive for clarity and rationality and efficiency. 'An efficient organization is the essential condition of most of the other reforms which we wish to advocate', the Oxford Report declared.[6] The others spoke in the same tongue. The reforms they advocated were enlightened, ameliorative, *improving* in the sense that Gladstone understood. Of two possible comparators, Radcliffe and Robbins, Noel Annan has written: 'They were sagacious, believed themselves to be liberal, were in fact sound conservatives on most issues, were loyal to any institution with which they were connected, and regarded those who criticized it as ignorant, malignant or ill-informed.' In the Oxford context much the same could be said of Kenneth Wheare, for example, or Norman Chester. Doubtless there was some of this in Oliver Franks, but he was either less conservative or more liberal. The urge to improve was stronger. His hearing was more acute. He had no difficulty at all in accommodating criticism of cherished institutions, so much so that he was the target of the classic calumny. 'It is a pity', wrote Max Beloff foolishly in 1966, 'that Lord Franks who has made important contributions to Britain's public life in more than one respect, should seek to be remembered in history as the Neville Chamberlain of Oxford's era of "appeasement".'[7]

Appeasement is supposed to be both futile and immoral. Franks Reports, on the other hand, were very moral documents. They were concerned with the operation of moral principles in 'the workaday world', to use a Franksian expression. They tackled awkward questions. What is fair? What is just? What, indeed, is right? On Oxford, for instance:

Our proposals for a new college contributions system are based upon the idea that there is a minimum level of endowment below which a college cannot adequately function as a 'state of the union'. It therefore seemed to us just to devise a scheme . . . by which all the well-to-do colleges will contribute to raise the endowments of the weak to a level at which they can live a decent college life.[8]

On Administrative Tribunals, the least appetizing of subjects, the proposals had the same distinctive thrust. They were explicitly designed to promote openness, fairness, and impartiality in the tribunal and public-inquiry mechanism, in which purpose they were remarkably successful. This trinity of attributes, the philosophical underpinning of the report, was formulated by Oliver Franks. Except perhaps in the field of intelligence (of which more below), the Grand Inquisitor had no truck with official 'mystery-mongering'.[9]

'The office of chairman', Franks had written in 1947, 'is primarily that of a judge, whose judgement is likely to be accepted if it adds wisdom to impartiality.'[10] The comparison is suggestive. In public he wore the countenance of the Inquisitor. In private he became more aptly the Adjudicator. Oliver Franks, it was thought, could adjudicate anything; but it was not expected that anything would include the Government itself. In 1982, however, after the convulsion caused by the Argentine invasion of the Falkland Islands, he was called upon to do precisely that.

The invasion took place on 2 April 1982. Overnight, *las Islas Malvinas* were transformed from a postage stamp into a political reality, just as the Argentines had always dreamed they would be. To the astonishment of the world and the mortification of the inhabitants, plain old Port Stanley suddenly took on a new identity as *Puerto Argentino*. Spanish was once again the language of the streets. An Argentine soldier reflected afterwards, 'When we first arrived in the Malvinas, the general feeling was that the war—such as it was—was over; it had been won for Argentina on 2 April.'[11] In Buenos Aires joy was unconfined. The junta led by General Leopoldo Galtieri had executed a daring and successful *coup de main*. After waiting 150 years they had regained possession of what was rightfully theirs. The British garrison had been expelled, the British Lion tamed, the Iron Lady humbled.

In London this impertinence triggered a profound political crisis. 'One felt they might do it,' Lord Whitelaw subsequently remarked, 'but one never really believed they would.'[12] On 5 April the much-admired Foreign Secretary, Lord Carrington, resigned. His ministerial team went with him. In the act of departure Carrington spoke resonantly of 'a great national humiliation'. Later he wrote: 'The nation feels that there has been a disgrace. Someone must have been to blame. The disgrace must be purged. The person to purge it should be the minister in charge.'[13] Would this be sufficient expiation? Would the Foreign Secretary be the first or the last to go? No one could foretell, but as a hastily assembled naval task force inched implausibly out of

Portsmouth it was hard to be optimistic. Within the week, half-buried in the accumulating pile of political debris, there was the promise of a truly eschato-logical purgative. On 8 April, in a written answer to a parliamentary question, the Prime Minister declared her belief that 'there should be a review of the way in which the government departments concerned discharged their respon-sibilities in the period leading up to the Argentinian invasion'. She would con-sider what form the review might take and in due course make a statement to the House of Commons.[14]

Subsequent events by no means fulfilled Argentine expectations. There was a real war. It was short and in its own terms decisive. British landings began on 21 May. The Argentines surrendered on 14 June. Some 900 servicemen perished. Nothing remained of *las Islas Malvinas* but a gleam in the eye. 'Still as Saxon slow at starting, still as weirdly wont to win.' In this miraculously transformed environment the Prime Minister announced the appointment of a Committee of Privy Counsellors under the chairmanship of Lord Franks, with far-reaching terms of reference:

To review the way in which the responsibilities of Government in relation to the Falkland Islands and their Dependencies were discharged in the period leading up to the Argentine invasion of the Falkland Islands on 2 April 1982, taking into account all such factors in previous years as are relevant; and to report.[15]

This committee started work on 26 July 1982. Five brief months later, on an uncommonly auspicious New Year's Eve, their findings were handed person-ally to the waiting Margaret Thatcher. How the heart must have raced at the sweet, secret moment of discovery! Tensely anticipated in every quarter, this particular Franks Report (formally known as the *Falkland Islands Review*), the most controversial of them all, was released on 18 January 1983, instantly appropriated, hotly debated, and as quickly forgotten.[16] Already an anachron-ism when it began, by the time of its first anniversary the Falklands War seemed to have passed into ancient history. With remarkable speed the report induced a profound sense of closure in the British body politic, if not the Argentine. To the intense disappointment of the Iron Lady's many enemies, Franks exposed misdemeanours aplenty but no high crimes. For those inclined to impeach, the sinking of the *General Belgrano* on 2 May 1982 remained the only hope, increasingly forlorn.

And yet it was, and is, a revelatory report. Professor W. J. M. Mackenzie's marvellous 'translation' of the 1961 Plowden Report on the control of public expenditure applies with equal force to Franks on the Falklands: 'Unluckily, it turns out that the real problem is about the nature of government in general, and of British government in particular. This is what we are discussing, but of course we have to wrap it up in Mandarin prose.'[17] The watchful Tony Benn was not joking when he said in the Commons debate that he knew more now about certain developments in the Labour Cabinet of which he was a member than he did at the time.[18] The report was an unseasonable tribune for open government, from the innermost counsels of state. It afforded detailed and punctual public scrutiny of diplomatic, military and, most notable of all, intelligence traffic between clearly identified agencies and precisely attributed individuals. It quoted verbatim from top-secret documents only months after they had been written. It gave an account of the structure and function of the unmentionable Joint Intelligence Organization. No British official publication this century has disclosed so much, so soon of that forbidden realm where the security classification is king. It is evident that the rigid prohibitions of conventional discourse were carefully but deliberately relaxed. The report makes an exceptional feast, 'for your eyes only'.[19]

The nature, purpose, and effect of the whole exercise became entangled in the grab for immediate advantage from it. Franks's committee found themselves in the unusual position of reviewing a putative diplomatic failure in the light of a decisive military success. Franks, who had been reading his favourite Barbara Tuchman, was reminded of the congressional investigation into the Japanese attack on Pearl Harbor on 7 December 1941. In an essay with the pregnant title 'Is History a Guide to the Future?', Tuchman had written:

Pearl Harbor is the classic example of failure to learn from history. From hindsight we now know that what we should have anticipated was a surprise attack by Japan in the midst of negotiations. Merely because this was dishonourable, did that make it unthinkable? Hardly. It was exactly the procedure Japan had adopted in 1904 when she opened the Russo-Japanese War by surprise attack on the Russian fleet at Port Arthur. In addition we had every possible physical indication. We had broken the Japanese code, we had warnings on radar, we had a constant flow of accurate intelligence. What failed?[20]

No proper British precedents suggest themselves, in spite of the Prime Minister's contention that committees of Privy Counsellors had been used before 'to look into matters where the functioning of the Government has been called in question and sensitive information and issues are involved', for example the embarrassing disappearance of two British diplomats (Guy Burgess and Donald Maclean) in 1951.[21] Perhaps the only possible comparison is with the Dardanelles Commission of 1916–17, established under the chairmanship of Lord Cromer 'to inquire into the origin, inception, and conduct of operations in the Dardanelles' in 1915.[22] Yet although there were certain similarities to the Falklands inquiry in terms of scope and substance and high political interest, there were important differences between the two. Most fundamentally, the Dardanelles campaign was universally regarded as a disaster— the very reason for the inquiry. Winston Churchill wrote at the time:

It seems to me very necessary for the Commission to bear in mind the circumstances in which their inquiry is pursued. The enterprise has ended in defeat and failure. The Army has been withdrawn. The positions which they had won by so much effort and sacrifice have been yielded to the enemy. The hopes, the legitimate expectations, the chances of battle have vanished away; only the slaughter, the suffering and the waste remains . . . A great volume of prejudice and not unnatural vexation has gathered round the story of the expedition. All tongues are freed. The natural tendency of the Commission is to look for faults and errors and it is not surprising that they should find them.[23]

The Falklands Committee were often to reflect on how different it would have been if that enterprise too had ended in defeat and failure. But they were permitted the unaccustomed luxury of keeping their reflections to themselves.[24]

The Dardanelles Commission were offered an obvious, indeed notorious, ministerial target. Churchill, as First Lord of the Admiralty and hyperactive member of the Dardanelles Committee, the war cabinet of its day, was widely held to be the ardent and characteristically unrepentant sponsor of the whole operation. Faced with this temptation the commissioners exercised considerable restraint, as the target himself acknowledged in welcoming their report as, 'at any rate, an instalment of fair play'.

They have swept away directly, or by implication, many serious and reckless charges which have passed current broadcast throughout the land during the long months of the last two years. They have reduced these charges within the limits of modest and sober criticism, and, further, by laying before the nation the general outlines of the story—a long, tangled and complicated story—they have limited the responsibilities which have been thrown on me and under which I have greatly suffered.[25]

Pre-empted by Carrington's resignation, the Falklands Committee were not led into any such temptation—not even by the biggest target of them all, Margaret Thatcher, 'she who must be obeyed'. The two functions mentioned by Churchill, however, found a distinct echo in the later report. Franks went so far as to include as a separate annex itemized 'Comments on some specific assertions', expressly to 'clear up damaging misunderstandings'. For instance, the interesting assertion that 'clear warnings of the invasion from American intelligence sources were circulating more than a week beforehand' was met by the equally interesting comment that 'no intelligence about the invasion was received from American sources, before it took place, by satellite or otherwise'.[26]

Father Franks too laid a story before the nation. Some seventy pages, the first three chapters, of a ninety-page report consisted of an historical analysis beginning in 1965 and becoming progressively more detailed as it approached the invasion date, culminating in an often hour-by-hour treatment of the last days. A fourth and final chapter addressed questions prompted by the central issue of the committee's remit, namely the way in which the responsibilities of government were discharged. The three historical chapters have been criticized on the one hand for beginning as late as 1965, and on the other for relegating Franks's supposedly more important task—adjudication—to the conclusion of the report. Neither criticism is particularly well founded. It is true that there was barely any acknowledgement of what might be called the prehistory of the invasion. This seems entirely understandable given the tenor of the terms of reference, the degree of urgency imparted by the Prime Minister's eager hope and the chairman's preference for the work to be concluded within six months, and the evident desirability of keeping the final product to manageable proportions for a potentially wide readership.[27] In fact the story that Franks did tell, so often skimmed as a kind of extended prologue to the final chapter (in extremity, the final paragraph), is absolutely central to an understanding of the report and the strange phenomena it described. The significance of this story lies first of all in the irretrievable fact of its telling, which was in itself a prime function of the inquiry. 'The Committee had to be set up,' *The Times* commented, 'if only to provide some objective commentary on a national drama which had brought the country to a pitch of emotional intensity unwitnessed for twenty-five years'—that is, since Suez.[28] More than this, Franks had to choose what kind of story to relate. The nature of his choice is the fascination of the report.

Comparison with the Dardanelles Commission is especially instructive in matters of personnel. The chairman, Cromer, expired in the middle of the proceedings in January 1917. At 75, he was two years younger than Franks, who remained in exceeding good health throughout. The secretary, E. Grimwood Mears, a former barrister, accepted the appointment on condition that he was knighted for his services; his wish was promptly granted. Anthony Rawsthorne, an experienced Assistant Secretary in the Home Office—a department relatively untainted by Falklands affairs—was well versed in committee work, a handy draftsman, and Positively Vetted; delighted with the appointment, he made no such stipulation. There were eight Dardanelles commissioners including the chairman, a motley group of varying distinction.[29] Not all were Privy Counsellors, whereas this was in effect made a requirement for the Falklands six, one of whom (Sir Patrick Nairne) was sworn in especially for the purpose. The Privy Counsellor is bound by a mighty oath of secrecy and truth. He may be entrusted with the most intimate secrets of state. He may see documents of the highest security classification. He may cross-question Prime Ministers past and present. What he may not do, in Oliver Franks's choice phrase, is blab.[30]

It is now clear that the Committee of Privy Counsellors represented the outcome of a whole series of calculations of the utmost political delicacy. The primary one was its very existence. 'As the Prime Minister probably recognises,' remarked Roy Jenkins, then leader of the Social Democrats, in the Commons debate on the appointment of the committee, 'an inquiry has always been part of the bargain. It was understood that there should not be criticism during the operation while British lives were at risk, but that she would agree to the fullest inquiry as soon as the operation was concluded.'[31] Prima facie evidence for such a bargain is provided by the advance commitment to a review, in many ways a surprising commitment made 'in the heat of the moment to re-establish the authority of a government at war', as *The Economist* underlined. In this sense, perhaps, the Government was forced to make a concession, as was persistently alleged by its critics.[32] If sedulous bipartisanship is a necessary condition for the successful prosecution of modern warfare, to concede an inquiry may be an essential device of political management. Certainly immense care was taken in consulting the leader of the Opposition (Michael Foot) and to some extent the leaders of the other political parties on the fundamentals of the exercise: the character of the review (not, for example, a judicial inquiry, or an investigation by a parliamentary select committee); the choice of chairman; the composition of the membership; and the terms of reference. Interestingly enough, on all four counts the Prime Minister's proposals were received with general approbation.[33]

The first and as it seems the only choice for the all-important post of chairman was Oliver Franks—'one of our most distinguished public figures', proclaimed Mrs Thatcher—and a Privy Counsellor since 1949.[34] Franks's name was originally suggested by his long-standing admirer and friend Sir Robert Armstrong, the Cabinet Secretary, who found a receptive ear. Armstrong was promptly dispatched to Franks's Oxford retreat in order to sound him out and at the same time discreetly test what has been called 'the condition of his marbles'. Any misgivings were speedily removed. The Franks family traditionally enjoys a vigorous old age. Oliver was a mere 77. His marbles, as Peter Hennessy has reported, were in perfect rolling order.[35]

Franks had served inconspicuously on the Political Honours Scrutiny Committee (PHSC) during Mrs Thatcher's period in office, but was not well known to her personally. Nevertheless it is likely that in prospect she approved of him rather more strongly than he of her. Unlike Locke, Franks was never 'suspected to be ill-affected to the Government'. In party political terms, he had remained, in his own word, 'a neuter'.[36] The PHSC, latterly a troika of some substance, has a duty to investigate the suitability of recommendations for honours of CBE level and above, and to refuse a certificate of authorization if it concludes that 'the past history of a person renders him (or her) unsuitable to be recommended'. Franks had been invited to become a member by James Callaghan in 1976, alongside the Conservative peer Lord Carr and the Labour peer Lord Shackleton, in order to cleanse a system that had begun to smell a little too strongly of personal patronage.[37] He took his duties as seriously as might be expected of one who had imbibed probity from the cradle. 'But as for those who look down with a great and lofty spirit upon prosperity and adversity alike, especially when some grand and honourable matter is before them, which converts them wholly to itself and possesses them, who will then fail to admire the splendour and beauty of virtue?'[38] In this role, from 1979, he had seen something of Margaret Thatcher, but scarcely more than her pubic face, which he found rather too headmistressy for comfort. Their first and only tête-à-tête took place several months after Franks had officially reported. In May 1983 he was summoned to the presence. The usual pleasantries—'three minutes of inanities'—were followed by two and a half hours of strenuous discussion launched by a meaningful probe from the Prime Minister: 'I don't think you said all that was in your mind with regard to intelligence.'[39]

Thatcher was right. For Franks, intelligence 'goes to the guts of things'. He therefore preferred not to talk about it. His answer to Barbara Tuchman's question, 'What failed?', was very like her own: 'Not information but *judgement.*'

We had all the evidence and refused to interpret it correctly . . . Men will not believe what does not fit in with their plans or suit their prearrangments. The flaw in all military intelligence, whether twenty or fifty or one hundred percent accurate, is that it is no better than the judgement of its interpreters, and this judgement is the product of a mass of individual, social, and political biases, prejudgements, and wishful thinkings; in short, it is human and therefore fallible.[40]

Franks profoundly agreed. In the course of the inquiry he had seen not only the final asessments but also the raw material from the Government Communications Headquarters (GCHQ), Cheltenham, on which they are based. He knew that the intelligence picture is not 'choate'. Rather, it is 'a Sargasso Sea of bits and pieces', out of which it may be possible to detect a pattern—or it may not. It is a matter of interpretation. What concerned Franks was how the interpreting was done, and by whom. Typically, his interest focused on the machinery of intelligence assessment. What he emphasized to Thatcher was the twin requirement of independence and responsiveness: independence from departmental axe-grinding (especially from the practised axe-grinders at the Foreign Office), and responsiveness to new patterns in ancient and unregarded seas. In short, it was a problem of 'the best mix of old hands and new minds'.[41]

Franks's colleagues were very largely selected for him. The composition of the committee was a juggling act of considerable virtuosity, much maligned. Margaret Thatcher suggested the idea of two Privy Counsellors from each of the main political parties, plus the former Permanent Secretary Sir Patrick Nairne as an 'independent' member (or a second independent member if Franks himself were so regarded). She nominated the former Conservative Cabinet Ministers Lord Barber and Lord Watkinson. Michael Foot nominated the former Labour Cabinet Ministers Lord Lever and Merlyn Rees MP.[42] All of these names were mutually agreed, apparently without difficulty, though their selection faced substantial criticism, then and since. They were stigmatized as a 'comfortable, conservative and clubbable' coterie, unlikely to pursue their inquiries with the necessary zeal; greybeards of 'the governmental purple', examining the performance of their fellows and colleagues, past and present: in a word, members of that deplorable fraternity, the Establishment. 'Privy Counsellors', wrote Simon Jenkins pithily, 'are not the most rigorous investigators of the nation's privy counsels.'[43]

There is undeniable truth to this disparaging assessment of the committee, but it does not take us very far. Privy Counsellors are honour-bound members of the Establishment. Oathing is a powerful force in any tribe. Committees of inquiry necessarily draw upon those who have previously lived the life. Who else would sit, unpaid, unsung, and who would give attention? The Falklands inquiry imposed an additional requirement, of especial concern to Robert Armstrong: familiarity with and sensitivity to the handling of intelligence, the last redoubt of state security.[44] *Quis custodiet ipsos custodes?*[45] From this perspective the credentials of the committee may appear, if not more impressive, then at least more appropriate. Franks had handled most things in his time, including the singular misfortune of having Burgess, Maclean, and Philby all at some stage in his Washington embassy. Barber would have seen enough as Chancellor of the Exchequer, Lever as a member of several important Cabinet committees. The others all had some continuous experience of security matters. Watkinson had been Minister of Defence; Rees, Northern Ireland Secretary and Home Secretary. Nairne, one of the most highly regarded Civil Servants of his generation, had a long pedigree in the Admiralty, the Ministry of Defence, and the Cabinet Office. Equally, his final tenure at the Department of Health and Social Security (1975–81) meant that he could in no way be associated with recent Falklands policy-making. He appeared to have been Private or Permanent Secretary to almost every important politician of the previous thirty years. Among them, at the end of the 1950s, was a young First Lord of the Admiralty by the name of Carrington.[46]

The disparaging assessment of the committee is more interestingly developed in what might be called the placeman theory. The theory states that 'all past prime ministers can happily sit quietly in their seats because they have a friend at court', with the corollary that Civil Servants had to have a friend too.[47] On this interpretation there was complete 'cover' for the entire pre-Thatcher period treated in the report: Lever for the Labour Governments of Harold Wilson (1964–70 and 1974–6); Barber for the Conservative Government of Edward Heath (1970–4); Rees for Wilson's Labour successor James Callaghan (1976–9), historically, the most vulnerable of the three to detailed disinterment. Nairne seemed to be a natural choice for the Civil Servants' friend. Watkinson, apparently, was friend to no one (though in office under Harold Macmillan); whether by accident or design, he did not take a leading part in the proceedings.[48]

The prospect of an inquiry in this field ranging freely across previous Administrations and rummaging through their normally inviolate papers was indeed an alarming one.[49] To the extent that the composition of the committee was designed to reassure, the placeman theory may have something to recommend it. Otherwise, like most conspiracy theories, it is appealing but overdrawn. The most important member of the committee, the chairman, was left out of the account. Nairne for one was miscast, his scepticism and tenacity underrated. Of the postulated connections, the most plausible was that between Rees and Callaghan, which was certainly very close. In truth Rees— mischievously described by one of his own party as 'the youngest and most militant member of the inquiry, which says a lot about its membership'— found himself in a most uncomfortable position.[50] Unlike the others, he was still an active member of a front-bench team in the House of Commons. He had to do his duty by the committee, but also by the Labour Opposition. If he sought in general to defend the record of the Callaghan regime against that of the Thatcher one, he had no wish to undermine the committee by presenting a minority report. In the subsequent Commons debate, on the other hand, he felt able to vote against the report to which he had put his name, on the curi- ous grounds that the committee had been critical enough already.[51]

Rees's colleague Lord Lever, avowedly 'nobody's man', accepted nomination to the committee only on condition that he would not have a party political game to play.[52] He did his bit, however, to protect Callaghan on at least one controversial issue. In November 1977, at a time of high tension in Anglo-Argentine relations, the Callaghan Government decided to deploy a small naval force of two frigates to the area and a submarine to the immediate vicinity of the Falklands, in advance of the next round of negotiations: 'a force of sufficient strength, available if necessary, to convince the Argentines that military action by them would meet resistance'—that is, a measure of prevent- ive deterrence. The decision was taken by the Defence and Overseas Policy Committee of the Cabinet—'OD' in Whitehall parlance—chaired by the Prime Minister. As Energy Secretary, with a departmental interest in the region's oil reserves, Tony Benn was present at one of the crucial meetings. With magnificent disregard for security, he recorded their discussion in his diary:

Before us was a secret Joint Intelligence Committee report marked 'Delicate Source— UK Eyes Only' which said that the Argentinian forces were strong enough to take over the Falkland Islands without a shot being fired. David Owen [the Foreign Secretary] reported that the Argentinians were likely to be very tough if the negotiations sched- uled for December in New York fell through . . . Jim [Callaghan], in a very John Bullish mood, said, 'World opinion may be against us, but they might feel differently if the Argentinians attack the Falklands.' So he asked the navy to send out two frigates and possibly a nuclear submarine *before* the negotiations began. A very tough line. We were all sworn to secrecy about the military operations. I don't like secrets.[53]

As Benn's account suggests, and as Franks confirmed, the deployment was made covertly. (It was revealed to the House of Commons by Callaghan him- self during the pre-invasion crisis of 30 March 1982.) The critical component was the submarine, whose presence could be concealed from friend and foe alike—gunboat diplomacy of immense sophistication.[54]

The naval force was in position by mid-December 1977. Over the following weeks the threat to the Islands receded. In due course both submarine and ships were withdrawn. Were the Argentines deterred by these means, as Callaghan has suggested? The answer appears to depend on the prior question of how much they knew at the time about British actions, for if Buenos Aires did not know of the deployment, the deterrent effect was at best potential and unprovable. Franks revealed that the many unbelievers included Lord Carrington, whose officials let him into the secret on 5 March 1982—a little late, it may be thought, though Franks refrained from saying so. What is clear from the scattered references in the report is that the issue was raised only in passing, if anything rather casually. Carrington asked whether the Argentines had known about the deployment and was informed that they had not, where-upon 'he took the view that this reduced its relevance to the situation he faced'. Accordingly, 'he did not pursue the matter'. Nor did his officials recom-mend that he should.[55]

In this way no submarine deployment was made, or even fully considered, at the very time it could have done most good. The preventive action taken by the Callaghan Government in 1977 became a 'non-precedent' for the Thatcher Government in 1982, almost by default. That was a great blunder, perhaps a fatal one, which Franks was apparently unwilling to second-guess.[56] It was also the symptom of a malaise afflicting the vital parts of the Iron Lady's administration, a malaise typified by her own ruinous question: 'Is he one of us?' Half-concealed for a long period—not least, by the Falklands vic-tory—the terminal nature of this condition was publicly and dramatically exposed in 1990, in the course of Thatcher's forced resignation.[57] Well before that, however, the syndrome had been described with clinical precision in the pages of the *Falkland Islands Review*.

Callaghan for his part—once described by Franks as 'a cautious and calcu-lating man who likes to foresee the consequences and repercussions of any action he undertakes'—claimed to have told the head of the Secret Intelligence Service, the late Sir Maurice Oldfield, of the decision to deploy as soon as it was taken. He has hinted that the information was passed on, but has provided no unequivocal statement of how and when. 'It was of course my purpose in telling Sir Maurice Oldfield of the position so that he should make use of the information. I have no doubt that he understood that, and I should be astonished if he did not make use of it.'[58] Merlyn Rees (then Home Secretary), who was there, was convinced that Callaghan arranged for the Argentines to find out about the deployment by instructing Oldfield to inform them 'in the most appropriate fashion', and that Oldfield complied; his recol-lection of the Prime Minister taking the old spy-master for a walk round the garden adds a touch of local colour to the story.[59] This interpretation has been supported by Denis Healey (then Chancellor of the Exchequer).[60] Harold Lever, on the other hand (Chancellor of the Duchy of Lancaster), who was also there, was equally convinced that Callaghan did no such thing, or at least that the Argentines were *not* informed; his recollection was confirmed by a fruitless search for clues among the documents made available to the Franks committee. This negative finding may not be conclusive, but it was good enough for Lever. In the circumstances he was anxious to minimize any embarrassment to Callaghan. Thus the deadpan first draft of the report, 'We have had no evidence that the Argentine Government *were informed* of this deployment', gave way to a more evasive final version, 'We have found no evidence that the Argentine Government ever *came to know* of its existence.'[61] Such is the tortuous process of report writing.

Did the Argentines know? As Franks might have said, it is impossible to be certain. Argentine testimony is every bit as contradictory as the British, and tainted by the ignominy of 1982.[62] However, there is a further twist. Both David Owen (the Foreign Secretary) and Ted Rowlands (Minister of State at the Foreign Office) agreed with Lever that the deployment remained secret until Callaghan's subsequent revelation of it—but they argued that the efficacy of the action lay precisely in that secrecy. In David Owen's version, 'Our naval deployment was an insurance policy, it did not of itself deter.' Of Carrington's failure to pursue the matter, Owen has observed: 'It was a serious error to conclude that because no Argentines had been told of the deployment in 1977, it had no relevance to the situation in March 1982. It was highly relevant. If a submarine had been on station, President Reagan could have told President Galtieri that a submarine was there and that Britain would torpedo any Argentine ships that approached the Falklands.'[63] On this argument, in tacitly endorsing Carrington's line of reasoning, Franks missed the point. What mattered was that a British Government had nerved itself to act, and in time. Owen, indeed, was puffed with pride that even our American cousins were not informed, a claim corroborated in a small way by Benn's intriguing disclosure of the classification of the intelligence report prepared for OD ('UK Eyes Only'). We glimpse the consoling power of independent action. At the going down of the sun, it is still possible to shuffle submarines back and forth across the imperial chessboard without reference to the Pentagon. American hegemony evidently chafes the spirit, however special the relationship.

According to its many detractors, a committee so constituted could be expected to produce only one kind of report. The letters column of *The Times* echoed to Correlli Barnett's ringing denunciation. 'In the Franks Report the British Establishment has sat in judgment on the British Establishment and found it not guilty.'[64] On this view the report, like the committee, was fatally compromised. It was 'a classic Establishment job', in the words of its most trenchant critic, Hugo Young.

Lord Franks's admirers saw the report as his last flawless exercise in mandarin ambiguity. But this was not its political impact, and nor, one must surmise, was it intended to be.

What the Franks Report was really addressing was another imperative familiar to mandarins, that of political reality. The fact was that the war had been won, and nothing could be allowed to interfere with this great event. Had the war been lost, the same set of facts would have been produced as a devastating proof of negligence. But, as was . . . later conceded from inside the committee, Lord Franks's strategic objective was to ensure that Mrs Thatcher's reputation should not be damaged. He could see no possible need, in the circumstances, for any other course of action.[65]

This is a grave indictment. It rests on the apparent exoneration offered in the report's conclusion, the notorious paragraph 339; or more precisely in the latter part of its last sentence, which by a quirk of fate appeared in splendid isolation on the last page. The offending passage ran: 'we conclude that we would not be justified in attaching any criticism or blame to the present Government for the Argentine Junta's decision to commit its act of unprovoked aggression in the invasion of the Falkland Islands on 2 April 1982.' Anticipating Hugo Young, Simon Jenkins charged that 'the only basis for this exoneration—admitted privately by some Franks committee members—was an understandable desire not to reopen political wounds at a time of rejoicing'.[66] To some degree the charge has stuck. In many quarters it was, and still is, something of a commonplace to dismiss the report as 'an unwarranted apologia'.[67]

The immediate impression of a final verdict delivered as a ringing declaration of faith in the victress received neat visual reinforcement from the suggestive layout of the report's final page. The headlines were set accordingly. 'Franks clears Maggie' was the reflex reaction, a reaction conditioned by the artful news management of the report's rush release: a tightly restricted distribution of advance copies, a prepared list of the numbers of 'key paragraphs', a spate of pre-publication leaks studiously designed to discount criticism of the Prime Minister herself and implant the idea of a long period of cross-party war guilt.[68] As to the source of the leaks, Franks was reminded of a remark by Harold Macmillan. 'Political casks always leak at the top.'[69] The ground had been prepared. The most celebrated variant of the 'Franks clears Maggie' approach was James Callaghan's well-made jest that 'for 338 paragraphs the Franks Report painted a splendid picture, delineating the light and shade. The glowing colours came out. When Franks got to paragraph 339, he got fed up with the canvas that he was painting and chucked a bucket of whitewash over it.'[70] The cartoonists had a field day.

Without subscribing to 'mandarin ambiguity', it is perfectly possible to see in the conclusion of the report something more than a political slogan. The paragraph should be taken whole:

Against this background [a recapitulation of the constraints on policy-making] we have pointed out in this Chapter where different decisions might have been taken, where fuller consideration of alternative courses of action might, in our opinion, have been advantageous, and where the machinery of Government could have been better used. But, if the British Government had acted differently in the ways we have indicated, it is impossible to judge what the impact on the Argentine Government or the implications for the course of events might have been. There is no reasonable basis for any suggestion—which would be purely hypothetical—that the invasion would have been prevented if the Government had acted in the ways indicated in our Report. Taking account of these considerations, and of all the evidence we have received, we conclude that we would not be justified in attaching any criticism or blame to the present Government for the Argentine Junta's decision to commit its act of unprovoked aggression in the invasion of the Falkland Islands on 2 April 1982.

The first thing to be said about this paragraph is that it was drafted collectively in committee: it was a composite effort, strenuously achieved. This was highly unusual. The bulk of the drafting was done by the secretary, Anthony Rawsthorne, who had been selected partly for that purpose. Patrick Nairne, a fabled draftsman, did most of the rest. The final paragraph must have seemed too important to be left to the secretary. Probably there were varying motives for accepting what ultimately emerged. Political loyalties naturally tended to reassert themselves at this stage. Different committee members attached special significance to different parts of the whole. For Rees, the first sentence was the key: it reiterated the report's critique of the Conservative Government then in power. For Nairne, as we shall see, the second and third sentences were crucial. For Barber and Watkinson, the last sentence accommodated their own reluctance to weaken Margaret Thatcher.[71] It was for the chairman, who was wont to exercise a tight rein on the proceedings, to ensure that collective responsibility ultimately prevailed. Oliver Franks always liked to produce a unanimous report. He took Radcliffe's view, that 'when several persons are charged with the responsibility for producing a joint report on matters that are both complex and wide-ranging, the right course is that sometimes individual opinions and preferences should be modified or abandoned for the sake of a presentation that can be put forward as the best collective view of the committee as a whole'. On the Falklands above all, he squeezed hard for unanimity. At a certain cost, he achieved it.[72]

How then did the committee reach this conclusion, and what exactly did it mean? *Pace* Hugo Young, Franks himself 'had no motive or desire to move one way or the other', and no grand design. 'I hadn't a clue where we would come out.'[73] Thatcher's reputation was not his prime concern. Of course he was alive to the political explosiveness of the inquiry. He questioned Robert Armstrong closely at the outset on the kind of job he was being asked to do. The advice he received was to provide a definitive statement that would take the issue out of domestic party politics, and 'turn it into political history'.[74] These were fundamental considerations from an influential source; but they gave no more than general guidance. In the case of the Iron Lady versus the Tin Pot Dictator, Franks was neither predisposed nor pre-ordained to acquit.

The committee spent their first six weeks combing the unprecedented mass of Government documents made available to them. Unlike the Dardanelles Commission, each member went through everything, individually. Apart from the direct benefits of this procedure, Franks wanted to impose a pause in order to defuse any partisan feeling in the immediate aftermath of the war. He also wanted to be quite certain that there had been full disclosure by the departments concerned, going so far as to check the serial numbers of telegrams and request written assurances from the Permanent Secretaries concerned.[75] Only after an intensive period of reading-in and discussion did the committee begin taking oral evidence. The witnesses included Margaret Thatcher herself, exhaustively prepared, who performed keenly to scholarship standard.[76] In general the Foreign Office proved to be more co-operative (or more cocksure) than the Ministry of Defence, which is alleged to have briefed its representatives to give nothing to the committee if they could possibly help it. Certainly the report's references to defence policy-making are noticeably sparer than those to foreign policy-making. In this respect among others the Defence Secretary, John Nott, escaped very lightly.[77]

The richest evidence in this inquiry did come from the documents. In forming their judgement the committee followed three self-imposed injunctions: to avoid the exercise of hindsight, to determine what was reasonable in the light of the circumstances prevailing at the time, and to allow for the fact that those involved were not dealing exclusively with the Falklands. This approach, crucial to the outcome of the report, has been found too lenient or plain misguided. According to Correlli Barnett, 'If you examine people's actions "according to their own lights" you are bound to exonerate them.'[78] That is disputable; and it is difficult to see how else the inquiry could have proceeded. 'Reasonable men', another phrase with a Shakespearian echo, may have been a construct of the supremely reasonable Oliver Franks, but the test of *un*reasonable behaviour surely remains a sensible criterion for appraising the responsibilities of government. The two questions formulated by the committee in order to make that appraisal, however, may be more arguable. Could the Government have foreseen the invasion on 2 April? Could the Government have prevented the invasion? The first of these questions was answered categorically in the negative. 'The invasion of the Falkland Islands on 2 April could not have been foreseen.' There is a misconception that the second was answered similarly. In fact it was not. 'No simple answer' was available. The report merely indicated that 'it is impossible to judge' whether an invasion on that date could have been prevented.[79]

It was on the basis of this approach, and these questions and answers, that the report concluded as it did. The questions it posed—questions of the committee's own devising—were highly specific. The answers it gave were carefully circumscribed. Both related to one particular date. Contrary to reflex reaction, the report's 'exoneration' of the Thatcher Government was, by deliberate intent, materially incomplete. As always Franks stuck strictly to his terms of reference. Put crudely, the report blamed General Galtieri rather than Mrs Thatcher (or Lord Carrington) for what happened on 2 April 1982. No explicit conclusion was drawn about what had happened earlier or what might have happened later. As Sir Patrick Nairne has explained,

we were not asked to review the discharge of the Government's responsibilities in rela-tion to the *general deterrence of Argentina* from invasion. Of course, the report says a lot about deterrent action, and we criticized the Government for some inadequacies and failings; but here the second and third sentences of paragraph 339 are crucial—and we might perhaps have given them greater emphasis. If the strategic deployment by *succes-sive* governments of our naval forces had given the South Atlantic a higher priority, and if in 1981–2 we had not been trying to persuade Argentina to 'cool it', Argentina *might* have been deterred from invasion; but, in the actual circumstances, the committee could not conclude that the Thatcher Government should be blamed for Galtieri's dash for the Malvinas.[80]

This explanation is cogent but evidently frustrating. There is a lingering feel-ing that by fixing his attention on 2 April Franks succumbed to an over-literal interpretation of his terms of reference. But the principal cause of the frustra-tion is a morbid fascination with the concluding paragraph.[81] That unhappy composite was the terminus and not the focus of the Falklands Review. 'It is essential that our report should be read as a whole', the committee protested. Their protestation was ignored. Paragraph 339 became the cynosure of the report: truly a case of the tail wagging the dog.

The contributory causes are more speculative. Perhaps the very terms of reference were flawed: deceptively open, yet framed knowingly or unknow-ingly to dam the flow of the inquiry. The suggestion is as intriguing as it is imponderable. Perhaps the committee's questions were deficient. Numerous alternatives have been put forward; often they were subsumed in the rest of the report.[82] Undoubtedly the answers repay careful study. The invasion was impossible to foresee, it was argued, because of the close timing of the de-cision. Prevention was difficult and uncertain because at any given moment the conceivable measures might be too provocative or too late. The committee estimated that the final decision to invade was not taken in Buenos Aires until 31 March at the earliest, though they noted correctly that an Argentine task force had put to sea on 28 March. We now know that the decision was taken rather sooner, on 26 March (still only seven days before the operation was launched). Firm Argentine evidence on this point was not then available.[83] More significantly, the junta had been scheming since January 1982 to execute such an operation several months hence, probably between June and October, but certainly before January 1983, the 150th anniversary of British occupation. All of these dates were common knowledge on the streets of Buenos Aires in February 1982. 'A positive act of will on the part of British intelligence must have been required to discount such evidence.'[84] In reality, 'unprovoked aggression' was foreseen by almost everyone; but it was expected later in the year. What remains to be explained is the scrambling of the original timetable in late March to produce an invasion in early April. There is no doubting the aggression. But was it truly unprovoked?

With a target of six months and a staff of two, Franks had neither the time nor the resources to unearth new evidence from the Argentine side. The committee (none of whom spoke Spanish) was barely competent to evaluate what was already available. Surprisingly, they did not seek help from such well-connected journalists as Jimmy Burns of the *Financial Times* or Simon Jenkins of *The Economist*. Concentrating on the British side, they monitored the quickening tempo of events in February and March 1982, and criticized the Foreign Office sharply for failing adequately to respond. Franks himself thought that there was a tendency for officials to be imprisoned in the continuum of their past. As Barbara Tuchman put it in a lecture entitled 'Why Policy-Makers Do Not Listen',

When information is relayed to policy-makers, they respond in terms of what is already inside their heads and consequently make policy less to fit the facts than to fit the notions and intentions formed out of the mental baggage that has accumulated in their minds since childhood.[85]

The report rightly identified the South Georgia crisis as pivotal, yet its analysis of British moves in late March 1982 is often wanting. This applies particularly to their unintended consequences, for it is the *interactive* nature of the crisis that impresses. South Georgia was in that respect a microcosm of the wider conflict. The decision to dispatch the venerable *HMS Endurance* there from Port Stanley on 21 March and the so-called Carrington ultimatum of 23 March, for instance, may not have been war-starters, but they were almost certainly crisis-stimulators, inducing the junta to accelerate their own timetable of operations.[86] The belated decision to dispatch a submarine to the Falklands on 29 March, to be on station some two weeks later (a decision leaked almost immediately by the *Daily Express*), can only have strengthened Argentine resolve to seize the day. A series of 'final warnings' from London, woefully tepid, scarcely gave them pause, and it is a mystery why Franks confined himself to a single, gnomic observation on the subject. On 23 March a junior Minister stated in the Commons that it was the duty of any government 'to defend and support the Islanders to the best of their ability'. On 25 March the Argentine Foreign Minister was informed that Britain was 'committed to the defence of its sovereignty in South Georgia as elsewhere'. On 31 March the President of the United States (Ronald Reagan) was asked to make clear to the Argentine Government that Britain 'could not acquiesce in action against the Falkland Islands', an instruction he comfortably exceeded by speaking in terms of a *casus belli* when eventually he got through to Galtieri the following day—too late.[87]

For the Falklands, it was usually too late. 'Has it ever occurred to you that nothing is ever done until everyone is convinced that it ought to be done, and has been convinced for so long that it is now time to do something else?'[88] The story that Franks elected to tell was a modern tale of knight-errantry. Great deeds were done and great opportunities missed. There is a certain incoherence to the action. The plot drifts, helplessly. A pervasive air of unreality is punctured intermittently by bursts of pure *realpolitik*. The denouement is bloody farce. Read from the beginning, the *Falkland Islands Review* is a marvellous chronicle of unripe time.

'Timing' dominates the report. For successive British Governments of varying political hues time was lost and gained, bought and sold, stolen and retrieved, occasionaly right and more often wrong. When an illicit Argentine presence was discovered on Southern Thule in the South Sandwich Islands in December 1976, London first demanded an explanation and then issued a formal protest, but took no further action. The then head of the Latin American Department of the Foreign Office has commented: 'It gave them a card, certainly. On the other hand it helped us in doing what we were constantly attempting to do, which was to *play for time*. To play for time in the hope that events would arrange themselves in such a conjunction that some kind of solution would emerge.'[89] Similarly, when the Minister of State was briefed for the fruitless Anglo-Argentine talks in New York in February 1982, he was told that 'if things were getting difficult, we would just have to *buy time*'. The Minister continued plaintively:

What was putting us in a very difficult position was this pressure on 'time'. Acceptance of the negotiating commission [an Argentine idea] meant that we must have regular meetings, every month, conclude everything and reach an agreement by the end of 1982. Knowing what Island and Parliamentary opinion was, and how difficult it would be to find a solution, this squeeze on 'time' placed us under very difficult pressure.[90]

Thus time might run on or run out, but in the years covered by the Franks Report it was never, ever, *ripe*. Most fundamentally, this applied to the formulation and concertation of ministerial views, specifically in OD—now only a shadow of its former self. The signal failure of this key Cabinet committee even to discuss the Falklands from January 1981 until April 1982 (to be precise, the day before the invasion) is perhaps the most remarkable feature of 'the nature of government' exposed with such startling clarity by the report.[91] If the first responsibility for that failure was the Foreign Secretary's, the final responsibility was clearly the Prime Minister's. It is scarcely necessary to read between the lines of the report, a technique recommended somewhat disingenuously by several commentators, to trace the process of decision-making to its source. Damningly, Franks also disclosed that during the same period there was no reference to the Falklands in full Cabinet until Carrington recounted the events in South Georgia on 25 March 1982. For the attentive reader it is all there, 'plain as a pikestaff'.[92]

Why was there no meeting of OD? Because 'the time was never judged to be ripe'. This was the assessment of the luckless Lord Carrington. The then Permanent Secretary of the Foreign Office, Sir Michael Palliser, who was not the only official to favour such a meeting—in September 1981 for example—has since ventured an explanation of his master's thinking:

Lord Carrington just felt that the *timing* was wrong. That reflected not in the least hostility to him *in the cabinet*—I really don't think that was there at all—but more a feeling that the only time when one would really get a British Cabinet to *focus* on the issue was at a time when it was manifestly going to cause real difficulty if they did not.[93]

Carrington had known what ought to be done since 1979, when he first recommended substantive negotiation on the root cause of the Anglo-Argentine dispute, sovereignty, with leaseback as the end in view: that is, sovereignty would be transferred to Argentina but 'leased back' to the UK for a specified period, possibly the lifetime of the existing inhabitants.[94] Thatcher decreed that the future of Rhodesia must be settled before there could be any discussion of the Falklands. Carrington delivered such a settlement—Rhodesia became Zimbabwe—in the process alienating not a few in his own party, a major source of the hostility mentioned by Palliser. By 1981 he had not changed his mind about what ought to be done, but he also knew that in order to do it he would need to carry his principal Cabinet colleagues with him, and that public (and Islander) opinion would have to be 'guided' or 'educated' to accept it—to say nothing of the difficulty of the negotiations themselves. He realized that he had no hope of meeting even the first of these requirements.[95] There was in existence a profound suspicion of the Foreign Office in general and the Foreign Secretary in particular, to which Margaret Thatcher was by no means immune. Peter Carrington was definitely not one of us. The feeling was well characterized by Carrington himself as a belief 'that there is something disreputable or even treacherous in trying to seek agreement with foreign governments'. Holders of this belief 'carry chauvinism and insularity to such a degree that one almost feels they disapprove of anyone in the Foreign Office talking to a foreigner. Negotiation, it seems, is feebleness and unpatriotic. But the alternative to negotiation is confrontation.'[96]

Confrontation was the province of the Defence Secretary, John Nott, Carrington's chief interlocutor on the issue. Sir Anthony Williams, then Ambassador to Argentina, later remarked that the problem of defending the Falklands—or deterring the Argentines—was not a Foreign Office problem at all. 'It was a Ministry of Defence problem, and particularly it was a Ministry of Defence *budget* problem. We [the diplomats] were asked to operate this Argentina difficulty within certain parameters. One of those parameters was that, actually, we had no money to spend. Indeed, such money as we were spending was being cut down.'[97] Public expenditure cuts were the order of the day. In the midst of a stringent Defence Review, locked in mortal combat with the Chiefs of Staff, Nott proved to be a singularly unaccommodating colleague.

Some six months before the invasion, therefore, Carrington decided definitively to perpetuate on old British cross-party tradition. He thought he had a little time. Hopefully, he opted to play for more. He would neither break off negotiations nor promote leaseback. For the Foreign Secretary it was a doomed gamble on a dwindling asset. As Michael Charlton has written, 'these were the months which the locusts ate'. From remote Buenos Aires Anthony Williams lodged his celebrated protest against a decision 'to have no strategy at all beyond a general Micawberism'.[98] The object of the game slipped elusively away. On 5 March 1982 Carrington declined to pursue the matter of a naval deployment. 'The last moment at which . . . it would have been possible to sail a deterrent force to be in place' and ready, according to Franks, was now past. 'The psychological moment' for which Carrington was waiting to face his colleagues with an incontrovertible policy choice never came.[99] On 2 April 1982 time abruptly ran out. For the way in which the responsibilities of government were discharged in the period leading up to the Argentine invasion, the moral of the *Falkland Islands Review* is clear. 'Time, by the way, is like the medlar; it has a trick of going rotten before it is ripe.'[100]

9 Envoi

As soon as the Falklands report had been delivered, Franks did what he always did on completion of a task. He went home to cultivate his garden. 'Reports are like children', he would say. 'You bring them up, send them away on a raft, and kiss them goodbye.' When he dispatched the first of the brood, Administrative Tribunals, he wrote to the secretary of the committee: 'For me it has been a most interesting experience, the subject itself, working closely with good legal minds, and the position of being appointed by Government, yet not of it. I hope it will remain pleasantly in your mind too, a good job very well done and strangely interesting.' The mild air of detachment was very characteristic. Similarly, he hoped that the secretary of the Oxford committee had found the exercise interesting; something good might come of it; but it was *now over*.[1] On a Franks report, Franks observed and enforced total silence. There would be no justifications and no recriminations. It was for the 'sponsors'—often the Government—to frame a response. Any attacks would fade with time. It was no good bothering about the slings and arrows of outrageous fortune. 'He does not nurse resentment, because it is beneath a magnanimous man to remember things against people, especially wrongs; it is more like him to overlook them.'[2]

Franks was now 78. It was time for Government to let him alone. Oxford, however, was not done with him yet. Early in 1987 he received a letter from the Vice-Chancellor, Sir Patrick Neill. It was a cry for help. The university faced a crisis—a crisis of its own making—over the arcane but incendiary issue of 'entitlement'. Predictably, the issue had a history. In fact the history had become part of the problem.[3] Entitlement had been a running sore in Oxford for over a quarter of a century. As the Franks Report had served to highlight, Oxford dons generally have a dual loyalty: to their college, and to the university as a whole. They are two-hatted monsters, in Franks's phrase, College Fellows and at the same time University Lecturers. However, when the actual position was investigated in the early 1960s it was found that a significant number of those holding university lectureships did not in fact belong to any particular college. In a collegiate university these unfortunates resembled nothing so much as unpersons (and in the Oxford equivalent of Newspeak, they were known as non-Fellows or, more euphoniously, non-dons). This was plainly an undesirable state of affairs, but it was not at all easy to remedy. The non-Fellows were clustered in new and rarified disciplines (nuclear physics, biological anthropology), or at any rate those without a large undergraduate following. They might be extremely distinguished in their own fields—many were—but they were of no immediate use to colleges full of students clamouring to read such common or garden subjects as Chemistry, History, or English Literature. As far as undergraduate teaching was concerned, non-Fellows tended to be in non-fields: for the most part, that was why they were non-Fellows.

Two other explanations suggest themselves. Both speak to human foible. A few non-Fellows actively preferred this non-existence. It relieved them not only of teaching, but also of administration—for most dons, a necessary evil. ('Rather like Maria Theresa, they may lament it, but they take it on', as the Franks Report had said.[4]) A few, also, had a reputation for being difficult, wayward, or simply obnoxious. It is possible that in some cases the reputation was well deserved.

In the internal market for college Fellows, therefore, the abundant supply was subject to certain serious limitations as to discipline and, perhaps, disposition. The inelasticity of demand was even stronger. College fellowships were the preserve of college Governing Bodies, that is, the collectivity of existing Fellows. Like all closed societies, the Governing Body regulated their own numbers and elected their own successors. No one could compel a college to elect a new Fellow. An unwary head of house could soon find himself bound, and in some cases gagged, by the majority of his colleagues. The university had no standing in the matter. The Governing Body was sovereign.

In 1965 a small bombshell exploded in Congregation. The dons decided that every University Lecturer of five years' standing was to be *entitled* to a college fellowship. This meant that fellowships would have to be found for those already in post, and promised to those who were newly appointed.[5] Where they were to be found, who would make the promise, and who would redeem it—none of this was very clear. 'Since the problem is insoluble,' wrote the Warden of Rhodes House (Sir Edgar Williams) sagaciously, 'men of goodwill continue to feel that it cannot be beyond the bounds of human ingenuity to discover a solution, whereas men of good sense find this blinkered buoyancy increasingly exasperating.'[6]

Years passed. There was some amelioration, but no solution. A back-list of 'entitled' non-Fellows remained. Gradually, exasperation mounted. 'The dispossessed became restive.'[7] The non-Fellows organized, and sought legal advice on their position. It transpired that the university was 'vulnerable'. The non-Fellows took some pleasure in intimating as much to the Vice-Chancellor (himself a QC). When the latter remarked that the university had not sought legal advice of its own, it was suggested to him that to do so might well help to 'persuade' the colleges to provide the necessary fellowships. Acting on this suggestion, the university received immediate confirmation of its vulnerability. The advice was as alarming as it was blunt: 'Every time the university appoints a lecturer for whom there is no college fellowship it commits a breach of contract and the breach continues for as long as no college association can be arranged.'[8] A crisis over entitlement had long been forecast. Now it had arrived.

Hence the cry for fireman Franks. Sir Patrick Neill, a courageous Vice-Chancellor, had persuaded the colleges to adopt a rota system of fellowship elections which would remove what he called 'the structural problem' of the future. What he wanted Franks to do was to resolve 'the personal problem' of the past: the rump of non-Fellows, forty-one in all, still without a collegial home. Impressed with the movement created by Neill, and conscious of his own reforming ancestry, Franks accepted the challenge without hesitation.[9] If he could 'place' each of the non-Fellows with a college, he would banish the spectre of entitlement once and for all. This extraordinarily delicate operation would have to be performed, as it were, without anaesthetic. Franks had no position, no powers, and no sanctions. All he had was a timely commission from the Vice-Chancellor. Two of Neill's predecessors, both admirers of Oliver Franks, were brought out of retirement to help him: the ebullient Lord Bullock, and the equable Sir John Habbakkuk. Inevitably they were referred to as the three wise men—in Bullock's version, 'one wise man and two boys'.[10] Their combined age was 226.

The personal problem had become acidulous with time. Understandably, all of the non-Fellows were acutely sensitive about their treatment. Many were resentful. Some were disaffected. One had been a non-Fellow for twenty years, another for fifteen. Several had been 'dined' by a college in the past, with a view to fellowship. Sometimes this process had been repeated with a second college, and then a third; but for whatever reason nothing had come of it. To be courted and spurned is a dispiriting experience, especially for those no longer young. Its legacy was a certain embitterment, and a wash of strong feelings about the colleges concerned. Yet the colleges themselves owed nothing to these unpersons, or so they thought. Some, it is true, were very popular. A female printmaker at the Ruskin School of Drawing was wanted by no fewer than twelve colleges. Others were wanted by ten, eight, or seven colleges. On the other hand eight of the non-Fellows were wanted by no one. This phenomenon Franks called 'bunching'.[11] It complicated the elementary difficulty with which he and the two boys began. There were forty-one non-Fellows and thirty-six colleges. Some Governing Bodies would have to be induced to swallow twice.

The preferences of both sides were revealed during the first round of the exercise. Franks convened his little committee for lunch. For these septuagenarians no introductions were necessary. 'I attach importance to our meeting', he told them gravely, and laid out the task before them. As he recalled it: 'We met. We scratched our heads. We wondered how to proceed.' They decided—it is difficult to believe that Franks had not already decided—to write to every non-Fellow and every college asking for their preferences, positive and negative, as to fellowships and Fellows.[12] When the replies were in, they began by interviewing each of the non-Fellows, 'partly to gain a personal impression, partly to understand more fully what their personal positions were, and partly to enlarge the degree of flexibility with which they regarded the future', as Franks explained at the time. His watchword was St Augustine's: *audi alteram partem*, hear the other side. Franks and his colleagues found these interviews 'fruitful'.[13] The non-Fellows found them stressful. Here they were, candidates once more, paraded in the university offices, given appointments at twenty-minute intervals, permitted to talk for nineteen, and deftly shown the door. The wise men were inscrutable as monkeys. They listened attentively, but what did they think? How could they know? And what would they conclude?[14]

The wise men chose not to interview all the colleges. They saw those who wished to see them, and summoned a number of others whose degree of flexibility left something to be desired.[15] In the remaining cases, the stated preferences of the Governing Body were such that there was little difficulty in identifying possible placements. A magnetic board had been set up in the office where the three men held their deliberations. As they shuffled and reshuffled the name counters, the kaleidoscope of non-Fellows and colleges slowly began to settle. It seemed that approximately half of the non-Fellows might be placed without much squealing from either side. This was the end of the first round. Franks collected the counters and put them in his pocket. A leak at this stage could prove disastrous.

The next round, they knew, would be stickier. The wise men decided to call a plenary meeting of all heads of houses—still a comparative rarity in this college-proud world. Some twenty years earlier the Franks Report had made a strong case for formalizing such a gathering in a Council of Colleges. The idea had not found favour, but the author of the report had not repented of it.[16] On this occasion, interestingly enough, 'they came like lambs', as Franks remembered, some alone, some with two or three or four minders. They took their places and waited expectantly. They did not yet know it, but they were about to be treated to a most unusual demonstration, perhaps the last of its kind. When the wise men came in, they rose to their feet. Franks bade them sit. Obediently, they sat. When all was quiet, he began to orate.

You will all remember how we were asked by the Vice-Chancellor and Council, with the assent of the colleges, to undertake the task of placing forty-one entitled non-fellows in fellowships in the colleges. We three were happy to emerge from retirement to do this, partly because in one way or another we have been associated and involved in the problem of entitled non-fellows for a long time, in fact ever since the Commission of Enquiry in 1964–6, and partly for another reason—we are concerned, concerned for the good name of Oxford; I mean the university and colleges taken together. I intend no criticism, but it is a fact that promises have been given to forty-one lecturers of the university and enshrined in the statutes of the university, and they have not been fulfilled, and this is a reproach to all of us in Oxford: it is why the three of us, when called upon, have felt it of great importance to try to help resolve this issue.

The room was loud with the sound of consciences being examined. Franks carefully introduced a personal note:

I myself have a further concern: it goes to the future of the collegiate system. At present we enjoy in Oxford a sort of federal union. The federal government is the university and the colleges are the states of the union, each with a real degree of sovereignty and enjoying within the union a large autonomy. I hold this to be a good state of affairs which should continue; it contributes greatly to the vitality of Oxford and that diversity in unity which gives strength, adaptability, and endurance. But I view with real apprehension what might happen if we three failed in our task and failed to place the non-fellows in the colleges. That failure would not be a secret. There would be those who would see to it that it was well known. There would, I think, in fact be a blaze of publicity, and therefore pressure that action should be taken. If Oxford cannot act, then others should make it act.

A shiver ran through the august assemblage. Franks added a touch of veiled menace:

These apprehensions of mine embrace the real possibility that the position of the non-fellows might be tested in the courts. And I say deliberately that I should not be sure of the outcome. Were it unfavourable, the distance from that to parliamentary legislation would not be great, and I do not believe that our collegiate system would be unaffected.

The heads of houses were now well ensnared. Franks proceeded to give them a brief progress report. He then turned to the need for 'accommodation'.

We pay great attention to what is said to us, both by the colleges and by the non-fellows, and we are most anxious not to send any non-fellow to a college which he does not wish to go to; equally anxious not to place any non-fellow in a college which does not want him, and in this I think we shall succeed. But the other side of the coin is that all, colleges and non-fellows alike, will have to be flexible in accommodating each other. I should like to add that so far as our talks have progressed, all concerned appear fully to comprehend the situation that they and we three are in. . . .

But the timetable matters. . . . We think for the sake of all that it should be completed with all deliberate speed. There is nothing to be gained by delay and there is something to be lost. This is why we have thought it right to press on. So far we have met with great help and support from the colleges and I am quite sure that we shall continue to do so. When we have made our placings or nominations and sent them to each college, we shall simultaneously send the total list to the Vice-Chancellor. This will mark the completion of what we were asked to do. We shall retire again into the shades. . . .

Now we are very glad to answer, if we can, any questions that occur to you. We said in the letter we sent you that it would be best not to discuss individual names or individual placings at a body like this and I think this is clear. These things are better done quietly and I think we can reach a quick end. There is no reason why the meeting should last all that long. We will be very pleased if we can answer any queries that arise in your minds.[17]

The oration was over. There were no questions. The heads and their minders filed out, a little stunned.

'Either by accident or design', according to Franks, the plenary meeting had an effect. After further contemplation of the magnetic board, the wise men duly placed the remaining non-Fellows. The picture was now complete. One Friday afternoon, with exquisite timing, they sent out letters of notification to all interested parties. Franks ceremoniously informed Bullock and Habbakkuk that their work was done, the committee was dissolved, and they should return once again to private life. They might even consider a short holiday. As for himself, he would be repairing to his beloved Scilly for the summer.[18]

Saturday passed uneventfully. The unnatural silence was finally broken on Sunday morning. Franks received an agitated telephone call from one head of house. He was sorry, but it could not be done—the college would not accept the placement made by the wise men. Franks suggested that he come and discuss it in person that very afternoon at, say, three o'clock. The head of house explained apologetically that he was ringing from London. Franks repeated his suggestion. Muhammad came to the mountain at three o'clock sharp. The nature of the difficulty was soon unfolded. This was a relatively new head of house whose Governing Body was acting up. The principle on which they wished to stand was that it was *their* decision; they could not have a lecturer foisted upon them. Franks heard the suppliance without comment. After a long interval he spoke. Indisputably, the college was right. It was their decision. 'The act of placing does not have finality', Franks wrote at the time. 'It does not usurp the right of the college not to elect.'[19] But the college should consider the consequences. The whole plot would unravel. The exercise would have to be done again. The non-Fellows would be restive—who could blame them? There would be inconvenience and discontent. The college should think about this and be prepared to explain it. That was all. The suppliant withdrew, shaken and grateful in equal measure. Franks boarded the train for Penzance.

'This was the dormouse raising its head from the teapot.'[20] The querulous Governing Body thought, and acquiesced. Nothing more was heard from any of the colleges. From the other side, one non-Fellow complained about lack of consultation, but subsequently found happiness in his placement. In spite of the fact that Franks had completely overriden a number of individual preferences, there was no further objection and no mutinous talk.[21] The festering problem of the previous quarter-century had been eradicated. The past had been successfully wiped clean. The whole operation had taken rather less than three months.

Compared to the economic recovery of Western Europe or the discharge of the responsibilities of government, entitlement was a small problem, and an intensely parochial one. Within that parish, however, it was at once enormously vexatious and ferociously difficult to solve. The solution offered by the wise men need not have been accepted by either side, as Franks well knew. He called it 'an exercise in moral suasion'. On the one hand, the non-Fellows had a grievance. They demanded to be heard. They came before the wise men, and, 'in the language of the late Cicero, in this way they were conciliated'.[22] On the other hand, the heads of houses were made to see clearly where their duty lay. It lay in self-sacrifice for the greater good—for the good of Oxford. After Franks had spoken there was no room for argument. The Sunday morning telephone call was only a momentary aberration. Late in life, so the story goes, the demented Lord Castlereagh was visited by the Duke of Wellington. 'Your Lordship is not in his right mind', said Wellington. 'If Your Grace says that it must be so', replied Castlereagh. It was much the same with Oliver Franks.

Although the placings had no finality, they did have moral authority. More exactly, they were clothed in Franks's moral authority. It is that fugitive quality which explains the remarkable phenomenon of universal compliance with his wishes. In common parlance, Franks lent his authority to the solution of the problem. That is to say, he lent himself. In a sense Franks *was* the solution. The exercise was deliberately conducted in such a way that to impugn the placings was to impugn the placer. But that was unthinkable; 'for what motive could induce one so imperturbable to behave disgracefully?'[23] If Oliver Franks was Solomonic, then so were the judgements that fell from his hand. In this respect the problem of entitlement, though small, was a representative one. Clearly Franks carried immense authority; the testimony on this is very striking. That authority was developed early, almost precociously. It was conspicuously present in Father Franks, the undergraduate, for example. Yet beyond the normal caste-marks—physical presence, intellectual rigour, personal integrity—the source of the authority is difficult to specify. One evening during the first stage of the exercise Alan Bullock was telephoned at home by a head of house who had just been interviewed by the wise men. There was something he had omitted to say. Would Bullock make the necessary representations for him? Bullock explained politely that Franks would certainly refuse to entertain anything which smacked of privileged communication. Instead he offered to arrange a further interview. The prospect of a second trial of strength with Oliver Franks was too much for the head of house. 'He terrifies me!', he exclaimed, and quit the field.[24] The episode is both revealing and misleading. One should never underestimate Franks's capacity to terrify grown men (less so grown women), though it must be said that old Father Franks was by no means as terrifying as young Father Franks. Terror is evidently not the answer to the riddle of moral authority; but the whole exercise does enable us to grasp the fundamental point that Franks's authority rested more on what he was than what he did.

What was Oliver Franks? With some men, the answer seems obvious. Winston Churchill was inspirational: he was the saviour of his country, and a beacon of hope. George Marshall was far-sighted: he was the organizer of victory, and the author of a Plan. Isaiah Berlin was profound: he was a brilliant thinker, and an enthralling exponent of ideas. Franks, by comparison, slips through the fingers. 'How are we to bury you?' asked Crito. 'However you like', said Socrates, 'provided that you can catch me.'[25] There was indeed something Socratic about Oliver Franks, who acted for much of his life as a kind of modern 'midwife of men's thoughts', as the great Athenian used to say of himself. He consciously attended to Socrates's question: how should one live? It might be said that Franks lived blamelessly. He was a virtuous man who did not cultivate virtue. Socrates believed that there was basically only one virtue, the power of right judgement. Franks may not have gone so far— prudence he possessed in abundance—but he did believe that judgement was the greatest human quality. 'We are all bad at it,' he said, 'but some are better than others.'[26] If ever Oliver Franks stooped to sin, it was to take a quiet pride in his own power of right judgement.

Above all, he was magnanimous. The magnanimous man is 'moderately disposed towards wealth, power, and every kind of good and bad fortune, however it befalls him'. Franks was the very picture of magnanimity.

He does not enter for popular contests, or ones in which others distinguish themselves; he hangs back or does nothing at all, except where the honour or the feat is a great one. The tasks that he undertakes are few, but grand and celebrated. He is bound to be open in his likes and dislikes . . . and to speak and act straightforwardly; and he cannot bear to live in dependence upon somebody else, except a friend, because such conduct is servile . . . He is not prone to express admiration, because nothing is great in his eyes. . . . In troubles that are unavoidable or of minor importance he is the last person to complain or ask for help, because such an attitude would imply that he took them seriously. He is the sort of person to prefer possessions that are beautiful but unprofitable to those that are profitable and useful, because this is more consistent with self-sufficiency. The accepted view of the magnanimous man is that his gait is measured, his voice deep, and his speech unhurried. For since he takes few things seriously, he is not excitable, and since he regards nothing as great, he is not highly strung; and those are the qualities that make for shrillness of voice and hastiness of movement.[27]

It was this magnanimity which so impressed itself on others. With it went a certain detachment—part philosophical, part spiritual—perhaps best described as a stoic acceptance of what is. One night in September 1987 Barbara died of lung cancer. She and Oliver had known for some time that she was unlikely to live, but had told no one, not even their daughters. The following morning Franks's neighbour found him digging the garden. 'My wife died during the night', he said, and continued his digging. There was a Quaker memorial meeting, full to overflowing. In response to one condolence Franks wrote: 'I am trying to get used to living without half myself.' They had been the best of friends for well over fifty years. For Barbara, as for Oliver, 'If I were pressed to say why I love him, I feel that my only reply could be: "Because it was he, because it was I."'[28]

Three years later there was another tragedy. In April 1990, on the eve of his inaugural lecture as Professor of Modern History at Royal Holloway and Bedford New College, Franks's son-in-law John Dinwiddy committed suicide. Dinwiddy was a world authority on Jeremy Bentham; his recently published study of Bentham's philosophy carried an acknowledgement to Oliver Franks, among others, for his comments on the manuscript.[29] Geoffrey Wilson, a close friend, went round to see Franks when he heard the news. He appeared to be perfectly collected, reasoning briefly as follows: 'This has happened. We must get used to it. We will get used to it. There is no point in getting emotional about it.'[30] Franks held fast to the last precept. When he himself recovered from a coronary (at 84) he discussed death and dying with his daughter Caroline with complete equanimity, noting matter-of-factly that he was 'very glad he did not die then'.[31]

The man whose outward emotions are as measured as his gait is always liable to the imputation of coldness, and so it was with Oliver Franks, who was widely thought to suffer from a kind of emotional anaemia. The only story consistently told against him was the quip that 'when you have broken the ice there is always the cold water underneath'.[32] The charges of 'thinness' or remoteness were variations on the same theme. 'Spontaneity makes actions attractive because they are not calculated actions', Noel Annan has written. 'Prudence is no doubt a Cardinal Virtue; but one can't help thinking that a world governed by her and her sisters, Temperance, Fortitude and Justice, would be dispiriting.'[33] Father Franks was not much given to spontaneity. On the contrary, he was a deliberate man, in action and perhaps in emotion too. The combination of extreme deliberation and formidable penetration easily made him appear slightly inhuman. This undoubtedly helped his moral authority; but it could also be enfeebling or even alienating, a reaction neatly captured in the epithet Olympian. Nor was that a complete misrepresentation. Franks was truly Olympian in the sense that he was rather unworldly. Unworldliness is a rare commodity in public life. It was one of Franks's most appealing qualities. His emotional condition was wrongly diagnosed. As he said of Dean Acheson, he had no incommunicable emotional depths. But he was not anaemic, he was reticent. The hallmark of his intensely private life was its simplicity—a Quaker tenet. 'We nearly all have something of the sailor or the gardener in us', Franks told the Pilgrim Society in 1948. John Locke presented his patron Lord Shaftesbury with a delightful little volume of his own composition on *The Growth of Vines and Olives*. Perhaps if things had fallen out differently Franks might have done something similar for his patron 'Lord'

Bevin. In every sense, he stood squarely in the tradition of looking after the garden he inherited.[34]

Oliver Franks was a good man. Goodness was the essential source of his moral authority. This was the first thing that was extraordinary about him. The second was his lay status. Franks was what Bentham called a 'lay-gent'—the most distinguished of his day.[35] 'I am no expert', he told the audience at a series of public lectures on the monetary system in 1960, in the wake of the Radcliffe Report. 'I am not an expert in economic theory. I never had, perhaps fortunately according to [the chairman], a training in economics. All I can claim is a good many years of being active in economic affairs.' Addressing a Civil Service College seminar on open government in 1978, he began by pointing out that he was not a lawyer; he had never held political responsibility; and he was not a constitutional historian.

On the other hand I was for nearly seven years a temporary civil servant in the war-time Ministry of Supply, and for nearly five years a member of the foreign service in Washington. I was chairman of a committee on section 2 of the Official Secrets Act of 1911 which reported in 1972, and I was a member of Lord Radcliffe's committee on Ministerial Memoirs. I have therefore visited the fringes of today's topic in various ways at different times . . .[36]

It was a lifetime's refrain. He might have been an expert philosopher. However, as the eighteenth-century solicitor Oliver Edwards said, 'I have tried too in my time to be a philosopher; but I don't know how, cheerfulness was always breaking in.' In retrospect the message is clear: philosophy was not enough. Adolf Hitler tossed Franks into a new career. Catlike, he landed on his feet.

Oliver Franks was the ideal layman.[37] He was interested in the subject at hand, whatever it was. He was unlearned—'nescient' in Bentham's word—but educable. He was knowledgeable on cognate matters. He was persistently inquisitive and profoundly reasonable. He had a remarkable talent for finding the right level of detail, as demonstrated in the entitlement exercise. He was adamant that a report on any subject should be intelligible to anyone 'willing to give some attention'—intelligible, that is, to the layman.[38] This whole profile was immensely reassuring. 'No lesson seems to be so deeply inculcated by the experience of life as that you should never trust the experts', wrote the noble Lord Salisbury. 'If you believe the doctors, nothing is wholesome; if you believe the theologians, nothing is innocent; if you believe the soldiers, nothing is safe. They all require to have their strong wine diluted by a very strong admixture of insipid common sense.'[39] Over four decades, the Franks brand of common sense had an enduring appeal for Governments of every ideological hue. The philosopher had become

> A Pillar of State; deep on his Front engraven
> Deliberation sat and publick care;
> And Princely counsel in his face . . .

Franks Reports exuded common sense. As to their insipidity, it has been well said that such committees are not only analytic but also catalytic: they 'have a role in appreciating a situation; and on occasion create a climate for action'.[40] Franks explored both possibilities. His affinity for the fundamental meant that little was overlooked. Often he was dealing with taboos of various kinds—national sovereignty, official secrecy, college autonomy, government efficiency. Reasoned discussion of the taboo is already an enlightened step. Demystification is vital to democracy. ('Knowledge is power', as Franks remarked boldly at the Civil Service College.[41]) In terms of analysis alone, the radical undertow of the reports is easy to miss. With the exception of official secrets legislation, moreover, Franks left nothing as he found it. Perceptions changed even when institutional practice did not. Franks may have become a pillar of state, but he kept a Nonconformist conscience. 'The Establishment smites the Establishment', proclaimed David Caute, of the Oxford report.[42] He was only half right. When it came to Establishments—to adopt his own formula—Franks was in them but not of them.

Franks probably had as much of an influence on people as he did on events. He was a natural exemplar. This personal influence can be sensed, but not easily charted. With some it was extremely powerful. One budding acolyte recalled:

I heard the name of Franks for the first time when a schoolmaster told me that as an undergraduate he had lived on the same staircase at Queen's College, Oxford, as a man called Franks while they were both preparing for their final examinations in philosophy and ancient history. Franks was represented to me as the perfect product of that particular Oxford training, a model of intellectual persistence and concentration. 'Learn to concentrate as Franks concentrates,' was the schoolmaster's last injunction to me.[43]

The tone of that recollection would have been instantly recognizable to an entire generation of public servants—loosely speaking, the wartime generation—among whom Franks was extravagantly admired almost without exception. Attlee's unreserved judgement was a representative one: for the majority of those who encountered him, however fleetingly, Oliver Franks was the ablest man they ever met. There was a period, extending from the mid 1940s to the mid 1960s, when it seemed to his contemporaries that he could do almost anything—Chancellor of the Exchequer or Governor of the Bank of England, as Rab Butler put it. Yet these were paths not taken. Franks forswore further influence on policy-making, of the kind exercised by Frank Lee on Europe, for example.[44] In the end, he offered no lessons to others except that of a life well led. 'Our great and glorious masterpiece is to live properly', said Montaigne. 'All other things—to reign, to lay up treasure, to build—are at the best but little aids and additions.'[45]

Franks had the greatness of his virtues, but was he a great man? In the first of his famous lectures on *Heroes, Hero-Worship and the Heroic in History* (1840),

Thomas Carlyle asserted that 'Universal History, the history of what man has accomplished in this world, is at bottom the History of the Great Men who have worked here. They were the leaders of men, these great ones; the modellers, patterns, and in a wide sense creators, of whatsoever the general mass of men contrived to do or attain.'[46] Was Oliver Franks a hero of this kind? Proverbially he was the avatar of that mysterious tribe, the Great and the Good, whose leading ethnographer in our own time is Peter Hennessy.[47] But the two categories are not commensurable. 'Greatness is not a specifically moral attribute', Isaiah Berlin has argued. 'It is not one of the private virtues. It does not belong to the realm of personal relations.'

A great man need not be morally good, or kind, or sensitive, or delightful, or possess artistic or scientific talent. To call someone a great man is to claim that he has intentionally taken (or perhaps could have taken) a large step, one far beyond the normal capacities of men, in satisfying, or materially affecting, central human interests. . . . In the realm of action, the great man seems able, almost alone and single-handed, to transform one form of life into another; or—what in the end comes to the same—permanently and radically alters the outlook and values of a significant body of human beings. The transformation he effects, if he is truly to deserve his title, must be such as those best qualified to judge consider antecedently improbable—something unlikely to be brought about by the mere force of events, by the 'trends' or 'tendencies' already working at the time—that is to say, something unlikely to occur without the intervention, difficult or impossible to discount in advance, of the man who for this very reason deserves to be described as great.[48]

Twice in his life Franks was associated with historically unprecedented transformations of this order: the European Recovery Programme, and, less tangibly, the Atlantic Alliance. In each instance his involvement was early, determinative, and effectual—in a word, galvanic. It is sometimes said that Franks was not creative. His part in these transforming events was highly creative. Complex international negotiation suited Franks's temperament. Always deliberate, he could be deliberately cautious or deliberately adventurous as the need arose. Caution was what Franks sufficiently possessed to be able (judiciously) to throw it to the winds. It is true that both the Marshall Plan and the Atlantic Pact were 'given' to him; but these were flying saucers, as Charles Kindleberger said at the time—ideas, grand but as yet unformed. Franks supplied the *phronesis*, the practical wisdom, to make them real. It was as if Marshall and Bevin sat, massively, on the bough of history while Franks worked the wood. Of course he was not alone in this endeavour. But his co-adjutors were remarkably few. Oliver Franks was one of the founding fathers: a small group of men, chiefly based in London and Washington, with outstations in Ottawa, Paris, Brussels, and The Hague, who were the modellers, patterns, and creators of the post-war world. But for them, it would have been different, and it might have been worse. There was, perhaps, a measure of greatness in that.

Notes

Preface

1. Michel de Montaigne, 'On Three Kinds of Relationships', in *Essays*, ed. J. M. Cohen (London, 1958), 251.

2. Stuart Hampshire, *Innocence and Experience* (Cambridge, 1989), 180.

3. Franks interviews.

4. Quoted in Christopher Ricks, 'Diary', *London Review of Books* (25 Jan. 1990).

5. Geoffrey Moorhouse, *The Diplomats* (London, 1977), 251–2.

6. Aristotle, *Ethics*, trans. Hugh Tredennick (London, 1976), 158.

1. *Entry*

1. *CYB 1929*, 215; recollections of R. S. Franks (his son), in notes made by Mrs Joanna Spencer (née Franks, his granddaughter).

2. Home Missionary Society minutes, quoted in H. G. Tibbutt, 'The Cotton End Congregational Academy, 1840–74', *Transactions of the Congregational Historical Society*, 18 (1958), 104.

3. Examiners' report for 1867, ibid.

4. *CYB 1929*, 215.

5. *CYB 1949*, 499.

6. Nathaniel Micklem, *Faith and Reason* (London, 1963). Cf. *CYB 1964–65*, 439–40; *DNB 1961–70*, 392; *Mansfield College Magazine*, 165 (1964), 208–9. The terminal 'e' in Sleightholme seems to date from this generation.

7. On his 'teaching ministry' (in Quaker parlance) see the tribute prepared by Helen Neatby of Sidcot Meeting in the *Friend* (21 Feb. 1964). Quakers were inclined to find his ministry 'a little too much like sermons'. Valerie Leimdorfer, letter to the author (13 Mar. 1990). Cf. *Woodbrooke International Journal*, 87 (1964), 2.

8. R. S. Franks, *A History of the Doctrine of the Work of Christ* (London, 1962); *The Doctrine of the Trinity* (London, 1953); *Enigma* (unpublished).

9. John Huxtable, letter to the author (30 Jan. 1990).

10. Basil Martin, quoted in W. T. Davies, *Mansfield College* (Oxford, 1947), 23. Cf. K. D. Brown, *A Social History of the Nonconformist Ministry in England and Wales* (Oxford, 1988), 232.

11. *CYB 1949*, 499; *CYB 1952*, 512; *CYB 1954*, 510–11; *CYB 1932*, 221. Ernest's son, Richard Lister Franks (born 1904), died of sarcoma in 1931.

12. R. S. Franks, *The Atonement* (London, 1934).

13. Mansfield College Council minutes (4 May and 21 June 1937). I am grateful to Elaine Kaye for information on the 'mini-inquiry', and for this characterization of it.

14. 'A Ninetieth Birthday', *Friend* (14 Apr. 1961). The 'birthday present' was a gift of some £3,000.

15. Report for 1896, quoted in F. J. Powicke, *A History of the Cheshire County Union of Congregational Churches* (Manchester, 1907), 253.

16. R. S. Franks, Jubilee Manual 1937, quoted in United Reformed Church Prenton, *A History of the Church* (Birkenhead, 1987), 4.

17. Report for 1902, quoted in Powicke, *Cheshire County Union*, 253–4.

18. Franks, Jubilee Manual.

19. J. W. Rowntree, quoted in H. G. Wood, 'Origins', in Robert Davis (ed.), *Woodbrooke* (London, 1953), 17. The Primitive Methodist was Dr J. Rendel Harris, so labelled by his Methodist cook. See also Arnold S. Rowntree, *Woodbrooke* (Birmingham, 1923).

20. R. S. Franks, 'Reminiscences', and T.W.G., 'Farewell to Mr Franks', *Old Woodbrookers Magazine*, 12 (1910), 6–8, and 13 (1910) 12–15; Woodbrooke Settlement Programme of Lectures (1904–10); Woodbrooke Council Annual Report (1910), Woodbrooke Library.

21. Davis (ed.), *Woodbrooke*, 38.

22. On appointment in 1904 his salary was £270 without residence; in 1908 this had risen to £350. In 1910 his successor was offered £500. Woodbrooke Settlement Committee minutes, Woodbrooke Library.

23. There are entries on two of them, Bernard (1880–1963) and Theodore (1888–1949) Shewell, in the *Dictionary of Quaker Biography* (LSF, typescript), Friends House Library, London.

24. 'Chips from the Log', *Old Woodbrookers Magazine*, 1 (1906), 8.

25. T.W.G., 'Farewell to Mr Franks', *Old Woodbrookers Magazine*, 13 (1910), 13–14.

26. *DNB 1961–70*, 392. For background see J. Charteris Johnstone, 'The Story of the Western College', *Transactions of the Congregational Historical Society*, 7 (1916), 98–109.

27. *Mansfield College Magazine*, 165 (1964), 208. Huxtable was the author of the principal obituaries of Franks. He became a friend and something of a disciple, and a considerable figure in his own right. See the obituary by Daniel Jenkins, *Guardian* (23 Nov. 1990).

28. A. J. P. Taylor, *A Personal History* (London, 1983), 16.

29. Codified and celebrated in an in-house history, in this case a very competent one: C. P. Hill, *The History of Bristol Grammar School*, rev. edn. (Gloucester, 1988).

30. BGS *Chronicle*, 25 (1949), 364.

31. Hill, *Bristol Grammar School*, 190. Norwood's 'ideology' is examined in Gary McCulloch, *Philosophers and Kings* (Cambridge, 1991), 41–65.

32. See J. E. Barton, *Purpose and Admiration* (London, 1932).

33. Quoted in Hill, *Bristol Grammar School*, 193.

34. Now exploded. See Martin Gilbert, *Churchill* (London, 1991), 19–34.

35. The information that follows is culled from the BGS *Chronicle* for 1915–23.

36. See William Beckford, *Vathek* [1786] (Oxford, 1983).

37. Interviews with Profs. T. F. Hewer and C. B. Perry (1 Feb. 1990); Gordon Taylor, letter to the author (16 Feb. 1990); W. Brunsdon Yapp, unpublished memoirs, BGS Library.

38. Erasmus, *Familiarum Colloquiorum Opus* (1526), quoted in 'Fives', *Encyclopaedia Britannica* (1966), iii. 357.

39. The following picture is drawn from interviews with the family.

40. See the interview with Peter Snow, 'Back to the Future?', *Oxford Today*, 3 (1990), 7.

41. Correlli Barnett, *The Swordbearers* (London, 1963), 11.

42. W. J. B. Owen (ed.), *Lyrical Ballads* [1798] (Oxford, 1969), 166–7.

43. From 'The Thorn', ibid. 66–76. For its provenance see pp. 138–9.

44. From 'The Quantock Hills, near Bicknoller', *Redland High School Magazine* (1922), 15. Cf. Rosalind Franks, 'The Middle School Expedition', ibid. (1919), 9–10. I am grateful to Mrs Anne Woolley, the School Secretary, for these references.

45. 'Franks', Entrance Book (1922–4), Queen's College, Oxford.

46. See Donald McFarlan, *White Queen* (Guildford, 1982).

47. BGS *Chronicle*, 16 (1922–3), 121, signed O.S.F. For his earlier editorials see ibid. 61 and 102.

48. The song is printed in full, without translation, in Hill, *Bristol Grammar School*, 272–3. I am grateful to the School Archivist, Michael Booker, for the supplementary information.

2. *Oxford Attained*

1. 'Oxford Letter', BGS *Chronicle*, 16 (1924), 304. Collections, mini-examination papers, are usually set at the beginning of each term, on the vacation reading.

2. Franks interviews. He recalled himself the *junior* scholar—an interesting slip in a memory of phenomenal precision. Cf. the junior History scholar at Christ Church in 1922, A. L. Rowse, *A Cornishman at Oxford* (London, 1974), 22–30.

3. Franks to his parents (n.d. [?14 Oct. 1923]), Franks Papers, Worcester College, Oxford.

4. Franks interviews; Franks to his parents (11 Nov. 1923), Franks Papers.

5. Franks to his parents and to his mother ([?]14 and 21 Oct. 1923), Franks Papers.

6. Douglas Jay, *Change and Fortune* (London, 1980), 24; Noel Annan, *Our Age* (London, 1990), 166.

7. For a picture of such a community (in this case Wesleyan Methodists), much admired in the Franks family, see Arnold Bennett's *Anna of the Five Towns*, first published in 1902.

8. Hewer interview (1 Feb. 1990).

9. 'Oxford Letter', BGS *Chronicle*, 16 (1924), 258; Franks to his parents (11 Nov. 1923), Franks Papers.

10. Franks to his mother and to his parents (21 Oct. and 11 Nov. 1923), Franks Papers.

11. Franks to his mother (n.d. [?18 Nov. 1923]), Franks Papers.

12. 'Oxford Letter', BGS *Chronicle*, 17 (1925), 45.

13. Franks to his parents (n.d. [26 Apr. 1925]), Franks Papers; 'Oxford Letter', BGS *Chronicle*, 17 (1925), 93–4.

14. Franks interviews. Cf. Sir Maurice Bowra, 'Oxford in the 1920s', in W. T. Rodgers (ed.), *Hugh Gaitskell* (London, 1964), 19–30; A. J. P. Taylor, *A Personal History* (London, 1983), 79–81. For the activities of the Old Bristolians see 'Oxford Letter', BGS *Chronicle*, 17 (1925), 236.

15. Oxford Bristolians Society minute book (1926–32), BGS Records Office.

16. 'Oxford Letter', BGS *Chronicle*, 17 (1925), 141–2.

17. See e.g. Jay, *Change and Fortune*, 31–2; Rowse, *Cornishman at Oxford*, 191–233. Cf. Evelyn Waugh, *Brideshead Revisited* (London, 1945).

18. Seminar on 'The Franks Report in Retrospect' (31 Jan. 1986), Nuffield College, Oxford. See also A. J. Ayer, *Part of my Life* (Oxford, 1978), 77.

19. Franks interviews. It is interesting to compare his bibliographical odyssey with Isaiah Berlin's in the same period. See 'The Pursuit of the Ideal' in *The Crooked Timber of Humanity* (Oxford, 1990), 1–19. Berlin read Greats at Corpus in 1930–2. His Oxford entrance papers were marked by Oliver Franks, who was suitably impressed by his quality of mind, though not the single continuous screed in which it was exhibited.

20. 'I have acquired myself a beautiful Kant': two volumes containing, *inter alia*, the *Critiques of Pure Reason, Practical Reason*, and *Judgement*. Franks to his parents (26 Apr. 1925), Franks Papers.

21. Set out in the *Critique of Judgement* (1790) and in the essay 'What is Orientation in Thinking?' (1786). I am indebted to the discussion in Onora O'Neill, 'Kantian Politics I: The Public Use of Reason', *Political Theory*, 14 (1986), 523–51.

22. Ayer, *Part of my Life*, 76ff.; Gilbert Ryle, 'Autobiographical', in Oscar P. Wood and George Pitcher (eds.), *Ryle* (London, 1971), 4. Cf. Isaiah Berlin, 'J. L. Austin and the Early Beginnings of Oxford Philosophy', in *Personal Impressions* (Oxford, 1987), 101–15. Ayer read Greats at Christ Church in 1930–2, Ryle at Queen's in 1921–3.

23. C. M. Bowra, *Memories* (London, 1966), 112–13. Cf. Berlin, 'Early Beginnings', 102; Alan Bishop, *Gentleman Rider* (London, 1988), 72–3.

24. Franks interviews.

25. Ryle, 'Autobiographical', 1–15; P. F. Strawson, 'Gilbert Ryle', *DNB 1971–1980*, 748–50.

26. Franks interviews; seminar on 'The Franks Report in Retrospect'.

27. From the papers in Moral and Political Philosophy, Logic, and Philosophical Books, published in *Oxford University Examination Papers* (Oxford, n.d.).

28. Rowse, *Cornishman at Oxford*, 228.

29. Franks interviews; E. M. Walker at Old Members' Dinner (25 Apr. 1928), *Queen's College Record* (1928); 'Oxford Letter', BGS *Chronicle*, 17 (1927), 391. The appellation means roughly 'the fine teacher'.

30. Franks interviews.

31. Ibid.

32. Ryle, 'Autobiographical', 8–9; Ayer, *Part of my Life*, 80.

33. He awarded himself 0 out of 10 for the second of these limericks. Franks to Rosalind (n.d. [Christmas 1927]), Franks Papers. Thomas Aquinas also wrote limericks. See Anthony Kenny, *Aquinas* (Oxford, 1980), 14.

34. Franks to his parents (16 Oct. 1927), Franks Papers.

35. Franks to Aunt Daisy (n.d. [Christmas 1927]), Franks Papers. He was still pining for Pontefract cakes in Washington 20 years later. See Barbara to Kitty Franks (27 Feb. 1949), Franks Papers.

36. 'Heidelberg Letter', BGS *Chronicle*, 18 (1928), 101.

37. Franks interviews.

38. Franks to his parents (24 Mar. and [?Apr.] 1928), Franks Papers.

39. Franks interviews. As Franks well knew, Goethe himself went over the Brenner into Italy in 1786, though he tarried in Florence for only three hours. See his *Italian Journey*, trans. W. H. Auden and Elizabeth Mayer (London, 1970).

40. Plato, *The Republic*, trans. Desmond Lee (London, 1987), 263. Cf. Glaucon's reply: 'My dear Socrates, if you make pronouncements of that sort, you can't be surprised if a large number of decent people take their coats off, pick up the nearest weapon, and come after you in their shirt sleeves to do something terrible to you.'

41. Stuart Hampshire, *Innocence and Experience* (Cambridge, 1989), 3.

42. Canon R. G. Lunt, letter to the author (4 Oct. 1987).

43. Franks interviews.

44. Quoted in Berlin, 'Early Beginnings', 111.

45. Franks interviews. In analysing the problem of choice, he drew a distinction between a decision *that* (a matter of morality) and a decision *to* (a matter of conduct). O. S. Franks, 'Choice', *Aristotelian Society Proceedings*, 34 (1934), 269–94.

46. See Plato, 'Cratylus', trans. Benjamin Jowett, in Edith Hamilton and Huntington Cairns (eds.), *The Collected Dialogues of Plato* (Princeton, NJ, 1963), 421–74.

47. This was nominalism. See Berlin, 'Early Beginnings', 107–8. In addition to Austin and Berlin, the group comprised A. J. Ayer, Stuart Hampshire, Donald MacKinnon, Donald Macnabb, and A. D. Woozley.

48. Ryle, 'Autobiographical', 6. The other members (not all synchronously, as Ryle says) were Christopher Cox, Frank Hardie, William Kneale, C. S. Lewis, John Mabbott, W. G. Maclagan, and H. H. Price.

49. Franks interviews. Franks was John Locke Scholar at Oxford in 1927. He lectured on Locke throughout the 1930s, and was still giving tutorials on his political philosophy half a century later, in retirement.

50. Prof. Donald MacKinnon, letter to the author (22 July 1989).

51. 'Modern Greats at Oxford' (1937), 29–30, Franks private papers.

52. Interviews with Lord Bullock, Charles J. Hitch, and Sir Geoffrey Wilson (20 Feb. 1991, 28 Aug. 1989, and 26 Apr. 1991).

53. University of Oxford, *Report of a Commission of Inquiry* (Oxford, 1966), para. 217.

54. Franks interviews.

55. Alastair K. Ross, letter to *Oxford Today*, 3 (1990), 61.

56. Lunt letter (4 Oct. 1987); *Oxford Magazine* (5 Nov. 1936). 'Being chuckle-headed' was an expression of J. L. Austin's. See Berlin, 'Early Beginnings', 101.

57. Franks, 'Choice'. I am grateful to Prof. Tony Woozley and the late Prof. Klemens Szaniawski for discussion of this paper.

58. 'Action, Perception and Measurement', 8–10 July 1938, *Aristotelian Society Supplementary Volume*, 17 (1938), 102–20.

59. Berlin, 'Early Beginnings', 115.

60. Franks quoted in Peter Boyle, 'Oliver Franks and the Washington Embassy, 1948–52', in John Zametica (ed.), *British Officials and British Foreign Policy* (Leicester, 1990), 190; interview with Lord Gladwyn (28 June 1990).

61. Beveridge to Waring (31 May 1926), quoted in Jose Harris, *William Beveridge* (Oxford, 1977), 313.

62. Gaitskell diary (28 Feb. and 1 Mar. 1956), printed in Philip M. Williams (ed.), *The Diary of Hugh Gaitskell* (London, 1983), 459–60; K. O. Morgan, *Labour People* (Oxford, 1987), 222, 224.

63. The soul (of society and of the individual) was a frequent topic of his early letters: 'It's really time someone talked to him for the good of his soul.' Franks to his parents (19 Dec. 1927), Franks Papers.

64. Jay, *Change and Fortune*, 60. Cf. Morgan, *Labour People*, 107–18.

65. Franks interviews; Demodocus quoted in Aristotle, *Ethics*, trans. Hugh Tredennick (London, 1976), 245.

66. From W. H. Auden, 'Spain'. See Annan, *Our Age*, 183–7. Auden later repudiated these lines because 'to say this is to equate goodness with success' (a dubious argument), and because he did not believe in them anyway: they just sounded 'rhetorically effective'. See the preface to his *Collected Shorter Poems* (London, 1966).

67. See Fernand Braudel, *Civilization and Capitalism*, trans. Siân Reynolds (London, 1981), a massive three-volume work originally commissioned in 1952 by Lucien Febvre as part of a series called 'Destins du Monde'. It was read and reread by Franks every three years or so.

68. See John Redcliffe-Maud, *The Experiences of an Optimist* (London, 1981), 29.

69. 'Disarmament Appeal', *Oxford Times* (21 Oct. 1932); Franks interviews. This group had nothing to do with the Oxford Movement led by their contemporary Roland Wilson (Oriel and Mansfield) and inspired by Frank Buchman's sonorous call for Moral Re-Armament. Franks himself frowned upon the Buchmanites' proselytizing and money-making. Cf. the obituary of Wilson by Kenneth Belden, *Independent* (4 Apr. 1991).

70. Franks *et al.* to Murray ([early] Mar. 1934); Murray to Meade (16 Mar. 1934), Murray Papers, 219, Bodleian Library, Oxford.

71. Franks interviews; *Queen's College Record*, 1 (1931), 5, and 2 (1933), 1.

72. Franks interviews.

73. Woozley letters (13 Sept. 1987 and 26 July 1989); Lunt letter (4 Oct. 1987).

74. Franks to his parents (7 Mar. 1935), Franks Papers.

75. Franks to his mother (21 Dec. 1927), Franks Papers.

76. Franks to his parents (6 Jan. and 12 Feb. 1935), Franks Papers.

77. George Steiner, 'An Examined Life', *New Yorker* (23 Oct. 1989).

78. Franks to his parents (26 Jan. and 5 Apr. 1935), Franks Papers.

79. Franks to his parents (27 Jan., 12 Feb., and 25 Feb. 1935), Franks Papers. In Mar. 1935 Franks was offered a university lectureship in Philosophy at Oxford, and the following month (while on holiday in California) the principalship of McGill University in Montreal, Canada. He accepted the former and returned home as expected.

80. Steiner, 'Examined Life'. Carnap himself came to Chicago from Vienna only after Franks had left.

81. On the Apostles see Annan, *Our Age*, 234–6.

82. Interview with Lord Dacre (Hugh Trevor-Roper) (12 Mar. 1991). I am grateful to Sir William Hayter for information on The Club. The fat and thin typology was suggested by a remark of Sir Raymond Carr's. In the early 1970s, besides these three, members included Sir Isaiah Berlin, Lord Blake, Lord David Cecil, Sir John Masterman, John Sparrow, Peter Strawson, Sir Kenneth Wheare, and Sir Edgar Williams.

83. 'Oxford Letter', BGS *Chronicle*, 17 (1927), 381.

84. See Aristotle, *The Politics*, trans. Jonathan Barnes, ed. Stephen Everson (Cambridge, 1988), 1.

85. Hampshire, *Innocence and Experience*, 123.

86. Franks interviews.

87. Barbara died on 5 Sept. 1987. I have drawn heavily on the obituaries in the LMH Brown Book (1988), 33–6; London Yearly Meeting Proceedings (1989), 220–1; and Sidcot School Old Scholars Report (1988), 60–1. For further amplification I am especially indebted to Dr Anne Whiteman.

88. Herbert George Tanner, *Some Recollections and Reflections* (privately pub., 1960), otherwise known as 'tripe, by a vegetarian' by the author, who was not lacking in a robust sense of humour. The following paragraphs are also based on interviews with various members of the Franks family.

89. John Morley, *The Life of William Ewart Gladstone*, iii (London, 1903), 552. Cf. Tanner, *Recollections*, 223.

90. See e.g. G. N. Clark, *Guide to English Commercial Statistics*, with a catalogue of materials by Barbara M. Franks (London, 1938).

91. On this last see E. J. R. Burrough, *Unity in Diversity* (privately pub., 1978), 8 ff.

92. Franks interviews; Tanner, *Recollections*, 60.

93. John Stuart Mill, 'The Subjection of Women' (1869), in Stefan Collini (ed.), *On Liberty and Other Writings* (Cambridge, 1989), 213. For a glancing reference to this 'passionate essay', which 'stirred English people first to controversy and then to thought and action', see Franks's foreword to Joan Bungay, *Redland High School* (Bristol, n.d.), p. ix.

94. See Barbara Tuchman (another favourite historian), 'In Search of History', in *Practicing History* (London, 1982), 18.

95. Interview with Sir Nicholas Henderson (15 Mar. 1990).

96. Interview with Sir Alec Cairncross (18 Apr. 1988).

3. *The Ministry of Supply*

1. Franks interviewed by Peter Hennessy (24 Jan. 1977), quoted in *Whitehall* (London, 1989), 92.

2. Committee of Vice-Chancellors and Principals to Sir John Anderson (23 Nov. 1938), LAB 8/214, PRO. 'Men of the professor type' was the expression used by the Government Code and Cypher School at Bletchley Park. The tale is brilliantly told in Hennessy, *Whitehall*, 88–119.

3. Lunt letter (4 Oct. 1987).

4. John Locke, *Two Treatises of Government*, ed. Peter Laslett (Cambridge, 1988), 339; Sir Oliver Franks, 'Central Planning and Control in War and Peace', three lectures delivered at the LSE (London, 1947), 12.

5. Jay interview (7 July 1988); Franks interviews. His sisters and brother felt the same. Joanna, a librarian, became a temporary Civil Servant in the Ministry of Aircraft Production until her brother amalgamated it with the Ministry of Supply in 1946; she remained in the Civil Service, rising to Under-Secretary in the Ministries of Power and Technology, and the Department of Trade and Industry. Rosalind, who had married a doctor, helped with the practice and raised a family. Martin continued steadfastly to practise his profession: as an engineer he was in a reserved occupation, under the control of the Admiralty.

6. Franks to his parents (5 Apr. 1935), Franks Papers, Worcester College, Oxford.

7. Henderson interview (15 Mar. 1990).

8. Franks interviews. 'A good war' was A. J. P. Taylor's verdict. See *The Second World War* (London, 1976), 234.

9. Hennessy, *Whitehall*, 100.

10. *The Memoirs of the Rt. Hon. the Earl of Woolton* (London, 1959), 163; Lord Franks, 'The Ministry of Supply', seminar at All Souls College, Oxford (22 May 1990), in discussion.

11. Franks interviewed by Peter Hennessy (11 Dec. 1984), unpublished transcript, 1–2.

12. Sir Oliver Franks, 'The Experience of a University Teacher in the Civil Service', Sidney Ball Lecture, 9 May 1947 (London, 1947), 1. 'Regulars' and 'auxiliaries' are Hennessy's terms: see *Whitehall*, 540–86.

13. Franks, 'Ministry of Supply', 3.

14. Ibid. 4.

15. Keith Middlemas, *Power, Competition and the State*, i (London, 1986), 23.

16. Franks to Welch (21 Sept. 1946), Franks File, BBC Written Archives Centre, Caversham Park, Reading.

17. The manifold difficulties and frustrations are discussed in Alex Danchev, 'British Strategy in the Second World War', in Warren Kimball *et al.* (eds.), *Allies at War* (forthcoming).

18. Stephen Wilson, brother of Geoffrey and a near contemporary at Queen's, was at this time a regular in the Ministry of Transport; Herbert Hart was an auxiliary in the War Office, and later Professor of Jurisprudence and Principal of Brasenose College.

19. Alec Cairncross, *Planning in Wartime* (London, 1991), 45–6. Cf. Franks, 'University Teacher', 9–10; Douglas Jay, *Change and Fortune* (London, 1980), 87–8.

20. *War Memoirs of David Lloyd George*, i (London, 1938), 146. According to this account, when President Wilson's emissary Colonel House visited the new Minister, the two men argued amicably over who should have the chair.

21. Jay interview (7 July 1988). The manpower figures are from Franks, 'University Teacher', 1–2.

22. Franks, 'Ministry of Supply', 3, 7.

23. Franks interviews. Cf. his remark on the early period of the war, 'if you had an idea what you wanted to do there was very little to stop you doing it'. Quoted in Peter Hennessy and Sir Douglas Hague, 'How Adolf Hitler Reformed Whitehall' (Strathclyde Papers on Government and Politics, 1985), 36.

24. Stuart Hampshire, *Innocence and Experience* (Cambridge, 1989), 18.

25. Franks interviews and 'Ministry of Supply', 17–18; Jay interview (7 July 1988), and *Change and Fortune*, 94.

26. Drop-forging is the process of shaping metal parts by forging between two dies, one fixed to the hammer and the other to the anvil of a steam or mechanical hammer.

27. Jay, *Change and Fortune*, 93.

28. His perspiration has always been the subject of apocryphal attention. 'One day the temperature was over 100 and all of us were sweating like horses. I looked at Sir Oliver. He was sweating too, but in a different, special way. A drop of moisture formed near his right cheekbone and, simultaneously, another near his left. Then those two drops moved neatly down his face in perfect

alignment. "Can you beat that," I said to myself. "He even sweats symmetrically."' A delegate at the Conference on European Economic Co-operation in 1947, quoted in Paul Bareau, 'Sir Oliver Just Keeps Climbing', *News Chronicle* (1 Nov. 1954). Franks himself considered this often-repeated story puerile.

29. Jay, *Change and Fortune*, 94. Franks recalled another solution: transferring unemployed tin-plate workers from Wales, which raised the equally contentious issue of differential regional wage rates. See 'Ministry of Supply', 7–8.

30. Jay, *Change and Fortune*, 99.

31. Beaverbrook to Churchill (17 July 1941), quoted in A. J. P. Taylor, *Beaverbrook* (London, 1972), 479. See, generally, pp. 477–505. Cf. Jay, *Change and Fortune*, 97–8.

32. *Time* (26 Sept. 1949). 'Britain's Ambassador Franks: Ice to Thaw Dollars' was the cover story.

33. Cairncross, *Planning in Wartime*, 13.

34. Jay, *Change and Fortune*, 97. On Beaverbrook's feud with Bevin see Alan Bullock, *Ernest Bevin*, ii (London, 1967), 114–18, 148–51; and Taylor, *Beaverbrook*, 498–501.

35. Franks, 'Ministry of Supply', 9.

36. Quoted in *Time* (26 Sept. 1949).

37. Franks, 'Ministry of Supply', 9–10.

38. Moran diary (23 June 1957), in *Winston Churchill: The Struggle for Survival* (London, 1966), 725–6.

39. Lord Bridges in Sir John Wheeler-Bennett (ed.), *Action This Day* (London, 1968), 220–1. The vast outpouring of writing and reminiscence from members of the circle has only recently abated. See e.g. John Colville, *The Churchillians* (London, 1981), and John Martin, *Downing Street: The War Years* (London, 1991). For a discussion of this literature and the difficulties it raises see Alex Danchev, 'Dilly-Dally, or Having the Last Word', *Journal of Contemporary History*, 22 (1987), 21–44.

40. The Beaver was Lord Beaverbrook; the Prof., Lord Cherwell (Frederick Lindemann). Father Franks seems to have had no other nickname except, fleetingly, No Lollie Ollie (in a later incarnation at Lloyds Bank).

41. Originally published in *Atlantic Monthly* (as 'Mr Churchill') and *Cornhill Magazine* (as 'Mr Churchill and F.D.R.'); reissued in book form as *Mr Churchill in 1940* (London, 1964); reprinted as 'Winston Churchill in 1940' in *Personal Impressions* (London, 1980; Oxford, 1982), 1–22. Berlin says, mistakenly, that it was a review of the *first* volume of the memoirs. He himself calls it an *éloge*: an address commemorating the illustrious dead (p. vii).

42. In 'The Anglo-American "Special Relationship" 1947–52', lecture delivered at the University of Texas (1989), 9.

43. Berlin, *Personal Impressions*, 23; Annan, introduction, ibid., p. xxi.

44. Franks interviews. He also described himself engagingly as 'a failed philosopher'.

45. Jose Harris, *William Beveridge* (Oxford, 1977), 364.

46. Franks interviews; Henderson interview (15 Mar. 1990). See Ch. 5.

47. Cf. Cicero, *On Duties*, ed. M. T. Griffin and E. M. Atkins (Cambridge, 1991). For editorial comment on the LSE lectures see 'Partners in Planning', *The Times* (28 Apr. 1947). Franks was attended to with great care by Patrick Nairne, one of the most successful Civil Servants of his generation. See 'Management and the Administrative Class', *Public Administration*, 42 (1964), 119–21; and his annotated copy of 'Central Planning'. Interview with Sir Patrick Nairne (16 Feb. 1990).

48. Franks, 'Central Planning', 25, 35, 37.

49. Franks interviews.

50. Berlin, *Personal Impressions*, 15.

51. Franks, 'Ministry of Supply', 20–1; interview with Lord Plowden (28 June 1990).

52. Franks, 'University Teacher', 16–17.

53. See ED(45) 1st meeting (14 Nov. 1945), T228/20, PRO. The other members were Sir Bernard Gilbert (Treasury), Sir Godfrey Ince (Ministry of Labour), Douglas Jay (now Economic Adviser to the Prime Minister), Sir Alexander Johnston (Ministry of Transport), and Sir John Henry Woods (Board of Trade).

54. Meade diary (17 Mar. 1946), printed in Susan Howson and Donald Moggridge (eds.), *The Collected Papers of James Meade*, iv (London, 1990), 231. Cf. ED(46) 1st meeting (15 Mar. 1946), T228/20, PRO.

55. See his remarks at a Permanent Secretaries' meeting convened by Bridges (2 Mar. 1946), T273/9, PRO, quoted in Hennessy, *Whitehall*, 124. In the event the plan for 1946 was rejected by Ministers.

56. Meade diary (30 June 1946), in *Collected Papers*, 286. Meade commented: 'This was a salutary dose of cold water, but I have not as a result changed my general attempts to set the stage for a "liberal-socialist" solution.'

57. For Berlin, a Zionist and a profound admirer of Chaim Weizmann, Bevin foundered on the rock of Palestine. See *Personal Impressions*, 50–3.

58. Valentine Lawford, 'Three Ministers', *Cornhill Magazine*, 169 (1956–7), 80.

59. Franks interviews; Francis Williams, *Ernest Bevin* (London, 1952), 237.

60. Interview with Lord Bullock (20 Feb. 1991); Alan Bullock, *Ernest Bevin*, iii (London, 1983), 83–4.

61. Lawford, 'Three Ministers', 79; Frank Owen, Sir Ben Smith, and Franks, quoted in Bullock, *Bevin*, iii. 85, 93.

62. Cf. Roy Jenkins's foreword to Edwin Plowden, *An Industrialist in the Treasury* (London, 1989), p. x.

63. Interview with Ambassador Lucius D. Battle (10 Apr. 1989).

64. Franks interviews.

65. Cf. John Redcliffe-Maud, *The Experiences of an Optimist* (London, 1981), 1.

66. Hugh Heclo and Aaron Wildavsky, *The Private Government of Public Money* (London, 1981), 14 (emphasis added).

67. Dalton diary (5 Mar. 1945), in Ben Pimlott (ed.), *The Second World War Diary of Hugh Dalton* (London, 1986), 840–1; Gaitskell diary (6 Aug. 1945), in Philip M. Williams (ed.), *The Diary of Hugh Gaitskell* (London, 1983), 6; Franks interviews. Cf. Hennessy, *Whitehall*, 570.

68. Franks interviews; Hall diary (29 Jan. 1953), in Alec Cairncross (ed.), *The Robert Hall Diaries*, i (London, 1989), 263. Cf. Middlemas, *Power, Competition and the State*, i. 368.

69. Franks, 'Ministry of Supply', 17. Wilmot was in fact a rather reluctant nationalizer. See the discussion in Kenneth O. Morgan, *Labour in Power* (Oxford, 1984), 110–17.

70. *Queen's College Record* (1946), 4; interview with John Prestwich (20 Feb. 1991).

4. *The Marshall Plan*

1. Max Beerbohm, *Zuleika Dobson* [1911] (London, 1991), 137; Franks interviews.

2. Minutes of the Governing Body, Queen's College, Oxford (30 June 1947), quoted in Kenneth O. Morgan, *Labour in Power* (Oxford, 1984), 271. The Archbishop of York sent his benediction a few days later.

3 Dean Acheson, *Present at the Creation* (New York, 1969), 233–4; Marshall to Lovett ([?]9 June 1947), *FRUS 1947*, iii. 247. The whole speech is printed in *FRUS 1947*, iii. 237–9.

4. Charles P. Kindleberger, 'Origins of the Marshall Plan' (22 July 1947), *FRUS 1947*, iii. 246–7; Leonard Miall, 'How the Marshall Plan Started', *Listener* (4 May 1961). On the hour and the myth see, variously, Alan Bullock, *Ernest Bevin*, iii (London, 1983), 404–22; Anne Deighton, *The Impossible Peace* (Oxford, 1990), 174–86; Alan S. Milward, *The Reconstruction of Western Europe* (London, 1987 edn.), 61–9.

5. Speech of 1 Apr. 1949, quoted in Bullock, *Bevin*, iii. 405. Cf. his first public response, embodied in FO to Washington (13 June 1947), T236/782.

6. Summary of third meeting with Clayton (26 June 1947), *FRUS 1947*, iii. 292; Foreign Ministry to Ministry of Economic Affairs (3 July 1947), 610.302, MBZ. The Benelux countries had made the same determination. See Ernst H. van der Beugel, *From Marshall Aid to Atlantic Partnership* (Amsterdam, 1966), 70.

7. FO summary, 'European Reconstruction' (17 June 1947), T236/782; Gallman to Washington (16 June 1947), *FRUS 1947*, iii. 254–5.

8. Hugh Seton-Watson, 'What is Europe, Where is Europe?', *Encounter* (July–Aug. 1985).

9. Franks interviewed by Edward Mortimer for the Channel 4 TV series 'Roosevelt's Children' (1987), unpublished transcript, 19–20.

10. Dixon diary (20 June 1947), quoted in Bullock, *Bevin*, iii. 409.

11. Report of Secretary of State's visit to Paris, CAB 21/1759.

12. Caffery to Washington (18 June 1947), *FRUS 1947*, iii. 260.

13. FO to Franks (19 Aug. 1947), FO 371/62576.

14. These attitudes are explored in detail in Michael J. Hogan, *The Marshall Plan* (Cambridge, 1987). For a rare dissenting voice see Lincoln Gordon, 'Recollections of a Marshall Planner', *Journal of International Affairs*, 41 (1988), 233–45.

15. A. D. Marris, *Prospects for Closer European Economic Integration* (London, 1948), 7–8. The author was Franks's deputy on the CEEC.

16. See Alex Danchev, 'In the Back Room: Anglo-American Defence Co-operation, 1945–51', in Richard Aldrich (ed.), *British Intelligence, Strategy and the Cold War* (London, 1992).

17. Summary of first meeting with Clayton (24 June 1947), *FRUS 1947*, iii. 271.

18. See e.g. Franks to Attlee (20 Sept. 1949), PREM 8/973; to Bevin *et al.* (27 Sept. 1950), in *DBPO* ser. II. iii, doc. 49, pp. 111–18. Robert Lovett at one point told the Belgian Ambassador in Washington that there was no prospect of 'an international dole'. Memo of conversation (25 July 1947), 840.50 Recovery/7-2547, RG 59, NA.

19. FO brief on Western Organizations (24 Apr. 1950), *DBPO*, ser. II. ii. 98; London Committee memo for Paris del. (15 July 1947), FO 371/62579.

20. Gallman to Washington (16 June 1947), *FRUS 1947*, iii. 255.

21. Dixon diary (2 July 1947), quoted in Deighton, *Impossible Peace*, 190.

22. Summary of second meeting with Clayton (25 June 1947), *FRUS 1947*, iii. 276–7.

23. Quoted in *The Times* (10 Feb. 1950).

24. Douglas to Washington (25 July 1947), quoted in Milward, *Reconstruction*, 62.

25. Charles Lamb, 'Poor Relations', in *The Essays of Elia* (London, 1889), 210–11.

26. Christopher Hitchens, *Blood, Class and Nostalgia* (London, 1990); Acheson talk to British-American Parliamentary Group (26 June 1952), Box 67, Acheson Papers, HSTL.

27. Franks interviews.

28. K. Morozov, 'The Marshall Doctrine', *Pravda* (11 June 1947), excerpted in Bedell Smith to Washington (26 June 1947), *FRUS 1947*, iii. 294–5.

29. FO *aide-mémoire* (25 June 1947), *FRUS 1947*, iii. 286.

30. Inverchapel and Balfour to FO (13 and 25 June 1947), FO 371/62399 and 1759; Summary of third meeting with Clayton (26 June 1947), *FRUS 1947*, iii. 291. Cf. Hogan, *Marshall Plan*, 52–3; Milward, *Reconstruction*, 64.

31. Eric Roll, *Crowded Hours* (London, 1985), 52; Caffery to Washington (1 July 1947), *FRUS 1947*, iii. 302–3.

32. Franks interviews. 'This really is the birth of the Western bloc', Bevin whispered to his private secretary during the final session. Dixon diary (2 July 1947), quoted in Bullock, *Bevin*, iii. 422. Cf. Jean Monnet, *Mémoires* (Paris, 1976), 316.

33. Unidentified official quoted in Richard Mayne, *The Recovery of Europe* (London, 1970), 115.

34. Communiqué (3 July 1947), translated ibid. 113; Marris, *Prospects*, 12.

35. Gottwald to Prague, pirated in Steinhardt to Washington (10 July 1947), *FRUS 1947*, iii. 319.

36. See Caffery to Washington (10 July 1947), *FRUS 1947*, iii. 317.

37. 'Had I been present at the creation I would have given some useful hints for the better ordering of the universe.' Alphonso X, King of Spain, epigraph to Acheson, *Present at the Creation*.

38. A. D. Marris quoted (anonymously) in Harry B. Price, *The Marshall Plan and its Meaning* (Ithaca, NY, 1955), 36; Franks interviews. Price interviewed most of the principals (but not Franks) in 1952–3. Extensive notes are in Box 1 of the Price Papers, HSTL.

39. Roll, *Crowded Hours*, 54.

40. See the statement reported at length in *The Times* (18 July 1947).

41. Franks interviews. The contact man was Ivan White, remembered as 'a rather dreadful PR officer'; in fact First Secretary and Consul. See also White interview for the Marshall Plan Project, COHRC.

42. Drew Pearson, 'Washington Merry-Go-Round', *New York Times* (3 Mar. 1947); Clayton interview for the Marshall Plan Project, COHRC; John Gimbel, *The Origins of the Marshall Plan* (Stanford, Calif., 1976), 269–70.

43. Moore to Wilcox (28 July 1947), *FRUS 1947*, iii. 239.

44. Kennan to Marshall, ([?]21 July 1947), *FRUS 1947*, iii. 335.

45. Anonymous delegate quoted in 'Green Baize and the Red Tide', *Newsweek* (25 Aug. 1947); Franks interviewed for BBC Radio series 'A Spark to Fire the Engine' (1986), prog. 1, transcript,

11, Marshall Papers, MRF. Cf. his interviews with Deighton, *Impossible Peace*, 192, 232; and Edward Mortimer, *Roosevelt's Children* (London, 1989), 55.

46. See Irwin M. Wall, *The United States and the Making of Postwar France* (Cambridge, 1991). Cf. Acheson, *Present at the Creation*, 219.

47. The conference resolutions are summarized in CEEC, *General Report* (London, Paris, and Washington, 1947), app. A.

48. Franks interviews; 'The Anglo-American "Special Relationship" 1947–52', lecture delivered at the University of Texas (1989), 8.

49. Milward, *Reconstruction*, 70. This scintillating and idiosyncratic book offers the only sustained treatment of the CEEC (see pp. 69–89). It is relentlessly critical, reacting in part against the blandness of van der Beugel, *Marshall Aid*, 68–97. Of the other participants, Robert Marjolin, *Le Travail d'une vie* (Paris, 1986), 184–91, is more analytical; Eric Roll, *Crowded Hours*, 50–6, more anecdotal.

50. Franks, 'Special Relationship', 10; Caffery to Washington (10 July 1947), *FRUS 1947*, iii. 316.

51. Franks interviews; Hogan, *Marshall Plan*, 60. In spite or perhaps because of this experience, Franks welcomed Hammarskjöld's election as UN Secretary-General (in Apr. 1953) with an exceptionally warm personal testimonial. Manuscript draft, n.d., Franks private papers.

52. Franks interviews. Cf. Milward, *Reconstruction*, 68–9.

53. Kirk and Caffery to Washington (19 and 20 July 1947), 840.50 Recovery/7-1947 and 2047, RG 59; Dr H. M. Hirschfeld (Dutch representative and Benelux spokesman) interviewed by Price (21 Nov. 1952), Price Papers.

54. Caffery to Washington (20 July 1947), *FRUS 1947*, iii. 333. Alphand was officially CEEC Rapporteur-General.

55. Franks interviews; Marris interviewed by Price (11 Nov. 1952), Price Papers. Monnet himself is silent: *Mémoires*, 316–17. His private views are set out in Clayton to Lovett (30 July 1947), 840.50 Recovery/7-3047, RG 59. For his practical effect see e.g. UK del. to London (11 Sept. 1947), FO 371/62582.

56. Sir Edmund Hall-Patch interviewed by Philip C. Brooks (8 June 1964), HSTL; Franks interviews; 'Portrait of an Expert', *Newsweek* (6 Oct. 1947).

57. Paul-Henri Spaak, *The Continuing Battle* (Boston, 1972), 10. The book is subtitled 'Memoirs of a European'.

58. Franks, 'Special Relationship', 10–11. Cf. Caffery to Lovett (27 July 1947), *FRUS 1947*, iii. 338–9; Marris, *Prospects*, 10.

59. Robert Frank, 'The French Dilemma', in Josef Becker and Franz Knipping (eds.), *Power in Europe?* (New York, 1986), 276. See in general John W. Young, *France, the Cold War and the Western Alliance* (Leicester, 1990).

60. Communication from M. Bidault (17 July 1947), *FRUS 1947*, ii. 992; draft record of second meeting of CEEC (17 July 1947), FO 371/62568. The atavism is well explained in John Gillingham, *Coal, Steel and the Rebirth of Europe* (Cambridge, 1991).

61. Minutes of fourth meeting of tripartite talks (27 Aug. 1947), FO 371/65201. See Milward, *Reconstruction*, 71–6.

62. Recalled by Sir Anthony Nutting in Michael Charlton, *The Price of Victory* (London, 1983), 148.

63. See the works by Gimbel and Deighton respectively.

64. Committee reports are printed in full in the *Technical Report*, and summarized in the *General Report*, apps. C, D, and E.

65. Ibid., app. B, para. 2.

66. Marris interviewed by Price (11 Nov. 1952), Price Papers.

67. Franks interviews.

68. Franks, 'Central Planning and Control in War and Peace', three lectures delivered at the LSE (London, 1947), 46, 52.

69. Marjolin, *Le Travail*, 119–22; Marris quoted in Price, *Marshall Plan*, 36; Monnet, *Mémoires*, 137–212; Eric Roll, 'The Marshall Plan as Anglo-American Response', in Stanley Hoffmann and Charles S. Maier (eds.), *The Marshall Plan* (Boulder, Colo., 1984), 39–45.

70. The Emergency Committee was replaced by the UN's Economic Commission for Europe (ECE), bypassed in its turn by the creation of the CEEC.

71. Interview with Lord Roll (15 Mar. 1990); Marris, *Prospects*, and interview with Price (11 Nov. 1952), Price Papers; Franks interviews. In 1952, with Franks's connivance, Dean Acheson tried unsuccessfully to involve Marris in 'the Iranian problem'. Memo of conversation (4 Feb. 1952), Box 67, Acheson Papers, HSTL.

72. Caffery to Washington (24 July 1947), 840.50 Recovery/7-2447, RG 59.

73. Marjolin, *Le Travail*, 186–7; Roll, *Crowded Hours*, 55–6. The Greek representative was M. A. Verdelis.

74. Hoffmann and Maier, *Marshall Plan*, 64. The Turkish representative was M. Numan Menemencioglu.

75. Quoted anonymously in Roll, *Crowded Hours*, 56. Freely translated, 'We'll be making it up!'

76. Caffery to Washington (6 Aug. 1947), 840.50 Recovery/8-647, RG 59.

77. Clayton to Marshall and Lovett (29 July 1947), *FRUS 1947*, iii. 339. Cf. Clayton to Lovett (1 Aug. 1947), 840.50 Recovery/8-147, RG 59.

78 William Diebold, 'The Marshall Plan in Retrospect', *Journal of International Affairs*, 41 (1988), 433.

79. Clayton to Marshall and Lovett (29 July 1947), *FRUS 1947*, iii. 340.

80. Nicholson/Plowden minute, 'European Economic Integration' (8 Aug. 1947), CAB 124/1050. See also Hall-Patch to Bridges (5 Aug. 1947), ibid.

81. The national positions are set out in CEEC, *General Report*, paras. 88–101.

82. 'Moreover, the position of Great Britain, which is not merely a European country but an international trader, presents very special difficulties.' FO *aide-mémoire* for discussions with Clayton (25 June 1947), *FRUS 1947*, iii. 287.

83. Statement to the Executive Committee, transmitted verbatim in Caffery to Washington (16 Aug. 1947), 840.50 Recovery/8-1647, RG 59.

84. CEEC, *General Report*, paras. 96 and 97. British official thinking (often his own) is summarized in Edwin Plowden, *An Industrialist in the Treasury* (London, 1989), 30–3; and discussed in Charlton, *Price of Victory*, 62 ff.

85. London Committee minutes (9 Aug. 1947), FO 371/62565.

86. Marris, *Prospects*, 17. See in general Alec Cairncross (ed.), *The Robert Hall Diaries*, 2 vols. (London, 1989 and 1991), *passim*; 'Lord Roberthall', *The Times* (19 Sept. 1988); R. W. B. Clarke, *Anglo-American Collaboration in War and Peace* (Oxford, 1982).

87. Quoted in Bullock, *Bevin*, iii. 98.

88. Hall-Patch to Bevin (7 Aug. 1947), FO 371/62552. A senior member of Franks's delegation (and later the UK study group on customs unions), Roger Stevens of the FO, was also strongly in favour. See his 'Politico-strategic implications of a European customs union' (22 Dec. 1947), FO 371/62555.

89. Franks quoted in Charlton, *Price of Victory*, 71; Franks interviews. He remarked of the Board of Trade that it 'remained Gladstonian for as long as it existed'—an implicit criticism of the GOM?

90. See Allan Bullock, *Ernest Bevin*, i (London, 1960), 387–8; iii. 318, 358.

91. REP minutes (12 Aug. 1947), Box 26, Lot 122, RG 353; Paul H. Nitze, *From Hiroshima to Glasnost* (London, 1989), 55; Nitze interview (31 May 1989).

92. 'The Germans were refused everything when they should have been given something and they were given everything when they should have been refused everything: I, for my part, would like to do something different.' Schuman to Jean Laloy, quoted in Robin Edmonds, *Breaking the Mould* (Oxford, 1986), 184. See Franks, 'Lessons of the Marshall Plan Experience', in OECD, *From Marshall Plan to Global Interdependence* (Paris, 1978), 22.

93. Quoted in Bernard Donoughue and G. W. Jones, *Herbert Morrison* (London, 1973), 481.

94. Franks quoted in Peter Hennessy and Caroline Anstey, 'Moneybags and Brains', *Strathclyde Analysis Papers*, 1 (1990), 8 (emphasis added); Franks to Makins (14 July 1950), in *DBPO*, ser. II. i. 259–60 (copied to Bridges and Plowden). Cf. Edmonds, *Breaking the Mould*, 316 n. 38.

95. Acheson, *Present at the Creation*, 387; Franks, 'The Movement towards Unity in Europe', lecture delivered at the University of Texas (1989), unpublished typescript, 16; Franks interviews.

96. Clayton and Caffery to Washington (20 Aug. 1947), *FRUS 1947*, iii. 364–7.

97. Clayton to Lovett (25 Aug. 1947), *FRUS 1947*, iii. 377–9. Cf. Caffery and Douglas to Washington (22 and 26 Aug. 1947), 840.50 Recovery/8-2247 and 2647, RG 59.

98. Memos of 27 May and 19 Sept. 1947, printed in Frederick J. Dobney (ed.), *Selected Papers of Will Clayton* (Baltimore, 1971), 201–4 and 219–22.

99. Clayton to Lovett (25 Aug. 1947), *FRUS 1947*, iii. 378; REP minutes (12 Aug. 1947), Box 26, Lot. 122, RG 353; Caffery to Washington (31 Aug. 1947), *FRUS 1947*, iii. 396.

100. 'Situation with respect to European recovery programme' (4 Sept. 1947), *FRUS 1947*, iii. 397–8, 402.

101. Ibid. 402; information from Prof. George F. Kennan.

102. Clayton to Lovett (25 Aug. 1947), *FRUS 1947*, iii. 378 (emphasis added). Lovett was less pleased to read a somewhat similar message, evidently planted, in the previous day's *New York Times*.

103. Lovett to Marshall (24 Aug. 1947), *FRUS 1947*, iii. 372–5.

104. Clayton to Lovett and Marshall (31 Aug. 1947), ibid. 392–3. These 'essentials' were adumbrated by Lovett on 14 Aug. 1947, and reiterated to the sixteen Western European Governments on 7 Sept. 1947. Ibid. 392–3, 413–14.

105. See Clayton to Lovett and Marshall (31 Aug. 1947), ibid. 393; Kennan, 'Situation with respect to European recovery programme' (4 Sept. 1947), ibid. 403.

106. Clayton *et al.* to Lovett and Marshall (11 Sept. 1947), ibid. 421–3; Hirschfeld to The Hague (12 Sept. 1947), 610.302, MBZ; William L. Clayton, 'GATT, the Marshall Plan, and OECD', *Political Science Quarterly*, 78 (1963), 502.

107. Hirschfeld to The Hague (12 Sept. 1947), 610.302, MBZ; UK del. to London (11 Sept. 1947), FO 371/62582; Milward, *Reconstruction*, 85.

108. Douglas to Marshall (9 and 12 Sept. 1947), *FRUS 1947*, iii. 420, 428–9.

109. Caffery to Lovett and Marshall (12 Sept. 1947), ibid. 426.

110. Lovett to Clayton and Caffery (7 Sept. 1947); Clayton *et al.* to Lovett and Marshall (11 Sept. 1947); Caffery to Lovett and Marshall (12 Sept. 1947), ibid. 416, 421–2, 427.

111. See Clayton *et al.* to Lovett and Marshall (11 Sept. 1947); Caffery to Lovett and Bonesteel (17 Sept. 1947); Caffery to Marshall (17 Sept. 1947), ibid. 422, 434, 436. The original European positions are summarized in Milward, *Reconstruction*, 84.

112. CEEC, *General Report*, para. 113. Cf. Marris, *Prospects*, 13.

113. Marris quoted in Price, *Marshall Plan*, 36; Roll and Wilson interviews (15 Mar. 1990 and 26 Apr. 1991).

114. Roll, *Crowded Hours*, 53–4.

115. Caffery to Lovett and Marshall (12 Sept. 1947), *FRUS 1947*, iii. 427. See also Clayton *et al.* to Lovett and Marshall (15 Sept. 1947), ibid. 432–3; Shakespeare, *Julius Caesar*, act IV, scene 1 (the Triumvir scene).

116. Berlin quoted in Sir Nicholas Henderson, 'The Franks way—Then and Now', *The Times* (17 Jan. 1983); Franks interviews.

117. Roll, *Crowded Hours*, 53; Franks interviews.

118. The CEEC's *General Report* was published *in extenso* in the *New York Times* on 24 Sept. 1947. The preamble guided much press comment thereafter. See e.g. the accompanying column by Anne O'Hare McCormick, 'A History-Making Plan for a Co-operative Europe'.

119. CEEC, *General Report*, preamble, paras. iii, iv, x, xii; Franks interviews. The phrases in italics are those to which Franks himself attached particular emphasis.

120. Charles P. Kindleberger, *Marshall Plan Days* (Winchester, Mass., 1987), 118. Cf. Milward, *Reconstruction*, p. xvii.

121. CEEC, *General Report*, preamble, para. xi; paras. 150–6; tables 11 and 12; app. D, table 3.

122. *New York Herald Tribune* (23 Sept. 1947). For a digest of American reactions to the official summary (not the full report) see Inverchapel to London (23 Sept. 1947), FO 371/62591; for an early British assessment see Sir Hubert Henderson, 'The European Economic Report', *International Affairs*, 24 (1948), 19–29.

123. CEEC, *General Report*, para. 168. Emphasized in 'Statement by the Rapporteur General', *Department of State Bulletin* (5 Oct. 1947).

124. Franks interviews and 'Unity in Europe', 8.

125. Count Carlo Sforza, in *Relazioni Internazionali* (24 Jan. 1948), quoted in Mayne, *Recovery*, 124.

126. Franks interviews.

5. *The North Atlantic Treaty*

1. Arthur Krock, 'In the Nation', *New York Times* (7 Oct. 1947); Malcolm Muggeridge, 'Paris Aid Talks to be Reopened', *Daily Telegraph* (13 Oct. 1947). The FO found the latter 'too well informed'. See Magowan to Makins (22 Oct. 1947), FO 371/62701.

2. Lovett to Clayton and Caffery (7 Sept. 1947), *FRUS 1947*, iii. 416; Robert Marjolin, *Le Travail d'une vie* (Paris, 1986), 189 ('une complicité tacite . . . entre les Européens et les représentants de l'Administration américaine, dans le dessein d'impressionner favorablement le Congrès'). Cf. Ernst H. van der Beugel, *From Marshall Aid to Atlantic Partnership* (Amsterdam, 1966), 92–5.

3. See Noel Annan, 'Dean Acheson', *Yale Review*, 77 (1988), 471.

4. Cf. Plato, *The Republic*, trans. Desmond Lee (London, 1987), book iv, 'Guardians and Auxiliaries'. See Walter Isaacson and Evan Thomas, *The Wise Men* (New York, 1986); and Godfrey Hodgson, *The Colonel* (New York, 1990).

5. Margaret Case Harriman and John Bainbridge, 'The Thirteenth Labour of Hercules', *New Yorker* (6 Nov. 1943). Cf. Isaacson and Thomas, *Wise Men*, esp. 60–4, 419 ff.

6. Franks to Lovett (22 Oct. 1947), *FRUS 1947*, iii. 446–8; Franks interviews.

7. Interviews with Ambassadors Lincoln Gordon and Philip M. Kaiser (22 Mar. and 25 Apr. 1989); Robert Hewitt, 'He's Speaking for Europe', *New York Herald-Tribune* (7 Dec. 1947); 'Some Person of Wisdom', *Time* (26 Sept. 1949).

8. *The Times* (18 Oct. 1947); 'European Construction', FO 371/62675. Cf. Michael J. Hogan, *The Marshall Plan* (Cambridge, 1987), 85–7; Alan S. Milward, *The Reconstruction of Western Europe* (London, 1987 edn.), 88.

9. Franks quoted in Edward Mortimer, *Roosevelt's Children* (London, 1989), 86.

10. 'The American Outlook in World Affairs', lecture delivered at the University of Leeds (1954), 7–11.

11. Franks interviews.

12. Hall diary (27 Sept. and 15 Oct. 1947), in Alec Cairncross (ed.), *The Robert Hall Diaries*, i (London, 1989), 7 and 12–13; Edwin Plowden, *An Industrialist in the Treasury* (London, 1989), 29–30. Ten years later, according to Moran, Franks said: 'I think the period 1945 to 1975 may be like 1815 to 1845. We have a good many old men at the top living in the past. . . . Nothing much will happen until a new generation takes over; we need younger men who are not obsessed with the past, men who are thinking where they want to go.' Moran diary (23 June 1957), in *Winston Churchill: The Struggle for Survival* (London, 1966), 726.

13. Gaitskell diary (30 July 1945), in Philip M. Williams (ed.), *The Diary of Hugh Gaitskell* (London, 1983), 14. Harold Laski advocated something similar and proposed himself, to no avail. Alan Bullock, *Ernest Bevin*, iii (London, 1983), 73.

14. Quoted ibid. 100.

15. Kenneth Harris, 'A Good Rough Weeder', *Observer* (8 Oct. 1967).

16. Henderson interview (15 Mar. 1990); Franks, *Britain and the Tide of World Affairs* (Oxford, 1955), 35 (the Reith Lectures of 1954).

17. Cicero, *On Duties*, ed. M. T. Griffin and E. M. Atkins (Cambridge, 1991), 46–7.

18. Franks interviews. 'An ambassador is an honest man sent to lie abroad for the good of his country' is attributed to Sir Henry Wotton.

19. Nancy Mitford, *Don't Tell Alfred* (London, 1960), 11, 20. In the novel Alfred is offered the Paris embassy. Gladwyn Jebb, who occupied that post and knew Mitford well, was sure that Alfred was not based on Franks. Gladwyn interview (28 June 1990).

20. Hall diary (24 Mar. 1948), in Cairncross (ed.), *Hall Diaries*, i. 20; Plowden, *Industrialist*, 29–30, and interview (28 June 1990); Prestwich interview (20 Feb. 1991).

21. Franks interviews.

22. *On Duties*, book i, may be read as a guide to discovering whether an action is honourable (*honestus*) or dishonourable (*turpis*). Seemliness (*decorum*) was a moral concept of great importance, embodying notions of what is fitting and what is, or ought to be, public.

23. *The Times* and *New York Times* (13 Feb. 1948); *US News and World Report* (27 Feb. 1948); Caffery to Washington (20 Mar. 1948), *FRUS 1948*, iii. 396.

24. Franks to his parents (n.d.), Franks Papers, Worcester College, Oxford; *The Times* and *Washington Post* (9 June 1948); *Time* (31 May 1948).

25. Franks memo, 'US opinion on the ERP—UK aspect' (30 Aug. 1948), T232/29; Lippmann

to Jordan (21 June 1948), FO 800/515; Broad to Hitchman (15 Dec. 1949), FO 371/78100. Cf. Lord Gladwyn, *Memoirs of Lord Gladwyn* (London, 1972), 226; Plowden, *Industrialist*, 40.

26. Kirkpatrick to Franks (29 Nov. 1948), FO 800/454. Cf. Franks quoted in Peter Hennessy and Caroline Anstey, 'Moneybags and Brains', *Strathclyde Analysis Papers*, 1 (1990), 2.

27. CM 2(48) (8 Jan. 1948), CAB 128/12. The alliance with France was the Dunkirk Treaty of March 1947. For this prehistory see John Baylis, 'Britain and the Formation of NATO', in Joseph Smith (ed.), *The Origins of NATO* (Exeter, 1990), 3–13; and Nicholas Henderson, *The Birth of NATO* (London, 1982), 1–12.

28. Inverchapel to Marshall (11 Mar. 1948), *FRUS 1948*, iii. 46–8.

29. The text of the Brussels Treaty is printed in Lawrence S. Kaplan, *The United States and NATO* (Lexington, Ky., 1984), 222–5.

30. Minutes of US–UK–Canada Security Conversations, 22 Mar.–1 Apr. 1948, in *FRUS 1948*, iii. 59 ff.; Cees Wiebes and Bert Zeeman, 'The Pentagon Negotiations', *International Affairs*, 59 (1983), 351–63. See the participants' accounts of Theodore Achilles, unpublished memoirs, 416-8G, Centre for NATO Studies, Kent State University; Robert Cecil, *A Divided Life* (New York, 1989), 85; Gladwyn, *Memoirs*, 215–16. Cf. the tenor of Donald Maclean, *British Foreign Policy since Suez* (London, 1970), 73, 109.

31. CP(48)75, 'European Economic Co-operation' (6 Mar. 1948), CAB 129/25; Franks interviews.

32. Lord Ismay, *NATO* (Paris, 1954), 3–11; NATO Information Service, *NATO Facts and Figures* (Brussels, 1981), 21; Henderson, *Birth of NATO*, pp. vii–x, 15–18.

33. The documentary evidence is still inadequate (and from the Soviet side unavailable). See Cecil's cool insider appraisal, *Divided Life*, 85–8; and Sheila Kerr, 'The Secret Hotline to Moscow', in Anne Deighton (ed.), *Britain and the First Cold War* (London, 1990), 71–87. Apparently authoritative book-length treatments of 'the Cambridge comintern' remain sensationalist or suspect. See, respectively, John Costello, *Mask of Treachery* (New York, 1988), and Verne W. Newton, *The Butcher's Embrace* (London, 1991).

34. Record of fourth meeting of US–UK–Canada Security Conversations (29 Mar. 1948), *FRUS 1948*, iii. 70. Cf. JCS memo, 'North Atlantic Pact' (5 Jan. 1949), *FRUS 1949*, iv. 12.

35. Transcript of 11th meeting of Washington Exploratory Talks on Security (14 Jan. 1949), C10, Lot 53D68, RG 353. The text of the North Atlantic Treaty, signed in Washington on 4 Apr. 1949, is printed in *FRUS 1949*, iv. 281–5.

36. Gruenther to Leahy (24 Mar. 1948), section 1, CCS 092 Western Europe (3-12-48), RG 218; Leahy diary, Leahy Papers, LC.

37. Lovett to Forrestal (23 June and 28 Dec. 1948), section 3, CCS 092 Western Europe (3-12-48), RG 218, and 840.20/12-2848, RG 59; Ohly to Forrestal (6 Jan. 1949), *FRUS 1949*, iv. 9–13; Achilles memoirs, 445-6H. Cf. Martin Folly, 'The British Military and the Making of the North Atlantic Treaty', in Smith (ed.), *Origins*, 33–48.

38. Bevin to Attlee (6 Apr. 1948), PREM 8/788.

39. Lovett daily log, Brown Brothers Harriman Historical File, New York Historical Society; Dulles memos, North Atlantic Treaty File, Box 37, Dulles Papers, Princeton University Library. Cf. Darryl J. Hudson, 'Vandenberg Reconsidered', *Diplomatic History*, 1 (1977), 46–63; Timothy P. Ireland, *Creating the Entangling Alliance* (Westport, Conn., 1981), 88–100.

40. Vandenberg Resolution, article 4, in Smith (ed.), *Origins*, 161.

41. Franks interviews.

42. Marshall to Caffery (23 June 1948), *FRUS 1948*, iii. 139.

43. Transcripts of the fifth (9 July 1948) to the 18th and last meeting (15 Mar. 1949) are in Lot 53D68, RG 353. Transcripts of the first four meetings (6–8 July 1948) do not appear to have been made. The record of an informal meeting at Robert Lovett's house on 20 Aug. 1948 is in the form of a lengthy memo of conversation by Lovett, printed in *FRUS 1948*, iii. 214–21. No record of any kind was kept of the informal meeting on 19 Feb. 1949, other than the reports of the respective Ambassadors. For internal evidence of going off the record see transcripts of fifth meeting, C10; sixth meeting, L8; eighth meeting, C2.

44. For a reconstruction of the atmosphere of the wartime Anglo-American combined committees, to which the NAT negotiations bore some resemblance, see Alex Danchev, *Very Special Relationship* (London, 1986), 114–32.

45. See Henderson to Galloway (23 Mar. 1949), enclosing Franks's 'corrected' remarks at 16th

meeting (7 Mar. 1949), 840.20/3-2349, RG 59. Agreed minutes of all formal meetings, with the notable exception of the 13th (25 Feb. 1949), are printed in *FRUS 1948*, iii, and *FRUS 1949*, iv. Cf. Escott Reid, *Time of Fear and Hope* (Toronto, 1977), 55–6, 260.

46. For diverting pen portraits of these men see Henderson, *Birth of NATO*, 42–3, 57.

47. Transcripts of fifth meeting (9 July 1949), A1, A5; 11th meeting (14 Jan. 1949), A2; 15th meeting (4 Mar. 1949), A8.

48. Achilles memoirs, 411G–449H; Henderson, *Birth of NATO*, 58–60; Lester B. Pearson, *Mike*, ii (New York, 1973), 51; Reid, *Fear and Hope*, 62–9.

49. The Working Party's first meeting was on 12 July, its 15th on 9 Sept. 1948. The Ambassadors' Committee met five times in July, once in Aug., twice in Sept. 1948.

50. The memos of the 3rd, 4th, 6th, 8th, 9th, 10th, 13th, and 14th meetings are printed in *FRUS 1948*, iii. 184 ff; the remainder, plus 'Action Summaries' of later meetings, are filed under 840.20 with the appropriate date, RG 59.

51. Achilles memoirs, 423-6G; Henderson, *Birth of NATO*, 56–60, 75.

52. Achilles memoirs, 411G–454H; Henderson, *Birth of NATO*, 59; Reid, *Fear and Hope*, 51, 63.

53. Achilles memoirs, 495I, 502I.

54. Henderson, *Birth of NATO*, 59.

55. Bohlen memos, Lot 74D379, RG 353; Charles E. Bohlen, *Witness to History* (New York, 1973), 367; T. Michael Ruddy, *The Cautious Diplomat* (Kent, Ohio, 1986), 84–91.

56. George F. Kennan, *Memoirs*, i (Boston, 1967), 404–14; David Mayers, *George Kennan and the Dilemmas of US Foreign Policy* (Oxford, 1988), 152–5; Anders Stephanson, *Kennan and the Art of Foreign Policy* (Cambridge, Mass., 1989), 135–44.

57. See Alex Danchev, 'Diplomacy's Wise Man?', *Wilson Quarterly*, 13 (1989), 104–6.

58. Henderson, *Birth of NATO*, 58; interviews with Lord Inchyra and Sir Donald Tebbit (30 May 1984 and 10 June 1988).

59. Interview with James Reston (28 Mar. 1989); Reid, *Fear and Hope*, 67 (citing Pearson).

60. Henderson, *Birth of NATO*. For Stephanson, the book has 'the self-congratulatory air of a successful schoolboy conspirator': *Kennan*, 322. It is interesting to observe how the cosy relationship of the former participants has now spilled over into print. Escott mentions Gladwyn, Gladwyn reviews Escott, Escott reviews Nicko, Nicko mentions Escott—all favourably, of course. See Reid, *Fear and Hope*, 27, 64, 68; Henderson, *Birth of NATO*, p. ix.

61. Achilles memoirs, 424G.

62. As late as Aug. 1948 the French confessed that they did not have an English-language text of the Rio Treaty, a vital source document, only a translation prepared in the Quai d'Orsay, 'which [they] believed was very poor'. Achilles note (10 Aug. 1948), 840.20/8-948, RG 59.

63. Henderson, *Birth of NATO*, 42.

64. Minutes of 14th meeting (1 Mar. 1949), *FRUS 1949*, iv. 130.

65. Henderson, *Birth of NATO*, 43.

66. Transcript of fifth meeting (9 July 1948), B5–6.

67. Interviews with Mrs Alice Acheson and Lucius D. Battle (23 Mar. and 10 Apr. 1989); Franks interviews.

68. Academicus, 'Britain Sends a New Kind of Ambassador', *New York Times Magazine* (2 May 1948). There is a similar description in the profile 'Sir Oliver Franks', *Observer* (10 Aug. 1947).

69. Transcript of 13th meeting (25 Feb. 1949), B7–8.

70. Franks interviews.

71. Franks to Bevin (29 Dec. 1948), FO 800/454.

72. Transcript of 13th meeting (25 Feb. 1949), A11–12. It was also Franks who drafted telegrams to the various European foreign ministries and arranged for their transmission under the special METRIC security system of accompanied diplomatic bags. See ibid., D3–4, F15–16; *FRUS 1948*, iii. 152.

73. Reid, *Fear and Hope*, 143.

74. US–UK–Canada Security Conversations, final draft paper (n.d. [agreed 1 Apr. 1948]), printed in *FRUS 1948*, iii. 72–5. See also Wiebes and Zeeman, 'Pentagon Negotiations', 357–9. The UN Charter is printed with a detailed commentary in Leland M. Goodrich *et al.*, *Charter of the United Nations* (New York, 1969). For article 51 see 342–53.

75. Inter-American Treaty of Reciprocal Assistance, signed at Rio de Janeiro on 2 Sept. 1947,

printed in *Department of State Bulletin* (21 Sept. 1947); and in part, with a commentary by Lovett, in *FRUS 1947*, viii. 90–3.

76. Draft treaty (19 Mar. 1948), file 283(s), part 1, RG 25, NAC; draft Pentagon Paper (24 Mar. 1948), file 12, vol. 6, Reid Papers, NAC.

77. Annex to memo by participants in Washington Security Talks (9 Sept. 1948), printed in *FRUS 1948*, iii. 237–48.

78. Ibid. 247; memo of 11th meeting of Working Party (16 Aug. 1948), 840.20/8-1648, RG 59.

79. Annex to report of Working Group to Ambassador's Committee, 'Washington Security Talks' (24 Dec. 1948), printed in *FRUS 1948*, iii. 333–43.

80. Acheson memo of conversation (3 Feb. 1949), and Bohlen to Acheson (18 Feb. 1949), 840.20/2-349 and 2-1849, RG 59.

81. Achilles memoirs, 428G; Henderson, *Birth of NATO*, 70; Goodrich, *UN Charter*, 314–17.

82. Franks to Bevin (29 Dec. 1948), FO 800/454.

83. Acheson memos of conversations (3 and 5 Feb. 1949), 840.20/2-349 and 2-549, RG 59; Tom Connally, *My Name is Tom Connally* (New York, 1954), 332-3; Arthur H. Vandenberg, Jr. (ed.), *The Private Papers of Senator Vandenberg* (Boston, 1952), 476.

84. Wrong to DEA (10 Feb. 1949), file 283(s), part 6, RG 25, NAC; Reid, *Fear and Hope*, 150.

85. Transcript of 12th meeting (8 Feb. 1949), C17–21. Cf. Reid, *Fear and Hope*, 149–51.

86. Minutes of 12th meeting (8 Feb. 1949), *FRUS 1949*, iv. 77–8.

87. Dean Acheson, *Present at the Creation* (New York, 1969), 281–2; Henderson, *Birth of NATO*, 90–1; Franks to FO (15 Feb. 1949), FO 371/79225.

88. Acheson memo of conversation (14 Feb. 1949), *FRUS 1949*, iv. 108–10.

89. Bohlen to Webb (16 Feb. 1949), ibid. 113–15.

90. Ibid.

91. Interviews with Alice and David Acheson (23 Mar. and 1 May 1989); Franks interviews; Allan Nevins, *Herbert H. Lehmann and his Era* (New York, 1963), 236, 280.

92. Acheson, *Present at the Creation*, 323.

93. Franks interviewed by David McLellan (27 June 1964), OHI 194, HSTL; Henderson *Birth of NATO*, 92–3; Franks interviews. Acheson also conferred with Franks on 10 Feb. 1949. See Acheson memo of conversation with the President (15 Feb. 1949), Box 64, Acheson Papers, HSTL; Reid, *Fear and Hope*, 97. He was deliberately vague about all this in his memoirs: *Present at the Creation*, 280–1.

94. Bohlen to Webb (16 Feb. 1949), *FRUS 1949*, iv. 115–16.

95. Acheson memo of conversation (17 Feb. 1949), ibid. 117.

96. [?]Franks–Acheson draft (16 Feb. 1949), embodied in Franks to FO (19 Feb. 1949), copy in Achilles Papers, 840.20/2-1949, RG 59. Cf. State Department narrative, 'The Drafting of the Treaty', North Atlantic Pact folder, Bohlen Papers, RG 59.

97. Acheson memo of conversation (17 Feb. 1949), *FRUS 1949*, iv. 117.

98. Transcript printed in Senate Foreign Relations Committee's Historical Series, *The Vandenberg Resolution and the North Atlantic Treaty* (New York, 1979), 85–127. See esp. pp. 106–20.

99. Bohlen to Acheson (18 Feb. 1949), 840.20/2-1849; Franks to FO (19 Feb. 1949), copy in Achilles Papers, 840.20/2-1949, RG 59.

100. Gross to Acheson (24 Feb. 1949), 840.20/2-2449, RG 59.

101. Acheson memos of conversation (25 Feb. and 7 Mar. 1949), Box 64, Acheson Papers, HSTL; Forrestal to Lovett (31 Dec. 1948), *FRUS 1948*, iii. 347. One year earlier the suggestion had been linked to negotiations for the Anglo-American *Modus Vivendi* on atomic consultation (or the lack of it). See Richard Hewlett and Francis Duncan, *Atomic Shield* (University Park, Pa., 1969), 275 ff.

102. Bevin to Acheson (17 Feb. 1949), FO 371/79226.

103. Nitze interview (31 May 1989). Cf. Hennessy and Anstey, 'Moneybags and Brains', 34–5. See also Philip C. Jessup, *The Birth of Nations* (New York, 1974), 97–9.

104. Hirschfeld and Marris interviewed by Price (11 and 21 Nov. 1952), Box 1, Price Papers, HSTL.

105. Transcript of 13th meeting (25 Feb. 1949), C5–9.

106. *Vandenberg Resolution*, 129–68, esp. 131–43. 'Restore and assure' security became 'restore and maintain' security, to conform to the language of the UN Charter.

107. Acheson, *Present at the Creation*, 284; Henderson, *Birth of NATO*, 112.

108. CP(50)220 (6 Oct. 1950), CAB 129/42; Bullock, *Bevin*, iii. 672.

109. The Brussels signatories undertook to 'afford the Party so attacked all the military and other aid and assistance in their power' (article 4, modelled on the Dunkirk Treaty, article 11). This was undeniably bold, but it was an entirely European affair.

110. On the 'inevitability' of agreement, cf. Henderson's first and second thoughts, *Birth of NATO*, pp. x, 113–14.

6. *Ambassador Ex and Plen*

1. The full title is Ambassador Extraordinary and Plenipotentiary. See *The Diplomatic Service List*, published annually.

2. Harold Nicolson, *Diplomacy* (London, 1939), 76–7. Of the introduction he was given at his Washington début, Franks observed: 'You have heard dressed up in polite and very friendly language the catalogue of my inexperience, on which I shall therefore no longer dwell.' Text of remarks at National Press Club (8 June 1948), FO 371/68045G.

3. David Reynolds, 'Lord Lothian and Anglo-American Relations', *Transactions of the American Philosophical Society*, 73 (1983), 1; Franks, remarks at National Press Club.

4. Max Beloff, *Britain's Liberal Empire* (London, 1987 edn.), 116–17. Cf. Donald Cameron Watt, *Succeeding John Bull* (Cambridge, 1984), 27, 175–7; Sir John Wheeler-Bennett, *Special Relationships* (London, 1975), 66–7. Franks's inaugural address to the Pilgrim Society was hailed by the chairman (a Bryce *aficionado*) as 'the voice of Bryce speaking once more'. Morgan to Sargent (14 Oct. 1948), FO 371/68045G.

5. For pithy characterizations of the succession down to Franks see 'Some Person of Wisdom', *Time* (26 Sept. 1949). 'The Holy Fox' was Churchill's coinage.

6. Cf. his own accounts: 'America and the Falklands', *The Economist* (12 Nov. 1983); 'The Washington Embassy', *Diplomacy and Statecraft*, 1 (1990), 40–8.

7. See Edmund Ions, *James Bryce and American Democracy* (New York, 1970); Reynolds, 'Lord Lothian'. Halifax's most recent biographer is not much interested in his embassy: Andrew Roberts, *The Holy Fox* (London, 1991). On Ormsby Gore see David Nunnerley, *President Kennedy and Britain* (London, 1972). Cf. their autobiographical writing: Lord Halifax, *Fulness of Days* (London, 1957); Lord Harlech, 'Suez SNAFU, Skybolt SABU', *Foreign Policy*, 2 (1971), 38–50.

8. Sir Nicholas Henderson, 'The Franks Way—Then and Now', *The Times* (17 Jan. 1983).

9. Nancy Mitford, *Don't Tell Alfred* (London, 1960), 69. Cf. the definitions in the first and second editions of the *Oxford English Dictionary* (Oxford, 1888, rev. 1933 and 1989).

10. Carlyle, 'The Hero as Divinity', in *Heroes, Hero-Worship and the Heroic in History*, ed. P. C. Parr (Oxford, 1910), 2.

11. Quoted in Roberts, *Holy Fox*, 50–1.

12. Franks interviews.

13. Society of Friends, 'Advices and Queries' (1964), 11, 15; Ray Monk, *Ludwig Wittgenstein* (London, 1990), 580. The Advices and Queries are 'Addressed to the Meetings and Members of the Religious Society of Friends, and to those who meet with them in public worship'.

14. E. I. Carlyle, 'Bryce', *DNB 1922–1930*, 133; Hall diary (Apr. 1951), in Alec Cairncross (ed.), *The Robert Hall Diaries*, i (London, 1989), 150.

15. Barbara and Franks to his parents ([postmarked] 20 June 1948 and 7 May 1949), Franks Papers, Worcester College, Oxford. Cf. Henry Brandon, *Special Relationships* (New York, 1988), 75–6.

16. Davidson and Henderson interviews (30 Oct. 1987 and 15 Mar. 1990); Wheeler-Bennett, *Special Relationships*, 16.

17. Ibid. 15–16.

18. Casey to Churchill (19 Dec. 1943), FO 954/30A; interview with Prof. A. H. Halsey (25 Feb. 1991).

19. Franks, 'American Impressions', lecture (London, 1954), 5, 21.

20. Davidson and Miall interviews (30 Oct. 1987 and 5 Apr. 1991).

21. Miriam T. Griffin, *Seneca* (Oxford, 1976), 77.

22. Franks interviews; Wheeler-Bennett, *Special Relationships*, 75. Morgan was married, successively, to two daughters of Senator Dwight Morrow, a partner in the banking house of J. P.

Morgan (no relation). On his own family background see A. N. Morgan, *David Morgan* (Newport, RI, 1977). I am grateful to Leonard Miall for information on the Morgan connection.

23. 'Some Person of Wisdom', *Time* (26 Sept. 1949); Kirkpatrick to Franks (29 Nov. 1948), FO 800/454.

24. Douglas at 1949 prize-giving, quoted in BGS *Chronicle*, 25 (1949) 476.

25. Kant, *Political Writings*, ed. Hans Reiss (Cambridge, 1991), 116, quoting Matt. 10: 16.

26. Franks to Strang (21 Dec. 1950), FO 371/81616.

27. R. W. B. Clarke, 'Western and Other Unions' (27 Sept. 1948), in *Anglo-American Collaboration in War and Peace* (Oxford, 1982), 207.

28. House friend is originally a term for the lover openly tolerated in a marriage. See Ginger, 'The House Friend', *New Yorker* (1 July 1985).

29. Cameron Watt, *Succeeding John Bull*, 161.

30. Interview with John Freeman (1 June 1983); Henry Kissinger, *The White House Years* (London, 1979), 95–6; Henry Brandon, *The Retreat of American Power* (London, 1973), 68–9, 128 ff.

31. Quoted in Alistair Horne, *Harold Macmillan*, 2 vols. (New York, 1989), ii. 307. Interview with Lord Harlech (12 Apr. 1983); Nunnerley, *Kennedy and Britain*, esp. 39–56; Robert F. Kennedy, *Thirteen Days* (London, 1969), 68–9; Theodore C. Sorensen, *Kennedy* (London, 1965), 559.

32. Printed in Arthur Salter, *Slave of the Lamp* (London, 1967), 185–6.

33. Alistair Buchan, 'Mothers and Daughters (or Greeks and Romans)', *Foreign Affairs*, 54 (1976), 659.

34. Dean Acheson, *Present at the Creation* (New York, 1969), 323; Brandon, *Special Relationships*, 76. Franks quotes and comments on Acheson's proposal in 'The Anglo-American "Special Relationship" 1947–52', lecture delivered at the University of Texas (1989) 13–14 ff.

35. Christopher Hitchens, *Blood, Class and Nostalgia* (London, 1990), 354; Noel Annan, 'Dean Acheson', *Yale Review*, 77 (1988), 468.

36. *Manchester Guardian* (10 Jan. 1949).

37. Franks interviews.

38. Franks interviewed by Prof. David McLellan (27 June 1964), OHI 194, HSTL. 'Like the finest champagne', was how he ended a 40th anniversary tribute. Speech at conference on 'Dean Acheson and the Making of US Foreign Policy', 6–7 Apr. 1989, Johns Hopkins School of Advanced International Studies, Washington, DC.

39. Franks himself stressed that the Canadian Ambassador Hume Wrong was another. For Acheson on Franks see *New York Times* (4 Oct. 1952); Princeton seminars, *passim*, Acheson Papers, HSTL; *Present at the Creation*, 323–4.

40. Max Beloff, 'The Special Relationship', in Martin Gilbert (ed.), *A Century of Conflict* (London, 1966), 169.

41. Henry Kissinger, 'Reflections on a Partnership', *International Affairs*, 58 (1982), 577; Nitze (then Director of the Policy Planning Staff) quoted in Peter Hennessy and Caroline Anstey, 'Moneybags and Brains', *Strathclyde Analysis Papers*, 1 (1990), 34.

42. Gaddis Smith, *Dean Acheson* (New York, 1972), 144–5; Battle interviewed by Marc Wall (24 May 1974), COHRC; Alice Acheson interview (25 Mar. 1989).

43. Quoted in Buchan, 'Mothers and Daughters', 660.

44. Acheson at Princeton Seminars (8 July 1953), Box 82, Acheson Papers, HSTL; Battle and Davidson interviews (10 Apr. 1989 and 30 Oct. 1987).

45. Academicus, 'Britain Sends a New Kind of Ambassador', *New York Times Magazine* (2 May 1948). Sir Isaiah Berlin swore that he was not the author.

46. Memo of conversation (27 Apr. 1951), Box 66, Acheson Papers, HSTL; *Britain and the Tide of World Affairs* (Oxford, 1955) 34; 'American Impressions', 20.

47. Memo of meeting (2 Apr. 1951), Box 66, Acheson Papers, HSTL.

48. Memos of conversation (26 Aug. 1950 and 2 Aug. 1951), Boxes 65 and 66, Acheson Papers, HSTL.

49. H. Freeman Matthews (Deputy Under-Secretary of State) interviewed by Richard D. McKinzie (7 June 1973), OHI 177, HSTL; Nicolson, *Diplomacy*, 78. See e.g. memo of conversation (7 Mar. 1950), in *FRUS 1950*, iii. 1628.

50. 'Special Relationship', 22.

51. Conveniently assembled in Christopher Hitchens, *Blood, Class and Nostalgia*, 23–4.

52. Lord Curzon, 'The True Imperialism', *Nineteenth Century* (1908), 157.

53. For a carefully balanced history of the crisis see Wm. Roger Louis, *The British Empire in the Middle East* (Oxford, 1984).

54. George McGhee, *Envoy to the Middle World* (New York, 1983); Houston-Boswall to Bowker (29 Mar. 1951), FO 371/91184.

55. McGhee, *Middle World*, pp. xvi–xvii, 334, 384; interview with Ambassador George C. McGhee (29 Mar. 1989). McGhee also attended some of Franks's lectures.

56. Robin Edmonds, *Breaking the Mould* (Oxford, 1986), 319.

57. Louis, *British Empire*, 655–6. Franks did not subscribe to these stereotypes. See his exchange with Bowker, in McGhee, *Middle World*, 385–7.

58. Cf. Buchan, 'Mothers and Daughters', 665. See also Richard Critchfield, *Among the British* (London, 1990), 380–1; Hitchens, *Blood, Class and Nostalgia*, 22–37.

59. Leggett to Fry (6 Feb. 1951), FO 371/91522.

60. Memo of conversation (27 Apr. 1951), Box 66, Acheson Papers, HSTL (emphasis added). The often-repeated story of Acheson telling Franks, apropos Iran, that 'the old Kipling approach did not work' appears to be based on a misreading (and paraphrasing) of this document by Acheson's first biographer. It is perhaps equally interesting, though no doubt less convenient, that Franks, not Acheson, was the author of the remark. Cf. Smith, *Acheson*, 339.

61. CM(60)51 (27 Sept. 1951), CAB 128/20 (emphasis added).

62. FO to Washington (30 June 1950), FO 371/81655.

63. The exchange is printed in Anthony Farrar-Hockley, *The British Part in the Korean War* (London, 1990), i. 98–9.

64. DO(50) 12th meeting (6 July 1950), CAB 131/8; Prime Minister's brief (5 July 1950), CAB 21/2248; CM43(50)3 (4 July 1950), CAB 128/18; staff conference (10 July 1950), DEFE 4/33.

65. Slessor to Elliot (14 July 1950), CAB 21/2102.

66. Dixon to Secretary of COS (21 July 1950), DEFE 11/196.

67. Franks to Attlee (15 July 1950), PREM 8/1405, part 1.

68. Makins to Strang (25 May 1951), FO 371/90931.

69. Franks to Bevin *et al.* (27 Sept. 1950), *DBPO*, ser. II, iii, 111.

70. Franks to Attlee (15 July 1950), PREM 8/1405, part 1. See e.g. Edmonds, *Breaking the Mould*, 229–30; Kenneth O. Morgan, *Labour in Power* (Oxford, 1984), 233.

71. F. M. Cornford, *Microcosmographia Academica* (Cambridge, 1933), 32.

72. Franks interviews. Cf. his interview with McLellan (27 June 1964), OHI 194, HSTL, and Hennessy and Anstey, 'Moneybags and Brains', 5–6.

73. In his letter he excused this direct approach on the grounds that Bevin was away from his desk, convalescing in Eastbourne.

74. Hall diary (18 July 1950), in Alec Cairncross (ed.), *The Robert Hall Diaries*, i (London, 1989), 124 (emphasis added). Hall observed that 'we could only do this if we found something to earn them with'. Franks's point was that confining oneself to naval support would not earn any.

75. BJSM to London (20 July 1950), DEFE 11/196; Franks to FO (21 July 1950), FO 371/84089. The talks lasted from 20 to 24 July. See *FRUS 1950*, iii. 1654–69.

76. Franks interviews; Franks to FO (23 July 1950), PREM 8/1405, part 1.

77. Quoted in Hennessy and Anstey, 'Moneybags and Brains', 5. Here Franks used words and phrases from the original telegram; he probably refreshed his memory from Peter Boyle, 'Oliver Franks and the Washington Embassy, 1948–52', in John Zametica (ed.), *British Officials and British Foreign Policy* (Leicester, 1990), 200–1.

78. DO(50) 15th meeting (24 July 1950), CAB 131/8; CM(50) 50th meeting (25 July 1950), CAB 128/19. The first British troops reached the UNC bridgehead at Pusan in late Aug. 1950. In July 1951 two British brigades and a Canadian/Australian brigade became the 1st Commonwealth Division in Korea.

79. Franks, 'Special Relationship', 19–22; Edward Mortimer, *Roosevelt's Children* (London, 1989), 31. Cf. Acheson, *Present at the Creation*, 387–8. Franks said simply: 'It was not part of our language.' On the suppressions of the post-war relationship see Alex Danchev, 'In the Back Room: Anglo-American Defence Co-operation, 1945–51', in Richard Aldrich (ed.), *British Intelligence, Strategy and the Cold War* (London, 1992).

80. Franks to Bevin *et al.* (27 Sept. 1950), in *DBPO*, ser. II, iii, 114. For a typical expression of British resentment see Strang to Franks (20 Dec. 1949), FO 371/74183.

81. Franks definitely claimed partnership in Sept. 1949, July 1950, Dec. 1950, and ritually on

departure in Dec. 1952. See also his 'Declaration of Interdependence', *Saturday Review of Literature* (13 Oct. 1951), which elicited a personal note of congratulation from the President. Truman to Franks (14 Oct. 1951), FO 371/90932.

82. FO to Washington (26 July 1950), FO 371/86979; Attlee to Bevin (10 Dec. 1950), FO 800/517.

83. See his farewell address to the Pilgrims, quoted extensively in *The Times* and *New York Times* (17 Dec. 1952).

84. Ernest R. May and Gregory F. Treverton, 'Defence Relationships: American Perspectives', in Wm. Roger Louis and Hedley Bull (eds.), *The Special Relationship* (Oxford, 1986), 181. Cf. Peter G. Boyle, 'The Special Relationship: An Alliance of Convenience?', *Journal of American Studies*, 22 (1988), 457–65.

85. 'Prefect' is Geoffrey Warner's term. See 'The British Labour Government and the Atlantic Alliance', in Olav Riste (ed.), *Western Security* (Oslo, 1985), 249.

86. *The Economist* (23 Aug. 1947). That journal had long railed against Britain's 'self-abasement' before and 'appeasement' of the US.

87. Dixon minute (28 Jan. 1951), FO 371/92067.

88. Strang minute (5 Jan. 1951), FO 371/92776. 'The Mad Haberdasher' (Truman) was the title of a contemporary Soviet play. See Adam Ulam, *Dangerous Relations* (New York, 1984), 271.

89. Roger Dingman, 'Atomic Diplomacy during the Korean War', *International Security*, 13 (1988–9), 50–91, the last word on the American side of the subject. See pp. 65–6.

90. Memo of conversation (26 Aug. 1950), Box 65, Acheson Papers, HSTL.

91. See e.g. Hall diary (8 Dec. 1950), in Cairncross (ed.), *Hall Diaries*, i. 135–9. The copious US record is in *FRUS 1950*, iii and vii.

92. See Acheson's accounts: *Present at the Creation*, 594–603; 'Winston Spencer Churchill', in *Sketches from Life* (New York, 1961), 61–84; Princeton Seminars (13 Dec. 1953), Box 83, Acheson Papers, HSTL. The President's memoirs barely mention the episode: Harry S. Truman, *Years of Trial and Hope* (London, 1956).

93. Franks interviews. Cf. Acheson, *Present at the Creation*, 482–3.

94. Jessup, memo for the record (7 Dec. 1950), in *FRUS 1950*, vii. 1462. As the memo correctly states, 'this information not incorporated in official account of meetings'.

95. Arneson, memo for the record (16 Jan. 1953), in *FRUS 1950*, vii. 1462–4; Acheson, *Present at the Creation*, 484; Truman, *Trial and Hope*, 435. The US record is in *FRUS 1950*, iii. 1761–74; the British in FO 800/445.

96. Joint Communiqué (8 Dec. 1950), in *FRUS 1950*, iii. 1783–7.

97. Anonymous [?Elsey] notes (n.d. [7 Dec. 1950]), Box 164, Truman–Attlee Talks, President's Secretary's File, HSTL.

98. Attlee to Bevin (10 Dec. 1950), FO 800/517; report to the Cabinet (12 Dec. 1950), CAB 128/18; statement to the Commons (14 Dec. 1950), *Official Report*, cols. 1355–7.

99. Dingman, 'Atomic Diplomacy', 55–69; Roger M. Anders, 'The Atomic Bomb and the Korean War', *Military Affairs*, 52 (1988), 1–6.

100. There is a mountain of literature on the Truman–Attlee talks, but as often happens, no settled interpretation. See Edmonds, *Breaking the Mould*, 221–4; Rosemary Foot, 'Making Known the Unknown War', *Diplomatic History*, 15 (1991), 421–2.

101. *Official Report* (14 Dec. 1950), cols. 1355–6.

102. First and fifth meetings (4 and 7 Dec. 1950), in *FRUS 1950*, iii. 1718–19 and 1771–3; Truman, *Trial and Hope*, 425, 428, 435.

103. Memos of conversation (5 and 7 Dec. 1950), in *FRUS 1950*, vii. 1382–6, 1390–2, and 1435–9.

104. Joseph Alsop, 'Our Trouble with the British', *Saturday Evening Post* (6 Oct. 1951); Truman, *Trial and Hope*, 435.

105. Memo of conversation (27 Apr. 1951), Box 66, Acheson Papers, HSTL; *FRUS 1951*, i. 802–901, *passim*.

106. Memos of conversation (11 and 13 Sept. 1951), in *FRUS 1951*, i. 880–90.

107. Summary (13 Sept. 1951), ibid. 890.

108. Arneson memos and US draft statement (17 and 18 Oct. 1951), ibid. 891–4.

109. See Harold Macmillan, *Riding the Storm* (London, 1971), 494.

110. Joint Communiqué (9 Jan. 1952), in *Department of State Bulletin* (21 Jan. 1952).

111. Quoted in David Henshaw, 'Whose Finger on the Button?', *Listener* (2 June 1983). Cf. John Baylis, 'American Bases in Britain', *World Today*, 42 (1986), 155–9; Simon Duke, *US Defence Bases in the United Kingdom* (London, 1987); David Gates, 'American Strategic Bases in Britain', *Comparative Strategy*, 8 (1989), 99–123.

112. *The Times* (17 Jan. 1983).

113. Memo of conversation (13 Sept. 1951), in *FRUS 1951*, i. 885; *The Times* (6 Dec. 1951).

114. Hilda to Neville Chamberlain (4 Nov. 1937), NC 18/2/1043, Chamberlain Papers, Birmingham University Library.

7. Oxford Regained

1. E. M. Forster, *Howards End* [1910] (London, 1989), 176; Franks interviews. Taylor's Law states: 'The Foreign Office knows no secrets.' A. J. P. Taylor, *English History* (London, 1975), 730.

2. Locke to Pembroke (8 Dec. 1684), quoted in John Locke, *Two Treatises of Government*, ed. Peter Laslett (Cambridge, 1988), 41; Franks interviews. Locke's house was that of Lord Shaftesbury, his patron.

3. Franks had sounded John Prestwich, a senior Fellow of Queen's, about the provostship, but his earlier apprehension proved correct: there was a feeling among the Governing Body that he was not sufficiently 'rooted' in Oxford for them to take a second bite. Prestwich interview (20 Feb. 1991).

4. Hall diary (29 Jan. 1953), in Alec Cairncross (ed.), *The Robert Hall Diaries*, 2 vols. (London, 1989 and 1991), i. 263.

5. Ibid.; Franks interviews.

6. Franks interviews; Colville diary (23 June 1952), and biographical note on Franks, in John Colville, *The Fringes of Power* (London, 1987), ii. 309 and 413. Cf. Peter Hennessy, *Whitehall* (London, 1989), 570; Middlemas, *Power, Competition and the State*, i (London, 1985), 368.

7. Montaigne, 'That no man should be called happy until after his death', *Essays*, ed. J. M. Cohen (London, 1958), 35.

8. Laslett, 'Introduction' to Locke, *Two Treatises*, 42. 'Fascinators' are a favourite category of Noel Annan's, but he does not mention Franks.

9. Hall diary (?? Apr. 1951, 14 Jan. 1953), in Cairncross (ed.), *Hall Diaries*, i. 150, 261; Franks interviews.

10. Shuckburgh diary (24 Sept. 1956), in Evelyn Shuckburgh, *Descent to Suez* (London, 1986), 360. Cf. Con O'Neill, 'Kirkpatrick', *DNB 1961–1970*, 616–17.

11. Acheson–Eden meetings (22 and 24 Feb. 1952), *FRUS 1952–4*, v. 134–5 and 155; Achilles memoirs, 486–9I; Princeton Seminars (14 Feb. 1954), Box 84, Acheson Papers, HSTL.

12. Ibid.; *The Times* (27 Feb. 1952); US del. to Washington (25 Feb. 1952), *FRUS 1952–54*, v. 158; Lester Pearson, *Memoirs* (London, 1974), ii. 77. Acheson's memoirs are more circumspect: *Present at the Creation* (New York, 1969), 625. After much huffing and puffing from London, Lord Ismay was appointed instead.

13. On thick concepts see Bernard Williams, *Ethics and the Limits of Philosophy* (London, 1985).

14. Franks, 'Mr Truman as President', *Listener* (14 June 1956).

15. Kenneth O. Morgan, *Labour in Power* (Oxford, 1984), 464–5. Cf. Acheson, *Present at the Creation*, 504–5.

16. Princeton Seminars (13 Dec. 1953), Box 83, Acheson Papers, HSTL.

17. Ibid. Cf. Franks on Bevin, in Alan Bullock, *Ernest Bevin*, iii (London, 1983), 83–6.

18. Acheson ('Dean, dear'), *Present at the Creation*, 271; Battle ('Luke, dear') interview (23 Aug. 1984). Cf. Pearson–Acheson corr. (15 and 23 Jan. 1952), Box 66, Acheson Papers, HSTL.

19. J. R. Winton, *Lloyds Bank* (Oxford, 1982), 157. Cf. Gillian Wagner, *The Chocolate Conscience* (London, 1987).

20. Franks interviews.

21. Seminar on 'The Structure and Government of the University since 1945' (7 Mar. 1986), Nuffield College, Oxford. Cf. John Redcliffe-Maud, *The Experiences of an Optimist* (London, 1981), 112–14.

22. [Sir John Masterman], 'The Retiring Provost of Worcester', *Oxford*, 28 (1976), 13.

23. Winton, *Lloyds Bank*, 158; interviews with Lord Richardson and W. de W. Symons (3 and 4 Apr. 1991).

24. Boswell letter (9 Feb. 1954), Franks File, BBC WAC. It was Franks's usual practice to forgo fees in favour of Oxford 'educational charities', that is, colleges.

25. Franks, 'Foreword' to *Britain and the Tide of World Affairs* (Oxford, 1955); Harman Grisewood memo (2 Sept. 1953), File R51/457, BBC WAC.

26. Franks, *World Affairs*, 5–6. Cf. Anthony Barnett, 'To be Absolutely Franks', *New Statesman* (21 Jan. 1983); Hennessy, *Whitehall*, 570–1.

27. Margaret Gowing, *Independence and Deterrence* (London, 1974), 184. Franks and Gowing were Oxford acquaintances of mutually high regard.

28. Franks quoted in Peter Hennessy and Caroline Anstey, 'Moneybags and Brains', *Strathclyde Analysis Papers*, 1 (1990), 10; and in Moran diary (23 June 1957), in *Winston Churchill: The Struggle for Survival* (London, 1966), 726.

29. Lewin memo (12 May 1954), File R51/457, BBC WAC; Franks, *World Affairs*, 62, 71. In the published version the title became 'The Issue before Us'.

30. Franks, 'American Impressions', lecture (London, 1954), 20–1. As printed, the text of the quotation is corrupt; it has been corrected here. After the couplet Franks omitted the following: 'She is the wandering Dutchman, the pilgrim and scapegoat of the world. Which flings its sins upon her as the old world heaped its sins upon the friars. Her lot is that of all courage, all enterprise; to be hated and abused by the parasite. But, and this has been one of the exasperating things in my life, she isn't even aware of this hatred and jealousy which surrounds her and, in the same moment, seeks and dreads her ruin.' Joyce Cary, *To be a Pilgrim* (1942), reprinted in *Triptych* (London, 1985), 498.

31. E. J. R. Burrough, *Unity in Diversity* (privately pub., 1978), 8–9, 233.

32. 'Report on the Structure and Organization of the Committee of London Clearing Bankers' (1974), copy in Franks private papers.

33. Franks *et al.* to Eugene Black (19 Mar. 1960), 21-page typescript, copy in Franks private papers.

34. J. Burke Knapp interviewed by Robert Oliver (July 1961), COHRC. See also 'Pushing India's Plan', *The Economist* (30 Jan. 1960).

35. e.g. 'The policy of the Atlantic Community towards the Developing Peoples', to the Investment Bankers' Association of America, New York (5 Oct. 1960); 'World Economic Growth: The Outlook', to the International Industrial Conference, San Francisco (11–15 Sept. 1961). Copies in Franks private papers. Franks was helped with the former by Robert Hall. See Hall diary (20 Sept. 1960), in Cairncross (ed.), *Hall Diaries*, ii. 244–6.

36. The Changing Economic Relationships of the United States and Europe', Semi-Annual Meeting of the Trustees of the Committee for Economic Development, New York (19 Nov. 1959), copy in Franks private papers.

37. Interview with Dr Lincoln Gordon (22 Mar. 1989); 'American Survey', *The Economist* (2 Jan. 1960). Franks thus anticipated the Brandt Commission by some 20 years.

38. Hall diary (19 Jan. 1956), unpublished. Cf. Gaitskell diary (1 Mar. 1956), in Philip M. Williams (ed.), *The Diary of Hugh Gaitskell* (London, 1983), 459–60; Hall diary (20 Jan. 1956), in Cairncross (ed.), *Hall Diaries*, ii. 59–60.

39. Cmnd. 827, *Report of the Committee on the Working of the Monetary System* (London, 1959). See also Franks's lectures in Bombay in 1960, *Some Reflections on Monetary Policy* (London, 1960). The other members were Prof. Alec Cairncross, Lord Harcourt, W. E. Jones, Prof. R. S. Sayers, Sir Reginald Verdon Smith, George Woodcock, and Sir John Woods.

40. Interview with Lord (Robert) Armstrong (8 Mar. 1990), secretary to the committee; Franks quoted in Hennessy, *Whitehall*, 571; Franks interviews.

41. Franks interviews; James Littlewood, letter to the author (31 May 1990). Littlewood was secretary to Franks's committee on Administrative Tribunals and Inquiries (1955–7).

42. Brian Aldiss, *Forgotten Life* (London, 1988), 135. Dr Winter, of Carisbrooke College (a fiction), lived 'secure in the Victorian brick wilderness' of Rawlinson Road, about a quarter of a mile from Oliver Franks.

43. Interview with Sir Maurice Shock (14 Feb. 1991); Franks interviews.

44. Noel Annan, *Our Age* (London, 1990), 19.

45. Untitled transcript, 9, in Franks private papers. Cf. Richard Critchfield, *Among the British* (London, 1990), 385–6; Hennessy and Anstey, 'Moneybags and Brains', 10; Moran diary (23 June 1957), in *Struggle for Survival*, 726; Edward Mortimer, *Roosevelt's Children* (London, 1989), 31.

46. Annan, *Our Age*, 378; Franks interviews. For 'the learned pedants of Oxford' see University of Oxford, *Report of a Commission of Inquiry* (Oxford, 1966), para. 18.

47. [Masterman], 'Retiring Provost', 13; Hugh Trevor-Roper, *Archbishop Laud* (London, 1940), 272.

48. Paul Johnson, 'Play Up, Play Up, and Lose the Game', *Independent* (15 Sept. 1991); Lord Halifax, *Fulness of Days* (London, 1957), 56; Trevor-Roper, *Laud*, 277.

49. Anthony Quinton, 'Sir Oliver Franks', *Oxford Magazine* (25 Feb. 1960).

50. Hayter interview (5 Mar. 1991); *Oxford Times* (11 Feb. 1960).

51. 'The Chancellor', *Oxford Magazine* (11 Feb. 1960); 'Send for Sir Oliver?', *The Economist* (13 Feb. 1960); Prestwich interview (20 Feb. 1991).

52. Trevor-Roper to David Stephens (26 Jan. 1960). I am grateful to Alistair Horne for making available his notes on this correspondence from the Macmillan Papers. Subsequent citations are from this source.

53. Dacre interview (12 Mar. 1991).

54. Trevor-Roper to Stephens (26 Jan. 1960); Berlin quoted in Alistair Horne, *Harold Macmillan*, 2 vols. (New York, 1989), ii. 269; Hayter interview (5 Mar. 1991). Cf. Bowra's evidence in Oxford Report, para. 490.

55. On Trevor-Roper's 'gratitude' see Annan, *Our Age*, 273–4; Horne, *Macmillan*, ii. 268.

56. Trevor-Roper to Stephens (8 Feb. 1960); Dacre interview (12 Mar. 1991).

57. Oxford Report, para. 51.

58. Frankophiles/phobes was a contemporary coinage attributed (falsely, he said) to Prof. H. G. Nicholas.

59. Trevor-Roper to Stephens (21 Feb. 1960). In 1980 he himself became Master of Peterhouse, Cambridge. 'As Professor he would have retired in two years' time; as Master he can go on for five. Also he does not need to bother about history any more, which will no doubt relieve him of doubts if any. Peterhouse is a small, very right-wing college where the fellows wear black armbands on the anniversary of Franco's death.' Taylor to Eva (16 Dec. 1979), in A. J. P. Taylor, *Letters to Eva*, ed. Eva Harazsti Taylor (London, 1991), 416.

60. Trevor-Roper to Stephens (10 Feb. 1960).

61. Harold Macmillan, *Pointing the Way* (London, 1972), 233; Horne, *Macmillan*, 269–70.

62. Godfrey Smith, 'Oxford Lines Up for the Battle', *Sunday Times* (21 Feb. 1960); Macmillan, *Pointing the Way*, 233; Randolph Churchill, 'It's Haroldus', *News of the World* (6 Mar. 1960).

63. Horne, *Macmillan*, 272; Dacre interview (12 Mar. 1991).

64. Macmillan, *Pointing the Way*, 233.

65. Trevor-Roper to Stephens (21 Feb. 1960); Hayter, Prestwich, and Symons interviews (5 Mar., 20 Feb., and 3 Apr. 1991).

66. Quoted in Churchill, 'Haroldus'. Roughly translated: 'Harold was considered worthy | to climb the summit: | And, O learned man, he is equally worthy | to preside over you.' For the flavour of the campaign see 'A Spare Chancellorship' and 'Vote Early and Vote Often', *The Economist* (27 Feb. and 12 Mar. 1960). The PM's tale is dashingly told by Alistair Horne.

67. *The Times* (3 Mar. 1960); Horne, *Macmillan*, 270; Churchill, 'Haroldus'; Hayter and Dacre interviews (5 and 12 Mar. 1991).

68. Quoted in Horne, *Macmillan*, 271.

69. Macmillan, *Pointing the Way*, 233–4; Godfrey Smith, 'Mr Macmillan in by 279 votes', *Sunday Times* (6 Mar. 1960); 'The Chancellor', *Oxford Magazine* (10 Mar. 1960).

70. Quoted in Smith, 'Mr Macmillan'.

71. Franks interviews; Wilson interview (26 Apr. 1991).

72. Edmund Burke, *Reflections on the Revolution in France*, ed. Conor Cruise O'Brien (London, 1986), 247–8 (quoting Spenser's *Faerie Queene*).

73. Hall diary (8 Dec. 1959), in Cairncross (ed.), *Hall Diaries*, ii. 220–1.

74. Hall diary (1 Jan. 1958, 17 and 27 Feb., 7 Apr., 8 Dec. 1959), ibid. 140, 188, 191–5, 220–1; Armstrong and Richardson interviews (8 Mar. 1990 and 4 Apr. 1991). It seems that Gaitskell himself might have preferred Plowden to Franks. He told Hall that the latter was 'too cold a fish' (27 Feb. 1959).

75. Hall diary (12 Jan., 29 July, 20 Sept., 19 Oct. 1960), in Cairncross (ed.), *Hall Diaries*, ii. 225–6, 244–6, 250.

76. Franks interviews.

77. Interview with H. G. Pitt (13 Feb. 1991); *Evening Standard* (25 Apr. 1961).

78. Hall diary (8 Dec. 1959, 21 and 28 Oct. 1960), in Cairncross (ed.), *Hall Diaries*, ii. 251–2; Roll and Plowden interviews (15 Mar. and 28 June 1990).

79. Pitt interview (13 Feb. 1991); Franks interviews.

80. Wallace Stevens, from 'Esthétique du Mal', in *Collected Poems* (London, 1984), 320.

81. Hall diary (28 Oct., 1 and 20 Nov. 1960, 5 Jan. 1961), in Cairncross (ed.), *Hall Diaries*, ii. 251–7; Pitt interview (13 Feb. 1991); minutes of College Meeting (25 Oct. 1961 and 21 Feb. 1962), Worcester College, Oxford.

82. Prestwich interview (20 Feb. 1991).

83. Interviews with Pitt and the Bishop of Newcastle (Alec Graham) (13 Feb. and 23 July 1991); [Masterman], 'Retiring Provost', 12–14; minutes of College Meeting (1962–76), Worcester College, Oxford.

84. Cf. John Locke: 'It is ambition enough to be employed as an under-labourer in clearing the ground a little, and removing some of the rubbish that lies in the way of knowledge.' 'Epistle to the Reader' prefacing *An Essay concerning Human Understanding*, ed. John W. Yolton (London, 1965), p. xxxv. Franks so described himself in his reminiscence, 'The Ministry of Supply', seminar at All Souls College, Oxford (22 May 1990), 2.

85. D. R. Thorpe, *Selwyn Lloyd* (London, 1989), 328–9; Donald Macdougall, *Don and Mandarin* (London, 1987), 141.

86. Oxford Report, preamble, paras. 1 and 2.

87. It even kept him awake at night. Steven Watson used to tell of a rare occasion when one of his fellow commissioners dared to be late. As they waited, Franks grew reminiscent. Unable to sleep the night before, he had turned to Barbara and said—at this point everyone was agog for an authentic example of Oliver Franks's pillow talk—'We *must* have a smaller General Board.' Pitt interview (13 Feb. 1991).

88. Oxford Report, paras. 5–9; interview with Brian Campbell (19 Feb. 1991). The donation was £5,000; the cost of publication, £6,500.

89. A. H. Halsey, 'The Franks Commission and its Aftermath', typescript, 11, to be published in the 20th-century volume of the History of the University, edited by Brian Harrison; 'Oxford after Franks', *Universities Quarterly*, 20 (1966), 258; interview (25 Feb. 1991). Cf. Oxford Report, para. 3.

90. Ibid., paras 5–9; Frank Kermode, 'The Future of an Elite', *Encounter* (July 1966); Robert Blake, 'The Effect of Robbins on Oxford', *Oxford*, 19 (1964), 60–8. Cf. Cmnd. 2154, *Report of the Committee on Higher Education* (London, 1963), para. 687.

91. Max Beloff, 'What's Wrong with Oxford?', *Encounter* (July 1966); Russell Meiggs, 'Oxbridge in the Dock Again', *Oxford Magazine* (6 Feb. 1964); interview with Dr Michael Brock (18 Feb. 1991).

92. Macmillan quoted by Lord Blake in a seminar on 'The Structure and Government of the University since 1945' (7 Mar. 1986), Nuffield College, Oxford; Franks interviews.

93. A. H. Halsey, 'Oxford after Franks', *Universities Quarterly*, 20 (1966), 257; Franks interviews; Campbell interview (19 Feb. 1991).

94. Oxford Report, preamble, paras. 3 and 8; *Isis* (11 May 1966); Franks interviews.

95. Oxford Report, paras. 45 and 47; interviews with Jon Davey, Jean Floud, Sir Maurice Shock, and Margery Ord (5 Feb. 1990, 13, 14, and 19 Feb. 1991). Floud drafted the chapter on admissions; Ord on academic life; Shock on costs. Steven Watson was the author of *The Reign of George III* (Oxford, 1960), one of the Oxford Histories of England, and editor, with W. C. Costin, of a well-used collection of constitutional documents.

96. David Caute, 'All Souls and Lord Franks', letter to *Encounter* (Sept. 1966); Oxford Report, para. 344 (emphasis added), and in general paras. 339–56. Caute was a dissident former Fellow: see his vitriolic 'Crisis in All Souls', *Encounter* (Mar. 1966).

97. D. J. Wenden, 'All Souls and its Finances since 1945', unpublished typescript, 10–11.

98. Statement to Congregation (2 June 1964), Oxford University *Gazette*, 94 (1964), 1203; Oxford Report, para. 3; 'An interview with Lord Franks', *Oxford Magazine*, 3 (Trinity 1966), 377–9.

99. Franks interviews; Halsey, 'Franks Commission', 8.

100. 'To be rather than to seem to be.' Cf. Cicero: 'The greatest effect is achieved, then, by being what we wish to seem; however some advice should be given so that we might as easily as

is possible be seen to be what we are.' *On Duties*, ed. M. T. Griffin and E. M. Atkins (Cambridge, 1991), 79.

101. Floud, Ord, and Campbell interviews (13 and 19 Feb. 1991).

102. Littlewood letter (31 May 1990); W. J. M. Mackenzie, 'The Plowden Report: A Translation' (1963), in Richard Rose (ed.), *Policy Making in Britain* (London, 1969), 273–82. I follow the wording of Mackenzie's para. 1.

103. J. R. Lucas, 'Under the Grill', *Oxford*, 30 (1965), 58; Brock and Halsey interviews (18 and 25 Feb. 1991); Franks interviews.

104. Andrew Adonis, 'Oxford's Crumbling Spires', *Financial Times* (11/12 Aug. 1991); Vernon Bogdanor, 'Complacency in the Quad', *Times Higher Educational Supplement* (22 Mar. 1991); Peter Snow, 'Back to the Future?', *Oxford Today*, 3 (1990), 6–10.

105. Seminar on 'The Franks Report in Retrospect' (31 Jan. 1986), Nuffield College, Oxford; Franks interviews.

106. Oral evidence by James Callaghan (7 Dec. 1971), in Official Secrets Report, iv. 188.

107. Littlewood letter (31 May 1990). For a magnificent portrait of the Dame see Crossman diary (22 Oct. 1964), in *The Diaries of a Cabinet Minister* (London, 1975), i. 23–5.

108. Lucas, 'Under the Grill', 57.

109. Franks interviews; Geoffrey Marshall, 'Kenneth Clinton Wheare', *Proceedings of the British Academy*, 62 (1981), 494.

110. Oxford Report, para. 481; interview with John Bamborough (20 Feb. 1991); Franks interviews.

111. Oxford Report, para. 490. See also paras. 465, 476, 480, and 484. For sharp contemporary commentary on the commission's proposals see the articles in *Universities Quarterly*, 20 (1966), 381 ff.; for a retrospective assessment see Halsey, 'Franks Commission'.

8. *Grand Inquisitor*

1. Franks's reluctant pen was not unusual. Peter Hennessy notes that 'only those reports bearing the names of Lord Radcliffe and Lord Annan . . . bore the unmistakable marks of their chairmen's personal draftsmanship'. *Whitehall* (London, 1989), 567.

2. Franks interviews; *Some Reflections on Monetary Policy* (London, 1960), 3.

3. Locke, *Essay concerning Human Understanding*, ed. John W. Yolton (London, 1965), p. xxxv. See e.g. Cmnd. 218, Report of the Committee on Administrative Tribunals and Inquiries (London, 1957), paras. 5–34, and app. II, 'A Note on the Terms of Reference'; University of Oxford, *Report of a Commission of Inquiry* (Oxford, 1966), para. 2; 'Interview with Lord Franks', *Oxford Magazine*, 3 (Trinity 1966), 377.

4. On openness and publication, cf. Tribunals Report, paras. 2–4; Oxford Report, preamble, paras. 5–7; Cmnd. 5104, Report of the Departmental Committee on Section 2 of the Official Secrets Act 1911 (London, 1972), preface, paras. iii and iv. The Falklands Report, the obvious exception, is discussed below.

5. Quoted in Noel Annan, *Our Age* (London, 1990), 301.

6. Oxford Report, para. 45.

7. Annan, *Our Age*, 11; Beloff, 'What's Wrong with Oxford?', *Encounter* (July 1966), 22.

8. Oxford Report, para. 52. Cf. para. 56.

9. Tribunals Report, paras. 23–5; Littlewood letter (31 May 1990); Geoffrey Marshall, 'Kenneth Clinton Wheare', *Proceedings of the British Academy*, 62 (1981), 494; William A. Robson, 'Public Inquiries and Government', in *Politics and Government at Home and Abroad* (London, 1967), 160–7. 'Mystery-mongering' is Robson's phrase.

10. Franks, 'Central Planning and Control in War and Peace', three lectures delivered at the LSE (London, 1947), 49.

11. Quoted in Martin Middlebrook, *The Fight for the 'Malvinas'* (London, 1989), 290.

12. Quoted in Michael Bilton and Peter Kosminsky, *Speaking Out* (London, 1990), 410.

13. Carrington interviewed by Robert Kee on BBC TV 'Panorama' (5 Apr. 1982), printed in *The Times* (18 Jan. 1983); *Reflect on Things Past* (London, 1989), 370.

14. *Official Report* [House of Commons unless otherwise indicated] (8 Apr. 1982), col. 416.

15. Ibid. (6 July 1982), cols. 51–2.

16. Cmnd. 8787, *Falkland Islands Review* (London, 1983), republished as *The Franks Report* with a

new introduction by Alex Danchev (London, 1992); interview with Anthony Rawsthorne (15 Mar. 1990).

17. W. J. M. Mackenzie, 'The Plowden Report: A Translation' (1963), in Richard Rose (ed.), *Policy Making in Britain* (London, 1969), para. 3. The original was Cmnd. 1432, *Control of Public Expenditure* (London, 1961).

18. *Official Report* (25 Jan. 1983), col. 831.

19. Cf. Nigel Clive, 'The Management of Intelligence', *Government and Opposition*, 22 (1987), 93–100; William Wallace, 'How Frank was Franks?', *International Affairs*, 59 (1983), 453–8.

20. Franks interviews; Barbara Tuchman, *Practicing History* (London, 1982), 250.

21. *Official Report* (8 July 1982), col. 469.

22. Lords Thomas and Hatch, *Official Report*, House of Lords (25 Jan. 1983), cols. 208 and 212; Cmnd. 8490, *The Final Report of the Dardanelles Commission* (London, 1917).

23. Churchill to the commission, quoted in Martin Gilbert, *Winston S. Churchill*, (London, 1975), iv. 9.

24. For their personal views on various aspects of the committee's deliberations I am grateful to Lord Franks, Lord Lever, Sir Patrick Nairne, Anthony Rawsthorne, and Merlyn Rees. Lord Watkinson makes reference to its work in his memoirs, *Turning Points* (Salisbury, 1986), 214–18.

25. Churchill in the Commons, quoted in Gilbert, *Churchill*, iv. 11.

26. Falklands Report, annex A, assertion 2.

27. *Official Report* (8 July 1982), col. 473; Falklands Report, para. 7; interview with Lord Armstrong (8 Mar. 1990).

28. 'The Franks Report', editorial, *The Times* (19 Jan. 1983).

29. They were Sir Frederick Cawley, a Liberal MP; James Clyde, a Liberal Unionist MP; Captain Stephen Gwynn, a journalist and Nationalist MP; Admiral Sir William May; Field Marshal Lord Nicholson; Sir William Pickford, a Lord Justice of Appeal; and Walter Roch, a Liberal MP.

30. Franks interviews. The substance of the Privy Counsellor's oath is given in Halsbury's *Laws of England* (London, 1974), viii. 708.

31. *Official Report* (8 July 1982), col. 484. Cf. James Callaghan and a Delphic Edward Heath, ibid., cols. 479 and 493.

32. 'Walking on Water', *The Economist* (22 Jan. 1983); George Foulkes, *Official Report* (26 Jan. 1983), col. 971.

33. Ibid. (8 July 1982), cols. 469–72; (26 Jan. 1983), cols. 995–6.

34. Ibid. (26 Jan. 1983), col. 995.

35. Peter Hennessy, 'The Lord who Sits in Judgement', *The Times* (17 Jan. 1983); Armstrong interview (8 Mar. 1990).

36. Fell to Sunderland (8 Nov. 1684), quoted in John Locke, *Two Treatises of Government*, ed. Peter Laslett (Cambridge, 1988), 23; Franks interviews.

37. Interview with Lord Carr (27 Mar. 1990); Peter Hennessy, 'Tower of Bauble', BBC Radio 4 'Analysis' (30 Mar. 1990); Adam Raphael, '"Sir" Rupert and "Lord" Archer Blocked', *Observer* (23 Dec. 1990). Carr and Franks were succeeded by Lords Pym and Grimond respectively.

38. Cicero, *On Duties*, ed. M. T. Griffin and E. M. Atkins (Cambridge, 1991), 77.

39. Franks interviews.

40. Tuchman, *Practicing History*, 250.

41. Franks interviews; Peter Hennessy, 'Intelligence Changes Recommended' and 'The Unlearnt Falklands Lessons', *The Times* (19 Jan. 1983 and 17 Jan. 1984). Cf. Michael Herman, 'Intelligence Warning and the Occupation of the Falklands', in Alex Danchev (ed.), *International Perspectives on the Falklands Conflict* (London, 1992), 153–64; R. V. Jones, *Reflections on Intelligence* (London, 1990), 26–8.

42. *Official Report* (26 Jan. 1983), cols. 995–6. Rees had also been a member of the Official Secrets inquiry.

43. Dick Douglas, *Official Report* (8 July 1982), col. 472; Hugo Young, 'An Establishment Job', *Sunday Times* (23 Jan. 1983); Simon Jenkins, 'The Pardoner's Tale', *Spectator* (2 Apr. 1983). For Franks's view of the Establishment see Hennessy, *Whitehall*, 545.

44. *Official Report* (8 July 1982), col. 469; Armstrong interview (8 Mar. 1990).

45. Who will guard the guards themselves? (Juvenal)

46. Interview with Sir Patrick Nairne (16 Feb. 1990); Carrington, *Reflect*, 147.

47. Alexander Lyon, *Official Report* (8 July 1982), col. 498. Cf. 'The Franks Report', *The Times* (19 Jan. 1983).

48. Private information. Macmillan, unimpressed, despatched Watkinson in the 'night of the long knives' in July 1962. See Alistair Horne, *Harold Macmillan*, (New York, 1989), ii. 341, 345.

49. See Edward Heath, *Official Report* (8 July 1982), cols. 495–6.

50. George Foulkes, ibid., col. 491.

51. Interview with Merlyn Rees (5 Feb. 1990); James Callaghan, *Time and Chance* (London, 1987), 234–5, 387.

52. Interview with Lord Lever (5 Feb. 1990).

53. Benn diary (15 Nov. 1977), in Tony Benn, *Conflicts of Interest* (London, 1990), 248–9. The submarine did not carry nuclear weapons; it was 'nuclear' only in the sense that it was nuclear-powered.

54. Falklands Report, paras. 64–6.

55. Ibid., paras. 148, 300, 329.

56. Ibid., paras. 327–32.

57. See Hugo Young, *One of Us* (London, 1991).

58. Franks, 'Disclosure and the Law', Civil Service College Working Paper 5 (1979), 2; Lord Callaghan, letter to the author (7 June 1990). Cf. *Official Report* (26 Jan. 1983), cols. 947–8; Callaghan, *Time and Chance*, 375; Michael Charlton, *The Little Platoon* (Oxford, 1989), 65.

59. Rees interview (5 Feb. 1990).

60. Denis Healey, *The Time of my Life* (London, 1989), 494.

61. Lever interview (5 Feb. 1990); Falklands Report, para. 66 (emphases added), and annex A, assertion 5.

62. See Charlton, *Little Platoon*, 116–17.

63. David Owen, *Time to Declare* (London, 1991), 350; 'How Franks Missed the Real Point', *Observer* (23 Jan. 1983). Owen's memoirs, evidently written with the original documents to hand, are the fullest available first-hand account. Cf. Ted Rowlands, 'Five Years before the Invasion', *The Times* (15 Jan. 1983).

64. *The Times* (26 Jan. 1983).

65. Young, *One of Us*, 284. His indictment of the Calcutt Report on Privacy is very similar: 'The Great, the Good and the Disastrous', *Guardian* (26 June 1990).

66. Simon Jenkins, 'Britain's Pearl Harbour', *Sunday Times* (22 Mar. 1987).

67. G. M. Dillon, *The Falklands, Politics and War* (London, 1989), 54. Cf. Jenkins, 'Pardoner's Tale'.

68. Philip Webster, 'Poor Intelligence Blamed by Falklands Report', *The Times* (17 Jan. 1983); Michael White, 'Anger at Whispering Campaign on Franks', *Guardian* (17 Jan. 1983); *Official Report* (18 Jan. 1983), cols. 171–6.

69. Franks interviews.

70. *Official Report* (26 Jan. 1983), col. 945.

71. Rees, Nairne, and Rawsthorne interviews (5 Feb., 16 Feb., and 15 Mar. 1990).

72. Cmnd. 827, *Report of the Committee on the Working of the Monetary System* (London, 1959), para. 15; Franks interviews.

73. Franks interviews.

74. Armstrong interview (8 Mar. 1990).

75. Falklands Report, paras. 4–7; Franks interviews; Rawsthorne interview (15 Mar. 1990).

76. Franks interviews. Confirmed by other members of the committee.

77. Interview with Simon Jenkins (28 June 1990).

78. Barnett to *The Times* (26 Jan. 1983). Cf. Falklands Report, paras. 13 and 14.

79. Falklands Report, paras. 266, 336, 339. Cf. 'Walking on Water', *The Economist* (22 Jan. 1983). Lever and Rees, especially, were keen to argue that the question of prevention was unanswerable. 'If I had agreed to my wife having a blue hat, not a red one, the marriage would have gone well.' Lever interview (5 Feb. 1990).

80. Sir Patrick Nairne, letter to the author (3 Mar. 1990).

81. Virtually the only commentator to wrestle free of para. 339 was Peter Jenkins (an opponent of the war), whose immediate verdict on the report was exceptionally favourable. 'An Acquital but a Grave Indictment', *Guardian* (19 Jan. 1983).

82. See e.g. Lords Hatch and Beloff, *Official Report*, House of Lords (25 Jan. 1983), cols. 212 and 222.

83. See Lawrence Freedman and Virginia Gamba-Stonehouse, *Signals of War* (London, 1990), 52 ff.

84. Jenkins, 'Pardoner's Tale'. Cf. Falklands Report, paras. 293–4.

85. Franks interviews; Tuchman, *Practicing History*, 289.

86. Charlton, *Little Platoon*, 116; Bilton and Kosminsky, *Speaking Out*, 39–40. Cf. Falklands Report, paras. 161–92, and 321–34.

87. Falklands Report, paras. 333–4. The transcript of the Reagan–Galtieri conversation is printed in Oscar R. Cardoso, *et al.*, *Falklands—The Secret Plot* (East Molesey, Surrey, 1987), 83–6.

88. F. M. Cornford, *Microcosmographia Academica* (Cambridge, 1933), 4.

89. Hugh Carless in Charlton, *Little Platoon*, 60–1 (emphasis added). Cf. Falklands Report, para. 279.

90. Richard Luce in Charlton, *Little Platoon*, 182–3 (emphasis added).

91. Falklands Report, para. 291.

92. Ibid.; Franks interviews.

93. Palliser in Charlton, *Little Platoon*, 138.

94. Falklands Report, paras. 73–6.

95. Carrington, *Reflect*, 348–64. As Sir Nicholas Henderson noted, the report did not confront the issue of 'education'. *Sunday Times* (23 Jan. 1983).

96. *Official Report*, House of Lords (25 Jan. 1983), col. 160.

97. Quoted in Charlton, *Little Platoon*, 127.

98. Ibid. 125; Williams to Fearn (2 Oct. 1981), quoted in Falklands Report, para. 104.

99. Ibid., para. 300; Palliser quoted in *Official Report* (26 Jan. 1983), col. 935.

100. Cornford, *Microcosmographia*, 32. The medlar is a small fruit tree.

9. *Envoi*

1. Franks interviews; Littlewood letter (31 May 1990); Campbell interview (19 Feb. 1991).

2. Franks interviews; Aristotle, *Ethics*, trans. Hugh Tredennick (London, 1976), 157–8. For a brief, delayed denial of the Falklands 'whitewash' charge, see Peter Hennessy, 'The Good and the Great', *Listener* (7 Feb. 1985).

3. The complete history is related in Michael Brock's 'Epilogue' to the 20th-century volume of the History of the University. I am grateful for the opportunity to read the draft typescript.

4. University of Oxford, *Report of a Commission of Inquiry* (Oxford, 1966), para. 491. 'Elle pleure, mais elle prend toujours', said Frederick II (the report explains) with reference to the partition of Poland.

5. For the statutory provision see the University's *Statutes, Decrees and Regulations* (Oxford, annually), title x, clause 1 (e).

6. Quoted in Brock, 'Epilogue'.

7. Franks interviews.

8. Quoted in Brock, 'Epilogue'.

9. Interview with Sir Patrick Neill (17 July 1991); Franks interviews. Cf. Oxford Report, para. 61.

10. Interviews with Lord Bullock and Sir John Habbakkuk (20 Feb. and 13 Mar. 1991).

11. Interview with J. D. Brown (secretary to the wise men) (16 May 1991); Franks interviews.

12. Bullock interview (20 Feb. 1991); Franks interviews.

13. Franks at plenary meeting of heads of houses (n.d.), Oxford University Registry transcript, 2; Franks interviews.

14. Interviews with former non-Fellows.

15. Franks interviews.

16. Oxford Report, para. 53; seminar on 'The Franks Report in Retrospect' (31 Jan. 1986), Nuffield College, Oxford; Franks interviews.

17. Plenary meeting transcript, 2–3.

18. Bullock interview (20 Feb. 1991); Franks interviews.

19. Information from Oxford University Registry.

20. Franks interviews.

21. Brown and Neill interviews (16 May and 17 July 1991); Franks interviews.

22. Franks interviews.

23. Aristotle, *Ethics*, 154.

24. Bullock interview (20 Feb. 1991).

25. Plato, quoted in Bernard Williams, *Ethics and the Limits of Philosophy* (London, 1985), 208.

26. Franks interviews.

27. Aristotle, *Ethics*, 155, 157–8.

28. Bullock and Wilson interviews (20 Feb. and 6 Apr. 1991); Michel de Montaigne, 'On Friendship', in *Essays*, trans. J. M. Cohen (London, 1958), 97. Unconsciously perhaps, Franks echoed Aristotle: 'for a friend *is* another self'. *Ethics*, 294.

29. John Dinwiddy, *Bentham* (Oxford, 1989); *Independent* and *The Times* (9 May 1990); *Political Studies*, 38 (1990), 543.

30. Wilson interview (6 Apr. 1991).

31. Interviews with Caroline and Emma Dinwiddy (7 Mar. and 4 Apr. 1991).

32. Retailed as 'a superficial and unthinking judgement' in E. J. R. Burrough, *Unity in Diversity* (privately pub., 1978), 8. The remark is attributed to Isaiah Berlin.

33. Noel Annan, *Our Age* (London, 1990), 35.

34. Franks, address to the Pilgrim Society (13 Oct. 1948), FO 371/68045G; Newcastle interview (23 July 1991). Cf. Society of Friends, 'Advices and Queries' (1964), 12.

35. Jeremy Bentham, 'The Elements of the Art of Packing, as Applied to Special Juries' (1821), quoted in K. C. Wheare, *Government by Committee* (Oxford, 1955), 15.

36. Franks, *Some Reflections on Monetary Policy* (London, 1960), 1–2; 'Disclosure and the Law', Civil Service College Working Paper 5 (1979), 1.

37. This ideal type is adapted from Wheare (later Franks's Oxford adversary), *Government by Committee*, 20–4.

38. Franks interviews; Peter Hennessy, *Whitehall* (London, 1989), 571.

39. Salisbury to Lytton (15 June 1877), quoted in Wheare, *Government by Committee*, 20.

40. Sir Geoffrey Vickers, *The Art of Judgement* (London, 1965), 50. Franks himself put it the other way round: that the scope for action (that is, implementation) depended greatly on the climate of the time. Franks interviews; Hennessy, *Whitehall*, 571–2.

41. Franks, 'Disclosure and the Law', 1.

42. Caute, letter to *Encounter* (Sept. 1966).

43. Academicus, 'Britain Sends a New Kind of Ambassador', *New York Times Magazine* (2 May 1948).

44. Peter Hennessy, 'Whitehall Watch', *Independent* (7 Jan. 1991).

45. Montaigne, 'On Experience', *Essays*, 397.

46. Carlyle, 'The Hero as Divinity', in *Heroes, Hero-Worship and the Heroic in History*, ed. P. C. Parr (Oxford, 1910), 1.

47. See Hennessy, *Whitehall*, esp. 546 ff.

48. Isaiah Berlin, 'Chaim Weizmann', in *Personal Impressions* (Oxford, 1982), 32–3.

Index